LONDON'S LOST ROUTE TO THE SEA

Inland Navigations

BETWEEN THE

River Thames & Portsmouth.

ALL Barge Owners, Merchants, and **Traders** in general, are hereby informed that the **Completion** of the **Navigation** into **PORTSMOUTH HARBOUR,** and from thence to **PORTSMOUTH QUAY** is rapidly proceeding, and will be **quite finished** and **open** for **Barges** of every description, prior to the **Fifteenth** of **April** next: in the meanwhile the various Trustees, Commissioners, and Committees of Management, are using their utmost endeavours by general Improvement of the whole Line, and by extreme **Moderation** in the **Charges** for **Tonnage,** to offer every Inducement to the **Owners** of **Barges,** to start with **Punctuality,** proceed with **Despatch,** and convey every Description of Lading on such **reasonable Terms,** as shall encourage all **Merchants** and **Traders** to freight their **Barges,** instead of risking the **Delay** and **Uncertainty** of Conveyance by **Coasting Vessels,** or the expensive mode of **Carriage** by **Waggons.** To promote which objects, and enable **Barge-masters** immediately to calculate their probable Expenses, that they may decide without doubt upon the **Price** per **Ton,** at which they can afford to convey every Description of Lading whatever ;

NOTICE IS HEREBY GIVEN,

THAT from the 15th day of April next, until the 15th day of April, 1831, the Trustees, Commissioners, and Committees of Management of the undermentioned **Inland Navigations** will only charge the following very **reduced Rates** of **Tonnage.**

From the River THAMES direct to PORTSMOUTH,

FOR TALLOW, SUGAR, PORTER, AND HEMP.

	S D
The River Wey Navigation	1 . 4
The Godalming Navigation	0 . 2
The Wey and Arun Junction Canal	0 . 9
The River Arun Navigation	0 . 3
The Portsmouth and Arundel Navigation	0 . 9
Total......	3 . 3 per Ton

FOR ALL OTHER LADING WHATEVER.

	S D
The River Wey Navigation	2 . 8
The Godalming Navigation	0 . 7½
The Wey and Arun Junction Canal	3 . 6
The River Arun Navigation	1 . 0
The Portsmouth and Arundel Navigation	4 . 0
Total......	11 . 9½ per Ton

From PORTSMOUTH into the RIVER THAMES,

FOR EVERY DESCRIPTION OF LADING WHATEVER.

	S D
The Portsmouth and Arundel Navigation	4 . 0
The River Arun Navigation	1 . 0
The Wey and Arun Junction Canal	2 . 3
The Godalming Navigation	0 . 7½
The River Wey Navigation	2 . 8
Total......	10 . 6½ per Ton

C. O. HODGSON,

Agent for the Wey Navigation, and Honorary Treasurer and Secretary to the above mentioned Inland Navigations.

RIVER WEY NAVIGATION OFFICE,
Guildford, 25th March, 1830.

N. B. All applications relative to Wharfs and Water-side Warehouses of every description throughout the whole Line, to be addressed as above, post paid.

Fig. 1.—Notice of completion of Cosham Cut and Toll Reductions, 1830

London's Lost Route to the Sea

An historical account of the
inland navigations which
linked the Thames
to the
English Channel

P. A. L. VINE

With 71 plates, 64 line figures, 16 maps

1996

This Book is dedicated to
the memory of

GEORGE O'BRIEN WYNDHAM
3rd Earl of Egremont
1751–1837

First published 1965
Second edition 1966
Third edition 1973
Fourth edition 1986
Fifth edition 1996

British Library Cataloguing in Publication Data

Vine, P. A. L.
London's lost route to the sea: an historical account of the inland navigations which linked the Thames to the English Channel.––5th ed.
I. Wey and Arun Canal (England)––History
I. Title 386′.09422 HE664.Z7W4

ISBN 1 873793 782

Printed in Great Britain
by Redwood Books, Trowbridge, Wilts
for Middleton Press
Easebourne Lane
Midhurst West Sussex

Contents

APPENDICES

List of Illustrations

Illustrations in Text

Note: The 64th illustration is numbered 32a.

Maps

Cartography by Roger Sellman
(except Nos 10 and 16)

Chronological Table

1545–75	Arun made navigable for barges from Arundel to Pallingham Quay.
1623	Attempt to extend Arun Navigation to Newbridge.
1635	Thames open for navigation to Oxford.
1641	First proposal to link the Wey and Arun rivers by canal.
1653	Wey Navigation opened to Guildford.
1663	Scheme to link Ouse, Medway, Arun, Rother, Itchen, Mole, and Wey rivers.
1722	Daniel Defoe visited Arundel, Guildford, and Petworth.
1735	New harbour at Littlehampton opened.
1763	Wey Navigation extended to Godalming.
1787	Arun Canal opened to Newbridge.
1790	Hardham tunnel completed.
1792	Dry dock built at Godalming.
1794	First attempt to extend navigation to Horsham. Rother Navigation opened. Basingstoke Canal opened.
1795	Godalming Navigation burst its banks.
1803	Surrey Iron railway opened.
1804	Pallingham Docks built.
1810	The Grand Southern Canal project.
1812	Second attempt to extend navigation to Horsham.
1816	Wey & Arun Junction Canal opened.
1821	Improvements made to the Arun Navigation. First dividend paid on Wey & Arun Canal shares.
1822	Chichester and Portsea Ship Canals opened.
1823	William Cobbett visited Newbridge. Portsmouth & Arundel Canal opened.
1825	Littlehampton chain ferry opened.
1827	Failure of the Grand Imperial Ship Canal project.
1829	J. M. W. Turner painted 'The Chichester Canal'.
1830	Portsea Canal closed.
1832	Godalming dock filled in.

1833 Survey of the Wey & Arun summit by George Rennie.

1837 Death of the third Earl of Egremont.

1838 Peak traffic on the Wey Navigation.

1839 Peak traffic on the Wey & Arun Canal and Arun Navigation.
New warehouse built at Newbridge.
Horseshoe cut at South Stoke dug.

1840 Traffic between London and the Portsmouth & Arundel Canal ceased.

1842 Wey & Arun Canal mortgage paid off.
Death of William Cutfield.

1845 London–Guildford Railway opened.
Drawbridge built across the Arun at Ford.

1846 Shoreham–Chichester Railway opened.

1847 Ford–Hunston section of Portsmouth & Arundel Canal ceased to be commercially used.

1853 Pump windmills at Bramley and Cranleigh auctioned.

1856 Ford–Hunston section of the Portsmouth & Arundel Canal became impassable.

1859 Railway from Horsham to Pulborough and Petworth opened.

1862 Cut made in the river Arun at Offham.

1863 Railway opened between Hardham Junction and Ford.

1864 Last barge built at Pallingham dock-yard.
Shalford gun-powder explosion.

1865 Guildford–Horsham Railway opened.
Payment of last dividend on Wey & Arun Canal shares.

1866 Railway from Petworth to Midhurst opened.

1867 Dashwood's voyage from Weybridge to Littlehampton.

1870 Wey & Arun Canal put up for auction.

1871 Wey & Arun Canal closed.

1872 Death of William Stanton.

1874 Payment of last dividend on Arun Navigation shares.

1888 Last barge left Fittleworth.
Arun Canal closed.

1889 Commercial traffic through Hardham tunnel ceased.

1892 Chichester Canal transferred to Chichester Corporation.

1896 Portsmouth & Arundel Navigation Company liquidated.
Warrant of Abandonment issued for Arun Navigation.

1902 Southampton Canal project.

1906	Last recorded trading activity on Chichester Canal.
1907	Littlehampton swing-bridge opened.
1924	Chichester Canal blocked.
1936	Warrant of Abandonment issued for Rother Navigation. Barge traffic to Arundel ceased.
1938	Swing-bridge at Ford rebuilt as a fixed structure.
1940	Last barge built at Dapdune Wharf, Guildford.
1949	Commercial traffic ceased on the Basingstoke Canal.
1950	Regular barge traffic above Guildford ceased.
1955	Pulborough–Midhurst Railway closed for passenger traffic.
1958	Regular barge traffic to Guildford discontinued.
1960	End of horse towage on the Wey Navigation.
1964	Wey Navigation transferred to the National Trust.
1965	Guildford–Horsham Railway closed.
1969	Commercial traffic ceased on the Wey Navigation. Godalming Navigation transferred to the National Trust.
1970	Wey & Arun Canal Society formed.
1976	Pallingham Quay Canal bridge rebuilt.
1982	Rowner Lock reopened.

Preface

Arteries of bygone commerce exert a particular appeal on those who would explore the labyrinths of history. Roman roads and packhorse tracks mark only the beginning of a study which reveals how greatly transport has influenced, and indeed still does, the manner in which we live. The crafts and customs developed by each mode of carriage have flourished and faded as new inventions have usurped the old. Much of the old remains, but unfortunately every day witnesses the destruction of some attractive link with the past—a weighbridge or a drinking-trough, a corn-exchange or a water-mill. Those that survive the onslaught of progress serve as monuments of former utility and will, it is hoped, be to some extent preserved.

Canals in particular make an attractive feature of vanishing England. Although a number are still active, several are on the point of extinction and many of the smaller navigations have already long been abandoned. The disused locks, deserted basins, and weed-covered waters form a melancholy and picturesque part of the landscape. It is, in fact, over ninety years since a barge sailing from the Thames to the English Channel traversed the Surrey and Sussex hills by means of the Wey & Arun Junction Canal. This waterway never achieved renown, suffered many adversities and enjoyed only a modicum of prosperity; yet it remains unique in the annals of canal history as being the sole navigation to have linked London with the South Coast. Built with the highest hopes, the canal promised to become part of a national highway to the sea, but with the defeat of Napoleon its expectations went unfulfilled. However, for fifty-five years it played a useful rôle in the development of local industries and agriculture by providing employment and bringing increased amenities to those who lived in the country villages and market towns of the Western Weald. Gradually railways circumvented its course, and when at length one intruded upon its banks only a brief struggle ensued before the canal fell into desuetude.

Today the crumbling ruins remain unknown or forgotten save to the countryside explorer and the local inhabitants whose ancestors worked the boats and locks for more than half a century. While the ravages of time and the encroachment of modern development have caused part of its workings to disappear, a sheltered situation has resulted in the survival of many interesting features. Aqueducts and bridges, cuttings and culverts, flood gates and lock-houses still adorn its reedy channel, the tranquil haunt of coot and moorhen. Doubtless posterity, musing upon grass-grown wharves and tangled towpaths, will point to the abandonment of Roman roads, canals, and railways as singular instances of the mutability of fashion and the rapid vicissitude of human invention.

The story of the Wey & Arun and the navigations which formed the link between London and the sea has hitherto been mainly ignored by the chroniclers of county histories, and it is indeed surprising that in spite of the wealth of literature about Surrey and Sussex there should have been so little written about the history of their waterways. The reason for this apparent neglect lies in the fact that the chronicler of individual canal histories must engage in pioneer research. Facts and figures have to be painstakingly gleaned from the dusty ledgers and account books of the individual companies, from parliamentary papers, petitions, minute books, shareholders' registers, newspaper files, and miscellaneous correspondence, while a field study of the works of the navigations and conversations with the inhabitants who live about their banks may help to provide missing evidence and local colour. Indeed, it is only since the publication of Charles Hadfield's *British Canals* in 1950 that there has been a comprehensive history of Britain's inland navigations.

I began searching for information about the London–Portsmouth route in 1943, after stumbling upon the Wey & Arun in the heart of Sidney Wood. Of the very many people who have helped me, I am particularly grateful to Charles Hadfield, Roger Sellman, and Richard Goodchild for allowing me to use information which they had obtained from earlier research; to Harry W. Stevens, formerly proprietor of the Wey Navigation, for his co-operation and hospitality; to *The Daily Telegraph* and *The Sunday Times*; to the proprietors of the *West Sussex Gazette* and the *Midhurst & Petworth Times*, the Archivists of the Surrey and West Sussex County Councils, the British Transport Historical Records, the Bodleian, the British Museum, the Guildhall and the House of Lords libraries for leave to study their records; to Frank Worley, the Chichester City Council, the Guildford Muniment Room and the Littlehampton Museum for the loan of illustrations; to Lord Egremont for permission to reproduce plate 1; to my parents for their encouragement; to Ean Begg, Alan Gordon, Gerald Griffith; Adrian Hamilton, Eleanor Cooke and Rose Hickey for their assistance in exploratory adventures; to Helen Leese, Jacqueline Metcalf and P who at various times have undertaken the typing of this and other manuscripts; to Roger Sellman for drawing the maps; to Eleanor Cooke for art work; to Diana Hanks for inspiration and participation.

P. A. L. V.
Pulborough
March 1965

Preface to Fifth Edition

THIRTY years have passed since I wrote the original preface and more than a decade since the appearance of the fourth edition. Official and public interest in Britain's waterways has undergone great changes, changes which many would never have foreseen. Pleasure boating is now a major recreational activity and canal restoration groups are active throughout the British Isles.

The work of the Wey & Arun Canal Trust in attempting to restore the waterway has gone from strength to strength. Each issue of their quarterly bulletin announces more significant steps which are detailed in the revised last chapter. I have also included a list of the in-text illustrations and restored the Wey Navigation Traffic Returns for the period 1846–1931 which were omitted from the fourth edition.

In addition to all those whose previous help and loan of illustrations has been acknowledged in the prefaces of the previous editions, I would like to again thank John Wood for his invaluable assistance and Kay Bowen for her able support.

P. A. L. V.
Pulborough
April 1996

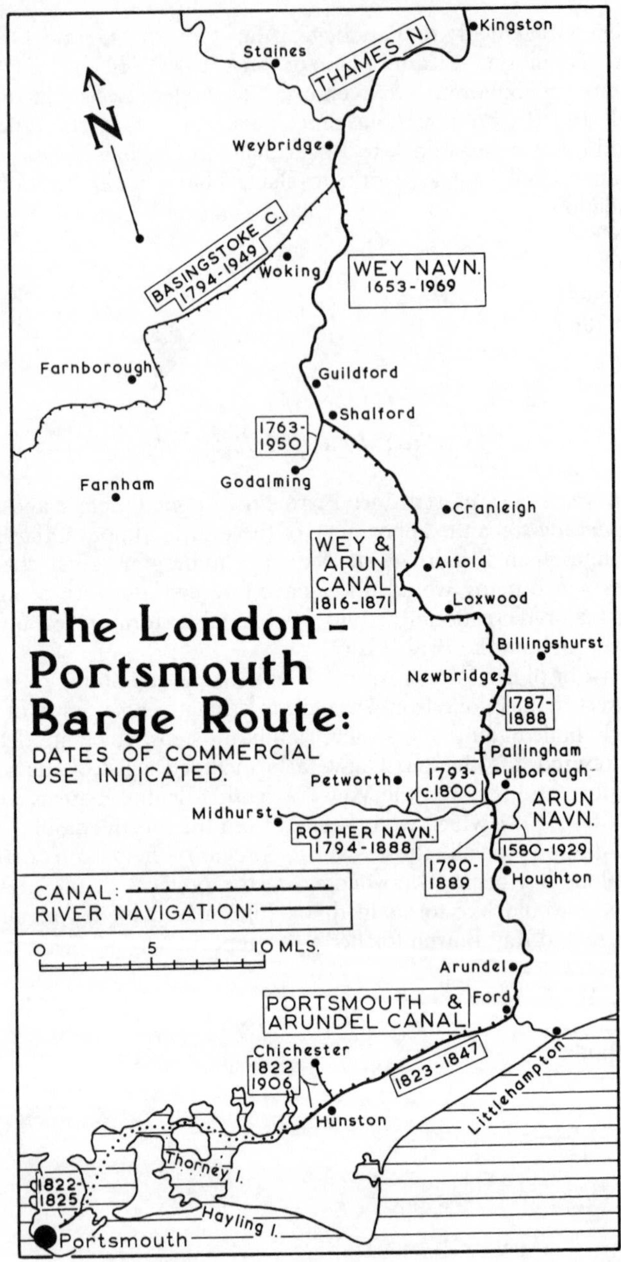
Kingston
Staines
THAMES N.
N
Weybridge
BASINGSTOKE C.
1794-1949
Woking
WEY NAVN.
1653-1969
Farnborough
Guildford
Shalford
1763-
1950
Farnham
Godalming
Cranleigh
WEY &
ARUN
CANAL
1816-1871
Alfold
Loxwood
The London-
Portsmouth
Barge Route:
DATES OF COMMERCIAL
USE INDICATED.
Billingshurst
Newbridge
1787-
1888
Pallingham
Petworth
1793-
c.1800
Pulborough
ARUN
NAVN.
Midhurst
ROTHER NAVN.
1794-1888
1580-1929
1790-
1889
Houghton
CANAL:
RIVER NAVIGATION:
0
5
10 MLS.
Arundel
Ford
PORTSMOUTH &
ARUNDEL CANAL
Chichester
1822
1906
1823-1847
Littlehampton
Hunston
Thorney I.
1822-
1825
Hayling I.
Portsmouth

Map 1

CHAPTER I

Land and Water Communication in Surrey and Sussex before 1789

Decay of Roman roads—early legislation—turnpikes—road conditions in the Weald—growth of water carriage on the Thames—obstructions to navigation—flash locks—rivers used for carrying iron and timber—introduction of pound locks—the grandiose schemes of the Restoration—beginning of the canal era and development of river navigations.

THE evolution of Britain's transport system has generally followed slowly in the wake of the nation's prosperity. Until the nineteenth century the chief highway of England was the sea, for it was only by water that heavy loads could be profitably moved any great distance. And it was not only coal and timber but all manner of merchandise that was carried in this manner. In *The Wealth of Nations*, Adam Smith strongly asserted that all goods could be transported more cheaply by water than by road except perhaps for live cattle, for the obvious reason that 'by land they carry themselves to market'.

The position hardly changed until the advent of the railway age, so that in 1811 it is no surprise to read in Jane Austen's *Sense and Sensibility* that all Mrs Dashwood's furniture, including the linen, plate, china, and books, had been conveyed from her Sussex home to Devonshire by boat. By road the cost would have been more than doubled. Sea carriage, however, held attendant war and weather hazards which caused delay and entailed higher insurance premiums, and where the sea was not within easy reach or there was no river which could be utilized, recourse had to be made to the pack-horse or the waggon train.

Each pack-horse usually carried about three hundredweight and had the advantage of being able to take the shortest route. The waggons might carry twenty times this weight provided there was a reasonable road, but even if there was, the journey seldom averaged more than two miles an hour.

The Romans built a network of roads in England for conveying troops and supplies. However, with the evacuation of the legions their *raison d'être* ceased and thirteen centuries of neglect caused them in many places to disappear. Stane Street, formerly connecting Chichester and London, vanished in the woods between Billingshurst and Dorking during the Middle Ages.

Parliament, indeed, paid scant attention to means for improving the state of the roads, and legislative machinery was lacking both for their construction and repair. An Act passed during Edward I's reign in 1285 was intended to provide travellers with a greater degree of safety, not, however, in respect of the huge pot-holes, but simply so that trees and undergrowth within two hundred feet of the highway between market towns could be cleared to prevent the concealment of robbers. However, an Act of Philip and Mary in 1555* decreed that as the highways were then 'very noisome and tedious to travel in, and dangerous to all persons and carriages', every parish should annually elect two surveyors to ensure that the parishioners, according to their means or abilities, provided labour and equipment for four days in every year for mending the roads. At last it seemed that the nation was becoming conscious of the deplorable quagmires which passed as roads, but, although the theory was sound, there was no effective method of making certain that the necessary repairs were carried out. Just as parishes varied greatly in extent and wealth, so did the enforcement and standard of work. The surveyors, unpaid and unqualified, rarely had power to levy assessments or hire supplementary labour. Peasants could not be expected to act gratuitously as skilled makers of highways and, in practice, farmers often chose four days in the year when little work was likely to be done on the land. In any case, the local inhabitants were more concerned in looking after the roads in the centre of the villages than in maintaining the outlying stretches; and as through traffic—contributing nothing towards the upkeep of roads of which it was the principal user—increased, neither the proper materials nor the skill were available to satisfy the needs for improved road-making. Seventeenth-century highways in the South of England were, in fact, as inadequate to meet the demands of the growing population as are parts of our present system to deal with the rapidly increasing number of motor vehicles. During the Middle Ages when there was little travel, this was of no great importance, but as trade developed under the Stuarts the shortcomings became increasingly apparent.

Not until the reign of Charles II were more serious attempts made to alleviate the situation. The introduction of turnpike trusts legalized the erection of toll-gates and made possible the better

* Amended in 1562 and 1575. Statute labour continued in force until 1835.

upkeep of roads with the proceeds of the tolls collected. The first Turnpike Act affecting Sussex was passed in 1696, but even when this system was organized on a larger scale during the following century it was much abused and the toll money often expropriated into the collectors' pockets, instead of being devoted to road repairs.

During the seventeenth and eighteenth centuries, four-wheeled waggons drawn by six or more horses gradually replaced the pack-horse teams that had travelled on the roads and over the hills of England since medieval times. These heavy waggons carried loads of wool, grain, farm produce, and timber from the market towns to the seaports and to London, and returned with groceries, coal, and general merchandise. In South-eastern England, cross-country traffic went from the forests loaded with oak to the naval yards on the Medway and returned with old ships' timber for the building of Sussex cottages and barns on the great estates. The roads which had sufficed for the farmer, the tinker, and the pedlar were inadequate for such traffic, as the iron-rimmed wheels churned the highways into morasses in winter and in summer left them a hard surface of irregular furrows.

Many travellers have recorded their impressions and the unpleasant experiences encountered on Sussex roads. In the harsh winter of 1644 the young wife of Sir William Springate made an heroic journey from London to Arundel where her husband, who was joint-governor of the Castle, lay dying of typhus. No coachman would carry her until she had paid one 'the very great price' of £12, which was not so surprising in the light of what happened, as the coach overturned and threw her into a hedge on one occasion and *en route* she suffered the misfortunes to be expected from such conditions. Daniel Defoe, journeying through Sussex in 1722, spoke of 'a lady of very good quality' being taken to church near Lewes, whose coach had to be drawn by six oxen as the way was too stiff and deep for horses. Arthur Young in his *Six Weeks' Tour Through the Southern Counties of England and Wales*, 1768, enumerated the few miles of good road which he found and of the rest said that 'it is a prostitution of language to call them turnpikes'.

So it was that the few families travelling by coach had more to fear from the state of the highways than from highwaymen. Wealden clay defeated the primitive road menders and also the attempts to transport increasing quantities of oak and cannon needed at the dockyards at Deptford, Woolwich, and Chatham. Defoe noted the prodigious size and quantity of the timber, yet added that it 'seemed in some places to be suffered to grow, only because it was too far off any navigation, that it was not worth cutting down and carrying away; in dry summers, indeed a great deal is carried away to Maidstone, and other places on the Medway; and sometimes I have seen one tree on a carriage, which they call there a tug, drawn by two and twenty oxen, and even then it is carried so little a way, and then thrown down, and left for other tugs to take up and carry on, that sometimes it is two or three year before it gets to Chatham; for if once the rains come in, it stirs no more that year, and sometimes a whole summer is not dry enough to make the roads passable'.[1] (See page 234 for references to Notes.)

A tariff for coaches, published during the Commonwealth, shows uniform rates everywhere 'except on Sussex roads which being worst and hardest for journeying shall be travelled as far as only is reasonable or shall be agreed or undertaken by the coachman upon hire'.[2] Land carriage was expensive besides. It was common for two scales of charges to be levied according to the season. For instance, in 1745 the tariff for goods by waggon between London and Pulborough was 2s. 6d. a hundredweight in summer and 3s. 6d. a hundredweight in winter. A pig might make the journey from Horsham to London for threepence in June but for fourpence at Christmas. A duck or rabbit was carried for only a penny less.

There was not, in fact, a proper highway to London between the Dover and Portsmouth roads and, except by sea, Sussex was virtually isolated from the capital. These conditions continued into the nineteenth century, although some remedial measures had been taken by Government in defining the classes of traffic to be permitted to use the roads. The Highways Act of 1753 set restrictions on the number of horses to a waggon and limited the weight to be carried by a single vehicle. Controversy arose over the merits of broad- or narrow-rimmed wheels and it was generally held that the wider the rim the better for the road but the worse for the vehicle. The General Turnpike Act of 1773 established an elaborate system of differential tolls under which vehicles with broader-rimmed wheels paid lower rates. However, what had become evident was that attention should be directed less to the traffic using the roads and more to the materials used for their construction. Investigations began into new forms of road surfaces and turnpike trustees started to interest themselves in engineering methods, but by this time water carriage had greatly increased.

River transport had, of course, existed in its simplest form since the days of the coracle, but in their natural state few English rivers were well suited to navigation. The Lower Thames had been used by merchants trading with Gaul before Julius Caesar's invasion, and during the Middle Ages commerce developed extensively on the river as London grew in size and importance. Cargoes of coal from Newcastle, cheese from Cheshire, or wool from the Yorkshire Dales would be unloaded in the metropolis and sent upstream by barge to be distributed locally by cart or pack-horse team. But it was not until the early part of the seventeenth century that a regular flow of boats was able to ascend above the Thames' tidal limits. From Richmond to Oxford a succession of obstructions in the shape of dams, shoals, fish kindles, and mills was a constant impediment to trade. Thacker quotes a series of extracts dating from before 1066 concerned with the need to destroy hindrances to the navigation.[3] However, if there was a good supply of water in the river, tolerable progress could be made. In 1432 the Countess of Warwick was able to sail by barge from Windsor to Abingdon, a distance of 60 miles, in 4 days. Although barge-owners often ran the risk of losing part of their cargoes through becoming stranded in the shallows, a certain amount of regular upstream traffic developed. William Paston wrote from Eton in 1479 saying that he was expecting figs and raisins to arrive by another barge, a statement open to varying interpretations but at least suggesting a fair amount of traffic. Complaints about the bad state of the navigation continued from one century to another; in the local courts lawyers engaged in constant disputes regarding the respective rights of millers, bargees, fishermen, and riparian owners. During Henry VIII's reign a number of regulations intended to improve the state of the river were sanctioned. Little was done at first, but gradually the more obnoxious impediments were removed until in 1605 it was recited[4] that the river was navigable for 'boates and barges of great contente and carriage' from London to within a few miles of Oxford (Burcot). It was, however, the extortions practised by the owners of the private weirs and locks which created the greatest hardship to those using the Thames. After the expiry of the 1694 Act which regulated the rates at each lock, charges were doubled and even trebled and this state of affairs, although remedied from time to time, continued until the jurisdiction of the Thames Commissioners was increased in 1751.[5]

The earliest types of lock were flash locks or navigation weirs. Built across the rivers in the form of dams, with a removable portion to allow the passage of craft, these locks varied from simple wooden structures with removable vertical planks and posts to more elaborate types built of stone and equipped with a gate which could be opened against the flow of the river by means of a winch on the bank. Their purpose was twofold. By raising the water level when closed, they increased the draught of the river upstream, and, when opened, the release of pent-up water produced a 'flash' upon which the craft could either ride downstream or be hauled upstream through the weir. As will be realized, negotiating these locks was often a hazardous task, especially if the difference in levels was considerable; and if water was in short supply, bitter opposition was often encountered from the mill or weir owners, who could demand an exorbitant toll for a 'flash' from their weir, knowing that the alternative might leave a barge stranded on the shallows below and prone to pilferage for days on end.

Once the value of water carriage had been discerned, ideas for the development of river navigations were quickly advanced. Those in Surrey developed as an extension of the Thames trade, in Sussex as an offspring of the coasting trade. However, the first schemes were on too ambitious a scale and very little success attended the efforts of the promoters. An attempt in 1600 to make the Medway fully navigable to Yalding failed, and Acts of 1627 and 1644 to extend the navigation beyond Maidstone produced little improvement. Plans for making the Wey navigable date from 1621 and a bill to link the rivers Wey and Arun reached the House of Lords in 1641 (*see* page 22). This was the first serious attempt to link one river with another by making a cut through the intervening land,* and although the bill failed, ten years later an Act for building the first part of the proposed navigation as far as Guildford was obtained.

The Restoration of the Stuarts brought a surge of enthusiasm for the concomitant development of highways and waterways. Along with the introduction of the turnpike system for improving and maintaining roads, many bills were introduced into Parliament for making rivers navigable; especially was this the case in the years 1661–4. Various ambitious schemes were devised for making London the centre of a network of inland waterways which would link the capital to the English and Bristol Channels. There were plans for joining the Thames and the Severn, and an unsuccessful bill was read in the House of Lords in March 1663, 'to make navigable or otherwise passable, divers Rivers,† from Greenstead, Arundell, Petersfield, Darkin and Farnham . . . to London and

* *John Taylor's Last Voyage*, also published in 1641, suggested that the Severn and the Thames could be joined by a cut of four miles.

† Presumably the rivers Ouse, Medway, Arun, Rother, Itchen, Mole, and Wey.

from Southampton to Winchester and Alsford'. In 1664 an Act was granted to make the river Mole navigable from Reigate to the Thames, but this was never executed. Work on the Hampshire Avon, authorized in the same year, was not started till 1675 and was finally abandoned uncompleted early in the eighteenth century.

It is indeed strange that interest in river navigation should have vanished even more quickly than it arose; among the reasons which caused many of the early Acts for the development of navigable rivers to remain a dead letter were not only an unwillingness to risk capital, but opposition from the mill owners. Improvements were made to the tideways of the Sussex rivers and to the harbours, but, except for the construction of an occasional flash lock, no serious attempts were made to develop navigation beyond the tidal reaches until long after the commencement of the canal era. Not until 1785 was authority obtained for the digging of the first canal in Sussex and five more years were to pass before an Act to make the Ouse navigable between Lewes and Lindfield was sanctioned. Within Surrey no major canals were ever built, for, as Stevenson pointed out, 'it is evident that all the canals which are or may be made in this county, if they terminate within it, must depend almost entirely upon the goods conveyed from the metropolis for their support; with the exception of the manufactories established near the river Wandle, there are none in the county which can supply a regular and ample carriage from the country to the metropolis. Of the advantages to the county itself from canals, there can be no doubt; the easy and cheap conveyance, even of coals and manure, would be a great means both of improving the land, and increasing the comforts of the inhabitants; but it may be doubted whether a county purely agricultural, except under very peculiar and favourable circumstances, can maintain a sufficient export trade to keep up a canal.'[6] The Basingstoke Canal, opened in 1794, ran mainly through Hampshire and only passed a few miles through Surrey before joining the Wey Navigation near Woking; the Grand Surrey Canal, whose Act was passed in 1801, was planned from the Thames at Rotherhithe to Mitcham, but only reached Camberwell; and the Croydon Canal, built at the same time, ran 9 miles from New Cross through part of Kent and Surrey to Croydon. Projects, however, were numerous. In 1778 a canal was planned from Kingston to Ewell, about 1798 from Deptford to Kingston with branches to Epsom and Croydon, and in 1811 from Thames Ditton via Leatherhead and Dorking to Holmwood. Of the Surrey rivers only the Wey was in fact made navigable.

CHAPTER II

The River Wey before 1789

The Wey river—Guildford's importance in Tudor times—Sir Richard Weston—the Wey Navigation Act, 1651—James Pitson—Scotcher's complaint—claims and litigation—Act of 1671—petitions for and against an extension—opening of Godalming Navigation, 1763—carriage of Government stores—Basingstoke Canal Act, 1778.

THE Wey rises near Selborne just within the Hampshire border. The Arun comes to life more than thirty miles to the east from amidst the hammer ponds of St. Leonard's forest. The Surrey rivers flow in a northerly direction towards the Thames, whereas the rivers of Sussex cut their way southwards through the chalk downs into the English Channel. Yet at their nearest points the Wey and Arun rivers lie only 10 miles distant and both have tributaries rising within 2 miles of each other. The early history of both waterways is relatively obscure, but they appear to have been navigable to some extent from time immemorial. The need for water transport was dire, and yet, as will be seen, it took 175 years from the time of the reading of the first parliamentary bill to unite the two rivers—time when such a link would have been of immense strategic value during the wars with France.

The Wey river, some 35 miles in length, enters Surrey near Farnham as little more than a stream and, after flowing southwards through Moor Park and close to ruined Waverley Abbey, turns east at Tilford, where it is joined by a tributary from Blackdown Hill. Continuing through Elstead and Peperharrow Park, under Eashing bridge and beneath the steep slopes of Charterhouse, the river reaches Godalming and is henceforth bridled by locks and navigable by barges. Past the water meadows of Peasmarsh and Shalford, where both the Bramley stream and the Tillingbourne lose their independence, mellow St. Catherine's Chapel dominates the scene shortly before Guildford is reached. Over flat fields the Wey goes out to the north, curving round Stoke Park, bordering the grounds of Sutton Place, and touching the village of Send; then, skirting Woking, the river encompasses the ruins of Newark Priory and, beyond Pyrford and the entrance to the Basingstoke Canal, divides the former racing track at Brooklands before reaching Weybridge and joining the Thames immediately below Shepperton lock.

The demand for a cheaper form of transport between Guildford and the metropolis 30 miles away was one of a combination of factors which led to the Wey becoming one of the first rivers in England to be canalized. Guildford had returned two Members of Parliament since Edward I's reign, and by the end of the sixteenth century had developed into an important market centre for farm produce and the manufacture of woollen cloth. But inevitably its trade was severely handicapped by the bad state of the roads which were quite inadequate to deal with the dispatch of vast quantities of grain to the London Corn Exchange, of vegetables to Covent Garden, and the carrying of coal from the Thameside wharves. Delays to waggons were so frequent in the winter months that produce had often either to be sold locally or carried by pack-horse to the capital, or at least as far as the Thames for transfer into barges. So although the distance by water from Guildford to London Bridge was half as much again as by land, the local merchants decided to ascertain the possibilities of improving the Wey for navigation; no easy matter. The river suffered regularly from flooding, its course was circuitous, and considerable capital was likely to be needed.

Doubtless a certain amount of water carriage was possible on the lower reaches of the Wey above Weybridge in the sixteenth century. As early as 1566 reference is made to a 'certen locke' and wharf to facilitate the carriage of wood 'between Woodham lande and Brooke lande upon the water of Weye to the intent that he [Lord Mountague] may the better with his barge convey and carry wood and timber from his wharf there to the City of London' and mentions that his barge was towed up to his wharf by men.[7] The Journals of the House of Commons reveal that in both 1621 and 1624 bills for 'prostrating weirs' upon the river were read and referred to Committee. The nature of these bills remains unknown. They certainly raised controversy. In 1621 Mr. Alford was not satisfied that the Hundred of Blackheath would benefit. As the Hundred of Blackheath included the Tillingbourne valley, where the Chilworth powder mills had been established in the sixteenth century, it appears likely that it was intended to make the river navigable only as far as Guildford. In May 1624, the bill was only carried by 82 votes to 77 on its second reading and although, on being reported with amendments, it was ordered to be engrossed, no Act materialized. It seems probable that the weirs would have been flash locks, as was the case on the Arun at that time (*see* page 22), and the bills may well have failed due to the opposition of landowners, millers, and the owners of fisheries.

It was then, however, that Sir Richard Weston became one of the strongest advocates for building the navigation. Sir Richard's lands at Sutton Place were regularly flooded by the Wey and during a visit to Flanders he was impressed at the way pound locks* were used to render the rivers navigable and to regulate their flow, and at the way they facilitated haulage and improved drainage. As an experiment Sir Richard erected a lock at Stoke and then, forming the idea of making a navigation to the Thames, induced Thomas, Earl of Arundel, to obtain a commission from Charles I, dated at Canbury, 8 September 1635, which empowered any 6 of 24 Commissioners, of whom Sir Richard was one, to survey the river and carry out the work. Although some agreements were made with the landowners through whose land it was to pass, the Civil War had begun before much progress had been made. Sir Richard's royalist sympathies precluded further progress and it was not until the Civil War was over that he was able to enlist the help of a man in favour with the ruling powers, James Pitson, a major in the Republican army, who undertook to apply for the Act in return for a share in the work.

A bill was presented to Parliament in December 1650 and on 26 June 1651 an Act was granted authorizing Guildford Corporation and others to make the Wey navigable at their own expense. The Corporation delegated their powers to Pitson and Richard Scotcher who took in Richard Darnelly and Sir Richard. These four apparently formed a partnership with a capital of £6,000 divided into twenty-four shares (moieties) of £250. Sir Richard subscribed £3,000, the others £1,000 each. Work was begun in August and rapidly pushed forward, 200 men often being employed at a time. Building materials were taken from the King's property at Oatlands and Richmond. Within nine months 10 miles had been completed at a cost of about £9,000. Twelve locks were built giving a total rise from the Thames to Guildford of 68 ft. The Act fixed the maximum toll to be levied for the 15 miles at 4s. a ton and, unlike the canal acts passed a century later, empowered the Wey Commissioners to build their own barges and carry freight at

* The pound lock was invented in China, the first known example in Europe being at Vreeswijk in 1373. Some historians have erroneously claimed that the Wey was the first river in England to have pound locks, but locks of this type were built on the Exeter Canal in the 1560s and on the Thames in the 1620s.

a predetermined charge. Boats were both horse-drawn (as they were until 1960) and towed by gangs of men, for which purpose the towpath was designated to be 18 in. wide on either side of the river.

Richard Scotcher, writing an essay in 1657 entitled *The Origin of the Wey Navigation*, described the financial confusion that followed. Scotcher, who wrote his account while lying in prison for debts incurred during his appointment as foreman and treasurer of the navigation (1652–4), laid stress on the villainy of Pitson, who, perceiving the need for more capital and the likely value of the navigation if completed, induced Sir Richard not only to provide much timber (valued at £2,000) for the work and to mortgage the lease of Sutton Place in order to advance more money, but to sell him a third part of his shareholding for a receipt for £1,000 of which he was to receive £500 and the balance to be used for the purchase of land and building wharves. According to Scotcher, Sir Richard never received the £500 and Major Pitson spent no more than £100 on the wharves, which he later sold for £1,400. Sir Richard died on 7 May 1652 and one of his fifteen children, George, was persuaded by Pitson to continue his financial support and act as foreman. George Weston, however, was soon in debt and forced to sell the family's remaining shares; two of these went to Pitson, who now had ten shares, and near-control of the undertaking. Before the end of the year, Weston had been arrested for his father's debts and lodged in prison. Thus it came about that, although the canalized river justified the expectations of its promoter, no profit ever accrued to the Weston family.

In the meantime, Pitson was busily engaged during 1652 in raising money. The original capital being expended, £1,200 was raised by twice asking the partners to pay a further £25 on each share. By the time this was spent, George Weston had been imprisoned and Richard Scotcher had become foreman, being persuaded to give up his own business in order to supervise the undertaking. 'For', said Major Pitson, 'it is better your own trade were in the middle of the sea, than that such a work should perish.'[8] Pitson continued to raise more money. There was yet another advance of £25 a share among the partners but one of them, a Mr Mills, refused on the grounds that he had bought his share under covenant on the understanding that the river would be made navigable without further charge.

In November 1653, just before Cromwell dissolved the Long Parliament, the work was finished at an estimated cost of £15,000.

Numerous payments, however, which cannot be accurately assessed, were still outstanding for land, labour, and materials. Three or four barges began to work the river, but due to the three previous winters and summers being very dry, the Thames was low and the bargemen 'could not cary above ten or eleven load, but they lay aground and were ffayne to bee at the charges of a lighting of them with boats, or else they could not pass'.[9] As a result they made little profit, but Scotcher had to pay for barge tackle and the wages of the bargees as well as the towing men, and his complaint was that while he paid out, he was never reimbursed proportionately by the other partners. Manning in his history of Surrey wrote, 'the utility of it was soon proved as it immediately produced £800 a year, and in a short time after £1500'.

During the period in which Scotcher was foreman, he claimed that he lost £3,366 besides the interest on his capital. He also complained that whilst he paid £150 for the bargemen's wages and for barge tackle, Pitson, on the other hand, collected £200 to £300 from the barge tolls and disbursed never a penny. Scotcher moaned bitterly of his treatment at the hands of the Commissioners appointed to investigate the management of the navigation: 'Only this have I to say . . . of all the proceedings of all the whole business from first unto last, that their leniency to one side, and their severity to the other side, the Commissioners will be a wonder unto their country in the judgement of indifferent and unbiassed men.'[10] The other partners were not heard for one reason or another and Scotcher concluded his account as follows: 'I have nothing more to say at present but only this, that Major Pitson was never called to an account, and yet had what he desired . . . and I shall justify what I have hear writ, if I may come to a ffaire tryall for it.'

The outstanding debts produced much litigation, threw the business into great confusion, and the river was very neglected until after the Restoration. In 1663 Pitson, who had successfully combated Scotcher's accusations, complained that William Dickenson, acting as trustee for John Weston, Sir Richard's heir, and others had fraudulently obtained possession of some land upon the banks of the new channel of the river, and had halted all traffic unless it paid them toll. In some weeks, 500 or 600 quarters of corn and shipbuilding timbers had been stopped. Their dispute stemmed from the fact that the Commonwealth being now over, the royalist landowners were rightly or wrongly trying to retrieve their lands. In March 1664 it was petitioned that 'Under a pretended Act of

Parliament made in the times of usurption, a great part of the river was cut through the King's own grounds, the locks and bridges being built from the King's Houses at Oatlands and Richmond, but His Majesty passed this by and appointed John Radclyffe to be conservator of the river for 31 years'. This bill was successfully opposed by John Weston and others and so thwarted a scheme by Radcliffe to obtain control of the river. Nevertheless, it was not until a second Act had been obtained at the fifth attempt* in 1671 'for settling and preserving the Navigation' that the additional works which had been in progress before were completed, many suits in law and equity having in the intermediate time taken place between the shareholders of the property. Nor were these disputes finally concluded until 1678, when they were terminated by a decree of the Court of Exchequer. The 1671 Act vested control of the river in six Trustees and appointed the two Chief Justices and the Chief Baron of the Exchequer to adjudge all claims. Eighty-seven claims were lodged but it is not clear how all were settled. An unusual provision in the Act was the right of Guildford to charge a penny toll on every ton to pay for the damage done to roads and bridges by carts using the river wharves and because 'the Corporation and Inhabitants would be burthened with poor more than before the Navigation by the poverty of the bargemen, their families, and others occasioned by the Navigation'. But if this statement was true in general, there were notable exceptions. John Williams, a bargeman of Stoke, claimed in 1671 that there was the large sum of £408 due to him for the provision of timber and stone used in building wharves. Again, it is to be noticed that when, after the Restoration, the proprietors vested their monopoly of carriage in Henry Goldwyer, bargeman of Guildford, and William Bromfield, they were able to repair damage of £200 caused by other boats.

Apparently both men leased out shares in the barges, for another claim in 1671 refers to John Skarvill, citizen and distiller of London, who sought a quarter of all profits of 'one barge of the usual burthen'. Skarvill had leased his quarter from Radcliffe for a period of 19 years from January 1665 (4,000 loads of timber passed down the river the previous year) for £325. On this basis, if the profits of a barge could be let at the equivalent rate of £58 p.a. for such a period, the purchaser, having in mind the attendant risks, presumably assessed the likely profits at a minimum of £100 p.a., and this gives a further indication of the amount of trade.

* Bills were introduced into the House of Commons in 1662, 1664, 1665, and 1669. See papers by Hector Carter and Michael Nash listed in Appendix A (III).

Because of the disputes the river had by 1677 fallen into ruinous condition and several thousand pounds had to be spent on repairs and negotiating agreements with the millers at Woking, Newark, and Stoke. However, barge traffic rapidly increased on the river after 1680 and Guildford continued to grow as a central distributing point for corn, beer, paper, hoops, bark, timber, and agricultural produce, much of which went to the London markets; the timber came not only from the neighbourhood of Guildford but was brought by 'country carriages' in summer from the woody parts of Sussex and Hampshire over 30 miles away. Of the flour trade Defoe says, 'This navigation is also a mighty support to the great corn-market at Farnham . . . for as the meal men and other dealers buy corn at the market, much of it is brought to the mills on this river which is not above seven miles distant, and being first ground and dress'd, is then sent down in the meal barges to London, the expense of which is very small.'[11]

There was also a certain amount of passenger traffic carried, for which a maximum charge of 1s. between Guildford and the City of London was stipulated in the original Act, but by the 1671 Act the maximum fare from London to Guildford was increased to 1s. 4d., although for the downstream journey it remained unchanged. In 1745 it is recorded that 'Guildford luggage boats left Queenhithe and other places',[12] but evidence has yet to come to light of regular passenger services.

At a time when, politically, the Seven Years' War was still causing Europe grave concern, the Industrial Revolution was already beginning to change the face of Britain. The demand for improved methods of communication was growing with the expansion of trade and commerce. In the North the Duke of Bridgewater was planning to usher in the canal era, and throughout the kingdom steps were being taken to improve the roads. In 1757 an Act was granted for repairing and widening the road from Dapdune wharf at Stoke through Guildford, Alfold, and Arundel. Efforts were also made to extend the Wey Navigation, but when a bill was first presented in 1759 three of the eight petitions to Parliament were against the proposal. The objectors included the traders of Haslemere who thought their trade would be greatly injured and the owners of the water-works by Guildford bridge 'whose profits were for the benefit of the poor' and who feared that any widening of the bridge might interfere with the mills which supplied the town reservoir.

The sponsors of the bill did not take this opposition seriously; 'Take no notice at home of the Haslemere affair', wrote Armstrong

THE

COMMISSIONERS

FOR extending the Navigation of the River *Wey*, from *Guildford* to *Godalming* in *Surrey*, do hereby give Notice, that the ſaid River is now open and navigable; and that they have this Day, at their Meeting, ſettled the following Rates and Duties upon all Goods to be navigated on the ſame, *viz.*

From the Wharf at *Godalming* to *Guildford.*

	£.	s.	d.
For all Timber and dry Goods *per* Load, — — —	0	1	5
For Coals *per* Chaldron, — — — —	0	1	3
For Chalk *per* Load, — — — — —	0	0	6
For Woollen Rags and other Kinds of Manure, — — —	0	0	9

From *Stone Bridge Brook* Wharf.

For all Timber and dry Goods *per* Load, — — — —	0	1	2
For Coals *per* Chaldron, — — — — — —	0	1	0
For Chalk *per* Load, — — — — —	0	0	4
For Woollen Rags and other Kinds of Manure, — — —	0	0	6

AND the Barge Maſters, having undertaken to carry Goods at nine Pence *per* Load Freightage, from *Godalming* Wharf to *Guildford*; and from *Stone Bridge Brook* Wharf to *Guildford* at ſix Pence *per* Load; this added to the reſpective Tolls above-mentioned, include all Charges of Carriage from the reſpective Wharfs.

May 29th, 1764.

Guildford: Printed by CHARLES MARTIN, at the *Angel* and *Bible* in *High-ſtreet*, M.DCC.LXIV.

Fig. 2.—Notice of toll and carriage charges on the Godalming Navigation, 1764

SURREY.

RIVER WEY from *Godalming* to *Guildford*.

[illegible]. Godalming Commissioners Account from the 25 Day of December 1766 to the 25 Day of March following.

Places of Loading and Unloading and Prices of Riverage.	No. of Loads.	at *per* Load.		£.	S.	D.
		S.	D.			
GODALMING - -	115	1	5	8	2	11
Stone Bridge - - -	- -	1	2	- -	- -	-
Coals to GODALMING	29	1	3	1	16	3
Rags to Ditto - -	- -	0	9	- -	- -	-
				9	19	2

RECeived the Day of 17 of the Sum of being in full of the above Account, for the Uſe of the Commiſſioners of the ſaid Navigation, by me

N. B. The above muſt be paid by the Day of next, or your Boat will be Stopped.

Fig. 3.—Godalming Navigation Account, 1766

from London to Yaldon, later clerk to the Godalming Commissioners, 'we not only shall get our Act passed but we can now tell with certainty when the money is ready to do the river.'[13] The bill, however, was lost and had to be re-presented the following year and before the Act was obtained Armstrong had to admit that they had had 'a very fatiguing affair of it'. The strong argument in its favour was that timber, bark, and manure could be more cheaply and speedily carried to Guildford. Evidence was given that the cost of bringing timber from places 10 miles south of Godalming would be reduced by 4s. a load as 'the farmers who are now obliged to lay out a night with their carriage might return home in one day by which six or seven shillings might be saved in each journey since they are obliged to drop timber on wastes which occasions delay and expense in reloading'. Great quantities of timber were dropped about Gosden Common, 3 miles from Guildford and less than half a mile from the intended navigation, and 'at present there are nearly 3,000 loads on and around Hambledon Common which sometimes remains there six months for the farmers will only carry it off just when they please'. A shipbuilder, Mr West, stated that he had had to stop building a 74-gun man-of-war for His Majesty as he could not get the timber he had bought carried. It was said that the lower cost of chalk would reduce the cost of manuring an acre by 6s. 8d., that the advantages would extend 16 or 17 miles from Godalming, and that the tanning trade suffered since great quantities of bark had to be left in Sussex as they would not answer the expense of carriage. So much in favour was the neighbourhood that petitioners came from as far afield as Midhurst, Petersfield, Petworth, Stopham, and Wisborough Green.[14]

The Wey Navigation Act of 1760 continued the waterway upstream for 4½ miles by means of four new locks which raised the river level 32 ft. The navigation was surveyed and built by Richard Stedman and John Smeaton; the latter had only recently completed building the third Eddystone lighthouse and 'on account of a large affair' with which he was concerned in the North excused himself from the undertaking early in 1761. To allow barges to pass freely, the central arch of Guildford Bridge was enlarged and widened and wharves were constructed at Shalford and Godalming. The work was completed in the autumn of 1763 at a cost of £6,450, which only exceeded the estimate by £850. Curiously, the navigation was controlled by a different body of Commissioners from that governing the Wey between Guildford and Weybridge and this has continued until the present day.

The completion of this last extension had important results in opening up the trade of Godalming and the country to the south and west. Corn and coal were the principal upstream freights. Downstream came timber, iron, and hoops bound for London, flour for the bakeries, manure for the farms, and bark for the Thameside tanning industry.

In 1767 proposals were discussed for the removal of the toll-gate between Guildford and Godalming on the Portsmouth road, apparently with a view to setting it up to the south of Godalming, because it was argued that the use of the road since the extension of the navigation had been greatly increased by the considerable fall of timber to the south and west of the town, by the carriage of hoops and iron to the wharf and by traffic to and from the forges on Witley and Thursley Heaths, all of which contributed nothing to the repair of the road.[15] In 1776, a year when 17,000 tons of merchandise were carried between London and Guildford, the Reverend W. Gilpin described the Wey as navigable as far as Guildford 'and beyond it, for timber, which is brought down the river from the contiguous parts of the country. Floats of timber are among the pleasing appendages of a river, when the trunks are happily disposed. This disposition, however, I fear, must be the result of chance, rather than of art. It is hardly possible to pack a float picturesquely by design. These cumbrous machines are navigated each by a single man with a pole; and as they glide gently down the stream, the tremulous reflections they form on the still surface of the water, and their contrast with trees, bushes, and pasturage, as they float along, are pleasing.'[16]

The American War of Independence gave a considerable impetus to trade, due in large measure to the transport of Government stores and ammunition from London to the great naval arsenal at Portsmouth. In 1780 both the Wey Navigations entered into an arrangement with the Government for the carriage of stores from London to Godalming by water and thence by land to Portsmouth. The navigations undertook to carry goods from Bull Wharf to Portsmouth within 8 days at 3s. a hundredweight or 5s. a hundredweight if all by road. In March it was reported that a quantity of Government stores had already arrived and that since many more were expected a warehouse was to be built at Godalming. Indeed between 1779 and 1782 receipts on the Guildford section of the navigation increased by 25 per cent and the amount of goods

At a Meeting of the Commiſſioners of the *Godalming* Navigation, held at the GEORGE Inn, in *Godalming*, in the County of *Surrey*, on Wedneſday the 24th Day of FEBRUARY, 1779.

RESOLVED, THAT one third Part of all Timber cut into Plank or Scantlings in their Wharfs, be charged for Wharfage Eight-Pence *per* Load, to make good the Loſs to the Navigation by ſuch converſion.

RESOLVED, That one half of all Timber cleft in their Wharfs, be charged for Wharfage Eight-pence *per* Load, to make good the Loſs to the Navigation by ſuch converſion.

RESOLVED, That all Timber brought into the Wharfs and cut there, and carried away by Land, ſhall pay for Wharfage, Carting, and Conveniencey of Sawing, Two Shillings *per* Load.

RESOLVED, That all Timber brought into the Wharfs with an Intent of going by Water, and afterwards ſent away by Land, ſhall pay Eight-pence *per* Load Wharfage.

RESOLVED, That all Slabs and Tops coming from Plank Logs, or Scantlings, that ſhall not be taken away within Half a Year from the Time of cutting them, ſhall pay for Wharfage, Eight-pence *per* Load, (Three-hundred Feet ſuperficial to the Load) and the ſame to be paid for every Half Year 'till cleared.

RESOLVED, That all Timber, Plank Treenels, Scantlings, Spokes, Poles, Poſts, and Rails, and other Goods that ſhall lye in the Wharfs Two Years, ſhall pay for Wharfage Eight-pence *per* Load at the end of the ſaid Two Years, and that after the Two Years, the ſame to be paid Yearly 'till taken away.

RESOLVED, That all Grocery, Shop-Goods, White Rags, &c. that ſhall be lodged in the Warehouſes and not taken away within One Month after Notice given, ſhall pay for Warehouſe-room Two-pence *per* Hundred ; and all Sacking Goods upwards bound, that ſhall be put into the ſame and not taken away within one Month after Notice given, ſhall pay One Shilling *per* Load ; and the ſame for every Month after 'till taken away.

RESOLVED, That no Saw-Pits be opened in the Wharf in future without Application to, and Conſent obtained of the Commiſſioners.

RESOLVED, That all Plank and Timber to be carried to the Loading Place or Saw-Pits be Truſſed in future, and not drawn on the Ground.

RESOLVED, That the Orders contained in the above Reſolutions do take Place from LADY-DAY, 1779.

EDMUND YALDEN,

CLERK TO THE COMMISSIONERS.

Fig. 4.—Godalming Navigation Resolutions, 1779

FEBRUARY 1, 1780.

NAVIGATION
OF THE
RIVER WEY,
IN THE
COUNTY OF SURRY.

MESSRS. COLLINS and DAVIS, beg Leave to acquaint the Honourable Board, that they have Barges ready at BULL-WHARF to carry any Stores or Goods in eight Days, and in Caſe of any Impediment in ten Days, that the Board may think fit to ſend by Them, at the Rate of three Shillings per Cwt. for Portſmouth; and that NICHOLAS PROCTOR, their Clerk, attends at BULL-WHARF every Day, to receive and take Charge of the Goods and Stores; and, in Caſe of any Stoppage on the Navigation, they will undertake to carry the ſaid Stores by Land the whole Way, at five Shillings per Cwt. during ſuch Stoppage.

And Meſſrs. COLLINS and DAVIS, further beg Leave to inform the Honourable Board, that, in Caſe of any Emergency ſignified to them by the Honourable Board, they will readily carry the ſaid Stores by Land the whole Way, in the moſt expeditious Manner, at the ſaid Price of five Shillings per Cwt. in like Manner as when there is any Stoppage on the Navigation.

Fig. 5.—Carriers advertisements for land and water carriage between London and Portsmouth, 1780

carried in the year rose from 22,000 to 36,000 tons. However, the Peace of Versailles (1783) coupled with the disadvantages of transferring goods from water to land half-way to Portsmouth caused traffic to diminish and in 1789 the Wey Navigation sold their three-quarter interest in the warehouse to the Godalming Commissioners at less than cost.

In 1776 plans were being made for a canal 44 miles long from Basingstoke to the Wey Navigation near Weybridge. A survey was made the following year and in spite of protests by the inhabitants of Reading on the ground that it might divert trade, an Act was obtained in 1778. However, the economic difficulties resulting from the war with America delayed its execution and little was done until about ten years later. Not, in fact, until 1794 was the canal completed, by which time the cost had reached about £190,000 against the authorized capital of £126,000, and its line had been shortened to 37½ miles by building the long tunnel at Greywell. As traffic between the Thames and the canal had to use a section of the Wey Navigation, future prospects appeared even brighter than the comments made in 1783 by the Basingstoke Canal Committee—'The River Wey . . . is well known to have very lately exceeded the most sanguine expectations of the owners.'*

* The history of the Basingstoke Canal is described in *London's Lost Route to Basingstoke*, P. A. L. Vine, 1968.

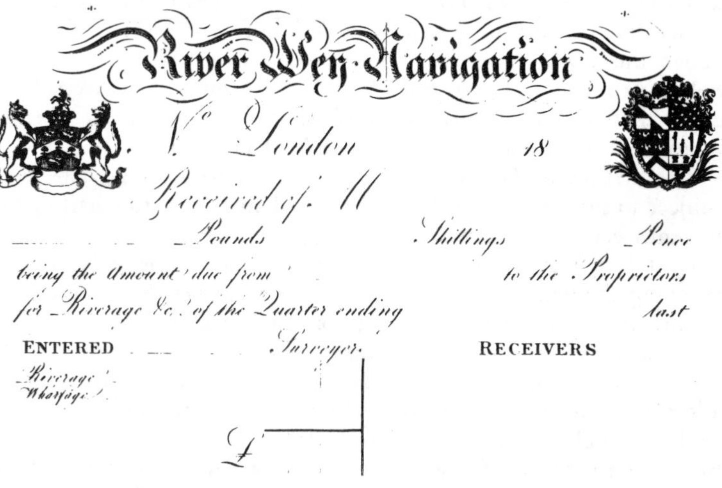

River Wey Navigation

No London 18

Received of M

Pounds Shillings Pence

being the Amount due from to the Proprietors

for Riverage &c. of the Quarter ending last

ENTERED Surveyor. RECEIVERS

Riverage

Wharfage

£

Fig. 6.—Wey Navigation Receipt, c. 1820

CHAPTER III

The River Arun before 1789

The Arun river—its variable outlet—signs of early navigation—Fitzalan's improvements—the water-bailiff's book 1637—bill to link Arundel with the Thames, 1641—incidents in the Civil War—shipbuilding industry—Littlehampton Harbour Act, 1732—Arun Navigation Act, 1785—opening of the Arun Canal 1787 and Hardham tunnel 1790.

THE river Arun, 47 miles in length, has its source in St Leonard's Forest and, after flowing westwards through Horsham to Bucks Green, makes a southerly turn to Newbridge and Pallingham. Passing under Stopham bridge, it receives the Western Rother and turns east to run beneath the site of the Roman fort at Pulborough. From the bluff on which the town stands stretches a great expanse of water meadow, flanked by sandy slopes of pine and confronted by the low, broad line of the Downs with its tree rings of Rackham and Chanctonbury. The river turns and makes for the sea, passing amidst the wild brooks between Amberley Castle and Bury, before forcing a passage through the Downs at Houghton, to pass through a roadless and secluded valley with steep slopes overhung by the substantial beeches of Arundel Park, until at length, jutting out above the town, tower the impressive battlements of the castle. Below Arundel bridge, the river runs for 7 miles in a deep, tidal channel edged by salt meadows and scoured by violent tides, before pouring into the English Channel at Littlehampton.

The Arun's outfall, like that of other Sussex rivers, has been subject to numerous transformations.[17] Until the latter half of the fifteenth century its estuary was some 10 miles east of its present site, at Lancing, where its waters mingled with the Adur before reaching the sea. Then its mouth became blocked by shingle and, as the inexorable eastward drift of the tides pushed the Adur towards Hove, so the Arun was thrust back westwards before the constant piling up of the shingle. Fresh exits formed near Worthing, Goring and Ferring; then finally, around 1500–30, it broke through near Littlehampton. Palmer's large-scale map of the Sussex coast, drawn in 1587, shows how narrow the Littlehampton mouth then appeared,* while stretches of landlocked water at

* About half a mile east of its present site.

Goring and east of Worthing reveal traces of the old course of the river. On Speed's map, 1610, no sign of these remains.

There seems little doubt that the Arun was partly navigable at the time of the Norman Conquest. Authorities are at variance upon whether Arundel boasted any river-traffic before this date, but the town is referred to as a port in Domesday Book time (*portum aquae et consuetudinem navium*) and it is reported by various chroniclers that about 1070, Roger de Montgomery, a Norman nobleman created Earl of Arundel by William I for his help at Hastings, imported small square blocks of Caen stone from Normandy for refacing the castle keep. Hadrian Allcroft presents a strong case for accepting Ford as the then port of Arundel, since the tide probably flowed no higher than this point before 1300 and the crossing-point would in any case have hindered the passage of boats heavily laden. Furthermore, the river would in any event have flowed an inconvenient half a mile east of where Arundel bridge now stands.[18]

Arundel grew in importance. In 1295 two Members were returned to Westminster. By the turn of the fourteenth century its markets and fairs were firmly established and on the hillside between castle and marsh 94 houses and 32 stalls were clustered together. Not, however, until the latter half of the sixteenth century were serious attempts made to improve the navigation of the river. In 1544 Henry Fitzalan had succeeded to the earldom at the age of 31 and it was he who, in the course of the next 30 years, set out to make the town a port for sea-going vessels and to reduce the widespread flooding. This work must have been a gigantic operation at that time, but it was surprisingly successful. The channel to the sea was cleared and widened and the river embanked as far up as North Stoke before the end of Henry VIII's reign (1547). The course of the Arun at Arundel was altered so that the river flowed to the edge of the town and by 1550 timber was being exported from the newly built wharves. During the early part of Queen Elizabeth I's reign, the work of making a new entrance—the narrow one shown on Palmer's map—to the river at Littlehampton was completed. The task of improving the upper reaches was then begun.

The water-bailiff's book of the river Arun[19] is the most accurate extant source of information regarding the early navigation of the Arun. Anciently, wrote the bailiff,[143] the navigation began at a place in the river called 'Turning-stream', which formed the junction of the Arun and Rother rivers, but that nowadays (1637) it started at Pallingham Quay, the river being cleared about the beginning of Queen Elizabeth's reign by Henry Fitzalan for the conveyance of timber by barge from Pallingham to Arundel.* 'It has likewise lately [1623] been endeavoured by some to have made it further navigable, even up to Newbridge, by expending a great sum of money,† a work very hard and difficult, the charge and labour lost, and the work now left undone, to the prejudice of the level, both below and above Pallingham.' In 1583 it is recorded that timber was transported from Ewhurst overland to the Arun for shipment.[20] Since Arundel is more than 7 miles further from Ewhurst than the Thames at Weybridge, it is a reasonable assumption that the timber was moved the shortest distance by land, i.e. to Pallingham which would have been 6 miles nearer and only 13 miles from Ewhurst.[144]

Navigation, however, above the tidal limit at Houghton must have been extremely slow and hazardous. The water-bailiff's duties included the supervision of no less than 29 'weares' ('many of which were in decay and ruinous') between Houghton and Pallingham; 15 of these were above Pulborough bridge. The fishermen had to open the gates of the weirs to let barges pass during the day. Between sunset and sunrise river traffic passed only up to Houghton since 'Bargemen ought not to passe with their Barges on the high streame from sun setting to sun rising, but in the tides way onely forth and back, and no farther, viz. as farre as the tyde flowes and lifts on ye sayd high streame'.[21]

The first serious proposal to link London and the English Channel by joining the Wey and Arun rivers was formulated in 1641, when a bill‡ was introduced into the House of Lords 'for the making a river navigable for boats and barges to pass from the Haven of Arundell through the Counties of Sussex and Surrey into the River of Thames'. The preamble of the bill explained the need for cheaper carriage and claimed that every barge carrying 20 tons would save the charge of keeping six score horses. The line of the navigation was to follow the course of the rivers Wey and Arun which were to be linked by a 2-mile canal from the tributary stream of the Wey at Cranleigh to a small branch of the Arun at Dunsfold; in such manner would communication be opened up between London and Littlehampton. The main object of the intended waterway was to provide for the carriage of chalk, timber,

* The Rother was also navigable in 1615 as far as Fittleworth, for a rude wharf supported by timber piles stood beside Fittleworth Mill. (Lady Maxse, *Story of Fittleworth*, 1935, p. 50.)

† £1,600.

‡ The text of the bill is given in Appendix I, pages 267–71.

and the products of the iron industry, none of which could be carried in winter by reason of the highways, 'it being almost impossible for carts and carriages to pass through, the ways being now extraordinarily foul and dangerous'.

It was proposed that the Lord Chancellor should appoint twelve commissioners representing Surrey and Sussex, to have 'full power and lawful authority to compound and agree with' all those affected by the perfecting of the 'free passage of the river or new cut or cuts to be made from London unto Guildford and so from Guildford unto Arundell and unto other parts of the said Counties of Surrey and Sussex as shall be thought fit and convenient by the Commissioners'. Any person being 'obstinate' and refusing to accept 'reasonable' compensation for compulsory purchase of land had to accept the Commissioners' recompense. To finance the undertaking the Commissioners were to have 'full power and lawful authority to tax and assess such of the inhabitants as shall in their opinion be likely to receive ease or benefit by the said passage and river, at such reasonable sums of money and payments as they in their discretion shall think fit'. Tax collectors were to be appointed by the Commissioners to collect these levies and any refusing to pay the sum demanded within twelve days 'shall be imprisoned without bail or mainprize by the discretion of the said Commissioners', until such time as they abided by their orders.

The bill also contained clauses to deal with dishonest tax-collectors (penalties of thrice the amount wrongly detained), and stipulated how appeals were to be made against the Commissioners' decisions (to be lodged with Justices of the Peace within six months and if no satisfaction received, upon suit to the High Court of Chancery). Any two Commissioners were to decide wharfage matters and tolls and the consent had to be obtained of not less than two before the local inhabitants could be taxed or imprisoned. And finally because the whole business was rather complex, 'and for that in the compassing, effecting and perfecting this great and beneficial work divers particular cases, questions and difficulties may arise which cannot at this present be foreseen and so expressly provided for by express and particular words, therefore to the end that the said great work may receive no delays nor hindrance but be advanced with all convenient and possible speed', the Commissioners could by a majority determine all matters concerning the work as they arose.

The bill had two readings, was then referred to Committee after which nothing further was reported. It may be assumed, however, that the bill was lost not only on the grounds that the Government was not prepared to grant such extensive powers in rather vague terms to a small body of men, but to the very uncertain state of the country at that time, only months in fact before King Charles made the disastrous attempt to imprison the five Members and the year before the outbreak of the Civil War. More particularly was Parliament hesitant to grant powers it had been at such pains to control when it passed, only thirteen years before, the Petition of Right, which forbade taxation without the consent of Parliament and arbitrary and illegal imprisonment. The Act would in any case have provoked strong opposition from the owners of mills and fish kindles which bestraddled both rivers, as did in fact occur when the Wey Navigation was built a decade later.*

An interesting series of incidents occurred during the Civil War. Sir William Waller, who commanded the Parliamentary forces south of the Thames, took Arundel Castle by surprise shortly before Christmas 1642. In December of the following year the castle was recaptured by the Royalists, due mainly to a severe frost which had enabled Lord Hopton to move his troops through 'the deep and dirty ways' before the opposition knew he had that place in prospect. However, Waller, who had been away in London, soon returned to the attack and, bringing his main force over from Farnham, retook the town a few weeks later in January 1644. That same month the Parliamentary Journals reveal that the 'Saint James, a Duyn Kirke ship, was stranded at Heene near Arundel Castle', and that the Government ordered that her valuable cargo be laid up in the castle. Heene is a district between Goring and Worthing, 12 miles from Arundel. Allcroft suggests that the vessel went aground in the silted channel at one of the former mouths of the Arun, whose locality was known as Arundel Haven, hence the confusion regarding the actual place. In spite of a request from Waller that the goods might be employed to discharge the arrears of pay due to his troops, the freight was reshipped and the *Saint James* sailed to London.

* The scheme appears to have been not unlike that advocated in 1656 by Francis Mathew when he addressed Cromwell's Parliament on the immense advantage of opening up a water communication between London and Bristol. He had proposed that the rivers Isis and Avon should be made navigable to their sources and that the 3 miles of intervening country should either be linked by a canal or a stone causeway. Mathew fully recognized the formidable character of his project and considered it quite beyond the range of private enterprise, but he ventured to suggest that it might not be too much for the Government to construct the canal and make other improvements with a reasonable prospect of success.

Until the sixteenth century no ships of any size were built at Arundel, as there were no suitable docks. In 1572 four coasting vessels were registered, only one of which was over 100 tons. However, by the turn of the century the improvements made to the Arun had resulted in a considerable increase in trade, and shipbuilding was flourishing as an industry certainly before 1630 when it is known that locally built vessels were exempt from 'anchorage' and 'bondage' on their first voyage.[22] The wide variety of merchandise imported into Arundel may be judged from the list of wharfage dues charged in 1643, which included playing cards, cod fish, glass, wrought iron, oysters, mill-stones, Purbeck paving-stones, tomb-stones, and French and Spanish wine. Ogilvy, in his *Britannia Depicta* (1675), wrote of Arundel as 'an ancient borough town seated on the N.W. of the Arun, over which it has a fine wooden bridge where ships of 100 tons may ride. It enjoys a good trade, several ships being built there, as of late "The Society", and "Mary", etc.' The only men-of-war built before the Napoleonic Wars were two advice boats mounting ten guns, each of 152 tons. The *Eagle*, built in 1696, was wrecked in 1703 on the Sussex coast and the *Swift*, built in 1697, came to grief the following year off the coast of North Carolina.

Defoe in 1722 mentioned that the town was decayed but that great quantities of large timber were shipped from there to the Thames at Woolwich and Deptford and up the Medway to Chatham, and to Portsmouth and even Plymouth, 'that is to say it goes to all the King's yards where the business of the Navy is carried on. The timber shipped off there is esteemed the best, as it is also the largest that is brought by sea from any part of England.'[23] An Admiralty report of 1728 stated that Arundel was eminent for building hoys and ketches because of the quality and vast quantity of oak timber which this part of England produces more plentifully than elsewhere.[24] Indeed, until the latter half of the eighteenth century much was also shipped to ports like Lewes and Rye for burning in the Wealden iron furnaces, ten of which produced 1,400 tons of iron in 1740. By 1788, however, only two furnaces were left and the last at Ashburnham was extinguished soon after 1810.

As has been related, the mouth of the Arun at Littlehampton was subject to continual silting. Its outfall was too narrow and additional new cuts made in 1600 and 1628 did not succeed in preventing its obstruction. Clearance was again attempted in 1657 but an Admiralty chart of 1698 shows that the waterway was practically blocked by shoals, a situation still prevailing in 1715 when the Mayor, Aldermen, Burgesses, and inhabitants of Arundel petitioned the House of Commons for an Act to raise money by charging tolls on all vessels entering the river, 'to make the same more navigable and keep in good repair, and also the Key [*sic*] in the Borough'. The petition referred to the many banks of gravel and sand preventing the passage of barges and to the mouth of the river being so stopped up that 'the navigation trade will be probably lost'.

However, not until the 1732 Littlehampton Harbour Act did Parliament authorize piers to be erected and a new channel cut through the beach half a mile westwards of the old harbour mouth. Tolls were to be collected for meeting the cost, and thereafter half rates were to be charged for preserving the harbour and the navigation to Arundel. On New Year's Day 1736, the *Grub Street Journal* announced that the new harbour at Littlehampton had been opened, that there were 7 ft of water at half spring tide and 9 ft when the tide was highest, and that it would probably prove the best harbour on the coast. But if the town's difficulties appear to have been temporarily alleviated in one direction, their solution only brought another in its stead, for three years later a fort with a battery of seven guns had to be erected to deter privateers!

The American War of Independence had begun before further efforts were made to improve the navigation. A petition presented to the House of Lords in February 1784 stated that the navigation was much obstructed by shoals and many other impediments and was so shallow in places that it was inconvenient for the carriage of merchandise.* The matter was not proceeded with until the following year, when leave was granted to bring in a bill which would improve the navigation above Houghton and authorize the construction of two canals between Coldwaltham and Hardham and between Pallingham and Newbridge wharf. The inhabitants of Pulborough and adjacent parishes protested against the proposed toll to be levied on goods passing between Houghton bridge and Pallingham since no toll was then payable and 'repeated declarations had been made that none was intended to be imposed'. Furthermore, it was claimed that great injury would be caused by the erection of locks and 'no possible advantage could accrue to the petitioners from the extension to Newbridge'. The petitioners won their main point and although the Arun Navigation Act, passed in

* William Jessop in a report on the Rother, 16 April 1783, mentioned that boats below Stopham carried only 15 tons.

May 1785, authorized the improvement of the tide-way above Houghton bridge, it specified that the navigation of the river between Houghton and Pallingham was to remain free of toll 'even if locks have to be, in time, erected between Houghton and Greatham Bridge'.

The Act, inscribed on over 50 ft of vellum, was considerably more specific than the unsuccessful bills which had preceded it. Maximum toll rates were quoted for different items between several places for various quantities. No barge was to pass through any lock with less than ten tons without leave. To prevent impositions by boatmen, maximum freight charges were specified, as well as penalties for overcharging. Concessional rates were granted to barges carrying sea-gravel for the repair of any of the roads leading in the direction of Newbridge wharf. Any damage to the navigation was to be regarded as a felony, but for wilful obstruction the worst fate that could befall an offender was one month in the 'House of Correction'.

The Arun Navigation Company was formed with an authorized share capital of £10,000 divided into shares of £100 each. On 6 June 1785 the first meeting of the proprietors was held 'at the house of Abraham Saker bearing the sign of the Swan at Pulborough', with Sir Harry Goring in the chair. £7,000 had already been subscribed and an initial call of £20 per cent made, when James Edwards, the surveyor, began work on the Arun Canal in August. The line chosen between Newbridge and Pallingham involved crossing the Arun river by an aqueduct at Orfold and building three locks. Water was to be supplied by water-wheel from the river, which was dammed immediately above the aqueduct.

The Company was very much a neighbourly and almost family affair. The majority of the fifteen shareholders were either local landowners or merchants, a third of whom lived at Arundel, and the remainder all within 10 miles of the line of navigation. Five shareholders in fact held over 70 per cent of the equity; two of them were brothers, one of whom had a daughter married to the son of another of the five.

The affairs of the navigation were managed by a Committee of three subject to the control of the general assembly of proprietors. To begin with, meetings were held three or four times a year at various inns but principally at Arundel ('Norfolk Arms'), Fittleworth ('Swan'), Pulborough ('Swan'), and once at Wisborough Green ('Three Crowns'). The minutes were brief. In June 1786

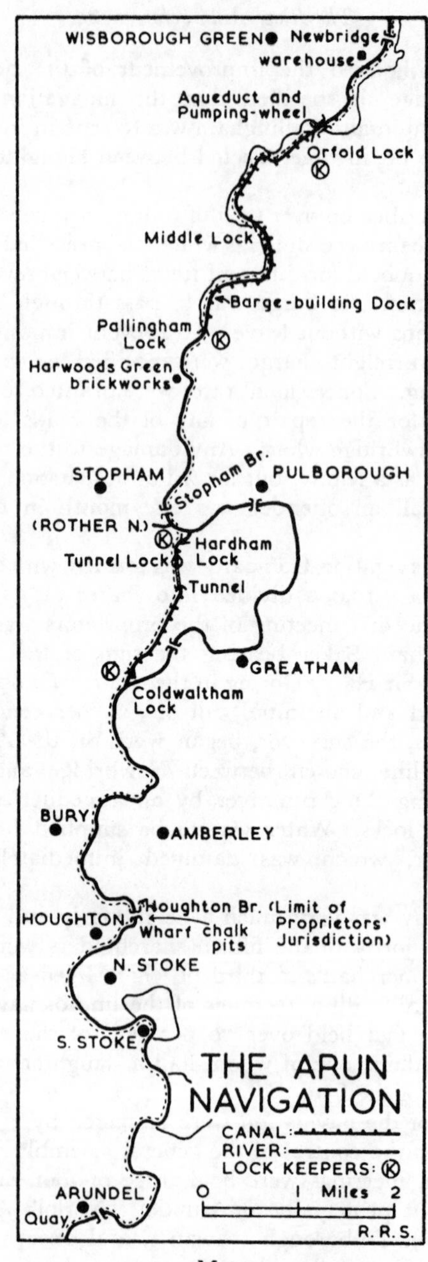
WISBOROUGH GREEN
Newbridge
warehouse
Aqueduct and
Pumping-wheel
Orfold Lock
Middle Lock
Barge-building Dock
Pallingham
Lock
Harwoods Green
brickworks
STOPHAM
Stopham Br.
PULBOROUGH
(ROTHER N.)
Hardham
Lock
Tunnel Lock
Tunnel
GREATHAM
Coldwaltham
Lock
BURY
AMBERLEY
Houghton Br. (Limit of
Proprietors'
Jurisdiction)
HOUGHTON
Wharf chalk
pits
N. STOKE
S. STOKE
THE ARUN
NAVIGATION
CANAL:
RIVER:
LOCK KEEPERS:
0
1
Miles
2
ARUNDEL
Quay
R. R. S.

Map 2

the Committee ordered that an advertisement be inserted in the *Lewes Gazette* to contradict injurious reports regarding the Company's standing, although in December it had to be admitted that 'immediately after the digging to Pallingham is finished, work should begin on the cut through Hardham Hill until the money is exhausted'. The upper navigation was opened without ceremony on 1 August 1787, but in the autumn work had to be discontinued on the lower section until £3,000 could be subscribed. No willing investor appearing, the money was borrowed at 5 per cent on mortgage of the tolls of the upper navigation. In June 1788 the Duke of Norfolk became a shareholder. At the end of the year the Committee rather optimistically, and perhaps imprudently, declared a half-yearly dividend of 2 per cent on borrowed capital. No further distribution was made for four years.

Fig. 7.—Seal of the Arun Navigation Company

It is also interesting to record that because the local roads were in such an atrocious state, the Company, in spite of its overdraft, was prepared to advance £600 to the parishes of Wisborough Green, Billingshurst, Slinfold, and Pulborough to put their high-roads in order. However, the offer was conditional on the principal being repaid in instalments within three years, and if the proposal was not acceptable, the clerk was ordered to indict![145]

A further £4,000, making the total expenditure £16,000,[25] was spent before the 13-ft high tunnel carrying the canal beneath Hardham Hill and the Roman road of Stane Street was completed during the summer of 1790. The tunnel section opened, the sinuous river channel round by Pulborough could be avoided and the distance between Arundel and Newbridge was shortened by 3 miles.

So it was that at the time of the outbreak of the French Revolution less than 15 miles separated the navigable portions of the Wey and Arun rivers, and yet the merging of their waters was only effected after an 'engagement' of nearly thirty years, during which time either one or both rivers were spurned by those trying to make a grander and more profitable union between the Thames and the English Channel.

An Abſtract, &c.

AT a MEETING of the PROPRIETORS of the ARUN NAVIGATION, held at the Norfolk-Arms, in Arundel, the 7th day of December, 1789, it was among other things) reſolved, That the following TOLLS ſhould be collected, from and after the Navigation be opened through Hardham Hill, viz.

For Tolls, Wharfage, Piling, Drawing, and giving Account, &c. at paſſing Palingham Lock, viz.

		l.	s.	d.	
All ſorts of Merchandize, in wood, downward,	at	o	4	o	per load
All ſorts of fire-wood —	at	o	1	6	per cord, or hhd.
All ſorts of chalk, ſoil, dung, or manure,	at	o	1	o	per ton
All ſorts of ſtones for making or mending roads	at	o	o	6	per ton
All ſorts of corn and grain	at	o	2	6	per load
All ſorts of coals by weight or meaſure,	at	o	2	6	per chaldron
Bark, not ſtored	at	o	5	o	per load
Ditto, ſtored	at	o	8	o	per load
Grocery & all other goods ſtored	at	o	4	o	per ton
All other goods upward, not ſtored	at	o	2	6	per load
Lime at per kiln of 240 nine gallon buſhels,	at	o	12	6	per kiln.

A 2 For

Fig. 8.—Arun Navigation toll rates at Pallingham Lock, 1790

CHAPTER IV

Plans and Projects (1790–1810)

The second phase of the canal era—Rother Navigation Act, 1791—canal planned from Petworth to Godalming—the third Earl of Egremont—his early life—agricultural reformer and patron of art—great benefactor—extensions proposed from the Arun Navigation to North Chapel and Horsham—Littlehampton Harbour Act, 1793—completion of the Basingstoke Canal 1794—first Surrey railway opened 1803—plans to link London and Portsmouth, 1803—relative merits of canal and railway—a public house at Newbridge—a bargeman's complaint—Rennie's Grand Southern Canal project, 1810.

By the time the first waters were pouring through the sluices of Pallingham lock, the canal era was entering its second phase. In the Midlands and the North the demand for improved means of communication, brought about by the Industrial Revolution, had acted as a powerful incentive to canal building. By 1790 canals had been built to link the Thames and the Severn, the Trent and the Mersey, inland navigation had been opened up between London and Liverpool, and a network of waterways spread around Birmingham and Leeds. The success of these ventures, which was bringing prosperity to Britain's trade by cheapening the cost of the transport of coal, ores, and merchandise, encouraged a spate of applications for fresh development despite the war with France.

The *London Gazette* on 18 August 1792 contained no less than nineteen notices of intended applications to Parliament for leave to make or extend cuts or canals in different parts of the kingdom, and during 1793 and 1794 thirty Acts were granted for some thousand miles of navigation requiring a total capital of nearly £5 million. Between 1789 and 1796 more than fifty new canals were authorized, and what became the 'Canal Mania' of 1792 was in many respects a counterpart to the railway boom of 1845. Most of the navigations built during this period became prosperous undertakings. There were, however, several companies floated on false expectations and inadequate surveys which, when the fever of speculation engendered by the 'Canal Mania' had subsided, ran short of capital and had to be abandoned. In the South, the Dorset & Somerset foundered for lack of capital when only 8 miles had been built, and the Salisbury & Southampton was never completed and only partly used after £90,000 had been expended.

The outbreak of the Napoleonic Wars in 1793 brought with it a financial crisis which, in turn, caused work on many canals to come to a halt. During 1794 the number of enactments fell by half that of the preceding year, and with no easing of the international situation the sponsoring of new projects was abandoned. In 1797 only one new canal was sanctioned. The canal boom was over. Coalition succeeded coalition and the face of war was seen on many fronts until the sight of Napoleon's forces encamped on the cliffs of France brought the threat of serious invasion to England for the first time since the Armada. More and more cargoes began to fall into the hands of the French privateers raiding in the Channel and along the east coast. As a result, merchants and carriers started diverting traffic to the inland waterways. In this situation carriers sometimes co-operated by lowering their charges, but the canal companies generally took full advantage of the situation and charged the maximum toll rates. However, between 1803 and 1805, the years when invasion threatened, several canal undertakings, including the Basingstoke, helped the nation by carrying military stores free of toll to the army encampments.

The military adventures of the first Napoleon resulted in events which made patent the many risks to which British shipping was exposed when sailing up the English Channel. Certainly the urge to improve overland communication between London and Portsmouth was strong and multifarious schemes for canals and railways were mooted. The precise nature of the impetus was constantly changing as commercial justification vied with temporary national need; consequently each project benefited and suffered from the prevailing political or economic temperature. Several plans were considered by successive War Ministers and it is surprising, having regard to the fact that no formidable natural barriers had to be overcome and that war with France was never far from the horizon, that the Government did not make any attempt to open up an inland water route of such seemingly strategic importance. In fact, the only action of this kind finally taken by the Government was to start building the Royal Military Canal from Hythe to Winchelsea in 1804 as a line of defence against invasion.

There is no doubt that in the south of England, where the motive force in projecting canals was agricultural rather than industrial, proposals were more in evidence than achievements. The Reverend Arthur Young, writing soon after the turn of the century, stated that 'the advantages which England has derived from extending its inland navigation, have been prodigious; and to agriculture it has been no less beneficial than to manufacturers and commerce' and added that the benefits Sussex had received and would gain from increasing her navigations were very considerable.[26] An Act had been obtained in 1790 for making the Ouse navigable from Lewes to above Lindfield, but financial difficulties prevented its completion until 1812. Lack of capital was indeed the problem and it was due to one man, the third Earl of Egremont, that waterways developed as they did in West Sussex. The Arun Navigation being completed, Egremont went ahead with his plan to make the Rother navigable at his own expense from the Arun at Stopham to Midhurst. William Jessop surveyed the line in 1790* and found that 'such navigation and cut may be made at an easy expense'. The original intention was also to improve the river from Greatham bridge to Stopham, but to this there were objections on the part of the Arun Navigation who were empowered, but had so far failed, to do this work under the provisions of the 1785 Act.

The Rother Navigation Act was passed in April 1791, with the object of supplying coal to the interior and exporting lead, corn, and Petworth marble. The Earl was the sole proprietor and had the advantage of being able to use the men from his Petworth estate to build the navigation. Young drew attention to the advantages resulting from the employment of a hundred or more Sussex workmen: 'In the usual method of cutting canals, these men are a constant nuisance to the neighbourhood, and the terror of all other descriptions of people. But in Lord Egremont's canal, the men are all drawn from amongst his own workmen, and have none of that turbulence and riot with which foreign workmen are inspired; and as these labourers use implements equal to the best navigation diggers, the employment of domestic workmen is an evident advantage; and still farther, the expenses of the job are much less to the employer, whilst the weekly wages of the men in this business, instead of 8s. or 9s. rise up to 14s. or 15s.'[27]

The line, completed in 1794† at a cost of £13,300, mainly followed the natural course of the river, rose 54 ft by eight locks, and had less than 2 miles of artificial cuts along its length of 11¼ miles. The navigation was a success.[146] The reduced cost and facility of freighting coal increased the productivity of the farmers, since it

* Jessop had also surveyed the river as far as Petworth mills in 1783.

† This date is inscribed on the parapet of the bridge at the entrance to the basin at Midhurst. The navigation was built by Charles and Samuel Jones.

proportionately lessened the demand for furze which had had to be grown to provide fuel for the kilns, and so enabled more grain to be sown. Corn, oak-bark, and cordwood for charcoal were exported in considerable quantities and Young commented that 'by this most useful and public spirited undertaking many thousand acres of land are necessarily rendered more valuable to the proprietors. Timber is now sent by water. Large falls have been exported which would scarcely have been felled, and the Government Agents and Contractors have made large purchases, in consequence of a more easy communication to the sea. An additional tract of country is also supplied with lime from the Houghton and Bury pits', the former of which supplied some 40,000 tons annually.[147]

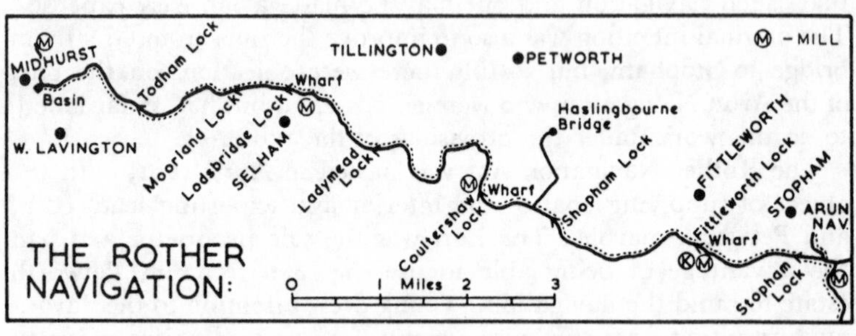

Map 3

A branch canal to serve Petworth was also built from the tail of the cut above Shopham lock to Haslingbourne bridge. This 1¼-mile extension which had been surveyed by Thomas Upton contained two locks and was completed in 1793 at a cost of nearly £5,000. It is unlikely, however, that this branch carried much traffic, for an Act was passed in 1800 which authorized a deviation in the turnpike road and enabled traffic from Chichester and Duncton to pass by Coultershaw mill instead of by Rotherbridge which was pulled down. Although Coultershaw was nearly 1 mile further away from Petworth than the wharf at Haslingbourne, two locks were saved. The old road had been devious, narrow, and incommodious, but it was not the main justification for building the Petworth Canal. According to Young,[28] Egremont originally intended extending the branch to Hampers Common, 'close to the town', which would have entailed 51 ft of lockage from Haslingbourne. Young commented that as farmers in the Weald required from 80 to 120 bushels of manure per acre of wheat, this proposal would enable waggons to load chalk from the Arun valley at Hampers Common instead of at Duncton, and so allow them to collect three or four loads instead of one in a day.

The fact that such a costly scheme was entertained reflects the enthusiasm of its promoter who, before the Rother Navigation had been completed, was already envisaging a direct communication with the Thames by linking Petworth (Hampers Common) and Stonebridge wharf. Young mentions in 1808 that 'a considerable part of the original plan still remains to be carried into execution; it is to connect London with Sussex and to lay open that market to the produce of this County and receiving its goods and merchandise in return. By a direct communication from Petworth to Guildford, by a collateral branch to Horsham, a very considerable proportion of the County would be benefitted; the ground has been surveyed and the levels taken.' William Jessop had carried out the survey by 1795[29] and a plan dated 1793[30] shows that a branch was also intended from Newbridge to Alfold to link with the line from Petworth.[148–9] The distance from there to Stonebridge was given as 23 miles requiring 133 ft of lockage and it was stated that the 12-mile collateral branch to Horsham would be on the level. That this plan appears to have been in Egremont's mind for some years is also evidenced by Marshall's reference in 1798 to the intention of making a canal from the Rother by Petworth to Godalming.[31]

George O'Brien Wyndham, the third Earl, was a remarkable man. Born in 1751, he succeeded to the title at the age of 11 and married only after several mistresses had borne him ten children. He was educated at Westminster, where he showed an aptitude for the classics and arts, and afterwards lived a gay social life in London, where he numbered Charles Fox among his friends. Until the age of 30 Egremont was very much the man about town, wearing sumptuous apparel at Court balls and seeking the company of beautiful women. He rivalled the Duc de Chartres for the favours of the courtesan, Mlle Duthé, to whom he gave a gilt coach and who was observed 'all bediamonded' in his box at the opera. In 1778 he visited Portsmouth where the King was reviewing the fleet. 'I went with a party, one of which was a lady with whom I was very much in love, without her husband, and lived in the same lodging with her.' He was also invited to dine with George III after the review, 'a thing unknown in those days', but this exploit was suddenly interrupted; 'I abandoned review, mistress and king and went post to the House of Lords' to oppose a private bill concerning a friend.[32] However, his excursions into the political field were few. His father, Sir Charles Wyndham, the second Earl, had been appointed one of the Secretaries of State shortly before his death, yet Egremont took no prominent part in politics; his appearances in the House of Lords became extremely rare after Pitt's accession to power—he disliked Pitt and mistrusted his colleagues.

His amorous intrigues came to a temporary halt when his engagement was announced in July 1780 to Lady Maria Waldegrave, a step-daughter of the Duke of Gloucester. Maria, who was immortalized on canvas by Reynolds, doubtless found Egremont hard to understand. Their relationship was not altogether happy, they parted, and he resumed his liaison with Lady Melbourne, whose influence, coupled with his natural shyness and disinterest in Court life, caused him to shrink from marriage and from London.

Egremont retired to Petworth and some five years later took as his mistress Elizabeth Iliffe, a girl still in her teens, whose parentage remains obscure. It seems to have been a union of real affection, though not of exclusive devotion, because there was a contemporary liaison with Elizabeth Fox by whom he had a son and a daughter. Not until July 1801, by which time he was 50 and Elizabeth Iliffe had borne him six children, did he marry her privately at Petworth, but the marriage that should have established her position destroyed it, and in May 1803 she left Petworth never to return. A daughter who died in infancy was the only product of the lawful union, and although his eldest son George, who took the name of Wyndham by royal licence, inherited the greater part of his estates, the earldom passed to his nephew, a fact which did not appear to cause him any great regret.

Egremont was immensely rich, certainly a millionaire and one of the wealthiest men in the kingdom. He inherited a considerable fortune which included lead and coal mines in Cumberland. His five principal estates in the British Isles covered 110,000 acres. It was indeed his vast financial resources coupled with his zeal for agricultural reform which prompted him for over thirty years to develop inland navigation in West Sussex. He was also extremely generous; his loans and small gifts exceeded a million pounds, and his donations to charities totalled some £20,000 annually. Indeed it was said that his name was associated with almost every institution in the country of which the object was to increase the sum of human happiness. He helped in other directions too. Men he respected were rescued from bankruptcy, a fellow peer was saved from ruin, a losing gambler assisted. He personally provided horses, uniforms, weapons, and equipment for the Petworth Yeomanry, which were raised in 1794 to defend the south coast against Napoleon. Egremont was appointed Colonel of the Sussex regiment. His suggestion that a retired regular officer might be more qualified was brushed aside by the Duke of Richmond, who insisted that 'to stand forth as Commander was of more consequence than any practical knowledge of cavalry business'. He also, rather reluctantly, accepted the Lord Lieutenancy of the county in 1819.

Egremont led a very active life and his principal interests were his estates and art. At Petworth he greatly increased cultivation, initiated experimental farming, developed stock-breeding, and kept a large racing stable which won for him five Derbys and five Oaks. He inherited a quantity of antique sculpture and paintings, many still in packing cases, and from this formed a collection for which Petworth House has become justly famous. His patronage was an invaluable support, both morally and financially, to contemporary artists, many of whom rose from obscurity to fame. In 1795 he commissioned Romney to paint his mistress and children, and in the course of the next 40 years 66 painters added 263 pictures to his gallery. Thomas Phillips contributed 34, Sir Joshua Reynolds 22, and Turner 20; the latter's friendship with Egremont enabled the painter to spend months at Petworth House where he had his own studio, good pike fishing, and the freedom to roam where he wished. And while we may regret that Turner did not do for the Wey and Arun what Constable did for the Stour, he did at least paint a fine water-colour of the Arun valley and have two attempts at the Chichester Canal.

The Earl's kindness and extreme modesty endeared him to many. His hospitality was famous and Burke spoke of him as 'delighting to reign in the dispensation of happiness'. Rarely did he formally entertain the great, but in June 1814, after Napoleon's abdication, he received the Prince Regent, the Tsar of Russia, and the King of Prussia with their suites; the picture *Allied Sovereigns at Petworth* by Phillips depicts the magnificent scene. Happier was he, however, when entertaining his own retainers and their families.

Egremont's main concern in all his enterprises was to improve standards. His enlightened disinterest in the profit motive is best illustrated in a letter he wrote in 1812, at a time when he was actively supporting the Wey & Arun Canal bill, in which he opposed the revival of schemes to make the Yorkshire Ouse and Swale rivers navigable in Acts passed in 1767. 'The Acts passed forty-five years ago were intended . . . for public benefit and not for private emolument. They gave power to subscribers to execute that public benefit and to levy tolls as proper remuneration for the money expended; and the subscribers on their part contracted an obligation with the public to carry that benefit into execution. The Acts have been in force during many years of the peace succeeding the Seven Years War when the rate of interest was lowest, and during the last fourteen years when the circulation of paper money arising from the restriction of bank cash payments has given such facility to speculations of internal improvement, that the attention of Parliament has lately been almost as much employed in watching and checking useless and improvident projects as in forwarding those which are useful and good. And now, at the end of these forty-five years the part of the objects of these Acts which has been executed is so inconsiderable that it bears no proportion to the original plan or to the just expectations of the public.'[33] To Egremont, the canalization of the Rother meant improving the trading facilities and living conditions of the locality, and nothing more. Indeed the tolls and wharfage rates which the Earl was empowered to demand on the Rother Navigation were much less than those authorized for the Arun or similar navigations and were specified in the Act as being for the repayment of money laid out by the promoter.

Trade on the Arun was encouraging. Despite a slow start, by 1791 some 14,000 tons a year were being carried and a modest working profit shown which unwisely prompted the proprietors to declare a dividend of 4 per cent the following year. However, its future prospects, in spite of a substantial overdraft, appeared bright and proposals were put forward for various extensions to the navigation. In December 1791 the Committee decided to petition Parliament for a bill to extend the canal from Orfold lock through Wisborough Green, Kirdford, and Shillinglee Lake to Fisher Street, North Chapel.[34] The purpose of the scheme was simply stated as 'public utility and improvement of land and estates', but more important must have been the fact that both Kirdford and North Chapel furnished substantial deposits of Petworth marble.*

The Arun proprietors were, however, worried by the amount of traffic which continued to ply the old river round by Pulborough

* It is possible that Lord Egremont had already been approached by the Government to sell the land for the factories which were set up about 1800 at North Chapel to supply charcoal to the gunpowder mills at Waltham and Faversham. In 1825, however, Cobbett noted that the factories had been closed for some time and the substantial brick and slate buildings sold for demolition.

and which threatened to increase with the opening of the Rother Navigation. They therefore decided to petition for an Act to continue the cutting from Hardham tunnel to the Rother above Stopham lock at Rail Picta, so that boats bound for Midhurst could avoid locking up and down, and thereby be encouraged to use their navigation. The treasurer was authorized to borrow £2,500 for these works, but the petitions which were heard on 28 February 1792 were, after being referred to a Parliamentary Committee, not reported and the extensions never made. A good deal of lobbying had in fact been going on behind the scenes. Egremont feared that the levels at Stopham lock might be seriously affected by the scheme and suspected that the Arun proprietors were anxious to collect tolls from all craft using the Rother navigation. The people of Pulborough were also bitterly complaining that the Arun proprietors were not maintaining the 'old river' to discourage barges from using the toll-free route.

Attempts were also being made to extend the Arun Canal as far as Horsham. On 9 July 1792 a well-attended meeting was held at the Town Hall, Horsham, under the chairmanship of the Duke of Norfolk, when it was resolved to make the Arun navigable from Newbridge to Weald Cross, Slinfold. Later it was agreed to extend this a mile further to Farthing Bridge on the main Guildford–Horsham road, less than a mile from the centre of the town. It was argued in favour of the scheme that it would improve the agricultural value of the lands and estates adjoining the river, which suffered from continual flooding, and that it would bring great benefits to the trade and commerce of Horsham. The survey made by John Rennie[35] showed the scheme to be practicable, the cost was estimated at £18,133 and leave to bring in a bill was granted by the House of Lords in February 1793. Over £15,000 had been subscribed, however, when, following a series of meetings, the Committee formed to carry through the project found that they could reach no satisfactory agreement with the proprietors of the Arun Navigation,[150] and the project was dropped in 1794. Marshall, in his *Rural Economy of the Southern Counties* (1798), advocated an extension of the Arun to Horsham either by improving the river or by cutting across the vale through Billingshurst, and from Horsham through the Surrey Weald to the chalk quarries at Betchworth and down the valley of the Mole to the market at Dorking.

The passing of the Littlehampton Harbour Act in 1793 enabled further improvement of the navigation between Littlehampton and Arundel, including the making of a towpath. Alterations were also made to the toll rates granted by the 1733 Act. Since £28,300 had already been expended by the inhabitants of Arundel and Littlehampton on repairs to the harbour (a huge amount for towns with a total population of less than 2,500), ships belonging to the port were exempt from toll.

Water communication was now open from the sea to Arundel for vessels up to 200 tons and for barges as far as Midhurst and Newbridge. The river between Arundel and Houghton, a distance of 8½ miles, remained an open navigation without a towpath. Barges either sailed or were punted up and down the river with the tide, the journey from Littlehampton to Newbridge taking about 2½ days, although 6 hours were saved if the tunnel was used. However, according to Young,[36] the 1s. toll for this cut drove much trade to the old river channel 'except in summer or in floods'. Sprit-sailed barges were mainly used and these could carry in excess of 30 tons, although the loads were related more to draught than to capacity, being dependent on the rains rather than the tides on the upper reaches of the river. Young also mentioned barges carrying 15 tons but stated that those carrying 25 tons were the best. Cargoes on the Rother averaged 20 tons, rarely exceeded 30, and between 1809 and 1815 35 tons was the highest recorded.

The short-sightedness of the Arun proprietors over the concessions and working arrangements which had led to the collapse of the attempts to extend the Arun Canal to North Chapel and Horsham had incensed Egremont, and it was doubtless their attitude which had prompted Young to say that the great advantage of the Rother Navigation being in the hands of one owner was that 'he feels a greater spur in the success of it than any company of merchants who live at a distance and subscribe their money. By vesting the undertaking in the hands of an individual, no opposition is likely to be met with nor is the business liable to be thwarted or counteracted.'[37] In fact, the lack of enthusiasm over the proposed extensions which Egremont wished to promote was occasioned to a large degree by the different outlooks, on the one hand, of a very wealthy landowner seeking the public good and, on the other, of the local merchants who were naturally more influenced by the profit motive and who had only received an annual return on their original investment of less than 1½ per cent over a period of ten years.[145] Egremont also appreciated that Sir Harry Goring, the chairman of the Arun Navigation and owner of the land in Wisborough Green through which any canal to Horsham would have to pass, was opposed to the scheme. However, the Arun's financial position was precarious. It was not even possible to pay those responsible for managing the navigation and in December 1793 it was resolved that 'the late Henry Digance and Thomas Seward be compensated for the time and trouble in superintending the works of the navigation by the issue of two shares each'.[38] Although toll receipts were satisfactory, nothing had been done to reduce the Company's huge mortgage, which was more than the original capital subscribed, with the result that interest charges accounted for half the revenue. The Company were reluctant to take action and proposals to suspend dividend payments (which had been paid at a rate of from 2 to 4 per cent between 1792 and 1796) were ill-received by some of the proprietors. At length, and only after some considerable hesitation due to personal animosity, it was decided 'to allow Lord Egremont to subscribe to the outstanding 26 shares at par on condition that he would lend his support to promoting the bill for the extension of the Navigation to Horsham'.[39] Moreover, it was an additional condition that Egremont would purchase at par any Arun shares which holders might wish to sell within the next ten years. Sir Harry Goring resigned the chairmanship in favour of the Earl, to whom he also sold his shareholding, thus giving Egremont 36 per cent of the company's capital. The Company's first action was to redeem £2,450 of mortgage bonds, but resolutions not to declare dividends until the debt had been considerably reduced were adjourned until 1800, though none were in fact paid after 1796 until 1821. In 1795 over 200,000 bricks had been sold for £294, but floods had caused much damage and £691 had to be spent on repairing the towpath during 1794 and 1795. A sub-committee was also set up to treat with any person who wished to license the tunnel for alleviating summer floods.

Meanwhile in Surrey and Hampshire the 37 miles of the Basingstoke Canal—whose Act had been passed in 1778—were finally completed in 1794. As all barges passing between the Thames and the canal had to use the Wey Navigation, the Wey tolls showed a considerable rise, though the charges they could levy on Basingstoke traffic using their river were limited by the Act. By 1800 over 21,000 tons were passing annually to and from the Thames which increased the Wey's traffic by more than half, the average yearly tonnage carried rising from 33,500 tons during the decade before the canal's opening to 54,500 tons during the ensuing decade.

However, even by the turn of the century, railways were being considered as an alternative form of transport to waterways. Already many canal companies and collieries employed horse-drawn waggons on rails for short-distance haulage. In 1807 Rudge wrote, in his *General View of the Agriculture of Gloucestershire*, that 'The time is probably fast approaching when the iron rail-road will supersede the further use of the canal, for the conveyance of materials and commodities of all kinds through the interior parts of the island; one horse of moderate strength will draw many tons of compact heavy substances with ease, and the frequent elevations which interrupt the level surface, may be managed with little trouble by the inclined plane, or by tunnels.'

In 1803 rival schemes were put forward to link London and Portsmouth. John Rennie's plan was to extend the Croydon Canal, then under construction. William Jessop, on the other hand, favoured an extension of the Surrey Iron Railway.

Rennie envisaged a large canal, 100 miles long with 41 locks and a long tunnel between Coulsdon and Merstham, running from the Croydon Canal via Redhill, Crawley, Ifield, Horsham, through Pulborough village and across the Arun above Arundel bridge to Yapton, Barnham, Mundham, Chichester, Emsworth, Havant to Portsmouth 'just above His Majesty's dockyard'. No details of expected traffic were given, but there was mention of naval stores, goods for the East India Company's ships at Spithead, chalk, and coal, and revenue was estimated at £100,000 a year. It was asserted that this canal would enable 60 tons of corn to be carried between the two ports for less than £50, as compared with the then current charge of £125. The cost was estimated at £720,649 for a broad and £571,621 for a narrow canal. Branch canals were also proposed to the Medway at Limpsfield and the Arun at Newbridge, Pulborough, and Arundel, but for these no estimates were given. A bill was presented to Parliament and subscriptions appear to have been sought, but with little success.

The *Lewes Journal*[40] commented that 'from a thorough knowledge of the country through which it is to pass, a country thin of population and with very few manufacturers, we confess ourselves at a loss to know from whence the tolls are to arise to pay the interest of the immense sum which will be required to complete the work'. A fortnight later, the *Journal* reported that the bill was lost for the present Session and so it remained for, as Rennie wrote later in 1810, 'A powerful opposition arose, which stopped the Bill in its early progress, and since then, the project, although not abandoned by its original promoters, has not been actively prosecuted.' One of the chief reasons for its failure was the doubts expressed about the wisdom of a tunnel 4½ miles long, not only on the grounds of cost and the possibility that the borings might meet quicksand where there ought to be rock, but of the difficulty of working through a tunnel of this length by man power. There were also loud protests from the millers on the Wandle and from various landowners.

As early as 1799 William Jessop had proposed a horse railway from Wandsworth to Portsmouth by way of Croydon, Reigate, and Arundel, and in May 1801 an Act was obtained for making the world's first public railway operated by a railway company. William Jessop, one of whose sons was to build the Wey & Arun, was appointed engineer. It was a double-track line laid with plate-rails on stone sleepers, on which four-wheeled waggons were drawn by horses provided by the merchants and carriers, who paid tolls calculated on tonnage, commodity, and distance. The Surrey Iron Railway was opened in July 1803 and ran from Wandsworth Creek as far as Croydon; but at a meeting on 3 June 1802 it was announced that 'it had been thought advisable to enquire whether the Iron Railway now establishing from Wandsworth to Croydon might not be extended through Surrey, Sussex and Hants, so as to open a communication with seaports in the Channel and particularly with Portsmouth'.[41] The plan proposed links with the Arun Navigation at Newbridge and the Ouse Navigation at Lindfield and also envisaged that at the London end the railway should leave the Surrey Iron Railway at Mitcham and cross the Thames by a proposed bridge that was later to be named after Waterloo; thence it was to run to Tottenham Court Road to join the intended London Railway, which was designed to link London Docks with the basin of the Grand Junction Canal at Paddington and which later became the Regent's Canal. The terminus was planned to be in Stamford Street, approximately where Waterloo Station now stands and the estimated cost was £430,000.[42] In 1803 Parliament authorized the extension of the Surrey Iron Railway through the Merstham Gap to Reigate (Croydon, Merstham & Godstone Railway Act). But in the event the urge to reach Portsmouth and even Reigate faded with Nelson's victory at Trafalgar and the high cost of construction. In fact the line never reached beyond Merstham (*see* Chapter V) although about 1810 a branch was built in the other direction from the Surrey Iron Railway to the canal basin at Croydon, where 'the trucks were generally drawn by large mules'.

In October 1803 Robert Marshall, lessee of the Godalming Navigation, published *An Examination into the Respective Merits of the proposed Canal and Iron Railway from London to Portsmouth*, in which he preferred canals to other modes of conveyance over level country where the land was of little value and the 'bowels of the earth contain valuable mines and quarries and with the advantages of plenty of water on a retentive soil, and', wrote Marshall, 'as did the Croydon Canal and its proposed extension to Portsmouth possess these advantages some hopes might be entertained of its success'. He estimated the total expense at £1,200,000, compared with £420,000 by railway. Arguments in favour of the railway were threefold; that the journey would be completed in one day instead of five, that it would take one-tenth of the time to build and that it would require forty as against seventy-five horses to operate. From about 1810 to 1835 the Croydon Canal and the Surrey Iron Railway operated in direct competition with each other, and the results over this period gave no positive proof that mule-pulled trucks were any more efficient than horse-drawn barges. In the event, both projects were dropped and the link between the two great cities postponed.

The Arun minutes referred only once to the possible need to call a special meeting and in 1804 at the height of the controversy the main item recorded was the decision to erect docks for the repair and building of barges at Pallingham. In 1805 the Magistrates refused to grant a licence for a public house at Newbridge unless the Proprietors of the Arun Navigation approved the application. No objection was raised to this proposal, for it would be 'a great convenience and accommodation, as well as to the merchants who are obliged from business to attend there and transact business in the wharf exposed to all weathers and without means of obtaining any refreshment within a mile and a quarter, as to the public'.[43] The 'Lime-burners' Arms' still exists in name today, although its site by the bridge was moved when barge traffic ceased.

In general the interests of the proprietors and their employees were protected by the Act and the Company's bylaws. In spite of a certain infamy occasioned by their poaching, the bargemen were independent, likeable, rugged types of men who lived a hard open-air existence. Their pleasures were simple in the extreme and few were literate. However, it is recorded[44] that in 1806 Henry Jupp, a farmer, took exception for some reason or other to a bargee, William Aldridge, and seized and impounded his barge-horse while he was passing through one of the locks. Aldridge complained to the proprietors, who resolved that Mr Jupp be summoned before a Magistrate so that a fine of not more than £5 and not less than £2 be imposed for the replacement of the horse, and that an action for damages be brought against Jupp as 'an example and caution to other occupiers of lands through which the towing-paths pass and to the public of the determination of the Proprietors to protect the bargemen in the legal execution of their duty'. In 1808 Richard Wardroper, a Midhurst solicitor, was appointed clerk on the death of Percival Hart and it was resolved that John Seward—the wharfinger at Newbridge—should be paid £30 per annum for superintending the navigation. The following year it was ordered that £500 should be paid from the tolls for assisting in the establishment of a road from Bury Gate via Pulborough and Billingshurst to Park Street Corner provided that only one turnpike gate was erected between each of the roads leading to Newbridge Wharf from Pulborough Street and Park Street Corner.[45] It was further agreed in 1810 to build a storehouse at Newbridge to allow lime kilns to be erected, and to enlarge the wharf by purchasing three acres from Guildenhurst farm.

Another abortive attempt to link London and the English Channel, only this time by a different route, occurred in 1807. It was planned to build a 35-mile barge canal from the Itchen at Winchester via Farnham either to the Basingstoke Canal at Aldershot or to the Wey Navigation at Godalming. The cost was estimated by the promoters at £200,000 with a 2-mile tunnel between Alresford and Alton, and £124,400 had been subscribed by 1809. However, the Basingstoke Canal Committee judged the likely cost to be twice the estimate and the Portsmouth, Southampton & London Junction Canal scheme foundered on the grounds of expense, the likely lack of water, and the problematical amount of trade in times of peace.

Then, in 1810, John Rennie published his proposals for the construction of the Grand Southern Canal from the Medway to Portsmouth. He suggested a line 95 miles long starting from Tonbridge and passing through Edenbridge and Crawley to Horsham, thence by Billingshurst and through the ridge at Pulborough, after which it was to keep to the hillside above the east bank of the river Arun until it joined the river Arun for 1¼ miles above Arundel bridge. Rennie avoided using the Arun Navigation because he thought it very bad, 'barges navigating it, experience great detention, from the floods in winter and droughts in summer and, as the length is greater by about eight miles, I can scarcely suppose any saving . . . in cost by the use of this navigation . . . when put in competition with the detention and inconvenience the trade of so great an inland navigation would be likely to sustain by the barges navigating the Arun between Newbridge and Arundel, on their voyage to and from Portsmouth. It is true, the Arun might be improved, but no improvement which could be made would ever render it so certain as the proposed canal, for the through trade; but a branch may be made to join it below Pulborough which will cost but little while it will open an extensive district of country to its benefits.'

The line from below Arundel was to follow approximately that of the later Portsmouth & Arundel Canal to Yapton, continuing through Chichester and Havant until it crossed into Portsmouth by an aqueduct and terminated in the Royal Dockyard. Near Tonbridge the canal would have been joined by the intended Weald of Kent Canal providing links to the sea at Rye and near Herne Bay. Branches were also suggested from Horsham to the Ouse Navigation at Lindfield; from Billingshurst (Rosers Farm) to Newbridge and to the Adur;[151] and from Chichester to the sea; while more direct communication with the Thames either by a canal down the valley of the river Mole or by the Surrey Iron Railway at Merstham was contemplated. The canal was to be large enough to admit Thames barges, have a 16-mile summit level fed by nine reservoirs in St Leonard's and Tilgate forests, and the estimated cost of the main line was £585,500, of which it is said that £650,000[46] was actually subscribed. The reasons why the scheme failed were multifarious. Besides powerful opposition from certain landowners, the route was extremely circuitous and, passing as it did through agricultural communities with few industries, many thought it unlikely that it would prove a profitable investment. And so, while the Grand Southern Canal project lay discarded, another plan for the linking of London with the English Channel began once again to be seriously discussed in the library at Petworth House.

CHAPTER V

The Wey & Arun Canal Bill (1810–1813)

Procedure for obtaining an Act of Parliament—public meetings held—publication of prospectus of the Wey & Arun Junction Canal—subscription lists filled—choice of engineer—Josias Jessop—the line surveyed—objections—petition for a bill—amendments—Act obtained—summary of the Wey & Arun Canal Act.

By 1810 the many ambitious proposals for linking London and Portsmouth had been discarded and 15 miles still separated the navigable portions of the Wey and Arun rivers. Lord Egremont, tired of twenty years' procrastination and seeking direct access to the Guildford and London markets for the produce of his estates, decided therefore to press ahead with the simplest scheme of all—to link the two navigations by the shortest practicable route.

Now the canals and river navigations of Southern England were, for the most part, projects conceived and financed locally by men to whom the practical advantages were as important as the long-term investment prospects. An Act of Parliament had invariably to be sought to raise the capital and to obtain the necessary authority to acquire land, cross highways, and divert streams. And since canal bills all contained clauses for levying tolls, they could only be introduced by petition to the House of Commons. Their progress was governed by the usual procedure for private bills until 1793, when it was realized that the rights of individuals to oppose bills were being entirely undermined, largely through ignorance of the exact nature of the intended schemes. New Standing Orders were therefore introduced demanding additional documents where the compulsory acquisition of land was involved. Promoters were henceforward required to submit an exact plan of the land to be taken, together with a book of reference showing the owners and occupiers of each parcel of land, a description of property to be demolished, a list showing whether the owners and occupiers assented, dissented, or were neutral to the project, a note of the sums individually subscribed, and an estimate of the cost. Compliance with these and other standing orders (viz. local publicity) was investigated by the Committee studying the bill.

The standing orders, which affected the Wey & Arun bill, had not, of course, applied to the Arun or Rother Navigation bills, which is one reason why information regarding the building of those navigations is difficult to trace.

The first course of action was for the promoters to put up posters and insert advertisements in the local press calling a public meeting so that the views of the neighbourhood could be obtained. If the meeting favoured the idea, money would be requested to meet the costs of obtaining the Act, in which case the subscribers were given the first opportunity of purchasing shares in the company should the Act be granted. The navigations already built in Surrey and Sussex were small and had been financed by the neighbouring landowners and merchants. To raise the capital for an undertaking as ambitious as the Wey & Arun, a wider appeal was necessary.

Initially, Lord Egremont sought the support of the principal landowners. The Duke of Norfolk, the Earl of Onslow, Lords Grantley, Midleton and King of Ockham were all willing to support the petition for a bill and of the 'prominent gentlemen' approached during the autumn of 1810, only General Norton at Shalford declined to give his signature. Towards the end of October, John Smallpeice, a Guildford solicitor, attended on the Reverend John Austin to advise him about convening a meeting to discuss the proposed canal. A week later notices appeared in the London, Surrey, and Sussex papers announcing that a meeting to consider the scheme would be held in Guildford on 24 November. However, the meeting was postponed until 1 December, and then *sine die* in view of the publication of Rennie's plan for the Grand Southern Canal (*see* previous chapter).

Six months later, however, on 17 May 1811, the following insertion appeared in the *Morning Post*: 'INTENDED SURREY AND SUSSEX CANAL—Notice is hereby given that a meeting will be held at the White Hart Inn, Guildford, on the 1st June next at 1.0 p.m. for the purpose of considering the propriety of making a navigable canal to connect the rivers Wey and Arun from Newbridge, Wisborough Green to Stonebridge, Shalford, a distance of only sixteen miles.' At the meeting, Lord Egremont announced the objects of the project and added that he had been authorized to state that in order to encourage the proposal the proprietors of the Arun Navigation only intended to charge 6d. a ton on goods going into the river Wey from the sea.[47] A further meeting took place at the Town Hall six days later to enable more people to express their views, and on 7 June the Mayor passed a resolution that such a canal would be advantageous to the town and neighbourhood. Five days later a similar expression of approval was shown by the town of Godalming.

A Committee of nine was thereupon formed to go ahead with the preparations for presenting a petition to Parliament. The next step was to choose an engineer to select the best route. Three men were therefore approached to undertake the preliminary survey. Josias Jessop, whose father, William, had surveyed the Rother Navigation twenty years before and whom he had assisted in building several Midland navigations, as well as the Croydon, Merstham & Godstone Railway;[152] Benjamin Bevan, who had been employed on constructing the Grand Junction Canal; and John Rennie, whose many feats of engineering had included the building of Waterloo Bridge, London Bridge, and the Kennet & Avon Canal. Jessop alone accepted. He came down from London to meet the Committee at Guildford and spent the next four weeks, accompanied by a surveyor, making his report.

By the end of August 1811, the Committee had studied Jessop's report and had decided to go ahead with the scheme. Notice of the intended application for a bill was sent to the *London Gazette*, the Surrey, Southwark, Middlesex & Sussex *Gazettes*, and the *Sussex Weekly Advertiser*, together with an announcement of the opening of a subscription list to the public. Gentlemen were invited to apply for shares in £100 units and pay a 2 per cent deposit on application to defray preliminary expenses. By the middle of the month the number of promoters in the venture had risen to nineteen, and in *The Times* on the 21st it was announced that £39,000 of the required £90,000 had been subscribed. At a meeting at the 'White Hart' on 12 October, with the Earl of Onslow as chairman, the Committee was further increased to twenty-three, of whom any five formed a quorum.

Matters now proceeded with more than usual rapidity. Clerks travelled by coach to the Temple and to Kingston, Petworth, and Lewes to affix Notices regarding the Parliamentary application to the doors of the County Sessions. Meetings between the projectors took place nearly every day and Smallpeice rode regularly over to Petworth House to consult Lord Egremont, whose advice was particularly valuable in connection with the negotiations between the promoters and the two big landowners, Lord Grantley and Sir Harry Goring, who strongly resented the line of the proposed canal passing through their estates.

The prospectus of the proposed Wey & Arun Junction Canal, after being redrafted by Lord Egremont, appeared in *The Times* on 17 October 1811.

'The advantage likely to accrue to the public from a communication by inland navigation between the river Thames and Portsmouth, has induced several noblemen and gentlemen of Surrey and Sussex to forward this desirable end by uniting the existing navigations from London through Guildford to the navigable part of the river Arun by a short cut in almost a straight line of seventeen miles, by which means two navigations, one of forty-nine miles, the other of twenty-four miles, both in a flourishing state, will form with the intended canal a direct navigable line from the metropolis of ninety miles to the sea at Littlehampton, only sixteen miles from Spithead, twenty-two from Portsmouth, on which the produce of Sussex, corn, flour, and timber, will be expeditiously conveyed to London; Guildford and Godalming will be supplied with cheaper coal—the present annual consumption being 10,000 tons. In return Portland stone, groceries, chalk and lime, iron-ware, slate, timber, manure, firewood, culm, bark and other articles can be carried. Government and East and West Indian stores will be forwarded (from the Capital) in sixty working hours, and from thence by one re-shipment—(which must take place even if the canal should extend to Portsmouth)—will be delivered alongside any ship at Spithead, the Motherbank or Portsmouth Harbour by the following tide by regular passage vessels, constructed and kept for that purpose. The Committee, having ascertained that 1,200,000 tons pass annually from the Thames to Portsmouth by land carriage and sea, they hope that they do not assume too much by hoping that not less than one-twelfth of this will pass through the projected canal, since goods will be delivered as cheaply as by the present coastal freightage and much more cheaply than by land carriage. The local traffic is calculated at 30,000 tons.

'The projected canal will pass through a country whose soil is principally clay, presenting no difficulties and with a plentiful supply of water in the driest seasons, without any tunnel, without injury to any mill, without destroying any house.

'The sum required to accomplish this most desirable and lucrative concern, is estimated by the engineer, Mr. Jessop, to be only £71,217; but as the Gentlemen wish to meet every expense they are convinced that £90,000 will amply cover every out-going.'

By now £51,000 had been promised. Lord Egremont headed the subscription list with £20,000; Lord Onslow had contributed £2,000; Lord King and eight others £1,000 each and there were thirty-seven, including the Commissioners of Arundel Port, who had their names down for £500 or more. *The Times* of 2 November announced that a further £13,000 had been subscribed. By the

16th the list was full with the names of 132 subscribers. The fact that the whole of the capital had been promised seventeen months before the Act was granted and within one month of the prospectus being issued shows the enthusiasm with which the project was greeted.

A contributor to *The Quarterly Review* in 1825 commented that canal interests were often 'compared to lotteries, containing a few large prizes, with many blanks' and that it had been asserted the profit made on all the canals in the kingdom did not amount to the legal interest on the sums expended in forming them. This, in fact, was almost true. The average return on eighty companies with a total capital of over £13 million was only about 5¾ per cent.

Discrimination in the growth possibilities of canal equities was not easy to exercise, and many investors when perusing the Wey & Arun prospectus were probably more conscious of the canal's potentialities in the event of war with France than with the normal commercial traffic it was likely to attract. On the other hand, this appeared to afford a good opportunity to buy shares which should, if the Committee's conjectures were correct, provide capital appreciation and a comfortable dividend (Jessop's estimate was 7 per cent). But the premises upon which these expectations were based proved as fanciful as the optimism of the promoters. However, many companies were at this time paying very substantial dividends; the Oxford Canal distributed to their shareholders in 1811 a dividend of 31 per cent. Again, more than twenty-five companies had their shares quoted at over twice their nominal value, although canal shares in general did not reach their peak level until twenty years later when the shares of the Loughborough Navigation soared to twenty times their issue price. It is a fact, however, that no canals constructed after 1793 were ever to reap excessive profits, for these disappeared when the cost of labour and materials rose during the Napoleonic Wars. New canal undertakings, finding that their expenses had been underestimated, were forced to borrow money or else abandon the venture. As in the case of both the Arun Navigation and the Wey & Arun, it was often twenty or thirty years after the opening ceremony before loans could be repaid; indeed in some cases, viz. the Portsmouth & Arundel, mortgages were never repaid from revenue.

The task of surveying the intended line was not easily undertaken. Large-scale and reliable contour maps were non-existent; the one-inch ordnance survey had not yet been completed; local knowledge was limited and only the regular boring of holes could acquaint the surveyor with the geological formations of the substrata. But, as happened in the case of the cutting along the summit level, there was no certainty of what lay twenty or more feet below the surface. An added difficulty was that until the Act was passed, the surveying engineer had no right to trespass. Jessop had to walk or ride over the whole of the route to gain a clear picture of the lie of the terrain before an alignment of the canal could be agreed. Naturally, access to private property was necessary and, where permission was not granted, the engineer's men were inclined to take matters into their own hands with the result that in some quarters opposition to the proposed canal became even more determined.

November, December, and the dark months of 1812 were occupied in discussions between the Committee, Jessop, and a number of irate farmers and freeholders who had suddenly realized the implications of a canal being dug across their lands. By the second week of January some changes had been decided by the Committee but not agreed since opposition was often only transferred from one landowner to his neighbour. Not all desired the facilities of water transport and its concomitant disadvantages. The chief objections were usually depreciation of property and loss of privacy for which compensation was hard to assess satisfactorily. Secondly, where the waterway was cut through their fertile meadows, landowners feared that drought might spoil the lushness of their pastures or alternatively that a burst embankment might damage land and even endanger life; thirdly, they distrusted the bargees who had little respect for the Game Laws; and, fourthly, they resented the interference and inconvenience caused by gangs of 'navvies' churning up their fields with all their building paraphernalia. There was certainly opposition to the scheme, but in many cases either Jessop or Smallpeice was at least able to turn an owner's dissent into a declaration of neutrality. An entry in the solicitor's accounts, dated 12 May 1812, however, shows that tenants and landlords could not always be pacified—'Attended on Mr. Jessop in consequence of his being served with notices not to trespass.' But by this time there was little more trespassing to do.

Sir Harry Goring insisted on changes to the suggested line to avoid the game preserves let to Mr Napper and General Onslow. To meet this objection and to avoid two aqueducts the Committee agreed to divert the course of the river for over half a mile. A more circuitous line was favoured through Sidney Wood to avoid Alfold village. Although this only increased the length of the canal by

Taking Levels and drawing Plans & Sections to be deposited with the Clerks of the Peace – 27 Days ——

Travelling & other Expences ——

Decr. 3 to 7 – To London to attend Petition in Parliament – 5 Days ——

Expences ——

1813 –

March 3 to 7th – To town to attend Bill thro' the Commons, 5 Days ——

Travelling Expences ——

21st to 26 – attendg. Bill thro' the Lords. 7 Days –

Expences ——

May 15th to June 19th & 21 to 27 – } marking out line of Canal 43 Days ——

Expences ——

July 11th 12th – To Guildford to attend meeting at the letting of the work – 2 Days ——

London 3 September 1813.

Received Three hundred & four pounds 5/. of Messrs. Price Hay & for the Wey & Arun Canal Compy. on acct. of Messrs. Haydon Sons.

Josias Jessop.

£304..5

Fig. 9.—*Josias Jessop's Account, 1812–3*

ANNO QUINQUAGESIMO TERTIO

GEORGII III REGIS.

An ACT for making and maintaining a Navigable Canal to unite the Rivers Wey *and* Arun, *in the Counties of* Surrey *and* Sussex.

[1 April 1813.]

WHEREAS the making and maintaining a Canal, navigable for Boats, Barges and other Veſſels, from the River *Wey*, at or near to a certain place called *Stonebridge*, in the Pariſh of *Shalford* in the County of *Surrey*, to the River *Arun*, at or near to a certain place called *Newbridge*, in the Pariſh of *Wisborough Green* in the County of *Suſſex*, in, to, or through the ſeveral Pariſhes of *Shalford*, *Bramley*, *Wonerſh*, *Dunsfold*, *Cranley*, *Hascomb* and *Alfold*, or ſome or one of them, in the County of *Surrey*; and alſo that part of the ſaid Pariſh of *Alfold* which is ſituate or lying in the ſaid County of *Suſſex*, and in, to, or through the ſeveral Pariſhes of *Kirdford*, *Wisborough Green*, *Rudgwick*, *Billingshurſt*, and *Pulborough*, in the ſaid County of *Suſſex*; would not only open a ſhort, eaſy Preamble.

A 2 and

Fig. 10.—Preamble of the Wey & Arun Canal Act, 1813

1½ miles it lengthened the summit level by 3 miles and added £15,000 to the estimated cost. However, variations could not always be made. At Wonersh, where Lord Grantley had taken particular exception to a canal dividing his estate, there was no practical alternative.

The Committee met a dozen times and more at the 'White Hart' between June 1811 and March the following year. Smallpeice travelled far afield—both to obtain the consent of owners to permit the canal to pass through their property and to persuade those who objected to change their minds. An extract from his accounts reads, 'Attending Mr. John Street; conferring with him to induce his father to withdraw his opposition . . . 6/8d.' He negotiated reciprocal toll agreements on through traffic both above and below Guildford, and with the Arun Navigation. Besides collecting the list of owners who consented, dissented, or were neutral, Smallpeice was required to obtain the signatures of those supporting the petition to Parliament for leave to bring a bill. The petition was drawn up by the close of January, and it was hoped to present it as a private bill during the next Session. Several owners of land, however, had yet to state their views and it seemed likely at that time that unless certain conciliatory measures were agreed, there might be parliamentary opposition. The Committee therefore decided to postpone the application until the following year and announcements to this effect appeared in the local papers towards the middle of February. Already the legal costs had amounted to nearly £500 and the total expenses to more than £1,000.

In May 1812 Jessop produced a revised estimate of £86,132 for making the canal along the realigned route through Sidney Wood. During August, the Committee considered Jessop's second report and decided to make fresh application to Parliament. In the meantime, every endeavour was made that autumn to induce the hostile faction to withdraw its opposition to the intended canal. When Lord Grantley and General Norton consented to remain neutral on the understanding that they would be generously compensated, others followed suit. By the time the petition was presented to the House of Commons on 8 December 1812, the majority of the dissenters to the scheme had been appeased.

The petition for the Wey & Arun bill was granted and the first reading took place on 3 February 1813. A petition asking to be heard against the second reading was presented on 8 February. Messrs Strong, Still & Co., acting for Lady Morshead and Mrs Thistlewayte, objected to the bill on the grounds that the proposed

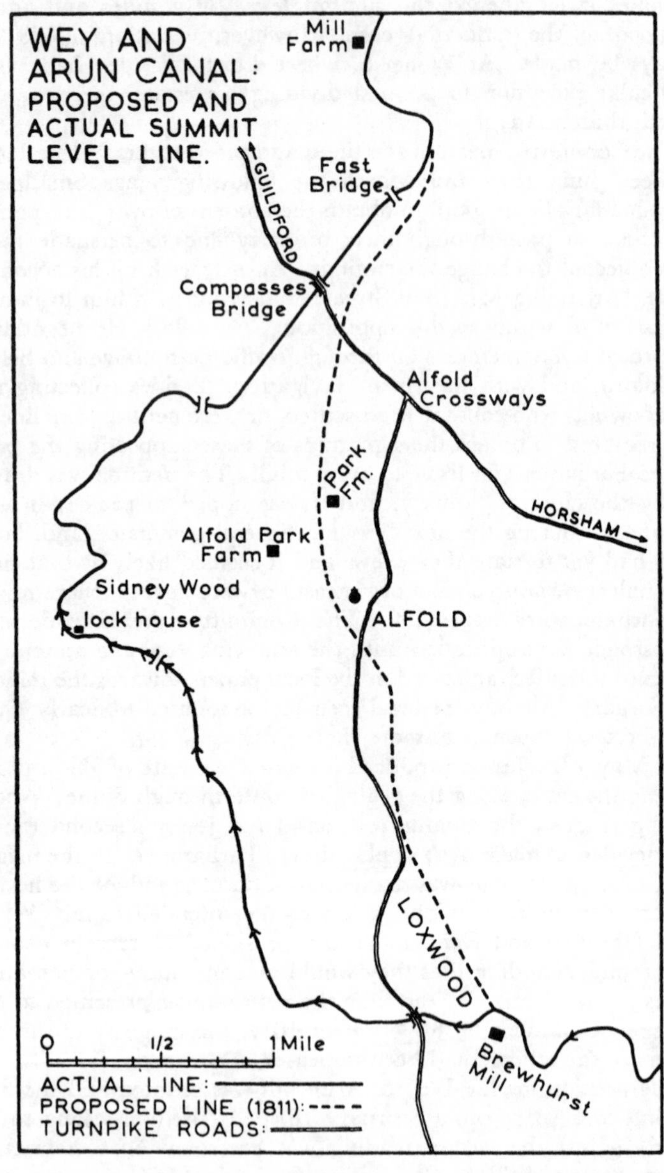
WEY AND
ARUN CANAL:
PROPOSED AND
ACTUAL SUMMIT
LEVEL LINE.
Mill
Farm
Fast
Bridge
GUILDFORD
Compasses
Bridge
Alfold
Crossways
Park
Fm.
HORSHAM
Alfold Park
Farm
Sidney Wood
lock house
ALFOLD
LOXWOOD
Brewhurst
Mill
0
1/2
1 Mile
ACTUAL LINE:
PROPOSED LINE (1811):
TURNPIKE ROADS:

Map 4

line of the canal differed very much from the plan they had originally seen, and that the existing proposed line through Sidney Wood could not in any circumstances be approved as it cut up the estate and would materially injure the interests of the parties whom they represented. Once again Jessop's reassurances, coupled with financial inducement, met with success. In some cases opposition was removed at this stage by offering to pay the landowners' costs; thus it is recorded, the 'Bramley gentlemen' withdrew their protests for the sum of £50. The second reading passed with only a few minor amendments. Thomas Lowndes, the owner of Vachery House, successfully pressed for a clause in the bill which allowed an option to let, rather than sell, his land for building the reservoir.

The third reading took place on 19 and 20 March; the bill was then formally read again in the House of Lords and 'An Act for Making and Maintaining a Navigable Canal to Unite the Rivers Wey and Arun, in the Counties of Surrey and Sussex', received the Royal Assent on 1 April 1813.

The Act contained 133 sections, designating both the means to be employed in building the canal and the manner in which it was to be maintained. The subscribers to the undertaking were constituted 'The Company of Proprietors of the Wey & Arun Junction Canal', and were now empowered to purchase all lands and acquire rights of way wherever necessary for the construction and maintenance of the waterway (1).* General Meetings were to be held annually in May (66); shareholders to have one vote for every share (63). The Committee of Management, elected from those possessing five or more shares, to control the workings of the Company (66). Commissioners to be appointed to determine the amount to be paid for the purchase of land and for damage to property (16). Where landowners disagreed with the valuation, appeal could be made to a jury of twelve, whose assessment would be final (22).

Sections were devoted to ways of obtaining capital (57), issuing shares (58), mortgaging (61) or letting (96) the tolls; to authorizing the Company to erect, if required, all manner of objects like water-tanks, watch-houses, weighing beams, dry docks, cranes, and fire-engines (steam-engines) (1); and permit the employment of rollers or inclined planes instead of locks (2). Maximum toll and wharfage rates were fixed; manure could be carried at 2d. per ton-mile; coal, corn, and timber at 4d. Boats carrying less than 6 tons could pass the canal for 1s., while passengers were not to be charged

* Figures in parentheses denote the section of the Act.

Wey & Arun Junction

CANAL COMPANY

SHARE No. 518

This is to Certify that The Reverend John Keate of Eton in the County of Buckingham Doctor in Divinity is a ——— proprietor of ONE SHARE in the WEY & ARUN JUNCTION CANAL numbered as above and Registered in the Register Book of the Company (Subject to the Rules, Orders and Regulations of the said Company) and that he his Executors, Administrators and Assigns are intitled to the profits and Advantages thereof. (last Install.t to be paid before June 24th 1815)

Dated this 25th day of August 1813

GUILDFORD

Clerk to the Company.

Fig. 11.—Wey & Arun Junction Canal Company Share Certificate, 1813

more than 2d. a mile (91); but the rate for through traffic to and from the rivers Wey and Arun was fixed at 1s. a ton (124). The channel and towpath of the navigation was to be limited to 20 yd width except at turning points, wharves and where its level rested more than 6 ft above or below the adjoining land, when the width could be increased to 50 yd (4). Where the canal divided an owner's land, a bridge was to be made (68) unless the land measured less than an acre or 50 yd in breadth, in which case it was to be bought by the Company and, if necessary, resold (11). Private wharves could be erected by landowners (101), who were granted the fishing rights (119) and allowed to keep a pleasure boat on the canal, gratis, unless passing through the locks (100).

The Company were entitled to make their own bylaws to protect their property, with power to impose fines of up to £5 in the event of contravention (81). Barges of over 25 tons burthen had to be manned by two able-bodied men, were not to be moored improperly so as to obstruct the navigation, fastened to bridges, or allowed to strike against lock-gates or wharves; failure to observe these rules empowered the Company to impose a fine. Section 116, however, threatened more fearsome measures. Anyone convicted of wilful damage to canal property was liable to be transported.

Special clauses had been inserted to protect certain property owners; one section was to indemnify the owners of Rowner Mill for loss of water (20); another restrained the Company from taking down Lord Grantley's fences at Bramley before erecting fresh ones 6 ft high (32). Watering places were to be made for cattle (49) and owners could erect additional bridges at their own expense (50). Finally, the Act specified that every barge should have its name and number painted on its prow in white (106), that mileposts should be placed at half-mile intervals along the banks (121), and that if the canal should not be completed within ten years, then the powers of the Act would become void, except for that part of the canal which had been completed (126).

CHAPTER VI

The Building of the Wey & Arun Canal (1813–1816)

Lord Egremont made Chairman—the purchase of land and payment of compensation—the line of the Wey & Arun—the first sod cut at Shalford—simple design of buildings—bankruptcy of the contractor—other delays—opening postponed—additional capital required—wages reduced—completion and opening celebrations.

THE first annual meeting of the Wey & Arun Junction Canal Company was held in Guildford on 9 May 1813. The shareholders were addressed in enthusiastic manner by Lord Egremont on the importance of the enterprise upon which they were about to embark and they in turn proceeded to elect the Management Committee. Lord Egremont was formally invited to be chairman of the Company at the Committee's inaugural meeting a fortnight later. Two local bankers were appointed joint treasurers and John Smallpeice became clerk to the Company. The next item on the agenda was to put in hand arrangements for raising the Company's capital and a first call of £10 per cent was ordered on each share. Further calls were intended on each succeeding quarter day so that the tenth and final payment would be made on 24 June 1815, by which time it was planned that the navigation should be completed.

The third step was to purchase land so that work on digging the canal could begin. It had been estimated that £9,500 would cover the cost of compulsory purchase and negotiations with owners were begun forthwith. The estimates were soon proved wrong. The men of property were loath to see their lands divided and, naturally seeking the highest price, were disinclined to accept the Company's offers, preferring the arbitrary valuation of the Commissioners, which body, being chiefly composed of landowners, was not unnaturally disposed to favour them. Either party could appeal to a jury, but, because of the cost involved, this rarely occurred. The Commissioners were first called together on 12 June 1813, and met often enough thereafter for there were many disputes to settle. Compensation was demanded by owners and

Wey and Arun Junction Canal.

C TWO SHILL P.Q. 8

I The Right Honorable George O Brien Earl of Egremont in Consideration of the Sum of Fifty Pounds paid to me by The Most Noble Charles Duke of Norfolk do hereby bargain, sell, assign, and transfer to the said Charles Duke of Norfolk his Executors, Administrators and Assigns Five Shares in the Wey and Arun Junction Canal, being Numbers 360, 361, 362 363 and 364 of the Shares in the said Navigation, To hold to the said Charles Duke of Norfolk his Executors, Administrators, and Assigns, subject to the same Rules, Orders, and Restrictions, and on the same Conditions that I held the same immediately before the Execution hereof: And I the said Charles Duke of Norfolk do hereby agree to take and accept of the said Five Shares, subject to the same Rules, Orders, Restrictions, and Conditions. Witness our Hands and Seals the seventeenth Day of July in the Year of our Lord, One Thousand Eight Hundred and thirteen.

Signed, sealed, and delivered, by the said George O'Brien Earl of Egremont in the presence of Jn. Smallpeice — Guildford — Sol.

Wm. Upton — Petworth Sussex Surveyor.

O'Brien Egremont

Signed Sealed and delivered by the said Charles Duke of Norfolk in the presence of Charles Greenaway Esqr. Going

Norfolk E M

** Two Witnesses required, who will add their *Residences* and *Additions*, and afterwards the Assignment must be registered at the Office of Mr. John Smallpeice in Guildford, the Clerk to the Company.

Russells Press, Guildford.

Fig. 12.—Share Transfer—Earl of Egremont to Duke of Norfolk, 1813 *(see page 55)*

WEY AND ARUN JUNCTION CANAL COMPANY.

Statement of RECEIPTS and PAYMENTS to 7th May, 1814.

	£	s.	d.
To Receipts on account of 1st. Call....	8729	18	3
2d. Ditto......	8600		
3d. Ditto......	8600		
4th. Ditto in part	7297	10	
Interest on Exchequer Bills paid off and exchanged for New Bills... ..	364	10	5
£	33,591	18	8

		£	s.	d.
By Payments to Engineer, Mr. Jessop		1041	15	
Surveyor, Messrs. Uptons......		526	1	3
Solicitor, Mr. J. Smallpeice for first application to Parliament and the Act...... ..		1791	3	11
for Printing, Books, Seal, use of Room for Meetings, and Postage, paid Messrs. Sparkes and Co......... ..		60	18	2
Contractor Mr. Keppell		2266	4	6
for Land and Timber		2727	4	8
		8413	7	6
By Purchase of Exchequer Bills, Brokerage, &c.........	19,200 0 0			
Interest accrued thereon.......	358 8 11	19,558	8	11
Balance in the hands of the Treasurers		5620	2	3
£		33,591	18	8

FUNDS now in the hands of the Company to answer accruing demands.

	£	s.	d.
In Exchequer Bills, ...	19200		
Interest due thereon	361	14	6
Cash in hands of the Treasurers	5620	2	3
£	25,181	16	9

GUILDFORD PRESS.

Fig. 13.—Wey & Arun Canal Company's first Annual Report, 1814

occupiers for damage to their property, for an orchard or garden destroyed, for loss of water to the mills at Brewhurst and Rowner, for crops trampled down by workmen or buried by earth from excavations. No houses or buildings were affected, but the Company had to pay heavy damages in some cases for depreciation and very unwillingly in the case of Lord Grantley, against whom the entry in the accounts regarding payment of £2,000 is followed by 'in lieu of a wall, stipulated to be built in his Lordship's park, but which his Lordship never intended to erect'. When all was settled the freeholders had received nearly £2,000 more than had been contemplated and the compensation paid for damages had greatly exceeded the estimate.

Constructing the locks was the most expensive item in building the canal, representing in fact 27 per cent of the total cost. The purchase of land and compensation amounted to 26 per cent, and digging, cutting, and embanking accounted for 22 per cent. In other respects estimates were relatively low. The thirty or so bridges were costed at £150 each, Drungewick aqueduct at £600, and the expense of diverting the Arun at only £2,200 a mile.

Josias Jessop designed all the aqueducts and bridges as well as the lock-keepers' cottages, though he only paid periodic visits to the line to see how the work was proceeding. The man on the spot was May Upton, civil engineer and the clerk of the works, who was later to build the Baybridge Canal to West Grinstead. His main task was to supervise the work of the contractor, Zachariah Keppel, a builder from Alfold, who in turn was responsible for engaging the men to carry out the excavations and have the works completed in a 'good perfect and workmanlike manner'. The 'navvies' (or navigators as they were called because they built the navigations) were easily recruited from among the local unemployed; Irishmen and French prisoners of war provided additional sources of labour.

After the land had been bought and before excavating could begin, the undergrowth had to be cleared, trees felled, and the topsoil removed. The timber was carefully stacked and later sold; in 1814 an auction at Billingshurst realized £871 and another the following year at Guildford over £250.

The Wey & Arun was dug for 18 miles across the wildest and most beautiful part of the Surrey and Sussex borders at a time when the Napoleonic Wars were drawing to a close. The first sod was cut at Shalford early in July 1813, and work began on the summit level that autumn. Gangs of sturdy labourers equipped

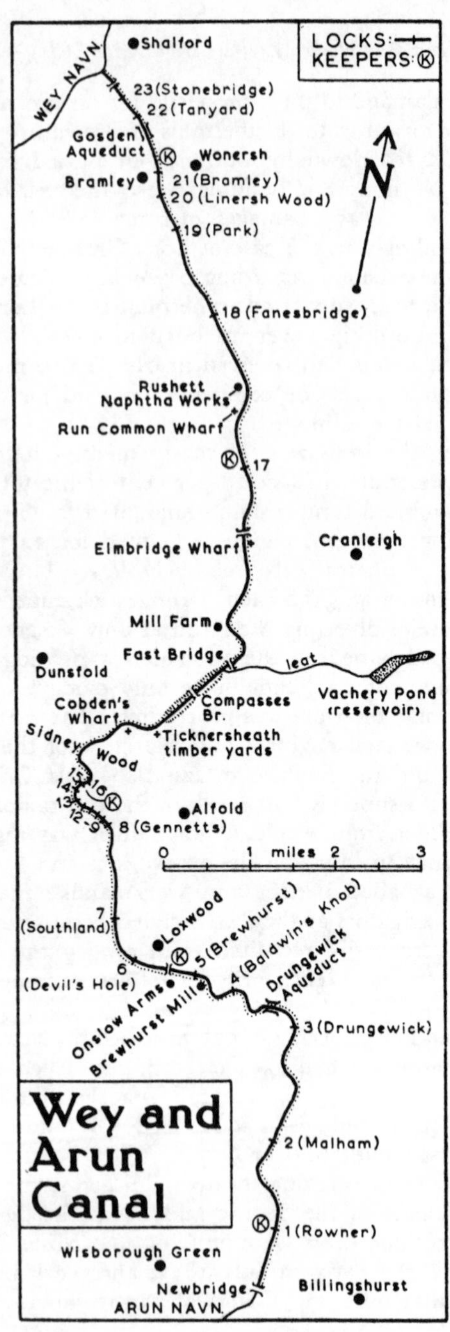

LOCKS:
KEEPERS:
N
WEY NAVN
Shalford
23 (Stonebridge)
22 (Tanyard)
Gosden Aqueduct
Wonersh
Bramley
21 (Bramley)
20 (Linersh Wood)
19 (Park)
18 (Fanesbridge)
Rushett Naphtha Works
Run Common Wharf
17
Elmbridge Wharf
Cranleigh
Mill Farm
Fast Bridge
leat
Dunsfold
Vachery Pond (reservoir)
Cobden's Wharf
Compasses Br.
Sidney Wood
Ticknersheath timber yards
15
14
16
13
12-9
Alfold
8 (Gennetts)
0 1 miles 2 3
7 (Southland)
Loxwood
5 (Brewhurst)
4 (Baldwin's Knob)
Drungewick Aqueduct
6 (Devil's Hole)
Onslow Arms
Brewhurst Mill
3 (Drungewick)
Wey and Arun Canal
2 (Malham)
1 (Rowner)
Wisborough Green
Newbridge
Billingshurst
ARUN NAVN

Map 5

with spades, picks, and shovels were soon forcing a channel through the countryside, while wheel-barrows went back and forth carting away the earth; following in their wake came the men to puddle the bed of the canal with clay, masons to build the bridges, culverts, and lock walls, and carpenters and ironsmiths to set in place the lock gates and paddles.

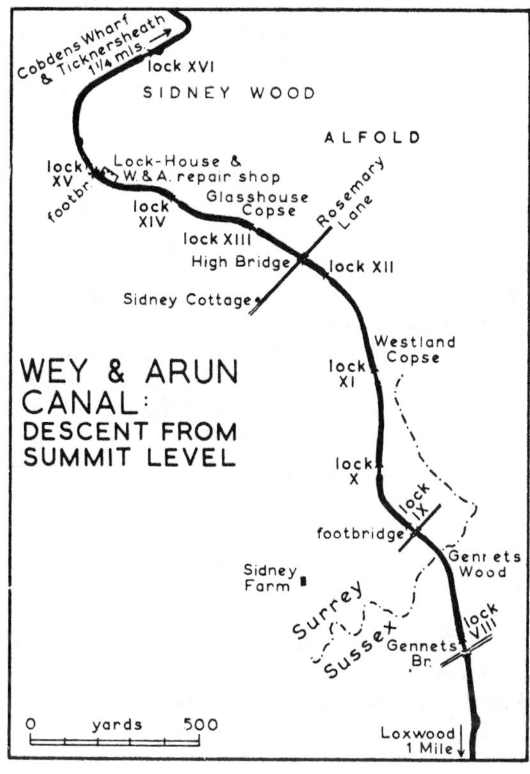

Map 6

The line involved the surmounting of few natural obstacles; leaving the Wey by Stonebridge wharf, Shalford, the waterway ascended through Bramley and Run Common by seven locks to its 5-mile summit level near Cranleigh. Here it crossed the Surrey/ Sussex watershed, 163 ft above sea-level, disappearing through a cutting at Alfold and crossing a valley into Sidney Wood; then, descending nearly 90 ft in less than 2 miles, it reached Loxwood and crossed the western branch of the Arun and the fertile meadows of Malham and Rowner to join the Arun Canal at Newbridge. Its width as planned was 30 ft and its depth 3 ft 6 in. except along the summit level 'to allow it to be drawn down a foot or more if necessary'; each of the 23 locks was to measure approximately 75 ft by 13 ft to allow the passage of barges carrying up to 50 tons. Besides the 35 bridges, 8 wharves, 5 lock houses, and 2 aqueducts were to be built along the towpath which passed under the majority of the bridges. By damming the stream and raising the height of the embankments of the lake in the grounds of Vachery House at Cranleigh, a reservoir was to be created for supplying water to the summit level.

The architectural design of the works along all the navigations between Weybridge and Portsmouth was almost solely functional. There was none of the elaboration which was to be found on the more majestic waterways where landowners would often only withdraw their opposition to the bill if a bridge or tunnel was built in a manner which harmonized with their property. (Lord Grantley's compensation would merely have resulted in a paling fence.) Embellishments found on the portals of Sapperton tunnel did not appear on the unadorned framework of Hardham tunnel, both of which were completed in the same year. The lock houses were simple, slate-roofed, square-shaped cottages. The aqueducts were unexceptional; those at Gosden, Drungewick, and Orfold had three small arches and were built mainly of brick. Only the narrow-waisted, hump-backed, low, stone bridges over the Arun Canal and the Rother laid a claim to beauty and permanence.

Every month Keppel drafted a report on the canal's progress. By the end of 1813 nearly 3 miles of bed and embankment had been completed. In May of the following year work was begun on the southern end. Sir Harry Goring at once wrote to the Committee objecting to workmen digging up his land. Although he was 'under the impression that it had been bought', it had not been paid for, and he intimated that it was his intention to resist further trespassing until the purchase price had been received. The Company, ever niggardly as regards finance, grudgingly paid out nearly £1,200 so that work could continue. Newbridge canal bridge was begun in June 1814, and that at Tickners Heath finished in July. Brickworks set up in Sidney Wood and at Alfold had by August made more than half a million bricks for the works along the northern end. Below Loxwood, however, locally quarried blocks of Pulborough stone were used for the locks and bridges, while additional bricks were brought up from Harwoods Green. Valleys started to be filled up in Sidney and Gennets Woods. That autumn Rowner and Malham locks were built and those from Gennets Bridge to High Bridge begun. At the same time, cuts were made across the sinuosities of the Arun below Drungewick and Loves Farm to divert the stream and avoid the necessity of additional aqueducts. Altogether nearly 2,000 yd of new course were dug for the Arun besides turning the course of the 'Loxwood' river in three places.

A third of the canal had in fact been completed when the Company suffered several setbacks. Firstly, Keppel, the contractor, having failed to appreciate the magnitude of his task, went bankrupt and was forced to retire from the scene by Christmas, leaving May Upton to carry on as best he could. Secondly, heavy rains during the winter months caused considerable delays; men had to be employed to pump out water from the works on as many as fifty-seven days between December and February. And, thirdly, progress was further retarded by the discovery that the bed of the 2,000-yd cutting was of sand so that it had to be doubly lined with clay, and it was evident that the canal would not be finished that year. Calls on the shares began to be made less frequently. Throughout 1815 Upton did his best to see that the work continued as smoothly as possible. Often letters seeking advice were sent to Jessop and from time to time he made the long journey from the Butterley Ironworks, his home in Derbyshire, to inspect progress on the line and the aqueducts at Gosden and Drungewick.

Slowly and surely the canal neared completion. Timber for the locks at the northern end arrived from Godalming during July and October, and was conveyed for at least part of the way by water. On 18 December 1815 the first tolls were taken when the canal was opened as far as Bramley. The Committee, however, were worried by rising costs and, in an effort to economize, it was decided to reduce the navvies' wages. Jessop, on hearing this news, tendered his advice to Smallpeice—'The lowering of wages may create a disturbance, in which case I think the Committee should dismiss the whole and stop their works, and in a few days there will be plenty of others who will be glad to be employed—for employment is everywhere very scarce. I should apprehend it will be of little use to reason with them on the low price of provisions and of every article of life, for they are not of a class to be moved by arguments against themselves, but they must give way to necessity.'[48] Indeed, at this time the country was convulsed by discontent and misery. Bread and Luddite riots occurred frequently, thousands of work-people were unemployed and the nation reeled under the heavy burden of taxation. The Sussex labourer received a wage of only 1s. 6d. a day if married or 7d. a day if a bachelor at a time when bread was 3d. a pound.

Large employers of labour in the early nineteenth century experienced difficulty in finding ready cash for the payment of wages, as for years the minting of silver and copper coin was insufficient for the national need. Indeed, because of the price of copper, no coinage was minted between 1807 and 1821. To overcome this shortage, many canal companies and traders produced tokens for local circulation. Those issued to the workmen on the Basingstoke Canal in 1789 showed a sailing barge on one side and a wheelbarrow on the reverse, together with the name of the contractor and the canal. It is possible that both the Wey & Arun and the Portsmouth & Arundel Companies did produce tokens embossed with their seals, but none has so far come to light.

The shareholders paid the tenth, and what they hoped was the final, call on 1 February 1816. The authorized £90,500 had been obtained but the Act had also stipulated that, should this sum prove insufficient, the Company had power to raise an additional £9,500 either by a further call of £10 per share or by mortgaging the tolls. At the general meeting in May it was announced that the canal would be open by Michaelmas, that the cutting, the reservoir, and two aqueducts were completed and that three million bricks had been made; that only Lock XVI and Fast Bridge remained to be built; also—and the sting was in the tail—that 'the price of land exceeding the estimate, the damages, the law and the failure of the contractor, have been very heavy additional expenses, amounting to £11,370, to make up for which the Committee are under the necessity of recommending another call of £10 per cent, which they hope will complete the whole'. Some shareholders, unable or refusing to pay more, forfeited fifty shares. Auctioned, they were resold for £94 each to Lord Egremont who now held 250 shares or 28 per cent of the equity.

By August the canal was finished and the summit level began to fill with water. The paraphernalia of the workmen was removed, the land bordering the canal began to be restored to its former state and all was ready for the Committee to plan the opening celebrations.

Although the Wey & Arun Canal had taken, from first to last, six years to complete, the actual building of the waterway had occupied only three years. Few canals had been planned, dug, and opened in less time. Some projects were begun but never finished. Many had seen a decade or more pass before being completed. On the other hand, the nature of the terrain offered no great engineering problems; no tunnel had to be bored through rocky hillsides, no aqueducts to be thrown across broad valleys, nor had there been any exceptional opposition to the scheme to hoist the parliamentary expenses.

The day appointed for the official opening, 29 September 1816, was one of great local rejoicing. The canal promised to reduce the price of fuel, and as its creators had worked painstakingly to achieve its completion, the local villagers and gentry were not adverse to applauding their exertions and according them public recognition for their enterprise. *The Times* published two reports of the opening ceremonies; one on 2 October reprinted from the *County Chronicle*, the second, three days later, from its own correspondent.

From all accounts it was an inauspicious autumn morning when the Earl of Egremont, accompanied by numerous friends and shareholders, attended by the Mayor and Aldermen of Guildford, assembled by the 'Compasses Inn' at Alfold. Hot punch, exchanges of congratulatory messages and salutatory greetings, and then the attendant company embarked by Compasses bridge on four gaily decorated barges. Lined up behind, as if to show the serious commercial intention of the canal, rode eight barges well laden with coal and stacked with timber. There was John Seward of Loxwood on *Active* and William Upton with a cargo from Petworth being wished the best of good fortune on their new venture. Clustered round the bridge were the villagers and some two hundred or more navigators who had helped to bring about the successful conclusion of the scheme. The two bands which had been hired to enliven the day's festivities struck up a lively air and to the sound of roaring cheers from every side the horses started off at a steady pace down the towpath. All along the route were gathered big groups and little groups of interested spectators. Parlour-maids waved handkerchiefs from farmhouse windows, farmers merrily raised their sticks, while urchins gleefully scampered to and fro to add to the discomfort of the grazing cows who were both frightened and bewildered by the unfamiliar sounds of drum and trumpet and intermittent cheering.

Towards noon the weather improved; and on reaching Stonebridge, the party was greeted by both a ray of sunshine and the barge of the Godalming Navigation Commissioners. As the colourful procession entered the river Wey upon the last stage of its journey, the crowds lining the muddy banks burst into spontaneous and hearty cheering. A local reporter, overlooking the river from a position on top of St Catherine's Hill, enthusiastically described the scene in the following words—'The sunshine which now broke out, combined with the unrivalled scenery of the favourite spot, the music, the numerous assembly of spectators and the merry peal of the bells of Guildford, Shalford and Godalming, all heard at this time, gave an effect to the scene which could not be contemplated but with the most lively and pleasing emotions.' Indeed the Canal Company had paid for bells to be pealed in no less than five churches to honour the occasion.

The party reached Guildford about 4 o'clock. The Mayor and Aldermen landed first, assumed their full regalia and with Lord Grantley, the High Steward, Mr Sergeant Best, M.P., the Recorder, and one of the town Members, Mr Sergeant Onslow, welcomed the arrival of the illustrious Lord Egremont and his friends. All then went in procession, with bands playing and escorted by troops, to the 'White Hart' hotel in the High Street, where the Company acted as hosts to some 130 guests.* At dinner Lord Egremont took the chair with Lord Grantley and Lord Onslow seated at his side. The dining-room had been decorated for the occasion and emblazoned with the Arms of Guildford and Arundel. The regimental band of the Second Surrey Militia played through courses of turtle soup, sole *à la délice*, roast chicken, and venison from the Petworth estates. Fifty bottles of port were drunk to appropriate toasts and the festivities were enlivened by their Lordships bursting into song. Surprisingly perhaps, the last guests had departed soon after 9 o'clock. Meanwhile, outside 'The Compasses', the navigators had devoured a roasted ox and, having drunk two hundred gallons of ale, were entertaining themselves rather than each other with ribaldry and songs. Tales are told, apocryphally perhaps, that several navigators fell into the canal that night and that more than one warm-hearted maiden ceased to be a maid. It had been an historic occasion for Alfold village.

* The guests included Lord Melville, Admiral Sir George Murray, and the Rt Hon. William Huskisson, M.P., who became President of the Board of Trade and who was killed by a locomotive at the opening of the Liverpool & Manchester Railway in 1830.

127	Dinners	31..15..–
4	Doz & 10 Port	17..8..–
3	Doz & 7 Sherry	13..19..6
1	Bottle Brandy	–..7..–
1	Bottle Rum	–..5..–
6	Doz & 8 Sodawater	3..–..–
3	Bottles Cyder	–..4..6
2	Doz Lemons	–..6..–
	Sugar	–..5..–
	Wax Lights	1..4..–
28	Servants Dinner	1..8..–

Fig. 14.—The White Hart Inn dinner bill included broken glass and wax lights

'And thus,' wrote *The Times* correspondent, 'has opened under the happiest and most promising auspices, a canal of 18 miles in length through a beautiful and picturesque country to which it is as ornamental as it promises to be beneficial, completed without exceeding the amount of money allowed by the Act, without expenses to the Company by the Committee of Management and with less ill-will and criticism and irritation than a business, including such a number and variety of interests, could be expected to produce during its execution.'

The Times had indeed used much space in telling its readers that a canal with great commercial possibilities had been opened and the townspeople of Guildford certainly became immediately aware of the first benefits of the Wey & Arun when the coal which had been carried in the wake of the procession was sold for 50s. a chaldron instead of the usual three guineas. At least the canal had opened on an auspicious note, but the wheels of fortune leave little to prophecy.

CHAPTER VII

An Unpropitious Start (1816–1823)

Trade begins slowly on the Wey & Arun—total expenditure—mortgage of tolls—proposals for a branch canal to Horsham—the Wey & Arun declares a dividend—toll rates reduced—reciprocal toll agreements—Arun Navigation Act, 1821—improvements carried out—poor state of Wey Navigation—proposal for a bridge at Littlehampton—Cobbett's *Rural Rides*.

THE period between 1816 and 1823 was one of disappointment and hopeful anticipation for the Wey & Arun proprietors. The canal was finished, although much clearing-up work had still to be done and during the first nine months of operation, 3,600 tons of gravel, clay, earth, chalk, bricks, and Pulborough stone were moved along the navigation. There was, however, little sign of the expected stream of barges nosing their way through the Surrey and Sussex countryside. No sooner in fact had the excitement following the canal's opening died down than trade languished and on a daily average only two or three cargoes were passing through. Little, it seems, was done to attract commerce or to establish industry upon its banks. During the first seven years of operation tolls averaged only £1,275 and the waterway carried less than 10,000 tons annually, a mere fraction of the 130,000 tons envisaged, and less than half that carried on the Arun Navigation, whose traffic had increased by 25 per cent.

So it was that the rosy prospects predicted by the Press assumed a different hue as optimistic assumptions proved fallacious. Indeed it was soon apparent that the prospectus issued in 1811 had become a cornucopia of extravagant statements, and the shareholders began to doubt if there was even a possibility of their aspirations becoming fulfilled. It was soon discovered that few London merchants engaged in the Portsmouth trade chose to ship their wares by barge to avoid the dangers of the Foreland passage when, of necessity, cargoes had to be reshipped at Arundel or Littlehampton. The Arun Navigation was also proving a hindrance to fully laden barges, which encountered a series of hazards in the sinuosities of the river and particularly in the low arches of Stopham bridge and the small dimensions of Hardham tunnel. The combination of winter floods and summer drought—and these impediments also occurred out of season—produced either insufficient headroom or draught, so that rarely could a barge carry more than 30 tons, whereas five or six times that amount could be loaded in one operation on coasters plying between Arundel and the London Docks. Moreover, the time for the journey being about the same whether inland or by the Straits of Dover, the former route had the disadvantages of tolls having to be paid to no less than six authorities in addition to freight charges. Finally, the end of the Napoleonic Wars had removed the risks engendered by French privateers and what was perhaps the strongest inducement had vanished.

Local traffic was also developing slowly. It was some years before a carrier started to operate from the banks of the canal and naturally much depended on those already established on the Wey, Arun, and Rother Navigations. It had been assumed that these barge-masters would be willing to expand their businesses but few had the capital to build new boats, and many were farmers using barges to move produce and fertilizers in similar fashion as today's generation employs lorries. Certainly until a demand was created there was little incentive for newcomers to establish themselves on the canal, and even those who did venture upon its waters were not always certain of obtaining sufficient back-carriage to justify their enterprise.

It had been envisaged that the canal would supply an annual quota of 10,000 tons of coal to Godalming and Guildford; but the merchants on the Wey Navigation, observing that their new competitors had caused the price of coal to fall in Guildford by 13s. a chaldron, hurriedly reduced their charges; and since the journey from London to Guildford was almost equidistant with that from the coast, and considerably quicker because there was only half the number of locks, by far the greater part of the coal brought to the city continued to come from the Pool rather than from colliers discharging at Arundel. Improvements had also been made to the Thames Navigation below Shepperton. By 1816 pound locks had been built to replace the flash locks at Sunbury, Molesey, and Teddington and provision also made for barges drawing up to 3 ft 10 in., both of which developments encouraged and speeded traffic to the Wey and Basingstoke Navigations.* There was little the Wey & Arun could do to redress the position. However, one of the conditions on which the Company leased the two chalk pits at Guildford Quarry to John Davis, the lime-burner,

* Richmond (half-tide) lock was not built until 1894.

in 1821 was that he should 'use and consume such coals and culm only as shall enter the port of Arundel and be brought thence by the Wey & Arun Junction canal'. As this was by way of an experiment the Company undertook to bear any working loss for the first year.

Despite the fact that the canal had been built during a time of falling prices, miscalculations regarding the cost of the canal's construction had proved expensive. Contrary to what had been previously thought, compensation had had to be paid to the owners of two water-mills, and building costs had been sizeably increased by the failure of the contractor. At the Company's annual meeting in 1817, it was announced that the total expenditure from the commencement of the undertaking to 10 May was £102,626, but that there were still considerable arrears of damages remaining to be paid to owners of land, for the payment whereof there was no fund but what arose from the tolls. Not until 1821 were all these claims settled. The authorized capital of £99,550 expended, the company was forced to borrow £7,000 at 5 per cent to meet these outstanding liabilities by mortgaging the tolls.* To add to these difficulties, large sums were having to be spent on improving the water supply which appeared to be quite inadequate for the canal's needs in dry weather.

Meanwhile, the town of Horsham was still seeking an economical means of importing coal and transporting its produce to London. The cost of land carriage remained high and more than twenty years had passed since the first abortive attempt had been made to extend the Arun Canal from Newbridge. It is true that Horsham had been included in the prospectuses of several of the projects to link London and Portsmouth, but these had all collapsed and the Adur Navigation Act (1807) had brought water transport no nearer than Bines bridge, 8 miles away. Now, however, there was the prospect of direct communication with both the Thames and the English Channel.

In 1812, two separate schemes were advanced, one of which came near to fruition. The first was designed to take advantage of the Croydon, Merstham & Godstone Railway which had been opened in 1805 as an extension of the Surrey Iron Railway. A survey had been carried out by Netlam and Francis Giles in 1811

* The second Portsmouth & Arundel Canal Act (1819) authorized the Wey & Arun to borrow on mortgage an additional sum of £10,000. Smallpeice told the Lords' Committee on the bill that £107,725 had been expended up to May 1819 and that the cost of new works and debts less tolls received left £8,716 outstanding.

and on 3 January 1812 the Duke of Norfolk took the chair at an enthusiastic meeting held in the 'King's Head' at Horsham, which had fervently supported the idea of a canal from Merstham to Newbridge via the town. However, the railway to Merstham had not been an unqualified success. It had only single-track working, the gradients were rather steep, and the traffic carried proved unremunerative. Plans deposited in September 1811 show that the intended navigation was to begin at the foot of an inclined plane leading to the railway and continue for 23 miles on one level through Nutfield, Outwood Common, Three Bridges, and Crawley to Ifield Ponds and Horsham Common where a chain of 17 locks was to carry the canal down to Warnham and Farthings bridge. From this point it followed the Arun valley to Newbridge. Three aqueducts were planned over the Arun, 1 reservoir at Merstham, 6 in St Leonard's forest and 32 locks over its total length of 37 miles. Critics of the canal scheme pointed to the nuisance of transferring all freight at Merstham and doubted the feasibility of cutting a passage there through the formidable chalk hills. A petition for a bill was presented to the House of Commons on 24 January, but was not reported.

The second and more practicable scheme envisaged a canal leading out of the Wey & Arun 4½ miles above Newbridge, from Drungewick to Broadbridge Heath Common. A bill was applied for on 18 December 1812, but was also not reported, the promoters being presumably advised to wait until the building of the Wey & Arun had been completed. In 1817 the project was reconsidered and at their meeting in June the Arun Committee reported that a canal from Drungewick Farm to the Roman Road running through Dedisham Farm, Slinfold, was likely to be carried into effect. The Committee stipulated, however, that they would only support the project provided that tolls of not more than 1s. 6d. a ton were to be charged, that the Wey & Arun were prepared to reduce their tolls between Drungewick and Newbridge to half those charged by their (the Arun) Navigation, and that the trustees of the Horsham & Guildford turnpike would either consent to a reduction of their dues or alternatively that the canal should be carried further on to avoid one of the turnpike gates on this road. The Arun proprietors were prepared to agree in turn that tolls on goods passing from the Arun to the intended canal should be reduced. However, it appears either that agreement could not be reached on these points (there was strong opposition from the turnpike trustees who were likely to lose revenue) or that other difficulties arose, because the project was once more dropped. The scheme was not seriously revived again until 1839 when the clerk, Richard Wardroper, was asked to ascertain 'what toll, if any, would be required for using the Wey & Arun from Newbridge to Drungewick for the purpose of carrying a branch towards Horsham';[49] of this idea no more is heard. The Baybridge Canal Act in 1825 did bring the Adur Navigation to within five miles of Horsham at West Grinstead wharf, but the fact remains that in spite of being situated on the river Arun, the town never had the direct benefit of water transport.

A bill was also introduced into the House of Lords by Lord Egremont in March 1816, entitled the 'Rother & Arun Navigation Bill', for leave to repeal and amend certain provisions in the 1791 Rother Navigation Act, but after a first reading it was not proceeded with. The bill on the face of it was a simple attempt to repeal a clause of the original Act which allowed timber to be charged by measure instead of by weight. Behind it lay a long-standing dispute between timber merchant Stoveld and the Earl over the payment of tolls which had, at times, so exasperated his Lordship that he had even considered abandoning the navigation.

Although the canal had been open five years, no dividend had been paid on the Wey & Arun shares, and the shareholders were becoming impatient at receiving no return on the capital they had invested. Partly to assuage their dissatisfaction and partly to mark the Committee's optimism upon the expected success of the connecting canal to Portsmouth (whose Act had been passed in 1817), the payment was sanctioned in 1821 of a maiden dividend of £1 per cent. As current expenses and interest on the mortgage totalled over £1,000 and toll receipts amounted to only £1,342, the payment of £905 from borrowed capital was something of a gamble. It so happened that the opening of the Portsmouth & Arundel Canal was delayed by two years and no further dividend was paid until 1828.

Maximum toll rates had been fixed by Act of Parliament. All merchandise entering the Wey & Arun could be charged 4d. per ton-mile and 2d. a ton-mile for manure, although special tariffs had been agreed with both the Wey and the Arun Navigations for through traffic; viz. all cargoes bound from the Wey to the Arun and vice versa were charged a flat rate of 1s. a ton. Initially 3d. and 2d. a ton-mile respectively were demanded by the Wey & Arun; then to encourage traffic further reductions had to be made. Reciprocal toll agreements were also entered into by the Portsmouth & Arundel Canal Company with both the Wey & Arun and the Arun proprietors by which it was agreed that all merchandise carried between Portsmouth and the Thames through the Wey & Arun would be charged 4s. 6d. a ton instead of the 6s. maximum allowed by the Act. This amount was to be chargeable 'during such time as this Nation or Kingdom shall be in a state of war with the several powers or Kingdoms of Europe, or the United States of America, or any or either of them, or any other State or Nations trading immediately with the Kingdom of Great Britain and Ireland'. Similarly, the Portsmouth & Arundel undertook to charge only 3d. a ton-mile on goods passing from the Wey & Arun. Efforts were made to induce both the Wey Navigations to follow suit but their agreement was only obtained after much exhortation in 1823.

In June 1819 the Arun Navigation, to encourage the coal trade, reduced their tolls from 3s. to 2s. 6d. per chaldron on traffic bound from Littlehampton to Elm Bridge wharf, Cranleigh, and to 2s. if landed at Bramley. Chalk was similarly reduced to 6d. a ton if carried to Tickners Heath wharf or beyond. But these reductions attracted little additional traffic and it was announced at the annual meeting at Guildford in 1822 that in view of the impending opening of the Portsmouth & Arundel Canal further toll concessions would be made to give an impetus to trade. The rate on corn, coal, and timber was reduced to 2d. a ton-mile, on manure and stone, etc., to 1½d. a ton-mile, but these prices were only to apply when barge-loads exceeded 30 tons and no water had to be drawn from the reservoir. On other commodities the toll remained at 3d. a ton-mile. The results again were not as successful as had been anticipated. During the first year of the lower tariffs' operation the amount of tonnage carried slightly increased, but receipts fell by over 10 per cent. In 1823 all tolls on coal and culm were reduced to 2s. a chaldron and those on chalk and lime were still further reduced.

In the opinion of John Rennie, the Arun was 'a very bad navigation and barges navigating it experience great detention from the floods in winter and droughts in summer'.[50] The winter floods of the Arun valley were certainly notorious and the accounts often revealed a drop in tolls during the months of January and February which was out of all proportion to the average, or to the receipts for the preceding or following months. It was obvious, therefore, that if a substantial through-traffic between London and Portsmouth was going to develop, the state of that waterway had to be greatly improved. Agreement was consequently reached in February

1818 to the effect that while the Portsmouth & Arundel Canal was being built, the Arun proprietors should carry out a number of improvements in return for being enabled to charge a toll of 1s. 6d. a ton (instead of 1s.) on traffic passing between the two navigations. The stipulated improvements were as follows:

(i) To build a towpath 8 ft wide along the east bank of the river from Houghton round the Horseshoe cut at North Stoke to the road at the foot of Burpham chalk pits, 'for the want of which the navigation is at times much impeded'.
(ii) To remove the bend for the space of 100 yd immediately north of Houghton bridge.
(iii) To remove shoals at Canterbury Roadway, Amberley Swamp, Pye Withey, the tail of Coldwaltham lock, Low Mead, and the tail of Pallingham lock.
(iv) To raise all bridges between Greatham and Pallingham lock bridge to permit barges to pass at all times.
(v) To clean out the bed of Hardham tunnel.
(vi) To make a cut at Hardham from the Rother to the Arun to take away flood water.
(vii) To raise and widen the central arch of Stopham bridge.
(viii) To make places between Low Mead and Newbridge for barges to pass abreast as may be convenient.
(ix) To erect a second pair of flood-gates at Orfold to create a 1-ft lock.
(x) To widen Orfold lock to 11 ft 6 in.
(xi) Either to lower the sill of Pallingham lock by 18 in. or else to build a second lock.
(xii) To deepen the navigation to not less than 3 ft 2 in.
(xiii) To widen the navigation to not less than 35 ft.
(xiv) Either to make a towpath or provide steam tugs for hauling boats along the navigation.
(xv) To erect guide-posts to enable barges to pass in time of floods.

I have listed in full the improvements required by the Portsmouth & Arundel since they clearly reflect the inadequacy of the Arun Navigation to cater for more than local traffic. Due to the delays in building the Ford section of the canal, no action was taken to carry out the work and a further survey was carried out by James Hollinsworth in the summer of 1820 from Burpham to Newbridge. This resulted in a second agreement being made in

January 1821, which amended the earlier one and fixed the date for completion of the alterations as 5 April 1823, reduced the maximum draught to 3 ft 1 in., and substituted for item (viii) the need for barges to be able to pass two abreast the length of the Arun Canal except for 250 yd near Lee Farm and for 200 yd at Orfold Hanger. Finally it was agreed that the Arun need contribute only two-fifths of the estimated cost (£300) for making the towpath round the Horseshoe cut. (The Arun Minutes mention that the balance was to be subscribed by both the Portsmouth & Arundel and the Wey & Arun.)

These two agreements were embodied in the second Arun Navigation Act passed in May 1821, which also discharged the Arun's liability to widen the river from Houghton to Burpham if the Commissioner of Sewers for the Rape of Arundel carried out the work before July 1822. The Act also empowered the Arun proprietors to appoint persons to act on the Portsmouth & Arundel Canal to prevent toll evasion and limited the time for completing the works to six years.

It was admitted that the cost of these alterations would be considerable, the estimated cost being £2,100 below Houghton bridge and £2,500 above. The Arun proprietors had to borrow £3,000 but the money expended was probably nearer £5,000. This was a particularly heavy burden for the finances of so small a company to bear and a blow for the shareholders who had seen their profits used for the last twenty-five years to pay off the original mortgage. The dividend—only resumed in 1821—had once again to be suspended though it was hoped that in view of the increased tolls to be levied on all London–Portsmouth trade this would not be for long duration. It was in fact to be ten years.

The alterations were begun in the autumn of 1821 under the direction of John Seward. The main arch of Stopham bridge was raised in July 1822 at a cost of £286 and a lower lock built at Pallingham. A cast-iron swivel bridge, thrown across the Arun at Low Mead [*sic*] lock, may have been a temporary bridge while the work at Stopham was being carried out. The evidence available suggests that the extension to Burpham was carried out by the Arun proprietors. I can find no trace of a second pair of floodgates being installed at Orfold but Orfold lock was widened, and the remaining alterations as far as can be ascertained were carried out by the summer of 1823. For his work Seward was paid £150. Until these improvements had been made, lack of draught had prevented barges carrying over 30 tons between the Thames and the Arun. Once completed, however, loads of 40 tons and more could be carried. In 1825 Isemonger's *Plymouth* passed from Littlehampton to Guildford with 38 tons of coal and in the following year the Arundel Company's *Norfolk* drew 3 ft 5½ in. while carrying 42 tons of corn through the Wey & Arun.

The tunnel was, of course, to remain the chief nuisance to larger-sized craft, for nothing could be done to increase its dimensions short of rebuilding it. The alternative route by Pulborough was equally useless for barges with high superstructures or bulky cargoes, since, besides being devious, it was spanned by two low bridges.

The Wey was also at this period a very primitive navigation. Charles Cracklow, the Wey agent, reported that in 1821 the wharves at Newhaw, Send, and Worsfold Gates were neglected, that Paper Court lock had been out-of-lease for many years, and that barge-horses had to ford the river both at Bowers and near Worsfold Gates. Cracklow re-established the wharves, built a wooden bridge at Bowers lock, negotiated the purchase of land for building a graving dock at Stoke, and restarted a weekly barge service between Guildford and London. Among the economies he introduced were reductions in the wages of the labourers, hitherto 2s. 6d. a day plus beer, which he claimed were higher than the general wages of the county and unnecessary in 'these times of cheap provisions and want of employ of labouring men'.[51]

In spite of his efforts and possibly because of his unpopularity, Cracklow was dismissed in 1822—the ailing Earl of Portmore 'had an unfeeling disposition towards him'—with the result that the navigation fell again into disorder. Lord Portmore died in November but neither his heir nor Langton, the other joint-owner, visited the navigation whose management rested entirely in the hands of their agent. However, neither of Cracklow's successors, Nicholson and Sandys, held office for more than a few months and it was not until the appointment of Charles Orlando Hodgson in 1827 that the Wey's fortunes began to revive (*see* p. 113).

In 1822 the towns and villages along the seaboard between Worthing and Bognor petitioned Parliament for a bridge across the Arun at Littlehampton. Rather surprisingly perhaps, this proposal aroused great opposition not only from the various navigation companies, but from the towns of Midhurst, Petworth, and Arundel who all feared a loss of trade. Lord Egremont also entered a petition against the bill, but the Arun Navigation Company was in something of a quandary since the Cutfield family, who held 44 per cent of the shares, lived at Climping and favoured a bridge.

Wey & Arun Junction Canal.

ABSTRACT of ACCOUNT for the Year ending 10th *May*, 1817.

		£	s.	d.
To Balance in the hands of the Treasurers, 1816		2,618	5	8
Receipts on account of 7th. Call		50		
8th. Ditto		50		
9th. Ditto		50		
10th. Ditto		100		
Received for purchase of 50 forfeited Shares	4700 0 0			
Moiety of Duty and expences	68 12 10	4,768	12	10
Receipts on account of 11th. Call (the Amount whereof is £9,050)		8,900		
£ 100 before paid in advance, £ 50 still unpaid)				
Received for Tolls on Canal		408	5	3
(from the opening, viz. 29th Sept. 1816)				
Interest on Exchequer Bills paid off and exchanged for new Bills		88	6	11
Exchequer Bills sold, and Interest thereon		5,123	15	1
		22,157	5	9

		£	s.	d.
By Payments Engineer, Mr. Jessop		89	5	
Surveyors, &c. Mr. M. Upton, Salary, &c.		345	5	2
........, T. P. Upton		280	10	7
........, J. Tewsley, for Surveying Timber		30	18	5
Clerk...., Mr. J. Smallpeice, 1 year's Salary to 1st. April, 1817		100		
........, Mr. C. J. Shebbeare Clerk to the Commissioners, a Bill		8	16	
Solicitor's Bills, paid for Abstracts &c.		83		8
Labor and Materials		13,615	4	6
Purchase of Land, &c.		571	2	6
In part of Purchase of Wharf at *Guildford*		12		
Owners and Occupiers of Land for Damages		2,518	1	5
Dean and Chapter of *Chichester* 1 year's Rent, deducting half a year's Property Tax		22	9	9
Overseers of *Rudgwick* for Poor Rates		2	4	7
Duty and Commission on Shares sold		156	12	3
Dinner Expences, &c. opening Canal		119	4	7
		17,954	15	5
By Purchase of Exchequer Bills	4000 0 0			
Interest accrued thereon	97 13 1	4,097	13	1
Balance in the hands of the Treasurers		104	17	3
		22,157	5	9

Russells' Press.

Fig. 15.—Wey & Arun Canal Company Abstract of Accounts, 1817

RIVER WEY, SURREY.--Mr Sparkes & Co. account of Riverage, for one Quarter ending the 29th of Sepr. 1813.

Places where Loaded and Unloaded.	No. of Loads.	At per Load.	£.	S.	D.
Nett Godalming	77	4-6	17	6	6
Do	16	2-0	1	12	—
Guildford	87	4-6	19	11	6
Dapdon		4-8			
Stoke	183	4-0	36	12	—
Bowers		3-0			
Triggs	5	2-6		12	6
Send Heath	6	2-6		15	—
Newark		2-0			
Pyrford		1-6			
Byfleet		1-6			
Newhaw		1-0			
Coxes		1-0			
Weybridge		0-6			
			76	9	6
Farm...			22		
Ballance £			54	9	6

This Bill to be Paid by the 16th Octr 1813

Settled Octr 26 — 1813
Guildford Wharf Wm Chandler

Russells' Guildford Press.

Fig. 16.—Wey Navigation—Barge Master's Account, 1813

A special meeting of the proprietors was therefore called in March and only after an animated exchange of views was the resolution that the bill should be opposed carried by 54 votes to 44. The bill was, in fact, lost, but in 1824 an Act was passed for establishing a ferry over the river Arun at Littlehampton and making roads to communicate therewith. Meanwhile Littlehampton harbour had been falling into decay again and in 1825 a third Act was passed for its 'more effectual security'.

It is interesting to record that on a cloudy summer day in 1823 —on the first of August to be exact—William Cobbett passed by Newbridge on one of his rural rides and noted its air of activity. 'Soon after quitting Billingshurst', he wrote, 'I crossed the river Arun, which has a canal running alongside of it. At this there are large timber and coal yards, and kilns for lime. This appears to be a grand receiving and distributing place.' And of course it was. The improvements ordered had borne fruit. Traffic had increased. Billingshurst and the surrounding farms and villages now looked to the wharf at Newbridge for the arrival of their coal and groceries, for their fertilizers and fancy goods from London, Guildford, and Arundel, and as the most convenient means of dispatching their own wares and farm produce to market. The following day Cobbett, having spent the night at Petworth, crossed the Rother Navigation at Coultershaw wharf and remarked that here, too, was 'another place of deposit for timber, lime, coals and other things'. At this time agricultural distress was at its worst, but Cobbett found that there was no misery to be seen in this district and found fifty people hay-making in one of Lord Egremont's fields. And because the farmers had no employment for many of their men, one labourer was seen to be cracking the big stones laid in the road with a sledge-hammer. Some days later, while riding from Hascombe to Ewhurst, Cobbett crossed the Wey & Arun between Goose Green (by Run Common) and Smithwood Common, but makes no other allusion than to say he crossed 'a canal'. It was clear that since the Wey & Arun's path lay through a sparsely populated and rural region, its immediate hopes of prosperity rested upon its use as a main line and for that reason were to be closely linked with the fortunes of the Portsmouth & Arundel Canal.

CHAPTER VIII

The London–Portsmouth Trade (1823–1838)

Portsmouth & Arundel Canal Act, 1817—the line and its estimated cost—second Act, 1819—unfortunate incident at the opening of the Chichester branch—celebrations on final completion—bullion barges—a connecting steam packet service—effect of opening on Wey & Arun—pollution of water suppl·es—Lord Egremont retires from the scene—doldrums—third Act, 1828—Cha. es Hodgson helps—joint committee formed to revive trade—Portsea Canal abandoned 1830—Palmer's exertions—the Company acts as carrier—toll concessions—end of through traffic.

WHEN finally in 1815 a bill materialized for a canal to forge the final link in the chain of direct inland navigation between London and Portsmouth, Gates, the Portsmouth historian, relates that 'it was received with great favour and some sanguine spirits prophesied that half the sea trade of London would pass along it. All in Portsmouth who were able to put money in it did so, and in a few days £20,000 worth of shares were subscribed in the borough alone.'[52] The same year Netlam and Francis Giles carried out a survey under John Rennie's direction. However, Lake Allen, a contemporary historian, suggests that there were less optimistic views of its prospects and remarks 'if the design is entered upon, it will have at least one beneficial effect, viz. that of employing a number of the poor and labouring classes of society'.

The Portsmouth & Arundel Canal Act was obtained in July 1817, by which time £101,250 had been subscribed, on payment of £1 per share deposit, towards the estimated cost of £125,490. The Company was floated with a capital of £126,000 raised in £50 shares. The principal shareholder was Lord Egremont (320) and 13 others held over 20 shares, including 125 owned by the Cutfield family; other shareholders included the Duke of Norfolk, Viscounts Keith and Exmouth and 'very many Gentlemen and Ladies of great respectability', among them Captain John Bligh. The first meeting of the Management Committee was held on 19 August 1817, when it was stated that the carriage of some 80,000 tons was to be expected and that the revenue was estimated at about £21,000 a year, of which the larger part should accrue from the 36,000 tons

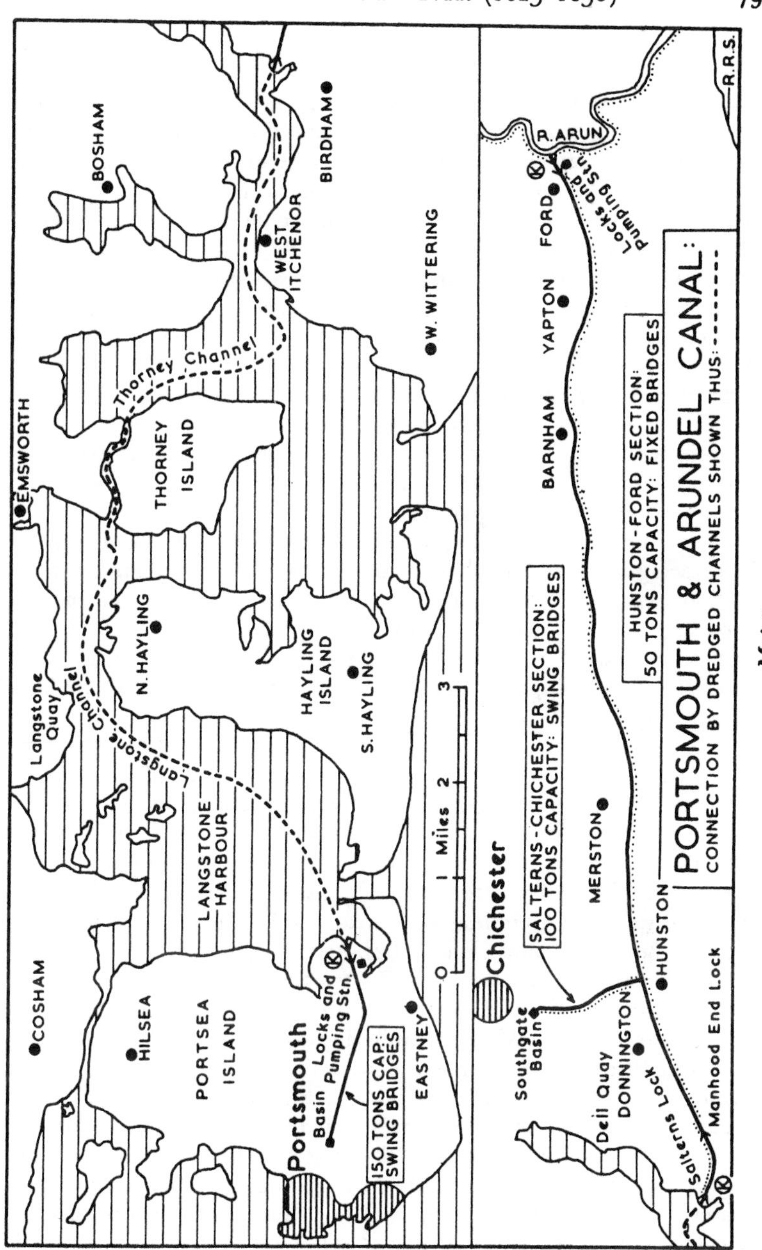
COSHAM
HILSEA
PORTSEA ISLAND
Portsmouth
Basin
Locks and Pumping Stn.
150 TONS CAP: SWING BRIDGES
EASTNEY
LANGSTONE HARBOUR
Langstone Quay
Langstone Channel
N. HAYLING
HAYLING ISLAND
S. HAYLING
EMSWORTH
THORNEY ISLAND
Thorney Channel
BOSHAM
WEST ITCHENOR
BIRDHAM
W. WITTERING
0 1 Miles 2 3
Chichester
Southgate Basin
Dell Quay
DONNINGTON
Salterns Lock
Manhood End Lock
HUNSTON
MERSTON
SALTERNS-CHICHESTER SECTION: 100 TONS CAPACITY: SWING BRIDGES
BARNHAM
YAPTON
FORD
Locks and Pumping Stn
R. ARUN
R.R.S.
HUNSTON-FORD SECTION: 50 TONS CAPACITY: FIXED BRIDGES
PORTSMOUTH & ARUNDEL CANAL:
CONNECTION BY DREDGED CHANNELS SHOWN THUS:

Map 7

formerly carried by sea, not only between London and Portsmouth, but between London and the western ports, since it was claimed that goods could be sent by canal as fast as by land and at one-sixth of the expense. Another major source of revenue was to be derived from carrying 12,000 tons hitherto conveyed by land together with 3,000 tons of Government stores from London. It was anticipated that the 2,500 tons carried between Arundel and Portsmouth would be sent by canal since goods had to be currently transhipped at Arundel from barges into sea-going vessels 'which are often delayed in Arundel river for several weeks if the wind sets on the shore'.[153] Local trade between Arundel and Chichester harbour was estimated at 6,000 tons and there were hopes of capturing the London fruit trade traffic 'because cargoes of a perishable nature are often injured by protracted voyages'. The Committee firmly believed that there was 'every reasonable expectation of a very abundant and satisfactory interest on the capital to be expended even in time of peace'[154]; but for long-term investors, they could not refrain from pointing out the 'inevitable and greatly increased value' of the shares should the country again be in a state of war. On 20 August 1818 Mr John Williams, one of the promoters, ceremoniously removed the first sod of turf at Ford, and then retired with his colleagues to the nearby 'Ship and Anchor'. It so happened that this section of the canal was the last to be completed.[155]

The main line ran due west from the Arun at Ford via Yapton, Barnham, and Hunston to Birdham, where it entered Chichester harbour; from there barges sailed or were towed by the Company's steam tug along dredged channels around Thorney and Hayling Islands and across Langstone Harbour to Milton Common where the Portsea Canal led to the terminal basins at the Halfway Houses, a total distance of 28 miles. At Hunston a short branch led into the city of Chichester, but the canal planned to cut across the neck of Portsea Island to give access to Portsmouth Harbour via Cosham was not executed until 1831. As the line passed through flat country, only six locks were required; two at each of the entrances at Ford, Birdham, and Milton Common, which raised the water-level 12 ft above high-water mark at spring tides. The only natural water supply was from the river Lavant, from which a feeder supplied the Southgate basin. The rest had to be pumped. The steam engine at Ford could lift some 96 hogsheads (5,000 gal.) of water a minute from the Arun and this rate was necessary since to prevent salt water entering the canal, no water could be taken from the river except between two hours after high water and one hour after low water.[156] To supply the Portsea Canal a huge well was dug above the second lock on Milton Common, from which water was pumped by the adjoining engine house.

Rennie based his estimate for a barge canal, with a depth of 4 ft 6 in. and a width of 33 ft, as follows:

	Distance (miles)	*Locks*	*Estimate* £
Ford to Birdham	12	4	72,270
Chichester branch	1¼	—	6,500
Thorney and Langstone channels	13	—	12,914
Portsea Canal	2½	2	18,618
Cosham cut	1¼	2	15,188
	30	8	125,490

It will be observed that the figure for the Ford–Birdham section alone was more than Jessop's estimate made four years earlier for the Wey & Arun, and the significant rise in costs as a result of the war can be judged when considering the much greater distance, lockage, and cutting involved in the latter.

The need to link Chichester with the sea stemmed from the fact that coastal vessels, particularly colliers, had to discharge their cargoes at Itchenor, for want of draught, into lighters which themselves had to be unloaded at Dell Quay, some 2 miles short of the city. Goods then had to be conveyed by waggon into Chichester, incidentally having to pass a turnpike gate on the way. In 1816, 18,000 tons of coal, besides 1,650 tons of merchandise, had been imported in this manner, and a branch canal would supersede this land carriage and enable barges receiving coals at Itchenor to proceed to the city direct. The earliest scheme for such a canal had been formulated in 1585, and again in 1801 and 1811 there had been similar proposals. However, the Committee reasoned that a ship canal would in most cases obviate the necessity for even one transhipment and thereupon decided in 1818 to apply for a second Act to enable both the Chichester and Portsea sections to be built as ship canals, 8 ft deep, for use by vessels of 100 and 150 tons burthen. The additional cost as estimated at £12,778. £2,540 was also allowed for a road to be built to the Southgate basin at Chichester. However, as it was also decided not to proceed for the time being with the Cosham cut, the total estimate for the line was only very slightly increased to £125,620. The Act was obtained in June 1819, and incorporated the agreement made the previous year with the Wey & Arun for mutual toll reductions. To enable land traffic to cross the Chichester Ship Canal, iron swivel bridges were made in 1820 by Tickell of Southampton, and these were named after the leading supporters of the project—Casher, Crosbie, Cutfield, Dudley, Egremont, and Poyntz.

The urgent need for the canal's completion, and indeed its *raison d'être*, had, however, virtually disappeared with the termination of the Napoleonic Wars. In their wake came economic problems and financial crises. Although in 1817 it was said that the estimated cost was higher than would be required due to the great reductions that had taken place in the price of land, labour, and materials, the reverse occurred and on more than one occasion work on the canal had to be suspended until more funds could be raised. The original Act had allowed £40,000 to be borrowed on mortgage of the works in addition to the capital. Although this sum had been confirmed by the second Arun Navigation Act, no lender could be found and it seemed as if the project was going to founder. Again it was Lord Egremont to the rescue, and on his personal guarantee the Government agreed to authorize the issue of Exchequer Bills[53] and work was able to proceed.

The navigation had, in fact, to be opened in stages. The *Brighton Chronicle* recorded that late in the afternoon on 27 December 1821 nearly one thousand spectators watched the filling of Southgate basin, but not until 9 April 1822 was the Chichester Canal officially opened. It was not an auspicious occasion. The procession from Milton consisting of three barges, two sailing vessels, and eleven rowing boats towed by the tug *Egremont* ran aground on a mud bank in Emsworth Channel and never arrived.[157] While John Williams and his party of 130 lay stranded, the yacht *Sylph* led a smaller procession of trading and pleasure craft up the canal to Southgate basin to be greeted by cannon fire, bands of music, and the acclamations of an impatient crowd.

The Company had to take great pains to try to refute the wild reports which spread after this unfortunate incident, but the navigation of the twisting tidal channels always remained a hazard on ebb tides and when the weather was rough. Some months later the *Hampshire Telegraph* reported that 'many thousands', lining the banks throughout its entire length, saw the Portsea Canal opened on 19 September 1822 when the steam tug *Egremont*, followed by several gaily decorated barges, passed in procession up the canal while bands of music played. John Frattle's sloop *Beehive*, which entered for loading, and the schooner *Richmond*, which discharged a cargo of coals at the basin, were listed as the first trading vessels to use the canal. The same report mentioned that only 550 yd of excavation and embanking remained to be completed. Yet eight more months were to pass before a barge could leave Portsmouth bound inland for London.

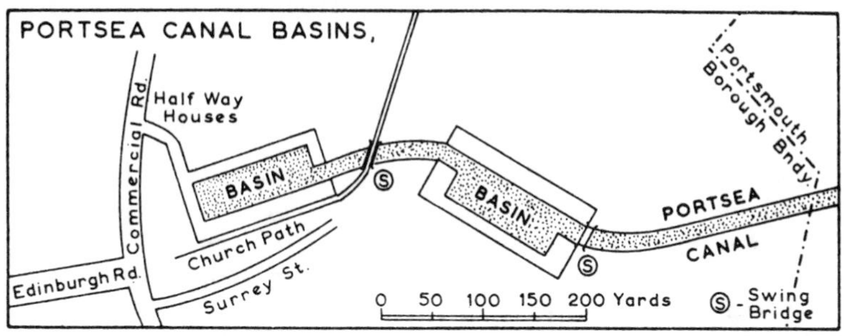

As designed by John Rennie in 1815. Only one basin was actually built.
Map 8

In the course of digging the canal, foundations of what were believed to be a medieval mansion of the Bohum family were found near Ford. Excavations at the canal basin at Chichester revealed Roman remains which included handmills, a funeral vessel, and a hoard of 700 denarii, and further south more Roman coins, lamps, and pottery were also found.[54] The canal was finally opened for traffic throughout its entire length on 26 May 1823. The inauguration ceremony occupied the space of two days. Nine days, however, were to elapse before a detailed account of the proceedings appeared in the London press. 'OPENING OF THE PORTSMOUTH & ARUNDEL CANAL, being the last portion of the whole line of inland navigation from London to Portsmouth', ran the announcement in the *Morning Post* on 4 June 1823. The reader can imagine the splendid sight as on that sunny May morning eighteen boats and barges, decorated with gay streamers and colours, assembled at the entrance to the canal at Ford; some were filled with the county's aristocracy and civil dignitaries, others laden with chalk for farmers on the line and five contained goods for Chichester, one of which had reached Ford from London in three days. Leading the way was the Earl of Egremont in his gaily painted pleasure barge, closely followed by that of the Duke of Norfolk with the Mayor of Arundel on board. The Mayor of

Guildford had many of his townsmen in his boat and there were numerous parties from the local gentry in others, all of whom were entertained by musicians who filled two more craft.

> 'The procession was handsomely decorated with colours, and it glided along upon the smooth surface of the canal through a country possessing every beauty, which high cultivation, interspersed with occasional plantations, could give it; while from the decks of the barges, the charms of a beautiful day were heightened by a very extensive and delightful varied prospect.'

At Hunston Common the flotilla was met by an 80-ton schooner and five sloops which had come up from Chichester harbour. The whole entourage then moved majestically along with bands playing and colours flying towards Southgate basin, where they were greeted with a discharge of cannon and by a 'very numerous assemblage of spectators, entirely covering the wharfs and adjoining land'. In the basin it was found that a sloop and two barges were in the midst of discharging their cargoes.

> 'The proceedings of the day passed without the slightest interruption and appeared to give entire satisfaction to everyone; it being a matter of no small congratulation to the tradesmen of Chichester that where five years before nothing but meadows and corn fields appeared, there is now a channel that will float their commerce to and from the Metropolis and the manufacturing districts of the country at comparatively little expense. At five o'clock, about seventy Gentlemen, amongst whom was the Noble Earl, sat down to an excellent dinner at the Swan Inn and the evening was spent in a way suited to the occasion.'

An elderly inhabitant reminiscing on the event in 1887 said: 'The first thing that took place was the digging of the canal, and when that was finished there was a grand "to do". It was a pretty sight, the vessels being towed down with scores of people on the decks, bands playing, and flags flying. There was a fair held there that very day, which was kept up afterwards for years. There was jumping in sacks, diving for oranges, donkey racing and so on.'[55]

The *Morning Post*'s report continued:

> 'On the following morning his Lordship and about fifty Gentlemen proceeded in one of the barges down the Canal into Chichester Harbour, and having embarked in the Company's Steam Vessel, to which a barge of forty tons burthen, and fully laden, was attached; the light barge also was, for the accommodation of passengers, made fast to her; and at about eleven o'clock, the Steam Vessel got under weigh; and

proceeded with this charge against a strong flood tide, making a good passage in five hours, through Chichester Harbour, Hayling Channel, and Langstone Harbour, to the Sea Lock of the Portsea Island Canal. The whole having passed the locks, proceeded through this branch, of two miles in length, between banks covered with spectators; to the amount of at least twenty thousand. On reaching the basin they were greeted with a discharge of cannon and the acclamations of the persons assembled, amongst which were at least three hundred who covered the masts, rigging and deck of a large collier brig that lay therein.

'The proceedings of this day also passed without any impediment, and the evening terminated with an excellent dinner at the George Inn, to which about sixty persons sat down to partake of some fine venison which his Lordship had handsomely presented to this assembly, as he had previously done to that of Chichester.'

The newspaper concluded its lengthy account with the comment that

'the arrival of the barge above stated at Ford from London in three days has proved the practicability of transporting goods from the metropolis to Portsmouth in four, as a barge can conveniently navigate from Ford to Portsmouth (which has been ascertained by repeated trials) in one day',

and the announcement that goods, with the exception of a few articles of special value, could now be conveyed by the Arundel Lighter Company, from the wharves of Randall, Howell & Co., Queenhithe, Upper Thames Street, and W. J. Hall near the Custom House, Lower Thames Street, London, to those of the Canal Company at the Halfway Houses, Portsea, for 22s. 6d. a ton including the expenses of shipping and landing; and that arrangements were being made by which goods 'destined for Western Ports in the British Channel, and for Guernsey and Jersey' as well as Paris (via the Seine) would be received and forwarded by vessels belonging to these places. A table of the various rates charged is given on the following page.

In a letter to the proprietors of the Wey Navigation, Williams explained the reasons why toll charges on the Portsmouth & Arundel had to be higher than on the other navigations. Expenditure on the canal itself, he wrote, totalled £170,000, £45,000 more than the estimate. Not only, he added, did enormous expense arise in supplying water to the canal by two steam engines and in providing a steam tug (which had cost over £5,000) to be kept constantly available, but also in keeping the tideway channels open, since the mud could only be excavated at low-water spring tides.[56]

Navigation	*Tolls from London to Portsmouth*		*Tolls from London to Chichester*		*On goods of much weight and little value*		*On goods of much weight and extremely small value*		*Government stores from London to Portsmouth*	
	s.	d.	s.	d.	s.	d.	s.	d.	s.	d.
Thames		8¼		8¼		8¼		8¼		8¼
Wey	2	8	2	8	1	8	1	0	1	4
Godalming		6		6		4½		3		4
Wey & Arun	3	6	3	6	2	3	1	6	2	3
Arun	1	2	1	2		9		6		9
Portsmouth & Arundel	5	0	3	0	3	0	2	0	3	0
	13	6¼	11	6¼	8	8¾	5	11¼	8	4¼
Freight	8	11¾	8	11¾	8	9¼	8	8¾		—
Total cost	22	6	20	6	17	6	14	8	8	4¼

Now that London and Portsmouth had at last been linked, what were the prospects of success? Williams had admitted even before the canal was fully open that tentative inquiries had shown the unwillingness of both the Government and merchants to change their normal method of transporting goods by coaster, since shipping charges had fallen as low as 10s. to 16s. per ton and that 'unless a strong case can be made it will be next to an impossibility to induce a departure from the old and beaten track'. Nevertheless, he remained convinced that the canal could beat the coaster out of the field if only all the connecting navigations would grant toll concessions;[57] and these were in fact granted. The distance from Portsmouth to London Bridge by river and canal was 116 miles; and since the coastal voyage to the capital was a hundred miles further, there appeared to be good reason for avoiding wintry seas, contrary winds, and the dangers of the North Foreland by conveying goods along this shorter but slower route—slower because barges rarely travelled by night, because progress was delayed by 52 locks and a tunnel, and because cargoes had to be transhipped at least once more than was usually necessary by coaster. Normally, four days were the minimum required to complete the inland journey.[58] Barges leaving Portsmouth at daybreak hoped to spend the first night at Ford or Arundel, the second above Loxwood, the third at Weybridge, so that the Pool of London would be reached late the following afternoon if conditions were normal. But they seldom were. Delays were manifold; shoals or floods in the Arun valley, shortages of water on the summit level, fog in the Thames, slackness by the barge captains—these were the causes of many.

Through traffic started, if not with a flourish, at least with enthusiasm, and in the first six months some 1,500 tons of corn and groceries reached Chichester and Portsmouth from the capital. On 15 September 1823 the *Sussex Weekly Advertiser* reported that 'The streets and various of the shops in the City of Chichester were on last Thursday evening, for the first time illuminated with gas, and presented a very brilliant appearance to a great number of perambulators.' On 17 November the same newspaper stated that the cutter *The Royal Gift* had arrived at the basin where its owner, a disabled naval warrior, gave a display of seamanship 'alike amusing to the visitors and profitable to himself'.

Trade, however, did not develop as had been expected. All the hopes and aspirations of the promoters were shattered when in 1824—which, incidentally, was the most successful year—only 3,650 tons and not the hoped for 55,000 were carried between the Portsmouth & Arundel Canal and London.[158] The chief trouble, the never-to-be solved trouble, was the failure of the carriers to obtain a back-carriage without which little or no profit could be made. Barges that conveyed over forty tons of goods down the Arun valley had either to return 'light' or with as little as two or five. Corn and groceries and, in smaller quantities, porter, wine, and pottery initially arrived with some degree of regularity from London; but consignments to the capital were harder to secure and consequently more variable, ranging from ships' timber and planks to more unusual items like furniture, soldiers' baggage, marble, and Indian cotton. However, what was lost in weight was to some extent made up in value. Every month or so until 1826 precious cargoes of bullion left the Halfway Houses bound for the Bank of England. Twenty-five or 30 tons was the usual consignment but one day in 1825* the *Union* and the *Portsea* went through together with 72 tons on board. Each bullion barge carried an armed guard of four 'redcoats' who slept on board at night. Long before the waterway was built the area had been associated with errant Huguenot glass-makers and smugglers who hid kegs of brandy in the recesses of the great chimneys of the Surrey farmhouses, and it is perhaps surprising that there are no reports of

* 10 February.

untoward incidents. An ambush in the depths of Sidney Wood might have been carried out with little difficulty, but how to get the booty away would have been a problem harder to overcome.[159]

An example of early enterprise in connection with the development of steamships occurred shortly before the canal was completed, when a company was formed for establishing a steam packet service between Portsmouth, Plymouth, and Falmouth with the object of forwarding as quickly as possible the cargoes coming down from London by barge. The shareholders included Lord Egremont and several of the Portsmouth & Arundel Management Committee and some £5,000 was raised.

The *Sir Francis Drake* began operations in 1824 equipped to carry 80 tons of merchandise as well as 15 cabin and 12 steerage passengers and, being fitted with the lower masts and the sails of a schooner, had only to use the 24 h.p. engine during calm or adverse winds. Her usefulness in connection with the barge trade proved, however, very limited since the charge from Plymouth to London for barge hire, canal dues, and shipment was 35s. a ton compared with 30s. by coaster. However, the packet operated fairly successfully despite boiler trouble until a superior vessel arrived on the scene early in 1826, which materially altered the prospects of the company. Knocked out of the Plymouth trade, fresh sources of revenue had to be found from the Channel Islands, by conveying voters to a Cornwall by-election and by providing excursion trips round the Eddystone lighthouse.

The opening of the Portsmouth & Arundel Canal brought an immediate increase in traffic to both the Arun and the Wey & Arun. Tolls rose by 47 per cent to £1,760 and by 60 per cent to £1,989 respectively during 1823–4. The Arun maintained this figure the following year, but it dropped to £1,450 in 1825–6 while the receipts of the Wey & Arun increased to £2,165 and £2,355. There was no doubt that traffic from the Portsmouth & Arundel had a more pronounced effect on the finances of the Arun than on those of the Wey & Arun, which received three times the amount of revenue from its southbound traffic than from that coming up from the coast. Yet the Arun was carrying a proportionately heavier traffic since its toll rates were roughly half those of the Wey & Arun, while for the through traffic between London and Portsmouth, it charged only one-third of the latter's toll for passing through the line.

Meanwhile, the Portsmouth & Arundel was faced with other worries. The Portsea portion of the canal was supplied with water from a huge well placed just above the entrance locks. Complaints had been received from thirty-six 'respectable inhabitants' that sea-water from the canal was percolating into their wells and polluting the water supplies. On 3 December 1824, a public meeting was held at the Beneficial Society's Hall in Portsmouth for the 'purpose of taking into consideration the means of obtaining compensation for the damage done by the canal', to prevent recurrence of similar evils, and to point out that as the canal bridges were incommodious and highly dangerous, they should be improved. Eighteen days later the proprietors held a meeting at the Old Town Hall, when considerable indignation was expressed at the conduct of the local people in the matter. It was declared that compensation had been given for injury in certain cases and that other complaints were being considered, but the Company 'was not to be dictated to by any set of individuals, however respectable'.[59] However, when the Company tried to obtain a third Act in February 1825, in order to raise more capital, petitions were entered against the bill mentioning both these complaints and, although amendments were made, the bill was lost—probably because of the waterway's financial position. Similar trouble was also experienced at Ford where salt water had spoiled crops on adjoining farmland.

In 1825 the through trade fell by half and the following year all traffic between the two great ports virtually ceased when the Portsmouth Barge Company was forced for economic reasons to sell its boats. In September 1826, Lord Egremont washed his hands of the concern and announced that he had voluntarily surrendered his holding now of 315 shares in the Company (issued at £15,750), that he would pay the Company's debt due to the Government (i.e. the mortgage of £40,000) which he had guaranteed, and that he would abandon any claim for its future reimbursement.[60] His sole condition, that the proprietors should cause the canal to be rendered complete and efficient, was probably enough to make the offer null and void! The *Hampshire Telegraph* imparted this offer to those persons interested in the canal's success with 'sincere satisfaction' and referred to it as a 'munificent gift'. The shareholders' thoughts on hearing the news may have been very different, but it at least enabled the Company to petition again for another Act.

Inevitably, the failure of the Portsmouth Canal affected the finances of the Wey & Arun, and during 1826–7 tolls fell by nearly 20 per cent. The Committee stated at the annual meeting in May that they attributed this 'amongst other causes incidental to the present state of trade and commerce to the failure of the Portsmouth Canal. There are, however, hopes that that line of canal may be restored, or a new one made, and in such case there can be no doubt but that the traffic on this canal will be increased.'[61] In February 1825, *The Times* had announced that a survey was under way for a canal of giant proportions from Deptford to the English Channel and rumours were now wildly circulating about the Grand Imperial Ship Canal project (*see* next chapter). The £100 and £50 shares of the Wey & Arun and the Portsmouth & Arundel stood relatively high at £25 and £15, respectively, for although the former had only just announced the resumption of a paltry dividend of 1 per cent and the latter had still not declared one, if a new canal should be built there was the prospect of a 'take-over' bid or advantageous compensation for those navigations whose lines might be affected.

However, no new canal materialized, and less than 1,500 tons of cargo passed between the Portsmouth & Arundel and London in the course of the next five years, 1827–31. In spite of its failure not all the proprietors had lost faith in their enterprise and it was left to George Palmer, the new manager, to make a final series of vigorous attempts to revive trade on the almost derelict waterway. The first step was to obtain more capital and in May 1828, a third Act was passed which empowered the Company to raise a further £50,000 in £25 preference shares on which 6 per cent was to be paid for ten years and 5 per cent thereafter; alternatively, the money could be obtained on mortgage or by granting annuities on the tolls. The preamble to the Act referred to expenditure and debts which the Company had neither been empowered to raise nor had the means of discharging, saying that this money had been insufficient to complete the canal so that the undertaking was still in an unfinished state and that parts had fallen into decay. A pertinent clause reflecting the apathy of the management was the provision that only three of the fifteen directors need constitute a quorum as 'it is often to be found difficult, and sometimes impossible "to assemble five of the Committee"'. The Cosham cut which was to provide a direct link with Portsmouth Harbour had not been made and several bridges over the Portsea Canal were still in a dangerous state. In view of the avidity with which the canal remorselessly swallowed up capital without providing any return, it was surprising that subscriptions were obtained for as much as £20,000.

The next matter was to secure toll concessions from the other five navigations between London and Portsmouth. A representative Committee was formed, the first meeting being held at Godalming on 13 October 1829 which was attended by Cutfield and Seward (Arun Navigation), Lord Selsey, Cartwright, Carter, and Palmer (Portsmouth & Arundel), Mangles and Newland (Wey & Arun and Godalming), and Hodgson (Wey). Further meetings were held at which it was agreed that mutual reductions would be made and that a delegation should approach the Thames Commissioners for a similar concession. The Commissioners were not sympathetic to the proposal, but in March 1830 the Company announced further reductions in tolls which enabled tallow, sugar, porter, and hemp to be carried to Portsmouth for only 3s. 3d. and other goods at 11s. 9½d. a ton instead of 13s. 6d.

Efforts were made in other directions to increase traffic. With a view to drawing public attention to the practicability of operating passage boats between London and Portsmouth, Hodgson arranged a one-day excursion cruise from Guildford in August 1829 with forty of the local gentry on board. As secretary of the London & Portsmouth Committee he also tried to induce the principal traders, like Birnie of Basingstoke, to extend their business, but with little success.

In June 1830 it was optimistically but rather falsely reported that trade was becoming very brisk—'The barges are going regularly and well loaded.' About 20 tons of marble from Asia and 84 tons from the Mediterranean were sent to King William IV at Windsor and, as well, 'above forty tons of gold and silver for the Bank of England have, with other goods, been sent by this conveyance from this port within a week'.* At the same time, great satisfaction was being expressed locally at the Company's decision to construct a quay for the loading and shipment of goods near Portsbridge which would enable the Portsea Canal, 'which had proved a great nuisance', to be closed. It was stated that the banks would be nearly sufficient to fill up the excavations and furnish materials for a road from the top of Surrey Street to Milton.[62]

By June 1831 the new cut at Portsbridge (Cosham) giving direct access to Portsmouth Harbour had been completed at a cost of over £1,000 and the basin at the Halfway Houses 'now rendered unnecessary, had been nearly filled up and the ground put up for sale'. The water supply had been improved by the purchase of a

* The Wey Navigation ledgers record the bullion, but not the marble.

mill and stream to supplement the existing supply and replace the steam engine at Ford. However, only four barges had reached London in the latter half of the previous year and the Management Committee lamented that they could not yet report a trade to Portsmouth. The coal trade to Chichester had also suffered due to the colliers' strike in the North and to Government proposals to reduce duties, but it was nevertheless claimed that the trade to Chichester alone was, after payment of all management and current repair charges, realizing a small surplus (tolls totalled £1,028 against expenditure of £987).[63]

The toll reductions proved in fact insufficient to encourage carriers to return to the canal and Palmer was left with no alternative but to persuade the other navigations to allow goods to pass toll-free. In this he was successful—with the exception of the Wey and the Thames Commissioners—and regular through traffic was restarted in October 1831. In spite of every effort the Thames Commissioners remained unco-operative, but the Wey agreed to charge only a nominal 7½d. per ton on all goods except bullion and since no carrier could be persuaded to venture upon the canal, Palmer decided there was no alternative but for the Company to hire their own boats. Three barges were obtained to form the nucleus of the reconstituted Portsmouth Lighter Company. With these Palmer managed to restart the London traffic, but although goods were transported virtually toll-free to London with a freight charge payable solely to the carrier, no more than eight cargoes reached the Thames during the ten weeks before Christmas; and whereas 189 tons were brought back to Portsmouth, the Hampshire merchants could be encouraged to ship only 22 tons to London. This latter amount was shared between six barges.

The toll concessions were continued the following year, but Palmer continued to be beset by misfortunes. His letters, written in a vivid, staccato style, revealed clearly enough the difficulties he had to face. In the spring of 1832 he wrote three letters in the space of four days which give a lucid picture of the state of the navigation. One to the Thames Commissioners, requesting six months' free navigation so as to create an extensive traffic on their river, referred to the fact that 'peculiar circumstances require peculiar aid'. Once again the Commissioners rejected his proposal.

A letter dated 4 April 1832, addressed to William Newland of the Wey & Arun, requested the waiving of the tolls for a further six months and continued:

Fig. 17.–J. A. Symington's drawing of a derelict lock on the Wey & Arun Junction Canal, c. 1900

PORTSMOUTH AND LONDON

FLY BARGES,

EVERY SATURDAY,

From BROOK'S WHARF, Upper Thames-Street.

Mr. Hawley Pr. Adml. Halkett

To Freight from London, by Fly Barge,

of 10th November 1831

1 Cask 1. 1. 14 0 2 6

26th December

2 Hampers 3. 3. 4 0 1 6

£ 0 4 0

JOSEPH PUSHMAN, Agent.

☞ **OFFICE—OYSTER-STREET, PORTSMOUTH.**

Fig. 18.—Invoice for Portsmouth & London Fly Barges, 1831

'My exertions shall not cease—I feel confident of success, tho' many circumstances have occurred to throw a damp on the trade, but winter and floods are now over.

'I am considered too sanguine—but I will be sanguine while I can see such a population to be supplied—dispatch and cheapness are wanting and if well regulated must command a trade—Impositions have been practiced by the masters of the Barges—

'The Barges hired were not adapted to the trade—tho' others more suitable could not be had—a new one is built by one of my friends and he will build another as soon as we find what improvements can be made—

'The Tunnel has been an impediment—but the new Barges will pass where others cannot—

'I wish for two Barges a week—if goods come a day after the time or if there happens to be a few more than can be taken on board they are obliged to wait a week—thus there is great delay—but when once they can go twice a week—they will find goods come faster. The hired Barges are so constructed that they could not carry according to the Register—Several floods have taken place and caused delay and a check to trade—

'The report of Cholera has operated against business—

'The Steamer's boiler is worn out—there must be a new one—It is true that the vessel's back is broken—We are obliged to hire until arrangements are made—

'I have got rid of Fowler*—he has been sadly negligent—The Office is moved to 18 Lombard Street, Portsmouth—Edgcombe is elected in his stead—I would give you more particulars—but really I am tired—tho' I seldom feel fatigue.'

A second and longer letter followed the next day in which Palmer admitted that the difficulties they had encountered could not have been guarded against in the infancy of a trade 'commenced by parties not practically acquainted with its details'. The vital need for back-carriage was stressed. So difficult was this to obtain that a man had even been sent over to France to try to arrange the import of eggs. In this the Company were successful and on 12 April the *Southampton* carried the first of many consignments to London. Palmer had also decided not to wait for the Committee's answer to his earlier letter since

'I conceive that I cannot be defeated by you—indeed my conviction has gone so far, that I have been tempted to an evasion, in my conversation to-day with the Chairman of the Thames Navigation Committee by saying that a free passage was granted by all the Navigations on the line—it is true that it has been granted tho' not a matter of fact, that it

* The clerk.

will be granted for another six months—however, I have ventured to imply as much, believing it to be your best policy to back my representations and knowing that unless the aid is given, the trade must cease.'

As a result of Palmer's efforts, the quantity of goods transported between the two ports rose to some 2,000 tons in 1832. Two-thirds of this traffic emerged from London, however, and consisted almost entirely of groceries for the Fleet. The struggle to find a back cargo persisted, as the following list of the very wide range of items carried up to London in 1832 reveals:

	Tons
Eggs	254
Rags	89
Flour	79
Soldiers' baggage	58
Old lead	35
Bullion	32
Empty casks	28
Burr stones	21
Fruit	17
Planks	13
Old canvas	12
Old cable	8
Beer or porter	6
Wine	5
Acorns	1
Sundries	12
	670

Every fourth barge had, however, left empty and the average load per barge of 8 tons up and 16 tons down was clearly uneconomic.[64] In spite of the fact that the Chichester section of the canal was making a profit receipts were insufficient to cover the cost of maintaining the canal, let alone meet the payment of interest on the preference shares. The canal's finances were tottering. The failure of trade led to further recriminations between members of the Committee and divided opinions amongst the shareholders. On 11 April 1833, shortly before the Annual Meeting, Palmer wrote to James Mangles, deputy chairman of the Wey & Arun, of the position:

'My intentions have been to induce every proprietor to know the real state of the concern in which his property is embarked and to urge some decided steps to be taken; I have also wished to show that the undertaking was feasible and to justify myself for being sanguine in my expectation.'

The optimistic manager was not entirely discouraged and continued:

> 'On looking calmly over what I have written upon the subject, I cannot but feel a satisfaction that it was taken up on good grounds and that however unfortunately things have turned out, there was and still is a fair prospect, tho' certainly not so good as I at first contemplated.'

Although the largest shareholder, he was by now tired of the wranglings and complaints of his Committee and intended resigning 'unless a more liberal course is taken' and 'rather than be any longer a galley slave to the Company'. Palmer claimed that the Wey & Arun Committee had been blind to their own interest, for

> 'the Wey & Arun depends for success on a trade from London to Portsmouth, without this it never can be anything but a poor concern, with it it may be made a rich one'.

In conclusion he added,

> 'I have had too much experience in canals to be daunted. I have exerted myself by day and by night. I have sacrificed my own business frequently to attend to the affairs of the Company and I can now retreat with honour. I only wish that every proprietor will take the trouble of making themselves masters of the actual state of things and either prosecute or abandon the concern altogether. I will neither drive a starved horse nor whip a skeleton.'

On the other hand, Admiral Halkett, in a letter to Mangles dated 29 April 1833, disagreed that Palmer had not met with the assistance which his exertions merited and that the Committee had still to learn how he could have received more pecuniary assistance.

> 'It is to be regretted that Mr. Palmer did not sooner acquaint you as a member of the committee that he was not supported. . . . I cordially wish that Mr. Palmer, yourself, and others in Town engaged in the concern would endeavour to recommend an efficient Committee. Many men of business unoccupied in Portsmouth would materially assist . . . it is most desirable to have you and Mr. Palmer present [at the General Meeting] and any other gentleman with knowledge in such affairs, or we will be at our last gasp.'[160]

They were certainly out of breath in their efforts to attract fresh traffic. The Wey ledgers mention various odd shipments. In 1833 oranges had been delivered to Guildford, bacon, butter, and pork to Newhaw, and a large quantity of old rope, hemp, and glue shreds to London. In 1835 the *Trout* carried 13 tons of live cattle up to Smithfield. The bullion traffic continued spasmodically until March 1838, but after 1826 it was rare for more than two consignments a year to pass.[161] Although the toll concessions continued to be granted to the London–Portsmouth barges, the tonnage carried between the two ports, which had risen to a little over 2,500 in 1833,

Fig. 19.—Seal of the Portsmouth & Arundel Navigation Company

had dwindled to a mere 750 by 1838 when the concession was withdrawn at the end of September and traffic between London and Portsmouth ceased.* Indeed the more widespread introduction of steam cargo vessels and improved land carriage had greatly reduced the need for an inland passage to obviate the route through the Straits 'against long easterly winds'. And as Finden wrote in 1838 in his *Views of Ports & Harbours*: 'As a commercial town Portsmouth does not rank very high.'†

In 1840 the tug *Egremont* was broken up[65] and in September the *Trout*, carrying only 6 tons of groceries, became the last barge to sail direct to Chichester from London. Although the ship canal remained busy, the section from Hunston to Ford remained open for only a dwindling and desultory local traffic. Pigot's *Directory of*

* It was stated in 1845 that the import of eggs from France to Portsmouth had fallen from 565 tons in 1837 to 130 tons in 1844 due to the opening of the London/Southampton railway.

† The number of mercantile vessels registered in 1831 was only 184 with a tonnage of 8,485 tons.

Fig. 20.—Chichester Canal, 1829

Sussex, 1839, in fact mentions that the canal passes through the village of Yapton and comments, 'but is of little advantage to the inhabitants, this being an agricultural district'. Yet one of the reasons advanced only twenty years before for building the canal had been to improve agriculture! Indeed, the Portsmouth & Arundel Canal had been a stupendous failure, costing more pounds to build than tons it was ever to carry throughout its length.

CHAPTER IX

The Grand Imperial Ship Canal Project (1825–1828)

Proposals for a ship canal from London to Portsmouth—its purpose—the idea of Mr Elmes or Mr Cundy?—formation of provisional management committee—five lines surveyed—publication of Cundy's reports and prospectus—letters to the press—the Rennies prick the bubble.

A HOST of schemes for railways or canals to link the ports of London and Portsmouth had been mooted since the turn of the century, but none was conceived on so ambitious or grandiose a scale as that which culminated in the project for the Grand Imperial Ship Canal. The proposed waterway, whose dimensions were planned on lines comparable to those of Suez,* was first brought into public prominence in February 1825, when *The Times* announced that a survey was already in progress for the purpose of making a navigable tide canal with 25 ft of water for first-class ships from Deptford to Arundel Bay (i.e. Littlehampton) at an estimated cost of £4 million.

Three reasons were advanced by the supporters of the scheme for its construction: first, to increase inland trade in Surrey and Sussex; secondly, to improve the supply of fish, provisions, and agricultural produce to the London markets, and thirdly to save time, life, and expense as a result of contrary winds, shipwreck, or capture by enemy privateers in the Thames estuary and English Channel. The reasons were sound. Whereas it could take up to twelve days or more to sail between London and Portsmouth, the voyage by canal might be accomplished in less than twenty-four hours. Shipwreck was ever occurrent for, as *Lloyds Register* showed, some 110 vessels were lost annually between the Isle of Wight and the Forelands, while the value of shipping captured along that part of the coast by the French during the Napoleonic Wars amounted to at least £3 million. In the event of hostilities the cost of moving naval and military stores to Portsmouth (land-carriage charges alone had exceeded £200,000 per annum in the previous war) would be much reduced.

* Opened in 1869.

The canal was to be designed to accommodate the largest ships afloat. It was estimated that East Indiamen and 74-gun ships would make the voyage between the two ports with the aid of steam-towage in as short a time as sixteen hours, while smaller vessels might perform the passage in ten or twelve. Critics of the scheme, however, thought it unlikely that in practice the distance could be covered in less than two days.

Two men claimed the idea as their own—James Elmes and Nicholas Wilcox Cundy. Certainly, in the autumn of 1824 Elmes laid a proposal before 'five or six gentlemen' for a 'tide-level' ship canal to be constructed throughout on one level. Elmes stated that the idea had originated with his father some years before and at this meeting produced a prospectus with a rough estimate and details of the cost and supposed advantages. The gentlemen in question thought it *prima facie* worthy of attention and directed their enquiries to ascertaining the revenue likely to be forthcoming from the work if carried into execution. Feeling that so magnificent an undertaking ought not to be pushed forward upon any insecure foundation it was, they claimed, their intention to refrain from calling upon the public for money until something satisfactory and incontrovertible had been established. Some weeks later, however, a placard appeared in various parts of the City announcing that Mr Nicholas Wilcox Cundy would in a few days submit to the public a prospectus for a Grand Ship Canal from London to Arundel Bay.

Now Cundy was an architect and civil engineer, besides being a loquacious gentleman who advertised himself as being a Member of the Royal Academies of Lyons, Bordeaux, Marseilles, Dijon, Rouen, and Paris, and he claimed in his turn that it was he who had first conceived the idea for such a canal, whilst travelling by coach up the Arun Valley one day in September 1824. It was perhaps more than a coincidence, however, that Cundy's placard should have been printed by the same Mr Moon of Threadneedle Street who had produced Elmes' prospectus and whom Elmes had, for some reason or other, quitted for another printer. The Rennies, George and John the Younger, relate that on learning of this, those who had entertained Elmes' proposition felt that they had no course left but to advertise at once and take possession of the ground. A prospectus was issued in March 1825, and as a result numerous applications for shares were received and duly registered: but, adhering to their original determination of not idly possessing themselves of other people's money, they altogether refused to receive the deposits which were in many instances pressed upon them. After several meetings, all strictly private (except one, it is stated, when Mr Cundy unexpectedly appeared and when nothing was done), a provisional committee was formed to investigate the project. Its members included Lord Palmerston, then Secretary for War, Vice-Admiral Sir George Cockburn, M.P., and Mr Horace Twiss, M.P., a future Under Secretary of State for Foreign Affairs.

Meanwhile Cundy, cold-shouldered but undeterred, had gone ahead with his own plans and in a series of reports set out his views regarding the feasibility of the undertaking. The line that he favoured was the more direct. He intended that the canal should have two main entrances from the Thames—one by the Victualling Office and King's Dockyard at Deptford, the other at Rotherhithe near Cherry Garden Stairs and opposite the London Docks. These cuts would unite near the Kent Road and the line proceed by Kennington church, South Lambeth, Battersea Marsh, Wandsworth, Merton, Malden church, The Gate on Epsom Common, Leatherhead bridge, Mickleham, Dorking bridge, Holmwood Common, Ockley church, Alfoldean bridge, Newbridge, and Pulborough to Arundel, where it would cross the Arun and follow close to the barge canal as far as Chichester and then by Langstone Harbour and Southsea Common to Spithead. From Cherry Garden Stairs the distance was 78 miles.

Tide-locks were to be constructed at each entrance 7 ft above the tide, and four huge locks—300 ft long and 64 ft wide—would have raised the canal 127 ft to the 21-mile summit-level. A similar number was planned for the descent to the sea. The canal's width was to be 150 ft and its depth 28 ft. The rising ground around Dorking would have entailed some 4 miles of cutting, averaging 130 ft in depth, and by Folley Farm (on the edge of Holmwood Common), the highest point on the line, 250 ft of sandstone, blue clay, and chalk were waiting to be cut away. A number of branches were also proposed: three to link with the Thames at Nine Elms, Vauxhall, and Kingston; others to link the canal with Ewell, Epsom, Reigate, Horsham, and Littlehampton. A large basin was to be built on Walworth Common and a harbour for 500 vessels was to be formed near Portsmouth by blocking Langstone Harbour to within 6 in. of high-water mark. Cundy's preliminary estimate of the cost was a modest and precise £3,979,420 with expectations of £518,025 in revenue.

Meanwhile, proposals for several alternative lines had been advanced by other projectors and public meetings held at which

Plate 1. The 3rd Earl of Egremont (1751–1837) with his daughter Mary, Lady Munster from a painting by Thomas Phillips

Plate 2. Barges moored below Thames Lock, 1929

Plate 3. Barges lying at the oil mill above Thames Lock, 1950. Horse towage continued until 1960

Plate 4. Laden barge approaching Guildford, 1842

Plate 5. Guildford railway viaduct and barge, 1849.
The wooden bridge carrying the line to Farnham was rebuilt in brick in 1912

Plate 6. Guildford Wharf, c.*1860*

Plate 7. Treadmill crane on Guildford Wharf, 1964

Plate 8. The Wey Navigation offices off Friary Street, 1964. They were demolished to make way for a supermarket in 1970

Plate 9. Unloading grain at Guildford Flour Mill, 1881

Plate 10. Sailing barges above Guildford Bridge, c.1790

Plate 11. Loading chalk at Guildford Quarry, c.1870

Plate 21. The Summit level in summer, 1952

Plate 22. The Summit level in winter, 1952

Plate 23. The Summit pound from Compasses Bridge, Alfold, 1934

Plate 24. The water conduit from Vackery Pond Reservoir flows into the canal near Fast Bridge, Alfold

Plate 25. Alfold Mill (demolished 1913) on the banks of the Wey & Arun Canal, c.*1905*

Plate 26. The lock-house in Sidney Wood was also the canal company's main workshop

Plate 27. Drungewick Aqueduct (1934). The ruins were demolished in 1957

Plate 28. Brewhurst Lock, Loxwood, 1952

Plate 29. Drungewick Lock, 1952

Plate 30. Love's Bridge, Wisborough Green, restored by the Wey & Arun Canal Trust, 1975

Plate 31. Rowner Lock and cottage, 1843

Plate 32. The canal bridge at Newbridge built in 1815 being strengthened before a culvert was introduced, 1953

Plate 33. Rowner Lock, c.1910

Plate 34. The warehouse at Newbridge Wharf, 1964

Plate 35. Orfold Aqueduct, 1964

Plate 36. Middle Lock at Lee Farm, 1952

the advantages of such a ship canal had been vigorously expounded. In March 1825 the Rennies issued a prospectus advocating a line 86 miles in length, 300 ft wide and 24 ft deep, from Deptford via Merton, Chessington, Epsom Common, Guildford, Alfold, Loxwood, and the Arun valley. Its main advantage was that the canal would only rise to 174 ft, thus involving no more than 6 miles of cutting over 50 ft deep along the summit-level. It was claimed that this could be executed with tolerable facility. The total cost was estimated at £7 million and the annual net revenue no higher than £350,000.

At a meeting held in the City at Freshfields the same month, at which Elmes and Cundy were present, the Committee agreed that no conclusion could be reached until a preliminary survey had been carried out, and it was therefore resolved that the Rennies should undertake this survey to assess the practicability of the whole venture, the relative merits of the suggested lines, and the probable cost. Accordingly, the Rennies invited Francis Giles to take the necessary levels and subsequently they themselves explored the lie of the land—according to Cundy—by carriage! To meet the cost of the survey, subscriptions of £1 each were invited from the public which gave each contributor the option to purchase 10 shares of £100 in the concern if a Company was formed. However, only £220 was received, of which £100 came from one of the Committee, Thomas Wilson, M.P. for the City of London.

There were, however, many who approved the project in principle even if they doubted its economic worth. Alexander Baring, M.P. for Taunton, to whom Cundy dedicated his Reports, had stated that it was 'a work that ought to be done (if practicable) at the expense, comparatively no matter what, if it can be accomplished, at either of the ravines at Guildford or Dorking; but if it was intended to go down the river Medway, it would be of no service: and although I have not connected myself with any of the new companies, I would be happy to give this great national work my personal attention and support'.[66]

Cundy quoted letters from Captain Robert King, 'an experienced nautical man', to confirm his opinion that his line was the only one which the public should adopt, and from Francis Giles, dated 11 March 1825, to say that the Dorking line was quite practicable (though he did not say it was necessarily the best).

The survey took many months to complete and it is not surprising perhaps that when at length the Rennies reported to the Committee that they had had five lines surveyed, it was in their opinion

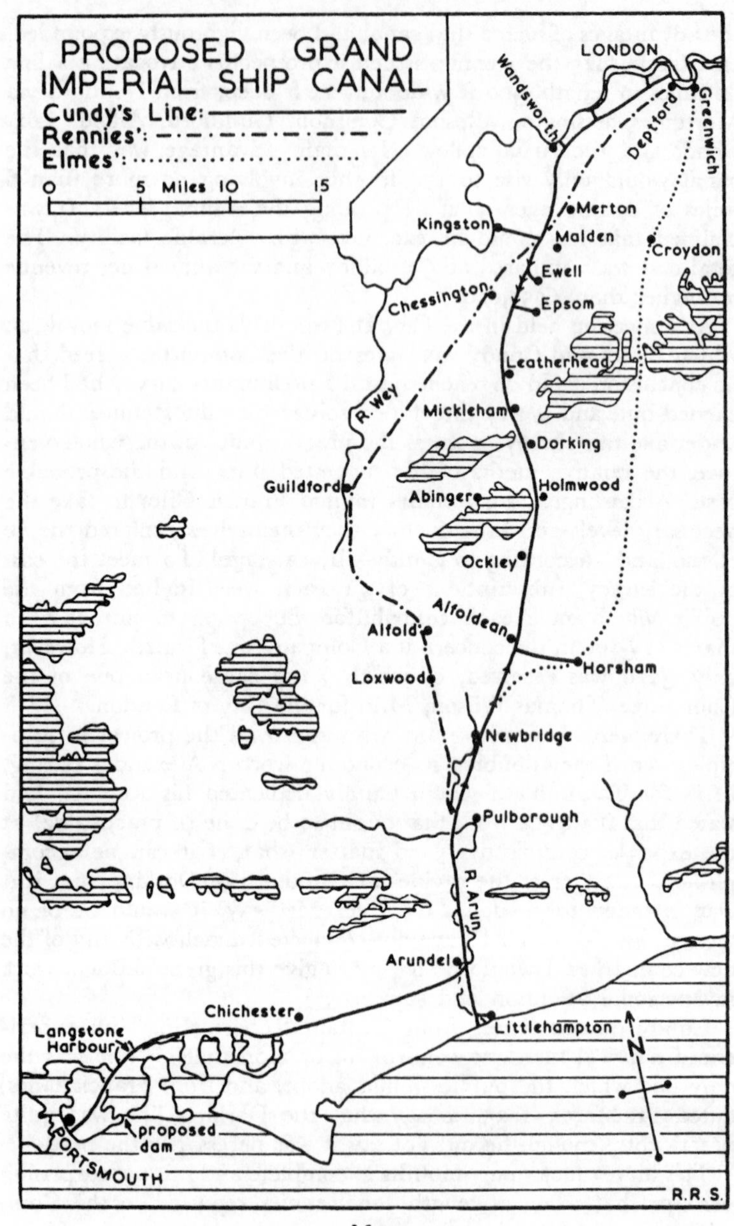
PROPOSED GRAND IMPERIAL SHIP CANAL
Cundy's Line:
Rennies':
Elmes':
0 5 Miles 10 15
LONDON
Wandsworth
Deptford
Greenwich
Merton
Kingston
Malden
Croydon
Ewell
Chessington
Epsom
Leatherhead
R. Wey
Mickleham
Dorking
Guildford
Abinger
Holmwood
Ockley
Alfoldean
Alfold
Horsham
Loxwood
Newbridge
Pulborough
R. Arun
Arundel
Chichester
Langstone Harbour
Littlehampton
N
proposed dam
PORTSMOUTH
R.R.S.

Map 9

the Guildford line which was 'decidedly the best having the least height, the easiest route and the best supply of water for the lockage'.[67]

The Rennies considered the Darent valley line from Dartford via Westerham, Limpsfield, Horsham, and the Arun valley impracticable on the grounds of its length (130 miles) and 500 ft high summit. The Medway valley line (length 160 miles and 550 ft summit) they also discarded for the same reasons. Elmes' Ravensbourne valley line from Greenwich via Croydon through the Merstham gap to Horsham was shorter and had in its favour a 50-mile summit-level, but the distance of 100 miles was still considerable and cuttings would have been required through hills rising to a height of 430 ft. The Rennies also dismissed as impractical Elmes' plan for a lockless canal on account of the great amount of excavation and expense, besides the risk that as its water supply was to be obtained from the rivers and streams it crossed, it would when executed be either dry in summer or flooded in winter.

It was true that the line chosen by Cundy was the shortest, but the Rennies regarded it with disfavour on the score of natural difficulty and enormous extra expense. Nor, when one considers the rudimentary instruments of excavation in use at that period and the lack of information regarding the various strata beneath the line's surface, was this surprising. However, the Rennies found George Morris' proposed deviation of Cundy's route from Dorking via Wotton and Abinger to Ockley more objectionable as, although the amount of cutting was decreased, it was three miles longer and, as a result of raising the summit to 200 ft above sea-level, the lockage was greatly increased. The Rennies admitted that they had had considerable difficulty in estimating the sum required for carrying out such a gigantic undertaking, though they thought that £6–£6½ million would suffice for the Guildford line and a 'much larger sum' if by Dorking.

Cundy completed his second report in September 1825, stating that 'on the Committee's instructions' he had carried out 'an admeasurement survey' of the intended line, that the deviations suggested by Giles were not advisable and that he regarded the route by Guildford as 'totally inadmissible', requiring a very long elevated summit and being unnecessarily circuitous. Nor, said Cundy, would it have saved any expense. 'Already', he announced, 'land has advanced in price, and property advertised for sale has been postponed in consequence, until the proprietors can ascertain the probability of the work being commenced.'

In his third report, dated July 1827, Cundy emphasized the advantages of the Dorking line over that advocated by Rennie and Giles via Guildford on the grounds that the saving of 6½ miles would result in less actual excavation, less land to be bought, and both quicker and cheaper carriage per ton-mile.

The ebullient Cundy, using every verbal artifice of persuasion, tried to get all and sundry interested in his scheme. When all three reports were published together in book form, however, *The Times* commented that 'Mr. Cundy's book was so complete an answer to itself that, to any mind capable of the least small reflection, no other need be given; but we know not with what best to recommend our readers to expend 10s. upon it, unless indeed they contemplated subscribing for shares, and then the purchase would be a cheap one.' Indeed, Cundy's arguments were cloyed with sentiment: there was an appeal to philanthropists, for 'nothing can be more gratifying than the prospect it presents of the preservation of human life from shipwreck'. And when East Indiamen, returning from a twelve-month voyage, laden with treasure, reached the Isle of Wight, it was to be supposed that the canal would 'relieve the merchant and the mariner's wife from thousands of fears and restless nights, when they hear the raging gales, or think of the dangers of war'. This was rubbish, and as *The Scotsman* was quick to point out, 'If mariners with valuable cargoes would not pay ½d. a ton for the use of the Caledonian Canal (which enables them to escape the storms of the Hebrides and Pentland Firth), what would prompt them to pay four or six times as much to avoid a smaller danger?'

Readers of Cundy's reports were, it is presumed, to have their confidence in his ability as an engineer increased by his invention of a counter-balance crane suspension bridge. Whether this was his own invention or not, whether in fact it even existed, is speculation, but he claimed that it could be suspended 64 ft over the canal and that such a bridge could be opened and shut by one man within two minutes.

One of his many optimistic assertions was that a coal-mine would be found under Holmwood Common, although a few sentences earlier he had been hoping to save the expense of a reservoir at Abinger by tapping the 'well-known inexhaustible springs' which abound there. Not perhaps the best place to work a coal-mine. However, if there should be no coal, Cundy assured his readers that there were 'immense beds of the finest iron, building and limestone (equal to the Portland)'. Besides his anticipated discovery of valuable minerals along the line, he drew attention to the plentiful supplies of timber, firewood, and charcoal that could be brought to the London markets.

PROSPECTUS

FOR MAKING THE

Grand Imperial Ship Canal

FROM

LONDON TO PORTSMOUTH.

IN 40,000 SHARES OF £100 EACH.

TO BE SUBSCRIBED IN FOUR YEARS, BY FIVE EQUAL INSTALMENTS OF FIVE PER CENT. IN EACH YEAR, AND BEARING AN INTEREST OF FIVE PER CENT.

TEN THOUSAND OF THE ABOVE SHARES TO BE RESERVED FOR HIS MAJESTY'S GOVERNMENT, THE BANK OF ENGLAND, THE HONOURABLE EAST INDIA COMPANY, AND OTHER INCORPORATED BODIES.

TO BE EMPOWERED BY ACT OF PARLIAMENT.

UNDER THE SANCTION OF

HIS ROYAL HIGHNESS THE DUKE OF CLARENCE,

LORD HIGH ADMIRAL OF ENGLAND.

Fig. 21.—Cundy's Prospectus for the Grand Imperial Ship Canal, 1827

Cundy did not neglect the likely romantic appeal of the waterway for 'it will form a beautiful lake, which will enrich the scenery' of the country, and be the attraction of thousands of parties of pleasure'. After further reflection, he decided that the lake would be 'unrivalled in England' and that numerous mansions and villas would be built upon its banks, leaving to the reader's imagination the possibility of Bacchanalian frolics.

Public interest reached its height in the autumn of 1827 when 1,500 copies of Cundy's reports were put on sale at half a guinea. This slim volume also included three plans, a memorial to the Lords Commissioners of the Treasury, and a draft of the intended Act of Parliament. At the same time, Cundy issued an elaborately designed prospectus, 'For making the Grand Imperial Ship Canal from London to Portsmouth', which purported to be sanctioned by H.R.H. The Duke of Clarence and named seven dukes, two marquesses, and five earls (including the Earl of Egremont) amongst the twenty 'Presidents for the time being'. The prospectus invited the public to subscribe three-quarters of the equity capital of £4 million, which was to be split into 40,000 shares of £100. The remaining quarter was optimistically reserved for the Government, the Bank of England, the East India Company, and other incorporated bodies. £1 per cent was to be paid on each share at the time of subscribing and an additional £4 per cent within one month of the Act being passed. Meanwhile, Cundy, who had named himself as sole 'Engineer', could draw whatever sums were necessary for making surveys and prosecuting Parliamentary proceedings, and similar expenses.

The prospectus stated that the canal could be completed within four years at an outlay of less than £4 million* and that the revenue would amount to some £700,000 a year. A bill was to be introduced into Parliament early in the ensuing session which, besides authorizing the making of the canal, would also include sections to:

(i) Grant remunerations to the Grand Surrey, Croydon, Wey & Arun and Portsmouth & Arundel Canal Companies.

(ii) Grant remunerations to the Commissioners of Arundel Port, Chichester, and Emsworth, and to the boatmen of Margate, Ramsgate, Deal, Dover, Folkestone, and Hythe.

(iii) Grant premiums for establishing fisheries in the English Channel for those pilots and boatmen who might sustain any loss and not be employed on the canal, etc., etc.

* A report in the *Morning Herald*, 3 November 1827, estimated the cost of Cundy's project at £4,976,120.

The conclusion, bursting with nationalistic fervour, read: 'This canal will pour into Great Britain a flood of prosperity hitherto unknown. It will call the attention of the arts, scientific and enterprising world to our shores, while the undertaking will remain an indestructible monument to the wisdom of Government and the promoters of this truly national and magnificent design.'

But although the prospectus said 'This national undertaking now remains no longer in doubt', the only doubt in the public's mind appeared to be whether anyone seriously believed the truth of these assertions. The public had grown shy of superlatives and wary of charlatans. Letters soon came pouring into the offices of the national and provincial press warning prospective subscribers of the dubious authenticity of these statements concerning patronage and cautioning them to wait until it was abundantly clear that the prospectus contained no misrepresentation calculated to induce a false estimate of the canal's success.[68] The writer of a letter signed 'NO ENEMY TO IMPROVEMENTS, BUT A FRIEND TO THE PUBLIC' referred to the extensive and profuse circulation of the prospectus but doubted that the Company had been formed and would not have been surprised if 'within six months the engineer, secretaries and other concocters of this Grand Canal will find themselves out of employment and the office in Parliament Street to let'.[69] It was pointed out that Mr Cundy, the architect of Pimlico and the surveyor to Earl Grosvenor, was in no way connected with 'Mr. Nicholas Cundy, the engineer',[70] and that the Duke of Wellington had never authorized the insertion of his name as a 'President, for the time being' of the Society for Constructing the Grand Imperial Ship Canal.[71]

An article in *The Scotsman*[72] referred to it as 'a magnificent but, in our opinion a very idle scheme', considered that its cost would exceed £10 million, its profits would not cover half its interest, and that even if the canal was cut, queried whether it would be used by shipowners when they could reach London by the Thames and whether an Indiaman of the first class would pay £1,200 for the privilege of shortening a twelve months' passage by two or three days.

The answer came on 22 November 1827, when *The Times* published the full story of 'The Portsmouth Canal' from its inception, which exposed at the same time the fiction of Cundy's prospectus. Below appeared a letter from the Rennie brothers, dated 15 October, giving the results of their surveys.

The Times' report concluded:

'As to the original supporters of the measure, they, perceiving that it was impossible to raise the immense sum of money required, even on the cheapest plan, without extensive aid from the Government, which it was not disposed to afford, abandoned the project, took not a farthing for expenses incurred upon themselves and left £220 to the inadequate remuneration of the Survey. They disclaimed any participation in the extraordinary statements which Mr. Cundy has from time to time put forth, and in the advertisements for deposits.

'At the same time they wish it to be understood that they are sensibly alive to the immense importance of the project; that they believe in its practicability; that the result of their calculations justified an expectation of about 5 per cent in time of peace, with a material increase in time of war, upon a capital of £6½ million, being the smallest amount for which Messrs. Rennie estimated the work could be executed, and that at a time more favourable to its execution they are willing to aid it with the produce of their labour.'

The financial world gasped and the plan was forthwith abandoned. Cundy's bubble had burst. Nevertheless, his petition for leave to bring in a bill was presented to the House of Commons on 15 February 1828, and referred to Committee, but it was not reported. Cundy himself, furious at the miscarriage of his plans, vigorously attacked the Rennies' report in a pamphlet, dated 1828, entitled *Mr. Cundy's Reply to Anonymous and Other Authors of Malignant Abuse and Misrepresentation on his projected line, furnishing Truth for Libel, etc.* The price was 2s. 6d. After a violent personal diatribe, Cundy declared that the Rennies' line would necessitate the demolition of Guildford Castle, the church, the county gaol, and some 500 houses. In addition, he included three letters to the editors of the *Morning Herald* and the *Public Ledger* which had not been printed and which replied to the letters in *The Times* and *Herald* papers. But the windmill, at whose sails Cundy levelled his quixotic tilts, had already broken down and he was left to devote his fertile imagination to devising railway lines. Six years later he was planning a Grand Southern Railroad to Portsmouth via Horsham, and in 1835 his was one of the five schemes considered by Parliament for the London to Brighton line. Rennie had, of course, already projected one to Brighton via Reigate which Cundy criticized on the grounds that it was more than probable that his tunnels would convert the railway into a river and the inclines would prevent trains exceeding the speed of coaches. Strangely enough, it was Stephenson this time whom Cundy accused of stealing his plans!

IMPERIAL SHIP CANAL

FROM

LONDON TO PORTSMOUTH.

MR. CUNDY'S

REPLY

TO

ANONYMOUS AND OTHER AUTHORS

OF MALIGNANT

ABUSE AND MISREPRESENTATION,

ON HIS

PROJECTED LINE,

FURNISHING TRUTH FOR LIBEL;

WITH PLAN OF SURVEYS, &c.

LONDON:

SOLD BY MESSRS. RIVINGTON, ST. PAUL'S CHURCH YARD; PARBURY, ALLEN, & CO. LEADENHALL STREET; RIDGWAY, PICCADILLY; EGERTON, CHARING CROSS; HEBERT, CHEAPSIDE; WILSON, ROYAL EXCHANGE; RICHARDSON, CORNHILL; AND SMITH, ELDER, & CO. CORNHILL.

1828.

Price Two Shillings and Sixpence.

Fig. 22.—Title page of Cundy's Reply to his critics, 1828

Number of Shares.	Names of Canals.	Amount of Share. £	s.	Average Cost per Share. £	s.	d.	Price per Share. £	s.		Div. per Annum. £	s.	d.	Dividend Payable.
1,482	Ashby-de-la-Zouch	100	0	113	0	0	80	0	0	4	0	0	Ap. Oct.
1,766	Ashton and Oldham	-	-	113	0	0	100	0	0	5	0	0	Ap. Oct.
720	Barnsley	160	0	-		-	220	0	0	10	0	0	Feb. Aug.
1,260	Basingstoke	100	0	-		-	5	0	0				
—	Ditto Bonds	100	0	-		-	-		-	-		-	April.
400	Chelmer and Blackwater	100	0	-		-	106	0	0	5	0	0	January.
1,500	Chesterfield	100	0	-		-	170	0	0	8	0	0	
500	Coventry	100	0	-		-	795	0	0	44	0	0	May, Nov.
1,851	Crinan	50	0	-		-	2	0	0				
460	Cromford	100	0	-		-	420	0	0	19	0	0	Jan. July.
4,546	Croydon	100	0	31	2	10	1	17	6				
11,810*l.*	Ditto Bonds	100	0	-		-	50	0	0	5	0	0	
600*l.*	Derby	100	0	110	0	0	130	0	0	6	0	0	Jan. July.
2,060	Dudley	100	0	-		-	52	0	0	2	15	0	Mar. Sept.
3,575	Ellesmere and Chester	133	0	133	0	0	72	0	0	3	15	0	September.
11,600	Grand Junction	100	0	-		-	243¼	241¼		13	0	0	Jan. July.
1,521	Grand Surrey	100	0	-		-	40	0	0	-		-	Apr. Oct.
120,000*l*	Ditto Loan	-	-	-		-	97	0	0	5	0	0	Jan. July.
2,849¼	Grand Union	100	0	-		-	21	0	0	1	0	0	1st Oct.
3,096	Grand Western	100	0	89	0	0 pd.	8	0	0				
749	Grantham	150	0	150	0	0	195	0	0	10	0	0	May.
	Hereford and Gloucester	100	0										
6,238	Huddersfield	100	0	57	6	6	15	10	0	0	10	0	September.
148	Ivel and Ouse Beds	100	0	100	0	0 pd.	115	10	0	5	0	0	Jan. July.
25,328	Kennet and Avon	100	0	39	18	10	25	10	0	1	5	0	September.
70	Loughborough	-	-	142	17	0	2100	0	0	180	0	0	Jan. July.
3,000	Macclesfield	100	0	100	0	0 pd.	60	0	0				
250	Melton Mowbray	100	0	-		-	200	0	0	9	0	0	July.
130	Nutbrook	109	0	-		-	-		-	6	2	0	
522	Oakham	130	0	-		-	32	0	0	2	0	0	May.
1,786	Oxford	100	0	-		-	500	0	0	32	0	0	Mar. Sept.
2,400	Peak Forest	100	0	48	0	0	65	0	0	3	0	0	June, Dec.
2,520	Portsmouth and Arundel	50	0	50	0	0	10	0	0				
21,418	Regent's	100	0	33	16	8	18	0	0	0	13	6	July.
5,669	Rochdale	100	0	85	0	0	70	0	0	4	0	0	May.
200	Stroudwater	150	0	-		-	480	0	0	23	0	0	May, Nov.
533	Swansea	100	0	-		-	200	0	0	15	0	0	November.
350	Tavistock	100	0	-		-	105	0	0				
4,805	Thames and Medway	100	0	30	4	3	4	0	0				
3,341	Ditto New	3	10	2	15	0 pd.							
—	Ditto 1st Loan	-	-	56	0	0	-		-	2	10	0	
—	Ditto 2d Loan	-	-	40	0	0	-		-	2	0	0	
—	Ditto 3d Loan	-	-	100	0	0	-		-	5	0	0	
—	Ditto 4th Loan	-	-	100	0	0	-		-	5	0	0	June.
1,150	Thames and Severn, New	-	-	-		-	30	0	0	1	10	0	June.
1,300	Ditto Original	-	-	-		-	25	0	0	1	10	0	Jan. July.
905	Wey and Arun	110	0	110	0	0	32	0	0	-		-	May.
20,000	Wilts and Berks	-	-	-		-	5	0	0	0	4	0	June.
126	Wisbeach	105	0	105	0	0	40	0	0	-		-	February.
6,000	Worcester and Birmingham	-	-	-		-	87	10	0	3	0	0	February.
800	Wyrley and Essington	125	0	-		-	115	0	0	6	0	0	February.

Fig. 23.—Table of Canal Share Prices, 1832 (see page 113)

Sir John Rennie, writing his autobiography fifty years later, made it clear that it was the size of the estimate that had caused the project to be dropped; at that time it was considered so large that 'all idea of prosecuting the undertaking further was at once abandoned. The world had not then been accustomed to the enormous sums since spent upon railways, and then they would never have believed that £16 million would be spent on the London, Chatham & Dover Railway, only the same length as the proposed canal.'[73]

Rennie added that the canal was perfectly feasible and would have been of great public advantage, but doubted whether it would have yielded a reasonable profit for the capital expended. In this connection it is not irrelevant to remark that the cost of building the Manchester Ship Canal was over £14 million whereas £8 million had been the original sum envisaged. In the historical light of canal engineers' estimates and the lack of data on which they were determined, it would have been surprising if the Grand Imperial could have been completed for less than £15 million, via the Dorking line.

And so the great scheme died.* It was never revived, though vague references appeared in the press from time to time; still, it is interesting to conjecture how such an enterprise, if it had been undertaken with Government help, would have fared and how undoubtedly it would have changed the face of the Surrey and Sussex countryside. It is possible, however, that its greatest value would not have been determined until 1940 when the Nazis occupied the French Channel ports. It is also possible that by that time road traffic requirements would have transformed the canal into an equally valuable motorway.

* A smaller, but similar project for linking the English and Bristol Channels also failed for lack of public support. A ship canal, 45 miles long, 90 ft wide, and 15 ft deep, with 58 locks, was planned for vessels of 200 tons to shorten the passage by over 250 miles and avoid the dangerous navigation round Land's End and the Lizard. An Act, obtained in July 1825, authorized £1,750,000 capital, but, although over £1,500,000 was subscribed, the canal was never begun. The estimate had risen to £3,135,000 when the scheme was unsuccessfully revived in 1888.

CHAPTER X

The Hey-day of Water Transport (1830–1840)

The flourishing 'thirties'—dividends and share prices—the Wey & Arun Committee—the clerk and the superintendent—lock-keepers and a tragic accident—local industries—carriers and cargoes—types of craft—passenger traffic—death of Lord Egremont, 1837—his funeral—receipts and tonnage increase—competition from land carriage—end of the canal era.

THE 1830s saw the hey-day of Sussex waterways; times when the future of even the Wey & Arun seemed reasonably assured; times when the wharves were stacked high with coal and timber and all was a bustle on the quayside as the barges were divested of their cargoes and the carts were loaded with wine and potted meats and groceries for the village stores; times when Turner, staying at Petworth House, would set off by coach and spend the day painting the Arun valley or the Chichester Canal. What Cobbett had seen at Newbridge could be seen at any of the main wharves between Weybridge and the coast; wisps of smoke rising from the kilns, horses stamping in their traces; the emptying of barrows and the rumbling of barrels; the swish of water and the thud of rope; the sound of Sussex oaths and childish laughter.

True, the rural navigations of the South never reached the same degree of prosperity as their counterparts in the Midlands and the North, but nevertheless many were profitable and even the little Arun Navigation began to pay increasingly large dividends, 7 per cent in 1831, 11 per cent in 1834, and 12 per cent in 1837. 1830 marks the time when Arundel reached the height of her prosperity as a port, in whose name 45 ships were registered. However, one of her parliamentary members was lost under the Reform bill and almost imperceptibly her importance began to wane as that of Littlehampton waxed. At the turn of the nineteenth century the population of Arundel was thrice that of Littlehampton, whose size trebled in the course of the next thirty years. But it was another forty before the census return of 1871 put Littlehampton ahead.

The Wey & Arun had recovered from the setback caused by the failure of the Portsmouth & Arundel and had resumed payment of a 1 per cent dividend in 1828. This rate was never exceeded

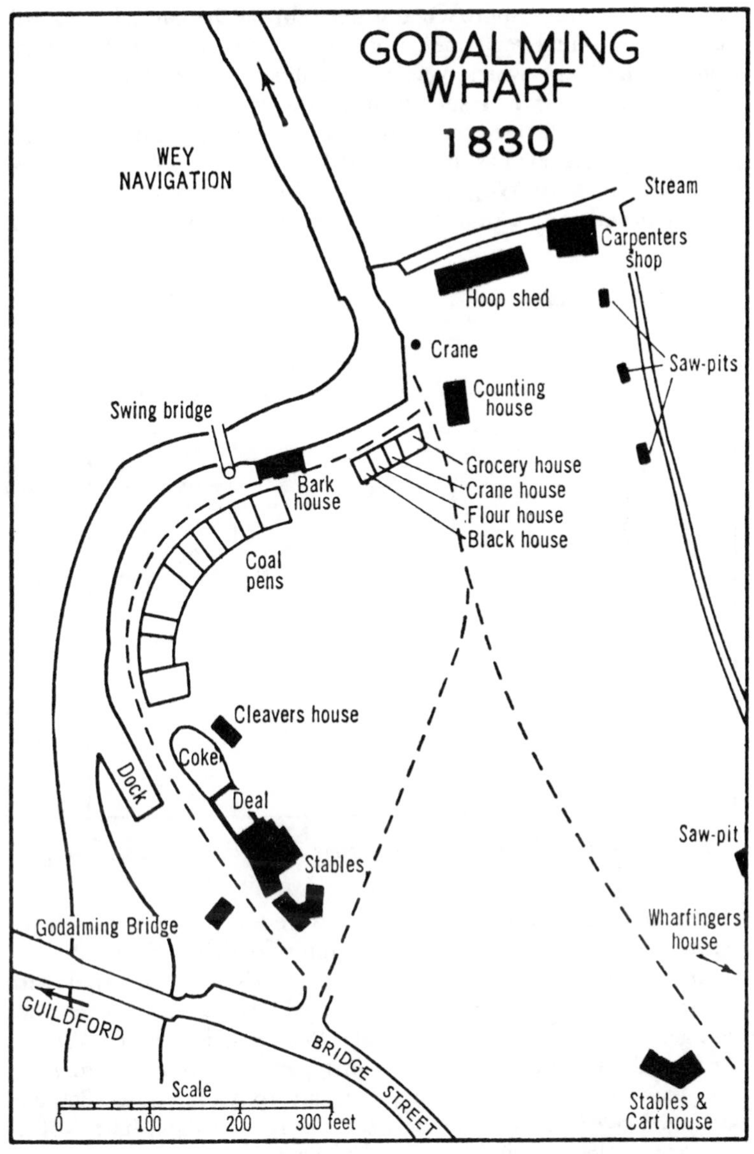
GODALMING
WHARF
1830
WEY
NAVIGATION
Stream
Carpenters
shop
Hoop shed
Crane
Saw-pits
Counting
house
Swing bridge
Grocery house
Crane house
Flour house
Black house
Bark
house
Coal
pens
Cleavers house
Coke
Dock
Deal
Saw-pit
Stables
Wharfingers
house
Godalming Bridge
GUILDFORD
BRIDGE STREET
Scale
0
100
200
300 feet
Stables &
Cart house

Map 10

(although earnings approached 3 per cent on the capital invested) due to the annual repayments of the debt incurred by the mortgage of the tolls, which was not finally discharged until 1842. Much of a waterway's success from the financial point of view depended on high receipts in relation to capital employed. The river navigations such as the Arun, Rother, and the Wey were more successful than the Wey & Arun and the Portsmouth & Arundel (which never paid a dividend) because they had been built at a

WEY AND ARUN JUNCTION CANAL.

Abstract of Account for the Year ending 1st May, 1834.

Date	Receipts	£	s	d
1833. May 1.	To Balance in the hands of the Treasurer ...	1055	10	4
1834. April 30.	Received for Tolls on the Canal during the Year ...	2157	18	4
	Rent for Wharfs, &c. ...	24	1	1
		3237	9	9

Date	Payments	£	s	d
1834. April 30.	By Payments, viz.			
	Clerk, Superintendant, Collectors, Lock-keepers, &c. Salaries ...	323	4	3
	Repairs and Incidental Charges ...	366	11	9
	Rent, Taxes, Tithes, &c. ...	339	18	4
	William Burch for a new Windmill Pump	173	9	7
	George Rennie, Esq. for Survey and Report relative to increase of the Supply of Water ...	60	18	0
	Printing and Stationary ...	2	13	10
	Interest on Mortgage of Tolls...	70	0	0
	Dividends paid on			
	8 Shares for 1828 ... 8 0 0			
	8 —— 1829 ... 8 0 0			
	8 —— 1830 ... 8 0 0			
	18 —— 1831 ... 18 0 0			
	48 —— 1832 ... 48 0 0			
	837 —— 1833 ... 837 0 0			
		927	0	0
		2263	15	9
	Balance in Treasurer's Hands ...	973	14	0
		3237	9	9

Fig. 24.—Wey & Arun Canal Company Abstract of Accounts, 1834

time when labour and material costs were less. Thus although the Arun Navigation's receipts were similar to those of the Wey & Arun (during the decade tolls averaged £1,700 compared with £2,180) its higher dividends reflected its lower maintenance charges and much smaller capital. Whereas in fact the Wey & Arun maintained a dividend rate of 1 per cent from 1828 to 1841, the Arun never paid less than 4 per cent from 1831 until 1866 and averaged over 11 per cent between 1831 and 1840. The Rother was rather less profitable. During the thirty years 1802–31 the average gross earnings amounted to about £550 per annum[74] on a capital expenditure of around £18,000 (*sic*).

The Wey prospered most of all the southern waterways, and this was due in some measure to the steps Hodgson had taken to revitalize the navigation. Action to prevent impositions by the bargees had proved successful and he could regard himself as an 'unflinching reformer against Russell and the other barge masters who formerly usurped supremacy of the navigation'. Whilst the Wey agent had little time for the numerous scoundrels connected with the barging business, he showed more than an average consideration for his own staff. At Christmas he provided them with supper and ale from his own stock, and suggested that the proprietors might like to give silk handkerchiefs to the wharfingers and lock-keepers as a token of their appreciation.[75]

However, the greatest source of trouble to the navigation was not the barge-owners but the owners and occupiers of the mills. The bone of contention was the millers' habit of drawing off so much water that barges could not pass the locks and then demanding excessive charges for providing additional water. Hodgson regarded them as 'a grasping set who, I fear, have not yet lost the title of the character old Chaucer ascribed to them'. The litigation which arose lasted three years before a compromise agreement was reached in 1832. For reasons which appeared to stem from disagreement with the Portmore family, and also perhaps because of the proprietors' apparent lack of interest in their undertaking, Hodgson resigned and sailed away to Jamaica in the autumn of 1831.[76] In fact, by this time the Wey's tonnage had begun to show an appreciable annual increase. Between 1832 and 1838 tolls rose from £5,842 to £7,763 and the amount of tonnage carried increased by over 40 per cent from 60,000 to 86,000 which was due partly to the Basingstoke Canal carrying materials for the building of the London & Southampton Railway.

Shares in the Wey & Arun, which had cost their original purchasers £110, had fallen to half their nominal value by 1820 and to a third ten years later although prices were stabilized around £25 between 1832 and 1841. However, the £100 shares were a limited market and dealings seldom occurred more than four or five times a year. Shares in the Arun Navigation were very rarely transferred. Only one hundred (or one-ninth of the number of Wey & Arun shares) existed, and of these eighty were held in 1833 by two families, the remainder being split amongst twelve proprietors. It is not therefore very surprising that during the decade of 1830 only seven Arun shares changed hands. The average price realized was £178, the maximum sum paid for any one share being £200.

Now let us turn to the management of these waterways. The Wey & Arun, like the Arun, was controlled by a body of men who received no salary and only a modicum of expenses. On the other hand, they seldom met more than three times a year, and being landowners rather than business men, their experience in company administration was negligible. As chairman, Lord Egremont took a considerable interest in the affairs of the canal, but the more mundane questions of toll rates and the settling of disputes were dealt with by the Management Committee, which was generally presided over by James Mangles, the deputy chairman. The day-to-day running of the canal really depended on the work of two men—the clerk and the superintendent. John Smallpeice was clerk to the Company from their incorporation until 1848. His part-time responsibilities were similar to those of the secretary of any public company, keeping the minutes of meetings, attending on the chairman and members of the Committee, issuing share certificates, maintaining the register of shareholders and the Company's books and ledgers—duties for which he received an annual salary of £100 and which he carried out at the same time as his other activities in connection with the borough of Guildford (he was a Conservative councillor and from 1812 treasurer of the County gaol at Sessions House, Newington) and his partnership in a family firm of solicitors.

The responsibility for keeping the canal in good working order devolved upon the superintendent. May Upton acted in this position until the appointment of James Stanton in January 1819. The post entailed keeping account of the tolls and expenses, directing the work of the lock-keepers and labourers, and reporting to the Committee on the state of the canal. It was indeed a never-ending, all-the-year-round task to maintain the canal efficiently, to see that the roads leading to the wharves did not become morasses, to keep the bridges, aqueducts, and culverts in good repair. The superintendent's salary never rose higher than a sovereign a week, but it was supplemented by a rent-free cottage and small garden. Stanton lived on Bramley wharf, and since the terms of his engagement did not preclude him from trading on his own account, by frugal living, tireless endeavour, and determined saving, he was able to purchase, within five years of his appointment, a barge of his own with which to develop a coal and timber business. Before the opening of the canal, the residents of Bramley had had their coal carted from Stonebridge wharf, but carriage by water direct from London or Littlehampton brought cheaper coal to the village.

Eliza began work for Stanton in 1822, and although she was on the small side, she loaded a wide variety of cargo, which included biscuits, corn, livestock, timber, tar, casks of wine, and, on one occasion, 1½ tons of books. Trade increased and he bought *Sarah.* By 1840 Stanton's barges were carrying over 1,000 tons up the Wey alone. His business flourished and on his retirement in 1857 *Lark*, *Active*, *Sceptre*, and *Providence* had been added to the Stanton fleet.

The wharfingers controlled the loading, unloading, and storage of goods at the principal distributing points along the navigations, maintained ledgers showing all goods loaded and unloaded, and rents for the use of lime-kilns, or for coal, grain, timber, etc., stored on the quaysides. The main wharves south of Guildford were situated at Stonebridge and Godalming on the Wey, at Bramley, Run Common, Elm bridge (for Cranleigh), Compasses bridge (for Horsham), Tickners Heath (for Dunsfold), and Loxwood on the Wey & Arun, at Newbridge and Pallingham on the Arun Canal, at Coultershaw (for Petworth) and Midhurst on the Rother, and at Stopham, Coldwaltham, Pulborough, Greatham, Bury, Houghton, and Arundel on the Arun.

On the main line between Weybridge and Coldwaltham fifteen lock-keepers had their little houses. The keeper's way of life was hard. He and his family lived in a small cottage, low-lying, often encompassed by mists and ever liable to be encircled by floods. Out in all weathers, his style of living was as simple as the design of his dwelling; his privations were many, his responsibilities great. Besides having to act as toll-collector, to check the loading of the barges, to oil the rack gear and carry out repairs, a constant watch had to be maintained on the water levels, which over a long stretch called for considerable local knowledge of sluices, streams, culverts, and weirs. During prolonged periods of rain or severe cold this involved much extra work as he had to be alert throughout the day and night, regulating paddles and looking for danger signs, especially where the canal level was higher than the adjoining fields and farmsteads. An embankment breached during a storm could cause a flood that would ruin crops and endanger life. Hardly a year passed when heavy rain did not so weaken an embankment that immediate action had to be taken to prevent a burst. In January 1795, disaster struck the Godalming Navigation, simply because a pair of small animals had tunnelled through an embankment. Very heavy snow had fallen and a severe frost followed which had blocked up all the canals in the kingdom. A mole and a rat had formed a tunnel through a high embankment; an unexpected thaw brought the water so rapidly from the hills that the sluices could not vent it, although every precaution had been taken to free them from ice; the water soon forced its way through the tunnel, and no exertions could stop the current. More than a hundred yards of the lofty bank were precipitated to the bed of the river, vast sheets of water and ice, extending from lock to lock, rushed through the gulf, flooding the adjoining fields, and a barge that had been frozen in met with the same fate.[77]

And there were other hazards. One slip and a barge might crush a leg against the lock wall; the snapping of a paddle shaft could easily result in broken fingers and all too often there were the poignant mishaps of children falling into the canal and drowning.[162] Sometimes acts of heroism saved a life and sometimes it was the lock-keeper himself who was the victim of tragedy. One winter's day the old keeper at Coldwaltham fell into the lock while walking across the gangplank and was drowned before the eyes of his helpless wife. However, there is no evidence to connect the unfortunate fellow with the individual referred to in an undated letter addressed to the wharfinger at Newbridge who, tired of the sight of water, sought relief in beer: 'Sir I rote to informed you the Conduct of the Lock Keeper at W—— [i.e. Coldwaltham] he is quite a disgrace, allyways in Toxacaped I think it quite time you knowed about it in the way he going on he is always at the Bear house A great pity better be at home with his family yours Tuly William Smith.'[78]

About 1840 the Wey & Arun and the Arun Canals were manned as follows:—

Section from	*To*	*Supervised by Lock-keeper at*	*No. of Locks*	*Length of Section (miles)*
Stonebridge	Birtley bridge	Bramley wharf*	5	2½
Birtley bridge	Compasses bridge	Lock XVII	2	5½
Compasses br.	Loxwood wharf	Sidney Wood	11	5
Loxwood wharf	Newbridge	Rowner lock*	5	5½
Newbridge	Middle lock	Orfold aqueduct	2	3
Middle lock	Stopham bridge	Pallingham*	1	4
Stopham bridge	Hardham tunnel	Hardham lock	2	¾
Hardham tunnel	Coldwaltham	Coldwaltham*	1	1¼

* toll house

The lock-house in Sidney Wood was also the Canal Company's main workshop. John Cole and his family lived there for over thirty years carrying out all manner of repairs, constructing lock-gates and building boats. The graving docks for refitting barges and annual overhauls were further afield at Stoke, Pallingham, and Arundel.* Although the lock-keepers did much of the day-to-day work, extra labour was always needed. A couple of carpenters and seven or eight labourers were employed to do the routine jobs of repairing fences and gates, trimming hedges, clearing ditches, and cutting reeds. At Stonebridge, for example, the entrance to the canal was continually silting up as a result of the flow of the Bramley stream and after an abundance of rain two men often had to be employed for a month at a time in scouring the channel. Other trouble spots were by Birtley Farm, by XVIth lock, and along the southern end of the summit level in Sidney Wood where the high embankments were in constant need of attention.†

Holiday periods or week-ends were the occasions most commonly chosen for carrying out lock repairs. Previously the blacksmiths—Kelsey of Bramley or Fielder of Loxwood—would have accompanied the carpenters to inspect the damage. A pair of gates might have to be lifted and rebedded, a paddle renewed, or some panels replaced. For both craftsmen, the installation of a pair of gates was the culmination of many weeks' work, for this was wood and iron working on the grand scale; massive oak timbers had to be fashioned to tenon and mortise before iron straps and hinges could be forged and fitted to the heel posts. Bricklayers, too, were always in demand especially after heavy frost when chamber walls might need to be repointed or sills rebuilt. Wages were low. Carpenters and bricklayers were paid from 2s. 6d. to 3s. 6d. a day, labourers 1s. 9d. or 2s., and the boy would probably receive 1s. There was, however, a free daily issue of beer.

The expense of maintenance work on the Wey & Arun averaged £300 per annum except during the peak period 1837–40 when the canal's greater activity caused this sum to be more than doubled. Although the Arun was mainly a river navigation, the outlay was almost as high due to the extensive damage caused to the towpath and embankments by severe winter flooding. On the credit side, rents for kilns and wharves, the sale of sedge, hay, bark, osiers, underwood, and withy faggots brought in a few pounds each year.

The Wey & Arun accounts bring to light a variety of items of extraordinary expenditure. Damage resulting from an overflow at the reservoir cost the Company £5, Richard Eager received ten

* The graving dock at Godalming, built in 1792, was filled in in 1832.

† Before the House of Lords' Committee in 1868, Pullen stated that the banks in Sidney Wood by XVIth lock had been washed away three times in the past and a considerable outlay had been required to restore the breaches.

guineas in 1822 as compensation for the digging of stones from his land at West Whipley Farm to patch a weakened embankment, and Mr Snelling was granted £50 compensation when a bank collapsed in 1843 at Rye Farm.

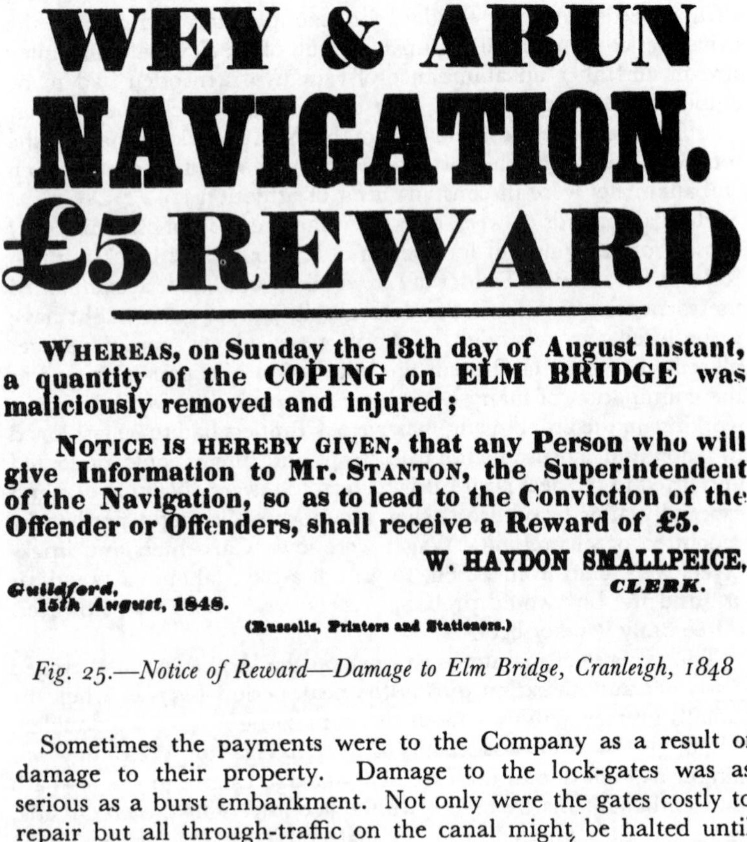

WEY & ARUN NAVIGATION.

£5 REWARD

WHEREAS, on Sunday the 13th day of August instant, a quantity of the COPING on ELM BRIDGE was maliciously removed and injured;

NOTICE IS HEREBY GIVEN, that any Person who will give Information to Mr. STANTON, the Superintendent of the Navigation, so as to lead to the Conviction of the Offender or Offenders, shall receive a Reward of £5.

W. HAYDON SMALLPEICE,
CLERK.

Guildford,
15th August, 1848.

(Russells, Printers and Stationers.)

Fig. 25.—Notice of Reward—Damage to Elm Bridge, Cranleigh, 1848

Sometimes the payments were to the Company as a result of damage to their property. Damage to the lock-gates was as serious as a burst embankment. Not only were the gates costly to repair but all through-traffic on the canal might be halted until repairs could be carried out. In 1835 John Davis' barge bumped into Lock X, in 1837 John Doick broke the lower gates of Wesby lock in number '23', and Charles Baverstock in '102' suffered the same mishap in Gennets Wood four years later. Baverstock's accident virtually closed the canal for nearly a fortnight, caused £75 worth of damage and loss of revenue to the Company of twice that amount; yet his fine when convicted for negligently bringing his barge into the lock was only £2 14s.!

Bridges on the Wey & Arun required more attention than should have been necessary; whereas all those over the Arun and Rother Navigations had been stone built, the majority of those over the Wey & Arun were constructed of brick, and some had been so poorly put together that within a few years they had degenerated into dangerous structures. Compasses bridge was a case in point; it had to be rebuilt in 1822 at a cost of nearly £300. Some of the lock walls, too, were never in good repair because the contractors had used insufficient mortar.

Sometimes expenditure was incurred in other directions. A handbill of 1848 offered £5 reward to anyone able to give information to Stanton which would lead to the conviction of the person who removed the coping stones from Elm bridge, Cranleigh. But not all the outlay was for reparations; a small percentage was devoted to capital expenditure. Increasing trade demanded the purchase of wharves and coal pens, the erection of lime-kilns and a store-room at Cranleigh wharf, and the building of two pump windmills (*see* Chapter XI) to improve the water supply.

Pilfering was always a problem and although the well-guarded bullion barges appear not to have been molested, many cargoes suffered. The commonest victims were the coal barges. To the villagers coal was dear and in short supply and it was sometimes not difficult to induce a bargeman to leave half a hundredweight of coal at a point on the bank—the loss being not easily discovered if stone ballast was shovelled under the remainder of the load. Local history also reveals that an Alfold schoolmaster, who had either found smugglers rare or their fees too high, took to stealing duty-paid spirits from the barges moored for the night in Sidney Wood.

Traffic was handled either by independent carriers, the majority of whom were small owner-boatmen, or by merchants and manufacturers who used water transport in connection with their own trade. The first carriers on the Wey & Arun had been those already established on the adjoining navigations. The carrying firm of Seward & Co. was already well known in Arundel, and about 1820 they started a regular service between Arundel and London, but the three barges, *Arun*, *Commerce*, and *Swallow*, seldom carried loads of more than 20 or 25 tons. However, by 1823 an amalgamation had taken place and Seward, Henly & Co. had increased the size of their fleet to ten barges. The improvements carried out to the Arun Navigation enabled cargoes to be increased to 40 tons and over and, later that year, after the opening of the Portsmouth & Arundel Canal, the Company was re-formed as the Portsmouth

Chichester, Arundel, Petworth & Midhurst
BARGE COMPANY.

N. B. THE BARGES load every WEDNESDAY and SATURDAY, at RANDELLS' WHARF, *Queenhithe, London,* and deliver Goods to the above and all intermediate Places without delay,

FOR READY MONEY ONLY.

Not accountable for Loss or Damage by Fire or Water, or from River Piracy, or for any Parcel above Five Pounds value unless entered as such and paid for accordingly; or for Leakage of Casks.

*** All Communications addressed to Mr. T. BONAMY, Agent for *Arundel* and *Chichester*; or RANDELL, HOWELL and RANDELL, *Queenhithe Wharf*; will be duly attended to.

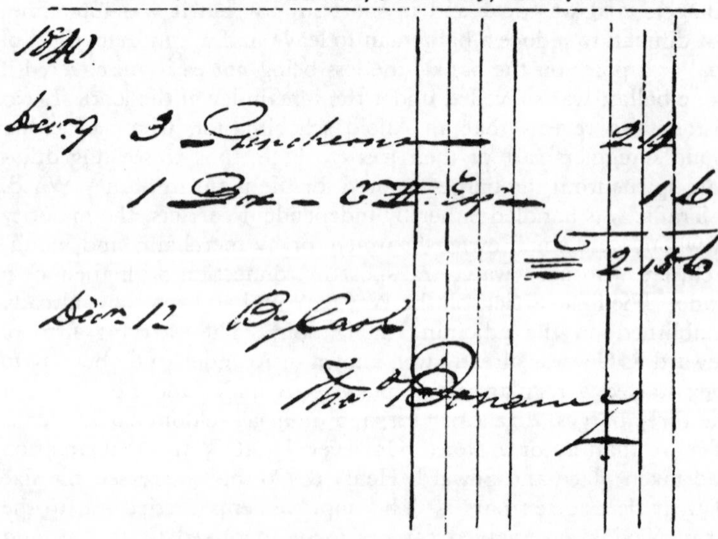

Fig. 26.—Invoice issued by Chichester, Arundel, Petworth & Midhurst Barge Company in 1840

Barge Company. However, within three years it had failed and the name was altered to the Arundel Barge Company, and in 1839 to the Arundel Lighter Company. A Sussex trade directory of 1839 shows that this was later changed to the 'London, Arundel & Chichester Barge Company', although remaining under the ownership of Seward & Co., whose barges loaded at Randells' Wharf, Queenhithe, on Wednesdays and Saturdays, as of yore. T. Bonamy was the appointed agent for Arundel and Chichester. A toll ticket issued in 1840 reveals a further variation in title to the 'Chichester, Arundel, Petworth & Midhurst Barge Co.' In 1844, however, Child & Henly, an Arundel firm of coal merchants who already ran their own river barges, acquired Seward's fleet and consequently the London loading point was changed to Bull Wharf, near Upper Thames Street. Two years later, Thomas Bonamy & Son, of Arundel, took over the concern and in 1848 restored its former title of 'The Arundel Barge Co.' Although the number of boats belonging to the Company was now reduced to seven, Bonamys remained the principal carriers between London and Arundel until the 1860s.

A Guildford *Almanack* of 1836 gives the names of five barge-carriers, including that of Seward & Co., and also names a Mr W. Mills as a barge-owner. Thirty years later the principal carrying fleet on the Wey was owned by William Stevens & Son of Guildford. Mr Murray Marshall of Godalming was the principal trader on the upper reaches of the Wey and shipped much timber from Arundel. Richard Isemonger's four boats catered for the needs of Littlehampton, and Stanton of Bramley usually had at least five in commission between the Thames and the English Channel. Most carriers owned only one or perhaps a pair of barges and generally served their particular neighbourhood. Nearly every riverside village boasted its own barge-master. Names like Barnard of Petworth, Doick of Hardham, Henly of Bury, Nye of Pulborough, Seward of Loxwood, Smart of Offham, Stanton of Bramley, Stone of Pallingham, and Strudwick of Fittleworth were as familiar to the neighbourhood as those of the baker, butcher, and wheelwright.[163]

Generally speaking, local traffic on the Wey & Arun could be divided into two classes—heavy and light. The most important branch was the coal trade and this came mainly from the South Wales coal fields to Arundel by lighter, whence slow-moving spritsail barges carried cargoes up to Cranleigh and sometimes as far as Bramley.[164] Stone and timber formed the bulk of the back traffic. The secondary trade comprised the smaller and less-sturdy boats laden with farm produce and general merchandise. Seldom carrying more than 20 tons, they usually travelled more quickly than their heavier counterparts and sometimes on the London–Portsmouth route these 'fly-boats' travelled both day and night using relays of horses.

Gradually local industries came to be developed along the banks of the canal. Below Bramley wharf there was a tannery to which bark was delivered. At Tickners Heath, brickfields and timber yards were established, while at Pallingham a flourishing boat-building and repair yard had been founded by the Stone family. On Rushett Common, by the parish boundary, stood James Tickner's vinegar works; close at hand on Run Common was the charcoal furnace belonging to Richard Medland which burnt some 2,000 tons of cordwood annually to manufacture naphtha, acetic acid and some 500 tons of charcoal. These products were rarely sold locally and had to be taken by water to Littlehampton from where they were shipped to London. As local timber became scarce difficulty was experienced in obtaining wood from further afield. Timber bought at Slinfold had, for instance, to be either carted to Newbridge or to Loxwood and loaded into barges bound for Run Common.[79]

Chalk was regularly supplied from the Guildford and Houghton pits to the canalside wharves where kilns had been established. The largest were those situated at Newbridge and Shalford, but they were to be found on most large farms like that of William Eager at Whipley Manor. Fertilizers were also required in other forms and sometimes the *Lark* carried as much as 45 tons of seaweed to Guildford.

Through traffic on the Wey & Arun was three times greater from the Wey than from the Arun; coal and groceries, however, came from both directions and Stanton at Bramley could choose his market. The Wey Navigation had a more evenly balanced trade. Barges carrying agricultural produce and timber to the Thames returned equally well laden with the needs of Guildford, Godalming, and the adjoining villages. In 1831, 827 boats entered the navigation at Weybridge with an average load of 38 tons and 867 at Guildford with an average load of 32 tons. In addition, a small quantity was loaded and unloaded between these two points, making a total of around 58,000 tons compared with the Wey & Arun's 17,000 and the Arun Navigation's 23,000 tons. Seven years later the Wey was carrying half as much again while the figures for the others had risen to 23,000 and 30,000 respectively.

To some extent this disproportionate amount of through-traffic in one direction was balanced by the fact that twice the amount of local traffic from the Wey & Arun passed to the Wey Navigation as from it. Indeed, the quantity of bark and barrel hoops which originated from the banks of the Arun and the Wey & Arun in 1831 accounted for nearly a quarter of the total traffic passing down the Wey into the Thames.

The types of craft used between London and Portsmouth varied from flat-bottomed barges on the narrower canal sections to barques and fore-and-aft rigged sailing vessels on the ship canals. There are few contemporary pictures of vessels used at that time. The best known is the square-rigged collier depicted by Turner on the Chichester Canal in 1829.[165] The designs shown on invoices and seals are not very reliable, being perhaps more picturesque than accurate. The simpler shapes and colours of the barges which ventured on the Wey and further south are disappointing in comparison with the gaily decorated narrow boats designed for the slimmer canal system of the Midlands. The dimensions of the Wey were too small for the Thames barges and the Medway barges could pass no higher than Arundel. The now forgotten Arundel barges had simple rigs consisting of either single or twin masts and lug sails. Smaller and not comparable to the masterly Medway flotillas, they were sharp forward and rigged with a sprit and foresail, without a mizen and so able to carry goods up the Arun as far as Pulborough. The considerable rise and fall of the tide made loading operations difficult and for that reason gang-planks 20 or 25 ft long were carried to reduce the pitch for the wheel-barrows. At Bury wharf, barges were moored at high water and left aground as the tide receded, a practice which continued until barge traffic ceased in the late 1920s. The size of vessels built at Pallingham was slightly less than 70 ft in length with a 12-ft beam and generally they had open holds so that away from home the crew either erected a tent or spent the night amongst the cargo under the open sky; only in severe weather did they shelter at the canalside inns. Sometimes a rude cabin was provided below deck, but never above, as on the Thames barges, because of the low headroom of the bridges. The deck fittings were functional rather than ornamental, with massive iron rings fixed fore and aft for mooring purposes.

There were three methods of navigating between Pallingham and the sea; by sail, by punting down with the tide (*see* Plate 53), and by horse haulage. The last method was used between Pallingham and the Thames, although the Portsmouth & Arundel barges had collapsible masts for sailing on the Arun. Serious efforts were made to obviate the use of horses. On the Portsmouth & Arundel a Mr Van Heythusen experimented with tread wheels as a means of propulsion and alleged that two men could propel one barge.[80] On the tideway between the Chichester and Portsea canals, much attention was paid to the possibilities of steam haulage to avoid the vagaries of sail. The first steam tug, owned by the Portsmouth & Arundel, was the *Egremont*, built in 1820 at a cost of £5,000 at Milton near Portsmouth. She was quite small, only 17 tons, with a single deck and mast and an overall length of 78 ft. Although steam vessels were a vital link between Chichester and Langstone Harbours their engines were unreliable and there is no doubt that they were a constant source of trouble. Certainly during the short history of the Portsmouth & Arundel Canal several tugs had to be used.[81]

Two of the smaller types of sailing barge, however, frequented the Chichester Canal and these are described by Frank Carr as follows:

> 'Between Poole and Chichester and within the waters of the Isle of Wight, were found a number of small ketch-rigged barges, not unlike the smaller Thames barges in build, but usually rigged either with "boomy" mainsails or with half-sprit mainsails. . . . They were employed in trading among the smaller ports within these limits, and carried a great part of the trade between the Isle of Wight and the mainland. They loaded about 100 tons. . . . In the waters of Langstone Harbour there were also small barges, known as Langstone barges, flat-bottomed, ketch-rigged, many of them with a sharp or "nip-cat" stern. Others had a transom stern, not unlike a Thames barge. They worked in the confined waters of Langstone, Chichester and Portsmouth Harbours, with an occasional longer voyage to Southampton Water. They had no leeboards, very little sheer and were pole-masted, but fitted with running not steeving bowsprits. They were employed mostly carrying shingle and coal.'[82]

Now, it is often forgotten that passengers were conveyed on canals. Yet this had been done in some form or other since the time of the first river navigations. During the early nineteenth century passenger-carrying reached its peak on the canals in the Midlands and the North, where packet boats were widely operated and well patronized. In Scotland in 1835, for instance, over 350,000 passengers were transported by packet boat between Paisley and Glasgow. The Wey Navigation Acts and both the Portsmouth & Arundel and the Wey & Arun Acts had laid down maximum passenger rates, and it is probable that people did occasionally travel up to London from the country by barge. However, contemporary descriptions of canal travel are extremely few and of those the majority refer to waterways in the Midlands or the North and have an industrial rather than a rural setting. Charles Dickens' account in *The Old Curiosity Shop* (Chapter XLIII) of Little Nell's chance journey by barge with her grandfather furnishes an interesting picture of canal life about 1840 and describes what was generally the only form of passenger travel by barge, for which, in spite of canal company regulations, tolls were rarely collected. It is believed that occasional passengers may have travelled with their cattle and garden produce from Wonersh and Bramley to Guildford on market days,* but there is no record of any regular passenger service being initiated and the toll cards printed from time to time by the Wey & Arun gave no rates for passengers, who could be charged twopence a mile. The Wey and some Sussex navigations, like the Ouse, were, on the other hand, only authorized to collect one penny a mile, but again it is very doubtful if any regular service was introduced or if passenger boats were built.

Lord Egremont was growing old, but his enormous energy seemed little impaired by advancing years. His birthdays had become the occasions for local celebration; particularly was this so when at the age of 83 a rustic festival on a gargantuan scale was held in Petworth Park for over 3,000 guests, whom he rode amongst and greeted.[83] However, on 11 November 1837, a month before his eighty-sixth birthday and only a week after he had journeyed back from Brighton where he had gone to pay his respects to the new Queen, Lord Egremont died. *The Times* obituary said: '. . . he was not eminent as a statesman or warrior; neither illustrious for eloquence or genius; he was remarkable for one quality alone, and that was his immense benevolence'. To do good seemed to be his great characteristic and it is readily understandable that biographers have echoed in various terms Arthur Young's adulation when he wrote:

> 'It is impossible not to feel great respect, in contemplating the energy of an individual of the highest rank and fortune, animated with such

* Collison Morley in *Companion into Surrey*, 1949, p. 52, mentioned that a barge took people to and from work every day between Cranleigh and Guildford. I do not know the source of this information but it is unlikely that such a service would have been run on other than market days since the 8-mile journey by water took three hours. The author does not refer to the matter in the 1938 edition.

ideas, and expending his income in so meritorious a manner, forming navigations, rewarding industry in the lower classes, improving the breed of livestock by bounties, encouraging all useful and mechanical artisans; setting on foot multiplied experiments to ascertain the comparative merit of different agricultural implements; introducing improvements, by extending the knowledge of new plants, animals, or implements, all of them in so many and various shapes contributing their assistance to national prosperity. The thought of one man having been instrumental in the improvement of his country, and still exerting himself in the same career, must be a constant fund of gratifications to every benevolent mind; and that long may he live to enjoy the fruits of his labour in the service of his country, is the wish of every man in the county.'[84]

The funeral took place ten days later at Petworth. As in his lifetime, so at his death, art and land played a leading role. The procession of mourners, led by Turner, included many of the artists to whom Egremont had been a friend as well as a patron. Behind the hearse four hundred labourers from the estate walked in pairs, clad in white smocks and black gloves. In addition, several hundred relatives and friends attended the large funeral—astonishing testimony to a beloved landlord and one of the greatest art patrons of all time.

Lord Egremont's development of the river Rother and his investment in the Arun Navigation had met with both financial and philanthropic success. However, his shares in the Wey & Arun showed at the time of his death a depreciation in value of nearly £20,000, although the canal had brought many comforts to the rural communities by providing them with the necessities of life hitherto denied them. It had also given employment to a variety of people and an incentive to establish local crafts and industries by providing communication with a wider market. In one respect only was his judgement proved at fault and that was his investment in the ill-fated Portsmouth & Arundel Canal, which caused him to lose over £55,000. In retrospect it seems strange that it should have been thought a feasible proposition to extend the Arun and Wey Navigations on a national scale when their disadvantages were well known. As early as 1809 W. Stevenson in his *General View of the Agriculture of Surrey* had been perspicacious enough to doubt 'whether a county purely agricultural, except under very peculiar and favourable circumstances, can maintain a sufficient export trade to keep up a canal'. Of course, at the time the canals were built it must be remembered that war with France was never far from the horizon and in such an event they would have clearly attracted more traffic. Furthermore, this particular link was only made when all other attempts to join the two ports had failed, and there was also Egremont's firm belief—written indeed into the 1817 Act—that 'it would promote the improvement and better cultivation of the circumjacent country by the conveyance of manure'. Altogether, Egremont's total investment in inland navigation exceeded £100,000,* which only rarely during the period of his lifetime yielded a return higher than 1 per cent in any one year.

In 1836, during a period when the nation's commerce was flourishing, freight rates on the Wey & Arun were slightly reduced, and the impetus given to trade caused toll receipts to rise from £1,938 in 1835–6 to £2,480 within three years and to £2,525 in 1839–40, the highest they ever reached. Even so, the total amount of merchandise carried hardly exceeded 23,000 tons, which was well below the original estimate envisaged even for local trade (30,000 tons) and was insignificant compared with the amount of traffic on the Kennet & Avon, which, linking the Thames and the Bristol Channel, for many years carried over 300,000 tons of goods annually.

The Arun Navigation's receipts, which had been £1,330 in 1830, exceeded £2,400 in 1839 and 1840. This rise in revenue encouraged the proprietors to improve the facilities at Newbridge. In 1837 a cottage was built for the under-wharfinger and in 1839 a large rectangular double-storied brick warehouse with a slate roof was constructed adjacent to the canal. Furthermore, the Company were willing to provide two horses for 'gratuitously assisting all waggons carrying coal and lime up the hill' from the wharf.

In 1838 the Commissioners of Sewers announced their intention of making the horseshoe cut in the river Arun at South Stoke—a matter which had been under consideration since Henry Palmer, civil engineer, had made an optimistic report way back in the summer of 1830. Although the cut would shorten the distance to Arundel by over a mile, the Arun proprietors adjudged the plan prejudicial to the navigation unless it reduced the floods. Cutfield and Seward represented the Arun at meetings with the other canal companies, after which a somewhat reluctant agreement appears to have been reached. In 1839 the work was completed and consideration was given by the Arun proprietors the following year to a suggestion by the Commissioner of Sewers that a cut

* Approximately, Rother £18,280, Arun £3,600, Wey & Arun £27,200, Portsmouth & Arundel £56,000.

should be made from Houghton bridge to the western tip of the horseshoe, which would have helped to reduce flooding as well as lopping another thousand yards off the distance. This project was only finally abandoned in 1849 because the consent of landowners could not be obtained.

Complaints about lack of draught were so serious in 1838 that the Arun Committee ordered that no dividend exceeding 5 per cent should be paid while the Arun Canal would not permit barges drawing 3 ft 1 in. to pass every twelve hours, nor until the reserves reached £300. Cutfield was also ordered to take whatever steps were necessary to allow barges drawing 3 ft 2 in. to pass. The following year it was felt that the Littlehampton ferry boat, when moored across the river, was impeding the flow of water up to Coldwaltham at neap tides and the ferry trustees were asked to 'remedy the evil'. Although the 1839–40 accounts showed an increase of £800 in maintenance costs, the Arun dividend was maintained at 12 per cent. Heavy expenditure on repairs was also incurred by the Wey & Arun; four sets of lock-gates were renewed between Bramley and the summit-level in 1840, and 154 tons of gravel laid along the towpath between Newbridge and Compasses bridge in 1841.

Before the coming of the railways, land and water carriage competed against each other without either method showing outstanding advantages. However, the length of turnpike roads in Surrey and Sussex increased by 40 per cent between 1814 and 1839[85], and during this period there was no doubt that better road surfaces and modes of conveyance were speeding up land transport. This was clearly illustrated during the building of the London & Southampton Railway, when it was stated that while the tonnage carried on the Basingstoke Canal had risen by 50 per cent, yet the revenue of the canal would have been still larger had not the competition of the road waggons much reduced the price of carriage.[86] A petition to the Thames Navigation Committee in 1829 referred to the 'lowering of many of the hills and general improvement on the whole line of roads between London and Portsmouth which enables the carriers to take heavier weights with fewer horses now than formerly'. To try to improve the national system of water communication, Hodgson had tried in 1830 to form a canal owners' club in London to enable the navigations to compete more effectively. A circular was issued, Lord Egremont was proposed as president, but lack of support prevented its formation.

River Wey Navigation,

Surrey.

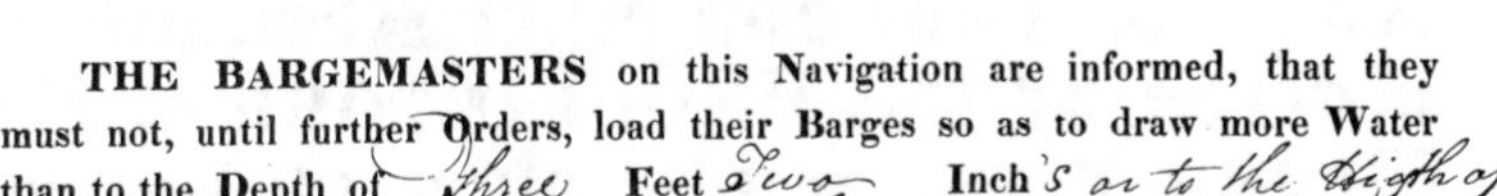

THE BARGEMASTERS on this Navigation are informed, that they must not, until further Orders, load their Barges so as to draw more Water than to the Depth of *Three* Feet *Two* Inch*'s or to the Hight of 7 feet 1 inch in Bulk from the Waters edge* ——

And the Wharfingers and Lock-keepers are to examine all Barges, to see that this Order is complied with.

The Bargemasters are also informed, that they are on no Pretence whatsoever, to draw open the Gates of any of the Locks or Pounds with Horses, or to open any of the Gates or Sluices; as the Lock-keepers have Directions to attend all Barges into and through every Lock, Pound and Gate.

The Bargemasters are hereby desired to attend to the producing of Invoices and Bills of Lading for the inspection of the Wharfingers and Lock-keepers of this Navigation.

And

The Bargemasters are also informed, that the Wharfingers and Lock-keepers are peremptorily Ordered to report to the Proprietors, the Names of those who shall act contrary to these Directions; and as the Proprietors are determined to protect their Servants in the due Execution of their Orders, it is expected these Regulations will be strictly observed.

By order of the Proprietors,

Fig. 27.—Notice to Bargemasters on the Wey Navigation, c. 1830

NOTICE.

In consequence of several additional Rates of Toll, and other Regulations ordered by the PROPRIETORS of the RIVER WEY, to take place on Barges navigating the said River on the 1st of July next, *a Meeting of the Timber, Corn, and Coal Merchants, Ironmongers, Grocers, Barge Owners, and others*, having Business on the said Canal, is requested to be held at the WHITE HART INN, GUILDFORD, on SATURDAY the 24th of JUNE, at three o'clock in the afternoon, to take the same Regulations, &c. into their consideration, and to consider the propriety of establishing a LAND CONVEYANCE between *Weybridge, Guildford*, and *Godalming*, and to adopt such Measures as the said Meeting may think proper.

JUNE 23, 1826.

[RUSSELL, PRINTER.]

Fig. 28.—Notice of meeting of merchants and barge owners to consider establishing a Land Conveyance, 1826

However, improved roads were not the only threat on the horizon as the darkening clouds of locomotion began slowly to gather in the late thirties. Horse-drawn trucks had been no threat to horse-drawn barges (*see* Chapter III) but the opening of the Liverpool & Manchester Railway in 1830 established the arrival of a new form of transport. In 1829 the energetic and prescient Hodgson proposed to introduce steam power to enable water traffic to compete with the projected steam land carriage and had gone so far as to write a paper and have drawings prepared of a steam-driven barge.[87] The proprietors did nothing, thinking perhaps on the lines of the Duke of Wellington that this mode of carriage would not 'force itself into extensive use'. By 1838 the first steam-hauled trucks to run on rails had appeared in Surrey as far south as Woking and on the London & Greenwich line. The following year the London & Croydon Railway, which had usurped the bed of the Croydon Canal, was opened. The halcyon days of the canal era were indeed over.

RECEIVED the 3rd day of August 1838.

of the Treasurer of the WEY AND ARUN JUNCTION CANAL COMPANY, Five Pounds, being the Dividend of £1. per Cent. upon my Share of the said Canal, ordered at a Meeting of the Committee of Management of the said Canal, on the Twenty-second day of May last.

Jos. Hodgson

£5 – –

Fig. 29.—Wey & Arun Canal Company Dividend Receipt, 1838

The table given below shows how toll receipts increased until they reached their peak in 1839 and then suddenly declined.

Year	*Arun*	*Wey & Arun*	*Wey*
1830	£1300	£2181	£5571
1835	1529	1938	6376
1838	2020	2479	7763
1839	2426	2524	7642
1840	2407	2189	6881
1841	1539	1713	5200

CHAPTER XI

The Two Windmills

Inadequacy of Wey & Arun's water supply—traffic halted during droughts—George Rennie's survey, 1833—construction of two pump windmills—their usefulness and uniqueness—their auction at Bramley, 1855—a steam engine?

THE Wey & Arun never came to be regarded in canal circles as a waterway of much importance. Its shares were rarely quoted in the national press, nor were its activities significant enough to warrant more than an occasional paragraph in the local gazettes. It was something of an anomaly. Built with the highest hopes, it suffered the ignominy of becoming a local line on a national route; a line reputed to disappear in winter beneath the swirling waters of the Arun floods and to resemble a bridlepath in times of drought.

No wonder that the London merchants regarded the waterway as a white elephant. It is, of course, interesting to speculate on how inland navigation might have developed in West Sussex if a canal to link the Wey and Arun rivers had been built soon after the opening of the Arun and Rother Navigations. Certainly the cost of construction would have been much reduced, its strategic value would have been proved during the Napoleonic wars, and the branch to Horsham would probably have materialized. However, the opportunity was lost and the Wey & Arun's chances of success were jeopardized not only by its high capital cost but by its heavy lockage and consequent water shortage. Even so, it is hard to visualize how any canal project to link the two rivers could have justified economically the additional expenditure required to overcome these disadvantages. It is doubtful, indeed, if it could ever have been more than a moderately prosperous undertaking, even if the more sanguine expectations of its promoters had materialized. The line was in itself devious and limited in scope by the size of the navigations at its northern and southern ends. Furthermore, by building as many as 23 locks, the number between Teddington and Coldwaltham was doubled and the venture imperilled from the outset. An engineer with greater foresight would have urged at the planning stage that the summit level should be dug deeper and the locks at the south end of Sidney Wood be placed together in a flight. If expense had allowed 10 ft of additional excavation it would have produced a 9-mile summit, obviated at least seven locks and provided an ample water supply. The seven locks XIV to VIII, which were built within 1,500 yd of one another at Alfold, could then have been constructed in a flight of seven chambers with eight gates and enabled the passage of craft to be speeded in both directions. A lift or inclined plane, provided for in the Act, would have been uneconomic and only worth consideration if the waterway had not been deepened, in which case an adequate water supply would have still remained a problem. As it was dug, the summit level was only one foot deeper than the remainder of the canal. Theoretically, nine barges passing through the locks at each end caused the water level to fall by 2 in. During busy summer months heavy demands had therefore to be made on the 50-acre reservoir (originally planned to cover 100 acres) at Vachery, and these could not always be met, with the result that barges might be delayed until the next rains.

Water was, of course, the predominating concern of the management of each and every navigation. Those in the south were no exception. They had either too much or too little, and usually when traffic was the reverse. The Arun installed a water-wheel by Orfold lock and dug a feeder stream from Wisborough Green to supply their navigation, but their main problem was usually too much water, for every winter the floods whirled around the abutments of the bridges and undermined the earthworks. The Portsmouth & Arundel provided pumping engines and had been involved in tiresome claims by those whose drinking-water and crops were affected by salt. The Wey were probably the least troubled, but they, too, after disputes and delays to barge traffic which lasted several years, had to sign an agreement (1832) with the millers at Woking, Stoke, and Newark for maintenance of the river level when water was low.

When the building of the Wey & Arun had been first contemplated, it was understood that abundant quantities of water would be available. The prospectus had stated that the line would pass through a country 'whose soil is principally clay, presenting no difficulties and with a plentiful supply of water in the driest seasons'. Although the Act had provided for the construction of a second reservoir at Ewhurst, when in 1818 negotiations were begun for the purchase of land financial considerations and strong opposition from the landowners caused the proposal to be dropped. However, soon after work was commenced on the 2,000-yd cutting at Alfold, the Management Committee received an ominous warning from the engineer—the clay soil had given place to porous sand. Although the bed and banks were carefully lined with extra thicknesses of puddled clay, the likelihood of leakage and evaporation was appreciably increased. The canal was filled without difficulty during the summer of 1816 and all went reasonably well until the fine weather in the summers of 1819 and 1820 caused barge traffic to be impeded by lack of draught. The first attempt at a panacea was to spend over £750 on deepening the reservoir. But the Company were dubious as to whether this in itself would be sufficient to alleviate the problem. The Abstract of Accounts for 1821 specifically exempted this item of expenditure from the proviso 'not likely to occur again'. For occur again it did, and hardly a year passed when there was not some cost incurred in trying to regulate and improve the water supply. This matter appeared regularly on the Committee's agenda. At the General Meeting in May 1827, it was reported that 'An increase in expenditure during the past year was occasioned by procuring an additional water supply from the Bramley stream. The Earl of Egremont, the Chairman of the Committee, with his wonted liberality, gratuitously granted the water, but the expenses attending the making of the aqueduct and course for the conveyance of the water into the canal have been considerable. This however is an expense which will not occur again, and the supply of water it is hoped may become essentially useful to the canal.' In truth, no more was done to the Bramley stream, but a further £90 was expended on Vachery Pond during the following year, and £65 the year after.

The position was obviously far from satisfactory. The Committee had tried to remedy the water shortage to the best of their ability, but the canal's present supply was still inadequate to meet the needs of regular barge traffic which was tending to increase each year. Whereas only some 60 boats had passed through the summit level during the busiest month in 1820, this number had practically doubled within a decade and was steadily increasing. So it was, then, that whenever there was a prolonged dry spell or a little more traffic than usual, the loss of water through evaporation and usage at the locks forced barge-masters to lighten their loads or risk becoming marooned in the shallows. The problem was a recurring one and there was no solution proposed which was not likely to weigh heavily on the Company's finances.

Finally, it was decided to invite George Rennie, one of the nine children of the renowned builder of London Bridge, to survey the adjacent countryside in order to find means of increasing the water supply. As a result of his two visits to the canal in July 1833, for which he received a fee of £60, the Wey & Arun became one of the few navigations in England to have windmills built upon its banks as part of its workings.* Since both the building of a second reservoir or the deepening of the summit level were impractical in relation to the Company's finances, Rennie recommended that water should be conserved from wastage by pumping it back to the upper levels after Locks XVII and XVIII had been drawn. The Company considered this a feasible proposition and tenders were subsequently invited for the design and erection of two suitable pumps. It appears from the correspondence among the Wey & Arun archives that a Mr William Birch was the sole person to have replied to this invitation. His first design was for a pump to be worked by either four men or a horse. This was rejected as being not only uneconomical but too slow in operation, as over two hours were required to replace one lockful of water. His second design was for a pump windmill and this was accepted.

The first windmill was erected by Lock XVII at the north end of the summit level and became known as Cranley Mill.† It was completed in 1833 at a cost to the Company of £285. The mill, constructed of oak and cast iron, stood on a brick foundation, rose to a height of 16 ft and measured 12 ft in width. Two 12-in. double-cylinder pumps raised 550 gal. a height of 7 ft a minute, i.e. 88 cu. ft; as 6,048 cu. ft (or 25,000 gal.) of water were required to fill a lock, the time taken to replenish that amount was about 70 minutes.

For the replenishment of the summit pound this was sufficiently fast, but for the smaller Run Common pound, a more powerful pump was required. In October 1833 Birch designed a more elaborate windmill which could be driven by either sail or horse, but the Committee decided on grounds of economy that wind power would be sufficient. By May 1834 Birtley Mill had been

* The majority of canals used primitive forms of pumping engine like those on the Portsmouth & Arundel Canal at Ford and Portsea, or at Crofton on the Wiltshire Downs which supplied the Savernake summit of the Kennet & Avon Canal. A 'wind engine' or six-sailed windmill was, however, temporarily in use on the summit level of the Thames & Severn. In 1790 it was sketched by Samuel Ireland who recorded that it was capable of throwing up 'several tons of water every minute' from a well beside the canal.

† Cranleigh was spelt 'Cranley' until 1867 when it was altered by order of the Postmaster-General to avoid confusion with Crawley.

WEY and ARUN JUNCTION CANAL.

WITH ADVANTAGE OF WATER CARRIAGE.

THE USEFUL

MATERIALS

OF TWO

WINDMILL PUMPS,

Situate on the Banks of the Wey and Arun Junction Canal, in the respective Parishes of Bramley and Cranley, near Guildford, Surrey.

To be sold by Auction (by order of the Committee of Management of the Wey and Arun Junction Canal Company) by Mr.

FRED[K]. KEENE

SUCCESSOR TO THE LATE MR. LOMAS,

AT THE JOLLY FARMER INN, BRAMLEY, SURREY,

ON TUESDAY, DECEMBER 6, 1853,

AT TWO O'CLOCK.

BIRTLEY MILL.

LOT 1.

All the useful Machinery, Sails, Fans, and Gear of Windmill (as marked) with the stout oak frame work, Cowl, &c.

LOT 2.

Two 12-inch double Cylinder Pumps, with iron Beam, Bearer, &c.

LOT 3.

All the Brickwork Erection of Mill and Shaft (as marked) with Door and Frame.

CRANLEY MILL.

LOT 4.

All the useful Machinery, Sails, Fans, and Gear of Windmill (as marked) with the stout oak Frame-work, Cowl, &c., &c.

LOT 5.

Two 12-inch double Cylinder Pumps with iron Beam, Bearer, &c.

LOT 6.

All the Brickwork Erection of Mill and Shaft as marked.

The Properties may be viewed Two Days prior to the Sale, and Catalogues had at the Jolly Farmer, Bramley; Onslow Arms, Cranley, and of Mr. Frederick Keene, Auctioneer, Estate Agent, and Valuer, 19, North Street, Guildford, Surrey.

(RUSSELLS, PRINTERS, &c., GUILDFORD.)

Fig. 30.—Handbill announcing auction of Birtley and Cranley Windmills

built at a cost of £500, but alterations had to be made which accounted for a further £170, and were not completed until the following year. Twice the size of its neighbour, it rose 24 ft above its brick-built base, which was 26 ft in diameter. Its 9-ft broad sails were 20 ft long and fitted with 160 shutters; a cap and fan tail completed its exterior. Standing by the side of XVIII lock, its twirling white sails and black oak frame must have made a picturesque sight.

For twenty years these two windmills played their part in trying to maintain a sufficient depth of water in all seasons. However, it is doubtful if they were ever really satisfactory. Repairs had to be done fairly regularly and the reliance on the elements for motive power was a constant handicap to their utility, especially as their use was most required during the hot summer months when there was the least wind to catch the sails. Certainly hardly a year passed without the Company having to provide extra assistance. In 1833 nine men were employed throughout October pumping water from both the Birtley and Run Common pounds. In 1836 James Mann, the Cranley carrier, used his barge to lighten those stranded in the summit pound. In 1838 a man was being employed to help lighten barges at the Company's expense and manual pumping had to be resorted to at both XVII and XVIII locks. At the same time, every effort was continued to increase and preserve the supply of water. Loss of water through the leaking of the upper lock-gates was minimized by the keeper going round after the passage of every craft and throwing in tan or sawdust from heaps deposited at the head of each lock. During 1837, a survey was made to determine if more water could be stored in Vachery Pond, and over £200 was spent in raising the banks still higher and in increasing its depth.

At length, the machinery inside the mills wore out. The Committee agreed that renovation was impractical, failed to give them away,[88] and finally decided to put them up for auction. Handbills were printed and displayed in the neighbouring villages advertising the sale of 'the useful MATERIALS of two WINDMILL PUMPS, situate on the banks of the Wey & Arun Junction Canal'. Each mill was to be auctioned in three lots with the advantage of water carriage; the first lot comprised the machinery, sails, fans, and stout oak framework, the second the two 12-in. cylinder pumps, and the third the brickwork. On 6 December 1853 the auction took place at the 'Jolly Farmer' Inn at Bramley. Birtley Mill fetched

£31, Cranley Mill £23, a total of £54 for two windmills which had cost nearly £1,000 to build.*

On 12 June 1855 a special general meeting was held at the Town Hall in Guildford to consider the propriety of erecting a steam engine for supplying water to the canal. Since the tolls had fallen during the preceding five years by nearly £500 to only £753, their lowest since the opening of the navigation, the urgency of the meeting was self-evident. The shareholders, however, receiving no dividend that year, were loath to increase expenditure on the waterway and rejected the motion with the opinion that, water or no water, trade was unlikely to increase.

But they were wrong. It so happened that the following year brought a windfall to ease the emptiness of the Company's coffers. A wet summer and the transport of materials for building a railway along the banks of the Rother caused the tolls to leap 40 per cent. The steam engine was forgotten.

* No trace remains of the two windmills which were dismantled in 1854. Their position was not marked on the Ordnance Survey and the last reference found is in the auction particulars of the canal in 1870 which refers in the schedule to 'site of wind pump' at Bramley, amounting to eight perches.

The pump windmills had no connection with Alfold mill that stood on the south bank of the canal between Three Compasses and Simmonds Bridges (*see* Plate 25). Its origin is shrouded in mystery but it seems probable that it was built soon after the canal was opened. However the mill is not shown on any tithe maps (although Mill Field is shown on one of 1841) and the 6 inch ordnance map of 1871 described it as 'disused'. In 1845 John Butcher was listed in the *Six Home Counties Directory* as the miller. In 1855 it was worked by Mrs S. Butcher and in 1865 by a Mr Chandler of Alfold. The mill was demolished in 1913. Evidence of the loading wharf and the short tunnel into the base of the mill from the canal has yet to be established. (K. G. Farries and M. T. Mason *The Windmills of Surrey and Inner London*, 1966, pp 38–40.)

Jack Hampshire recalls what happened in 1913. 'During the time the paving stone job was in progress father had taken on a contract to dismantle an old windmill that stood on the south bank of the Wey and Arun Junction Canal. The mill had to be taken to pieces very carefully and each piece had to be marked and numbered. The small parts and the machinery had to be put into crates, and the centre shaft and sweeps transported on a tug to London docks for shipment to America.' (*I worked with traction engines*, 1967.)[166] Farries and Mason add that Jabez Nightingale of Cranleigh demolished part of the mill.

CHAPTER XII

Competition with the Railways (1840–1865)

The advent of rail transport—its development in Surrey and Sussex—opposition to the Shoreham to Chichester line—drawbridge over the Arun—closure of Ford–Hunston section of the Portsmouth & Arundel Canal—rumoured take-over of the Wey & Arun Canal by the Direct London & Portsmouth Railway Company—reductions in toll rates—share values fall—diminishing dividends—gunpowder cargoes—hazard and tragedy—changes in management—a railway along the Rother and another to the sea—Lord Grantley's opposition to the Horsham & Guildford Railway bill—building and opening of the line.

THE year 1840 saw the opening of the first railway in Sussex and marked the beginning of the end of the canal era. Henceforth the barge had to give precedence to the truck in much the same way as the stage coach was being usurped by the railway carriage. The change-over was none the less gradual and not, in the case of waterways, by any means complete. However, no sooner had railways become accepted on a national basis than there was a scramble to promote companies for building lines in all, and often parallel, directions. Between 1843 and 1845, over 160 railway Acts were granted and by 1847 some thousand miles of waterway had fallen under the control of railway companies.

The canal proprietors did what they could to oppose the flood of railway bills. In some cases not even a formal protest was made, so inevitable was the bill's success; a few navigations seized their last chance of financial gain either by accepting compensation as the price for withdrawing opposition or by concluding an advantageous sale to the newly formed railway companies. Sometimes a victory could be achieved and the railway bill would be thrown out, but this was seldom due to the persuasions of the navigation companies but rather because either the line chosen was not considered the best or because the opposition from the landowners was too powerful. Rarely could canals successfully compete against railways on equal terms. Exceptionally, one body of proprietors perceived that so far as picturesqueness was concerned, they could defy the proposed line of a railway. 'There will always be', said the Committee, 'many who will prefer travelling by a route through richly diversified scenery to one well known to be so very bleak and barren.' This was a most attractive waterway in Scotland, but even so the railway usurped the passenger traffic without great difficulty.

While the railways secured unquestionable superiority for passenger traffic, the waterways possessed, and still do in fact possess, certain positive advantages over any form of land carriage; nevertheless, lacking as they did uniformity in width, depth, and gauge of locks, the navigations were ill equipped to meet rail competition as a whole. Even in so short a distance as between Guildford and Chichester, locks of six different dimensions had been built, so that only barges able to enter the smallest chambers could pass. Unlike their competitors, most canal proprietors were, until 1845, hampered by being empowered only to collect tolls and not to act as carriers. Several companies, the Portsmouth & Arundel and the Thames & Severn included, ran their own boats out of sheer desperation and without parliamentary approval. No prosecutions followed, but the Act as it stood made the quotation of through-rates for long-distance carriage a complicated and discouraging procedure. Once the Act for the competitor railway had been passed, the navigation might sing its swan song and spend two or three very profitable years carrying the materials for the building of its usurper. Once this windfall had been gathered, however, it was seldom long before expenditure swallowed up revenue.

The development of the railways was a slow and rather haphazard process. Several private bills had often to be promoted before an Act could be obtained, and more than one Act granted before a line was built—no less than four attempts being made and three Acts passed between 1846 and 1861 before a railway reached Bognor in 1864. There was no planning on a national scale any more than there had been with the waterways, and even some of the main trunk lines were built in bits and pieces with several years intervening before a further Act enabled land to be acquired and additional capital to be raised so that the next link could be completed.

Within a decade of the opening of the Stockton & Darlington Railway, serious attention was being directed to making a railway from London to Brighton. In 1835 as many as six projects were laid before Parliament; some like Rennie's advocated a direct line involving substantial engineering works; others like Stephenson's and Gibbs' an easier but more circuitous route. None, however, satisfied the Parliamentary Committee, but the following year

Stephenson's bill for a line via Leatherhead, the Mole gap, Horsham and the Adur gap to Shoreham and thence to Brighton was passed by the Commons though rejected by the Lords. The intended line would not have passed within ten miles of the waterway, but William Cutfield, the treasurer and most active officer of the Arun Navigation, succeeded in concluding agreements with the projectors of both Stephenson's and Gibbs' lines, that should either bill be successful, the railway Company would pay £1,200 to the navigation for loss of trade.

However, the Act passed on 15 July 1838 was for the line chosen by John Rennie, which followed the route of the present Brighton line and which did not interfere, even indirectly, with the navigation's trade. Work began in July 1838, but not until May 1840 was the first section of railway completed in Sussex between Brighton and Shoreham harbour. In September 1841 the main line from London Bridge to Brighton was opened, the link with Victoria station not coming until 1860. In Surrey, the London & Croydon Railway had bought and closed the Croydon Canal (opened in 1809) as early as 1836 in order to build part of their line along its bed. Compensation had been fixed at £40,000 as compared with the cost of £27,000 but even so this was an advantageous settlement, for the canal Company had never paid a higher dividend than 1 per cent. In May of the same year Richard Smallpeice, the Mayor of Guildford, took the chair in the Council Chamber at a meeting to consider a railroad to Guildford, from which it was clear that this was felt to be as desirable as had been the water-link with Arundel twenty-five years earlier.

The railway reached Woking in 1838, Guildford in 1844, and Godalming in 1849. Consequently toll receipts on the Wey, which had attained their peak in 1838, were halved within a decade, and the quantity of cargo carried—in spite of tolls being reduced by one-third—dropped from 86,000 to about 50,000 tons during the same period. The Basingstoke Canal suffered even more severely and although both navigations cut their tolls, the Thames Commissioners controlling the third part of the route to London would not reciprocate. The war of the freight rates between goods truck and barge had begun in earnest, though its outcome was hardly in doubt. Tariff cutting sometimes retained traffic at the price of reduced receipts, but the railways always had the advantage of offsetting any loss against their profitable passenger traffic. Only in those districts where railways were slow to develop did the navigations continue to contrive to pay their way.

The completion in 1840 of the trunk line from London to Southampton, which was in direct competition with the Basingstoke Canal, was followed the next year by that to Brighton and Shoreham, and preparations were begun for extending the railway westwards towards Portsmouth. The majority of traders and townspeople along the south coast from Brighton to Bognor and Chichester naturally favoured the proposals, which soon, however, began to create quite a storm from a number of different factions. Indeed, no less than twenty petitions were entered against the Brighton & Chichester Railway bill, including one by the Wey & Arun, but not by the Portsmouth & Arundel who, although most directly affected, had little traffic to lose and no money to meet legal costs. The opposing interests can be divided into four groups. First, there were the big landowners like the Duke of Norfolk and George Wyndham; secondly, the trustees of the turnpike roads between Brighton and Worthing and of the Littlehampton ferry, who clearly stood to lose revenue; thirdly, towns such as Arundel and Petworth, who feared the loss of their market trade; and, fourthly, the Littlehampton Harbour Commissioners and the navigation companies, whose finances would also be directly affected.

In 1843, the Committee set up by the Arun proprietors to report on the intended Shoreham–Chichester railway estimated the loss of revenue at £155 per annum. Although it appeared likely, in view of the Brighton line's success, that however strongly the bill was opposed it would be passed, the Arun Committee decided to fight in the hope of obtaining at least similar compensation from the railway for loss of traffic as had been offered previously by two of the promoters of the Brighton line—compensation, however, which the London & Brighton Railway had shown no wish to make. The Company therefore agreed to petition against the bill and 'to contribute one-sixth of the expenses (up to £100) towards protecting the interests of the navigation and its links'.

In 1844, James Powell, the clerk to the Arun Navigation, spent a very busy spring writing letters to all the M.P.s and peers in Sussex requesting support, drafting petitions, and hiring gigs in order to attend special meetings.[89] Consultations and conferences; meetings and minutes; meticulous in every detail, he took the trouble to point out to William Holmes 'that the petition will go free of post if the ends of the envelope are left open as for a newspaper and it is marked "Parliamentary Petition"'. 'Away six days attending the House of Commons' read his accounts; away again for five days, and then the discovery that both the Duke of Norfolk and the Duke of Richmond had agreed to support the bill. Indignantly he wrote to Holmes in March: 'I think it is monstrous that the Duke of Norfolk should be favoured and placed in a position different from the mass. I really believe that there is more injury inflicted by private bills in one year than by general laws in six.' In fact an attempt to throw the bill out of the Commons at the second reading had been lost on 26 March by 99 votes to 48. The Wey & Arun were not so active: 'I am not aware that Mr Smallpeice has moved at all' wrote Powell on 28 March, and at a meeting held of the interested parties it was agreed that only the petitions of the Arun Navigation and the Port of Arundel Commissioners should be supported by counsel before the House of Commons Committee.

The basis of the Arun's petition was that the proposed railway bridge at Ford would materially obstruct the progress of large vessels up the river Arun and that the railroad was unnecessary as the existing means of communication in the neighbourhood were quite sufficient. In the hope that it could be shown that the bridge at Ford would reduce the draught on neap tides, readings were taken every fifteen minutes at Coldwaltham lock. And, indeed, the Parliamentary Committee ruled that, unless the Arun could show that the railway would impede the flow of water, they had no case since any indirect loss of revenue was not within the scope of compensation. Evidence on this latter point was not therefore heard and, since the lock readings had proved nothing, counsel on behalf of the Arun Navigation had very little to say.

In May, Powell informed the chairman, William Shaft, that he 'dreaded the expense of going to the Lords'. Petitions against the bill were heard by the House of Lords Committee during June, but by this stage the navigation interests had dropped their case. However, the promoters of the bill produced evidence that 2,320 tons of goods were carried annually by barge between London and Arundel* at a cost of 28s. a ton in 'uncertain time' and that a further tenth of this amount passed by road. In any case as the most powerful objectors to the bill had been, so to speak, bought off, the Arun's opposition could do no more than protect its interests by pressing for insertion of clauses in the Act to prevent interference to the navigation, and on this point they were well supported by the Admiralty. To counsel's question as to whether there was any doubt that the traffic on the canal would be transferred to the railway, witness replied that the railway would take

* Average during 1836–43.

away much of the Arun's traffic, not only on grounds of expense but because 'there is great delay occasioned every now and then from impediments in the navigation. If you take the average of the year, there is a stoppage of six or seven weeks annually and they never can get any goods down under from 27s. to 37s. per ton.'[90] A Bognor ironmonger said it took three weeks or more to get goods down from London by water carriage at a cost of 31s. 8d. a ton which was, he admitted, less than half the cost of carting them. A Littlehampton grocer said that timber imported from the Baltic was then taken by barge to London for 27s. a ton compared with 50s. by waggon; although it was expected that the cost by rail would be only 17s. a ton. The Duke of Richmond's steward commented that the occupation bridges over the Portsmouth & Arundel were a great inconvenience both to the public and farmers alike and that an extra horse had to be used to draw loaded waggons over them. The railway would be of great benefit since it took five days to drive cattle to London from Chichester and the 18,000 cattle sent annually to Smithfield became slimmer by a stone on the journey.

The railway Company won the battle, but only at a price. By the time the Act was passed, in July 1844, it contained no less than 374 sections which filled 133 pages. Clauses had been inserted which provided that the piers of the bridge should be wholly constructed of piles to prevent the least obstruction to the ebb and flow of the tide (239), that no work below high-water mark should be done without the Admiralty's consent (240), that lights should be hung out from sunset to sunrise (241), that a £10 fine would be imposed if any barge was detained for longer than twenty minutes (242), that the navigation should be kept clear during building operations (243), that if necessary the bridge was to be kept open one and a half hours before and after high water except for ten minutes before and four minutes after train times (245). Although the Arun Navigation failed to win any financial compensation, the trustees of the Littlehampton ferry, whose receipts for the past ten years had averaged £450 per annum, were to be paid the difference each year if they fell below that level in the following five years (255).

The drawbridge at Ford stood close to the entrance to the Portsmouth & Arundel Canal and was built entirely of timber, beams 60 ft long being imported from the Baltic for the piles. Although it only carried a single track, it had the widest movable span ever constructed at that date. The opening section was designed by John Rastrick so that a 63-ft portion of the bridge moved sideways

Fig. 31.—Ford Railway Bridge closed to shipping, 1846

Fig. 32.—Ford Railway Bridge open to shipping, 1846

LORD & LADY GRANTLEY *with* MR. C. F. NORTON *request the Pleasure of* the Revd Miss Talbott's ***Company to a Fête Champêtre, at Wonersh, on Thursday, the 26th Instant, at Two o'Clock.***

Wonersh, 18th May, 1831.

⁂ It is requested that this Card may be delivered at the Porter's Lodge.

☞ *Boats will be provided to convey the Company to Wonersh, and will start from Guildford Bridge at One o'Clock precisely.*

N. B.---In the event of the Day fixed for the Fête proving unfavorable, it will be postponed to the following Day.

Skinner, Columbian Press, Guildford.

Fig. 32a.—Invitation by boat to Wonersh House, 1831 *(see page 161)*

while the 144-ft middle section could be run back on twelve 6-ft wheels to occupy part of the space vacated, and leave the channel unobstructed. This middle span had a central tower 35 ft high, from which supports maintained the correct alignment of the structure. It took two men and a boy about five minutes to open the bridge, which weighed 70 tons and had to be moved by gearing operated by handwheels. An unpleasant mishap took place at the drawbridge on the night of 27 November 1851, when a passenger train collided with a cattle train, smashed three waggons, and lost

18 Account of ***Mr.*** Hoops received in

B - 2 - 3 - 4 - 5

Guildford Wharf ______________ ***to M***

Wharfinger.

Fig. 33.—Receipt for hoops at Guildford Wharf

its engine and tender down an embankment. The fireman was terribly injured and died without recovering consciousness. Two passengers were also hurt. The driver, Pemberton, whose negligence in disregarding the signals caused the accident, attempted to commit suicide by cutting his throat with a clasp knife; the guard got the knife away but the driver then broke clear and flung himself into the Arun, from which he was finally dragged ashore by the scruff of his coat.[91] After the inquest, the wretched Pemberton was sent for trial on a charge of manslaughter.

In 1862 a double-track 'lift-and-roll' iron drawbridge replaced the timber bridge to meet the heavier traffic requirements imposed by the building of the railway from Hardham junction to Ford. The bridge, designed by Jacomb-Hood, had a centre span 90 ft long although the navigable passage was in fact reduced to 40 ft. The opening of the bridge for river traffic generally meant that the line was blocked for at least half an hour as, before it could be moved, all wires passing over the bridge had to be disconnected by hand, the fishplates detached and the gas and water stopcocks turned off. Nine men were required to work the gear mechanism and a house had to be built close by on the east bank of the river to quarter the staff who were forced to perform the operation at all times and in all weathers. However, this rather laborious work had seldom to be carried out more than four or five times a week so that the bridge staff had also to undertake general maintenance duties. The bridge was strengthened in 1898, but otherwise remained unaltered until the gradual decrease of river traffic after the Great War made the moving span unnecessary and it was replaced by a fixed structure in 1938.[92]

On 8 June 1846 the railway was opened from Shoreham to Chichester and the Ford–Hunston section of the Portsmouth & Arundel Canal became defunct almost immediately, the only traffic remaining being the occasional delivery of coal and manure to waterside farms.[167] The Company ceased to hold annual general meetings after 1845, although they were formally advertised in the local press. Committee meetings stopped being regularly held in 1847, which I would regard as being the last year when the Ford–Hunston section was commercially used.[168] Certainly no tolls for this section appear to have been collected after this date. When in 1851 a general meeting was convened regarding the sale of some land in Portsea, a new clerk had to be appointed in place of his predecessor, who had died. The paucity of meetings must in fact have caused the various promoters of the railway bills to Bognor quite a problem.

Although the Portsea Canal had been closed in 1830, little, if any, of its land had been sold. However, in 1844 it was planned to use a short stretch of the bed near its terminal point for the extension of the railway from Havant to Portsmouth and reference was made to the fact that the waterway was both deserted and abandoned in the parliamentary proceedings.[93] The actual year when the Ford–Hunston section ceased to be navigable is more difficult to ascertain. It had fallen into semi-disuse before the opening of the railway to Chichester, for it was stated to a Parliamentary Committee that this part was used on average perhaps once a week.[94] John Rastrick, engineer of the London & Brighton Railway, stated in March 1846 that the canal was 'very little used' and that a proposed rival railway from Chichester to Bognor intended using part of the canal for their line.[95] It was his intention, however, to cross the canal near Woodgate by a bridge 12 ft above the surface of the water with a 25-ft span.

Mr Humphrey Brown, a traffic estimator, stated in connection with the Direct London & Portsmouth Railway bill, 1845, that 12,000 tons of merchandise passed between Portsmouth and Godalming and intermediate places by barge.[96] This estimate might lead one to believe that the Portsmouth & Arundel Canal still carried a fair amount of traffic. However, the canal was not mentioned by name and Brown admitted that the source of his information was solely the ledgers at Stonebridge wharf and at Godalming. During further cross-examination, he stated that 'goods went direct from Portsmouth to Godalming every day by water'. I doubt, and so did counsel for a rival railway company petitioning against the bill, whether this was true. The amount of cargo carried by water between the places situated on this route probably totalled this figure—2,905 tons being carried by the Arundel Lighter Company alone beyond Guildford and back in 1844—but the bulk of any traffic originating at Portsmouth came by coaster to Arundel and then up the Arun Navigation by barge, or by road to Godalming.

Nevertheless, De Salis in his *Chronology of Inland Navigation* (1897) states that the Ford–Hunston section did not fall into disuse until about 1853. However, the Bognor Railway Act of that year proposed crossing the line at North Mundham by a swing bridge with a 14-ft span only 2 ft above the water, and it is curious that no reference is made to the canal in the Act if the proprietors of the line had considered the bridge likely to be opened for barges. Yet in spite of a further Act in 1855 to extend the time required for the purchase of land, the railway was not begun. There is no reason to assume that this was because of the difficulty of negotiating with the moribund Canal Company, who appear to have taken no interest in the proceedings, no reply being given by the clerk as to assent or dissent to the scheme. Still, it would be interesting to know the reasons why, when the 1861 Act was passed for a railway from Barnham to Bognor, section 40 stipulated that a swing bridge should be built over the 'disused' portion of the canal and that if 'in the event of the navigation being required for water traffic or if converted into a road or railway', a penalty of £10 would be imposed on every occasion that the swing bridge impeded traffic. A similar clause was included in the Hayling Railways Act, 1860, which provided for ships and vessels 'Navigating the cut made by the Portsmouth & Arundel Navigation' to pass unhindered 'as reasonably required'. According to the clerk of the Company, no meetings of the Portsmouth & Arundel were held after 1855 and I think it must be concluded that these sections were either included by the promoting railway companies to protect their interests in the event of a possible revival of water traffic, or possibly after informal meetings with the main shareholders.

Disused does not, of course, mean unnavigable, but it is probable that the canal became impassable about 1856, which was the year that Stanton, the Bramley lock-keeper, was quoted as saying that the canal had last been used and which was in 1867 'trodden in by cattle, filled in in places and quite dry'.[97] The reference in the winding-up petition of 1888 also mentions that this section had not been used for 'thirty years and upwards'.[169]

In the middle forties, the years of the railway 'mania', a considerable number of railway lines were projected across Surrey and Sussex, one of which, had it come to fruition, would in all probability have caused the Wey & Arun to be closed many years earlier. In 1845 Portsmouth became the goal of three different railway companies, each of whom promoted bills—the London, Brighton & South Coast from Chichester, the London & South Western from Guildford, and the Direct London & Portsmouth from Epsom.

It was the last scheme which gave rise to the rumour, mentioned by Powell in a letter to George Marshall in November 1845, that the Wey & Arun was to be sold to a railway company. The plans of an alternative route drawn up in December show that the main line of the Direct London to Portsmouth Atmospheric Railway was intended to leave the London & Brighton at Redhill for Emsworth where it was to join the Brighton's extension to Portsmouth. *En route* its path lay by way of Cranleigh and along the banks of Vachery Pond before it crossed the Wey & Arun west of Loxwood and proceeded along a very rural route via Kirdford, North Chapel, and Selham. Branches were planned from West Dean to Chichester and from Loxwood to Guildford. This latter line was designed to cross the Wey & Arun twice, once just north of Compasses bridge and again between Bramley wharf and Gosden aqueduct. The three bridges over the canal would have had at least a 12-ft clearance, but since the line was to run almost directly parallel to the canal for 6 miles from Mill Farm at Hascombe to Shalford some approach must certainly have been made to the Canal Company. However, the minute books of the Wey & Arun are incomplete and the railway was never built, so I have been unable to trace whether any formal offer was made to purchase the canal. When six months later, in June 1846, the Direct London & Portsmouth

Railway obtained their Act, the branch to Chichester had been dropped and the route altered to start from Epsom and proceed via Leatherhead, Dorking (with a branch to Redhill), Albury, Wonersh, Bramley, Shalford, Godalming, and Haslemere to Portsmouth, where it was to use half a mile of the bed of the Portsea Canal before terminating at Landport Road. This new route would have crossed the Wey & Arun at Wonersh by a viaduct 160 yd long, rising 20 ft above the surface of the canal. Not surprisingly, perhaps, the Act also contained clauses to enable a tunnel to be built where the railway would pass near Lord Grantley's mansion at Wonersh Park, to provide for the fish ponds there to be crossed on piles, and to enable John Sparkes to sell Gosden House and ten acres of his property to the Company.

Not only the Wey & Arun, however, was in jeopardy. In December 1845, the Arun proprietors received notice of the Dorking, Brighton & Arundel Railway Company's intention of incorporating portions of the Arun Navigation towing-path between Wisborough Green and Coldwaltham into a line they proposed making from Dorking to Arundel and Littlehampton, but no application to Parliament was made. This is not surprising. The route chosen from Horsham involved no less than twelve bridges over the Arun and Rother Navigations between Pallingham and South Stoke as well as level-crossings close to Stopham and Houghton bridges. In July 1845 an Act had been passed for a railway from Three Bridges to Horsham, and in November 1846 concern was also being expressed as to how a projected Horsham–Chichester railway would affect the Arun Navigation. Several Acts were indeed obtained for railways which were in fact never commenced. The financial difficulties which brought about the collapse of the 'mania' prevented work even being started on the Direct London & Portsmouth (whose estimated cost was £1½ million) and it was not until a later Act was passed in 1859 that this line was built via Guildford.

Although both the northern and southern perimeters of the London and Portsmouth water route were by 1850 circumscribed by railways, the local traffic of the Wey & Arun and the Arun was not directly threatened. Nevertheless, the general economic depression of the early forties, coupled with the loss of traffic from the Wey Navigation and the growing competition from door-to-door land transport, caused receipts for both navigations to drop substantially. The record results declared by both Companies in the summer of 1840 had dwindled by one-third within three years, and although

REDUCED RATE OF TOLLS *payable on the Wey & Arun Junction Canal.*

FOR all Coals, Corn, Timber, and Poles (when there is no Draft on either the Summit Pond or Reservoir) in Barges of all sizes	*3s. ⅌ Ton, for the whole Line.*
For the same Goods (when there is such Draft) in all Barges under 30 Tons burden . .	*4s. 6d ditto.*
Ditto, ... in all Barges of 30 Tons, and upwards .	*3s. ditto*
For Bark and Hoops, at all times in Barges of not less than 40 Tons, fully laden . .	*3s. ditto*
Ditto, ... for any distance less than the whole line	*2d.-halfpenny ⅌ Ton ⅌ Mile*
For all Timber and other Articles above-mentioned (except coals) when there is no Draft as above, in Barges of all sizes not passing the whole Line, such Tonnage not exceeding 3s. ⅌ Ton in the whole	*Ditto*
For all Timber and other Articles above-mentioned (except Coals) when there is such Draft in Barges of not less than 30 Tons burden, not passing the whole line of Canal, such Tonnage not exceeding 3s. ⅌ Ton in the whole	*Ditto*
Ditto in Barges of less than 30 Tons burden not passing the whole Line of Canal, such Tonnage not exceeding 4s. 6d. ⅌ Ton in the whole	*3d. ditto*
For all Dung and Ashes and for all Chalk, Marle, Stone, Slate, Bricks, Tiles, Sand, Lime and Lime-stone, whether used for Manure, or not, and for all other Articles to be used for manuring Lands, in Barges of not less than 30 Tons burden . . .	*Three-half-pence ⅌ Ton ⅌ Mile*
Ditto, . . . in Barges of less than 30 Tons burden	*2d. ditto, ditto*
For all other Goods, Wares, Merchandize, and Commodities whatsoever	*3d. ditto, ditto*
For every empty or light Vessel of any sort, and for every such Vessel carrying not more than 6 Tons of Manure, or 4 Tons of any other lading, for each of the first Locks at each end of the Line of Canal, when there is no Draft as above . .	*One Shilling*
For every such Vessel, when there is such Draft, for each of the 6 Locks at each end of the Line of Canal	*One Shilling*

N. B. The Tonnage per Mile for any distance short of the whole Line of Canal, is in no case to exceed the Amount of Toll for the whole Line.

Guildford, 25. May, 1822. JOHN SMALLPEICE,

Clerk to the Company.

Fig. 34.—Wey & Arun Canal Company toll rates, 1822

TOLLS CHARGED ON DIFFERENT GOODS,

ON THE WEY AND ARUN JUNCTION CANAL.

		S	D	
Coal	at	2	0	per Ton for the whole line,
	or	0	2½	per Ton per Mile, not to exceed 2*s* 3*d* for the whole line.
Timber, Hoops, Bark, and Corn . .	at	2	3	per Ton for the whole line,
	or	0	2½	per Ton per Mile, not to exceed 2*s* 3*d* per Ton for the whole line.
Grocery	at	2	3	per Ton for the whole line,
	or	0	2¼	per Ton per Mile.
Fire Wood	at	1	1½	per Ton for the whole line,
	or	0	1½	per Ton per Mile, not to exceed 1*s* 1½*d* per Ton for the whole line.
Chalk and Lime	at	0	1½	per Ton per Mile.
Manure from London	at	0	1	per Ton per Mile for the whole line.
Sea Gravel and Sea Weed	at	1	0	per Ton for the whole line,
	or	0	1	per Ton per Mile, not to exceed 1*s* per Ton for the whole line.

Light Barges 1*s* at each of the first Locks at each end of the line of Canal.

Timber, Hoops, Bark, & Corn, DURING SHORT WATER.

		S	D	
In Barges not having 15 Tons	at	4	6	per Ton for the whole line,
	or	0	3	per Ton per Mile, not to exceed 4*s* 6*d* per Ton for the whole line
Except as back carriage to pass	at	2	3	per Ton for the whole line,
	or	0	2½	per Ton per Mile, not to exceed 2*s* 3*d* per Ton for the whole line.

Light Barges 1*s* at each of the Three Locks at each end of the Line of Canal.

Guildford 1st June 1844 John Smallpeice Clerk

[Russells, Printers.]

Fig. 35.—Wey & Arun Canal Company toll rates, 1844

the years immediately following the opening of the L.B. & S.C.R. (formed in 1846) had caused no material decrease in the Arun tolls, they fell again by 20 per cent in 1849 and were to fall by a further third by the end of 1852, in which year receipts from the Arun dropped below £1,000 for the first time since 1820 (or possibly 1795). Receipts from the Wey & Arun also steadily diminished, averaging £1,235 per annum between 1846–50 compared with £1,610 per annum during the previous five years, which, however, represented a decrease in tonnage of only 1,500 tons to around 15,000.

TOLLS

PAYABLE ON THE WEY AND ARUN JUNCTION CANAL,

On and after the 1st June, 1855.

	s d		d		s d	
COALS..............	at 1 0	℔ ton passing the whole line,	or 1	per ton ℔ mile not to exceed	1 0	℔ ton
TIMBER............	at 2 0	℔ ton ditto	or 2	per ton ℔ mile not to exceed	2 0	do.
GROCERY..........	at 1 6	℔ ton ditto	or 1½	per ton ℔ mile not to exceed	1 6	do.
BARK..............	at 1 6	℔ ton ditto	or 1½	per ton ℔ mile not to exceed	1 6	do.
HOOPS & CORN....	at 1 6	℔ ton ditto	or 1½	per ton ℔ mile not to exceed	1 6	do.
SLATE & IRON	at 1 6	℔ ton ditto	or 1½	per ton ℔ mile not to exceed	1 6	do.
BRICKS & TILES ..	at 1 0	℔ ton ditto	or 1	per ton ℔ mile not to exceed	1 0	do.
CHALK & LIME....	at 1 6	℔ ton ditto	or 1	per ton ℔ mile not to exceed	1 6	do.
FIRE WOOD	at 1 6	℔ ton ditto	or 1½	per ton ℔ mile not to exceed	1 6	do.
SEA GRAVEL AND SEA WEED	at 1 3	℔ ton ditto	or 1	per ton ℔ mile not to exceed	1 3	do.

DUNG (from London) at 1d. per ton per mile—not to exceed 1s. per ton for the **whole line.**

LIGHT BARGES 1s. AT EACH END OF THE LINE OF CANAL.

Fig. 36.—Wey & Arun Canal Company toll rates, 1855

There was no real remedy, but in an endeavour to keep their share of the local trade various experiments were tried by way of lessening toll dues. In 1842 the Wey & Arun toll on groceries was lowered by ¼d. a mile and a ton of seaweed—newly introduced as manure—could pass through the line for 1s. This latter charge appeared to meet with some success, for during three subsequent winter months 220 tons were carried inland, including 130 tons to Guildford and 43 tons to Bramley.* Reductions from 2s. 7½d. to 2s. 3d. a ton were made the following year on general merchandise and for one year it was decided to allow a 100 per cent rebate for barges loaded with over 6 tons of back-carriage. Some toll rates fluctuated a great deal. That, for instance, on coal, which formed

* The seaweed trade ran into difficulties in 1846 when the Duke of Norfolk forbade fishermen to remove it from Littlehampton beach.

the largest item carried on the canal, dropped from 3d. a ton-mile in 1822 to 1½d. in 1844, 1¼d. in 1849, and 1d. in 1850.

Not unnaturally, some navigation companies were reluctant to make toll concessions and were accused by the merchants and carriers of being blind to their own interests in view of rail and road development. This attitude was well illustrated by a meeting of coal and timber merchants, millers, barge and mill owners held in January 1845 in the Council Chamber at Guildford to 'memorialize' the proprietors of the Wey Navigation. It was pointed out

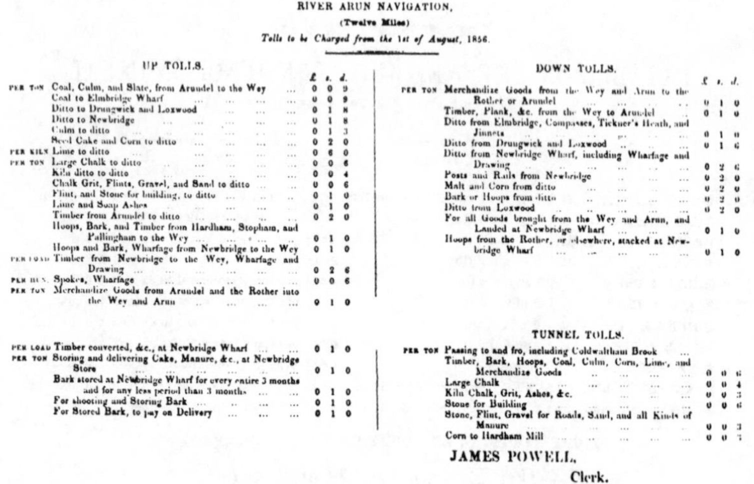

RIVER ARUN NAVIGATION,

(Twelve Miles)

Tolls to be Charged from the 1st of August, 1856.

UP TOLLS.

		£	s.	d.
PER TON	Coal, Culm, and Slate, from Arundel to the Wey	0	0	9
	Coal to Elmbridge Wharf	0	0	9
	Ditto to Drungwick and Loxwood	0	1	8
	Ditto to Newbridge	0	1	8
	Culm to ditto	0	1	3
	Seed Cake and Corn to ditto	0	2	0
PER KILN	Lime to ditto	0	6	0
PER TON	Large Chalk to ditto	0	0	6
	Kiln ditto to ditto	0	0	4
	Chalk Grit, Flints, Gravel, and Sand to ditto	0	0	6
	Flint, and Stone for building, to ditto	0	1	0
	Lime and Soap Ashes	0	1	0
	Timber from Arundel to ditto	0	2	0
	Hoops, Bark, and Timber from Hardham, Stopham, and Pallingham to the Wey	0	1	0
	Hoops and Bark, Wharfage from Newbridge to the Wey	0	1	0
PER LOAD	Timber from Newbridge to the Wey, Wharfage and Drawing	0	2	6
PER HUN.	Spokes, Wharfage	0	0	6
PER TON	Merchandize Goods from Arundel and the Rother into the Wey and Arun	0	1	0
PER LOAD	Timber converted, &c., at Newbridge Wharf	0	1	0
PER TON	Storing and delivering Cake, Manure, &c., at Newbridge Store	0	1	0
	Bark stored at Newbridge Wharf for every entire 3 months and for any less period than 3 months	0	1	0
	For shooting and Storing Bark	0	1	0
	For Stored Bark, to pay on Delivery	0	1	0

DOWN TOLLS.

		£	s.	d.
PER TON	Merchandize Goods from the Wey and Arun to the Rother or Arundel	0	1	0
	Timber, Plank, &c. from the Wey to Arundel	0	1	0
	Ditto from Elmbridge, Compasses, Tickner's Heath, and Jinnets	0	1	0
	Ditto from Drungwick and Loxwood	0	1	6
	Ditto from Newbridge Wharf, including Wharfage and Drawing	0	2	6
	Posts and Rails from Newbridge	0	2	0
	Malt and Corn from ditto	0	2	0
	Bark or Hoops from ditto	0	2	0
	Ditto from Loxwood	0	2	0
	For all Goods brought from the Wey and Arun, and Landed at Newbridge Wharf	0	1	0
	Hoops from the Rother, or elsewhere, stacked at Newbridge Wharf	0	1	0

TUNNEL TOLLS.

		£	s.	d.
PER TON	Passing to and fro, including Coldwaltham Brook			
	Timber, Bark, Hoops, Coal, Culm, Corn, Lime, and Merchandize Goods	0	0	6
	Large Chalk	0	0	4
	Kiln Chalk, Grit, Ashes, &c.	0	0	3
	Stone for Building	0	0	6
	Stone, Flint, Gravel for Roads, Sand, and all Kinds of Manure	0	0	3
	Corn to Hardham Mill	0	0	3

JAMES POWELL,

Clerk.

Fig. 37.—Arun Navigation toll rates, 1856

that, unless toll reductions were granted, trade would be transferred to the newly opened railway leaving 'the barge owners scarcely anything to do, their barges a valueless burden to them and their men going to the Parish'. Criticisms were levelled at the proprietors for doing nothing to assist the millers on the Wey to compete with the London millers, who were using steam power; cheaper rates would, it was said, encourage timber from the neighbourhood of Pulborough, Petworth, and Midhurst 'which now goes to Arundel' to be brought by inland navigation rather than by sea to London. An immense quantity of hoops was being carted to London by waggons and were 'the owners of coppice lands generally enabled to send them to London at a reduced rate, there is no doubt but a much larger quantity would be made, instead of cutting so much stuff into faggots. The same applies to spokes, fellies, posts, and rails which might be cut out of small timber otherwise consumed at home as firing.'

By reducing the toll on manure the merchants felt confident that not only would a greater quantity be brought down from London but more agricultural produce would be sent up, and this would encourage farmers to grow more mangel-wurzels for sale in the waterside markets in the Borough and Hungerford. Furthermore, it was clearly short-sighted policy that farmers should have to pay 6d. a ton on seaweed as soon as it entered the Wey Navigation, when it cost as little as 1s. 6d. a ton to carry it all the way from Littlehampton to Stonebridge, a distance of over 40 miles.

Another grievance was that the toll to Guildford was the same as to places 7 or 8 miles nearer the Thames and while this had been done to compete with coals coming from the Wey & Arun, it was small comfort to merchants who had to pay the same rate for coal coming only 4 or 5 miles from the Thames. There was, in fact, said the petitioners, hardly one single commodity, ranging from linseed oil, iron, and rags for paper making, on which the tolls could not be usefully lowered—and the Wey Commissioners soon had no alternative but to do this. The Godalming Navigation also reduced the toll on hoops by a third in 1845 and sanctioned reductions on a wide range of goods (including bargate stone) in 1850 and 1852 when it was reported that 'a falling off of traffic on the Wey & Arun had made Stonebridge Wharf scarcely self-supporting'.

Similar concessions had to be made on the Arun Navigation. At the request of several timber merchants, the toll on timber was reduced from Newbridge to Pallingham in 1844, but the anticipated increase in traffic did not materialize as timber could almost as easily be carted to and shipped from Pallingham quay, in which event only tolls for using the tunnel were chargeable. It was therefore agreed to increase the tunnel toll to 9d. since barges could only proceed by Pulborough when there was 'plenty of water'. In 1845 goods were charged 1s. a ton as far as Cranleigh and 9d. a ton if bound for London. In July 1847 it was agreed to permit guano and ammonia to be stored at Newbridge, but four weeks later the merchant was allowed to erect his own store-room since 'the guano in the Company store is very offensive'. The toll on oil-cake was reduced in 1848 and that on slate in the following year. However, reduced toll rates halted the drift in cargoes away from the Wey & Arun and the Arun only at the expense of diminishing income.

In 1849 the Godalming Navigation reported that the bark traffic had been lost to the railroad[98] and by 1850 the situation had so deteriorated that it was the belief of the Arun proprietors that unless steps were taken to compete with the railway companies the business of the navigations would very much decrease. Letters were written to the adjoining navigations and a collective reduction in tolls suggested which must have produced some results, for the toll on all traffic from the Arun and Rother to the Thames was lowered to 6d. a ton. An analysis of merchandise carried on the Wey & Arun in 1850 showed that coal barges represented half the total traffic but only 45 per cent of income. The table was as follows:

Cargo	*Tonnage* (*tons*)	*All Cargoes* (*per cent*)	*Tolls* (*£*)	*All Tolls* (*per cent*)
Coal	7,488	49½	468	45
Timber	3,810	25	286	27½
Groceries	1,172	8	73	7
Hoops	1,120	7½	70	7
Corn	131	1	8	1
Sundries	1,400	9	131	12½
Total	15,121	100	1,036	100

Canal companies all over the country had seen their shares steadily decline in value as the railways began to carry a larger and larger proportion of freight traffic. Wey & Arun shares, which had stood at £25 in 1840, had fallen to £10 within a decade and barely fetched 65s. in 1860. On the other hand, although shares of the Arun Navigation, which had been standing at £200 in 1840, had dropped to £120 by 1851, they still fetched £75 in 1861 and £50 in 1869, in which year the Company were still paying a small dividend, although their traffic had been adversely affected by the opening of the railway along the Rother to Petworth (1859) and Midhurst (1866) and the extension of the line from Pulborough to Ford in 1863.

One of the reasons advanced for extending the Wey Navigation to Godalming had been the carriage of gunpowder from the Chilworth powder mills. The Act of 1760 stated that no barges with 28 lb or more of gunpowder might lie within half a mile of Guildford under penalty of £5, and it was the usual practice for barges laden at Stonebridge with 10 or 20 tons of powder to come down by day and moor for the night just below Stoke lock. A report in the local press, however, reveals that this was not always done.

One winter's night about 1862 a barge loaded at Stonebridge wharf and bound for Barking arrived at Guildford, and the boatman, to be near his home, moored his boat at the wharf just below High Street bridge. About 9 o'clock a fire broke out in Smith's timber yard only 50 yd downstream—a fire that extended to the water's edge and destroyed the contents of the yard. The officers of the navigation, hurrying to the fire, discovered to their horror the proximity of the fateful barge which was transgressing the law. The boatman, ordered to remove it, could only contemplate advance and exclaimed, 'You would not have me pass by that fire?'

COALS!

LONDON & SOUTH-WESTERN RAILWAY STATION

Guildford.

MESSRS. E. & A. PRIOR

Continue to supply Coals, Coke, &c., of the best quality, at the lowest Market Prices.

TERMS:—CASH.

All orders executed with punctuality addressed to Mr. MOUNTAIN, Railway Station, or No. 2, Farnham Road, Guildford.

Fig. 38.—Guildford coal merchant's advertisement, c. 1850

Made to retrace his steps, he went back under the bridge and Guildford escaped what might have been severe destruction.

It was not long after the Guildford scare that a grim tragedy did occur, a forerunner of the better-known Regent's Park explosion of 1874. One fine August day in 1864, a newly delivered barge—the last, incidentally, to be built at the Pallingham boatyard—belonging to Samuel Sharpe of Chilworth, had been loaded with gunpowder at Stonebridge wharf, and was only a mile or so from the mills when an explosion took place which was distinctly heard as far away as Pallingham. The two men on board were blown to pieces and the vessel sank. It was no more possible to ascertain the cause of the disaster than it was to explain the one which occurred ten years later. Such were the hazards of the gunpowder trade. Nevertheless, these dangerous cargoes continued to be carried by water to the magazines at Woolwich, Purfleet, and Barking Creek until 1921.

During the period covered by this chapter, various changes in the management of the navigations had occurred. On the death of Lord Egremont the chairmanship of the Wey & Arun had passed to James Mangles, M.P., until 1838, to John King of Loxwood until 1844, and then to William Newland of Guildford. In 1848 John Smallpeice retired and was succeeded as clerk by W. Haydon Smallpeice; and so the father who helped to give birth to the project for uniting the two rivers passed on his responsibilities to his son, who was to see the canal's darkest days and, as the official liquidator, watch its demise.

In May 1842 William Cutfield, the treasurer and largest shareholder in the Arun Navigation, died. No new chairman of the Arun had been appointed after Lord Egremont's death, but there was no doubt that, both before and after the Earl's death, Cutfield had been the driving force behind the Company. The minutes refer to his 'unremitting attention to the management of the navigation and the necessity of forming a management committee to fulfil what Mr Cutfield had gratuitously performed'. Henceforth, a three-man Management Committee were to meet biannually until the election of William Shaft as chairman in 1855.

The general managers, too, were growing old. In 1857 James Stanton ceased to be superintendent of the Wey & Arun after 38 years' service. His successor, Thomas Pullen, went to live in the Company's cottage by Elm Bridge Wharf, where he was later referred to in the House of Lords as having kept a shop 'or something of that kind' and whose services were according to Richard Holmes 'entirely useless'. In the summer of 1856 Richard Seward, who had been superintendent of the Arun since 1825, had his salary increased to £105 p.a. 'in consideration of his long service and of his being liable to an increased income tax'. By the end of the year, however, the proprietors are expressing their regret at the decease of their 'old and valuable wharfinger'. In 1857 John Sprinks was chosen as his successor at a salary of £75 p.a. after six applicants had been interviewed. Sprinks' appointment was a great success and he combined a great number of offices in one. Holmes described him 'as a very acute and intelligent kind of man, which I did not find the generality of people on the Wey & Arun were except the clerk'.

As the 1860s drew near, the expansion of the network of railways in Surrey and Sussex continued apace and plans were afoot to construct three branches which would come into direct competition with the navigations. The first to be built was the Mid-Sussex line which was opened from Horsham to Pulborough and Petworth in October 1859.* The Arun proprietors had tried more than two years previously to come to some arrangement with the railway Company and rather optimistically had offered to withdraw their opposition to the bill if the Company would agree to make up any deficiency between receipts and expenditure of the navigation which prevented the payment of a 5 per cent dividend in any year after the opening of the railway.[170] Since only $5\frac{1}{2}$ per cent had been paid for the previous year it was hardly surprising that this offer was not even entertained; the only alternative was for the Arun to petition against the bill in an attempt to procure compensation. In this they were entirely unsuccessful, the House of Lords' Committee ruling that the Canal Company had no right to be heard against the preamble, only the clauses. The promoters had originally intended to build their line from Horsham to Billingshurst with branches to Petworth and Pulborough. However, this former branch, which would have crossed 18 ft above the Arun Canal a short distance above Orfold lock, was strongly opposed by Colonel Wyndham on the ground of the line's proximity to Petworth House. Consequently, the line was made direct to Pulborough and built along the south bank of the Rother via Hardham to Petworth. The river Arun was bridged by a single span of 120 ft at Pulborough, and Hardham canal tunnel crossed only 8 ft above its crown. As a result the Rother Navigation and the Petworth estate were spared interference, but the townspeople of Petworth had a mighty long walk to the station, which was situated by Coultershaw wharf.

The building of the Mid-Sussex Railway brought increased revenue to both the Arun and the Wey & Arun and even when completed took little traffic from the Arun, for whom the main blow was the authorization, on 23 July 1860, of the extension from Hardham through the Arun valley to Ford, by the L.B. & S.C.R. (Deviations) Act.[171] However, this new line brought one benefit to the navigation. In order to save the expense of two swing bridges over the sharp bend in the Arun at Offham, the railway Company had to cut a new channel for the river which, while enabling them to build fixed bridges, reduced the distance by water between Bury

* Shortly after the line was opened an engine ran away from Petworth after her boiler had been lit and left with the regulator wide open. She was steaming slowly through Horsham with the remains of three sets of crossing gates on her buffers when she was caught.

wharf and Arundel by three-quarters of a mile. It was also intended to build a tramway from Arundel station to the wharves on the east bank of the Arun, but this was never constructed.

A few days later, on 6 August, Parliament sanctioned the building of a branch line from Horsham to Guildford; thus it came to pass

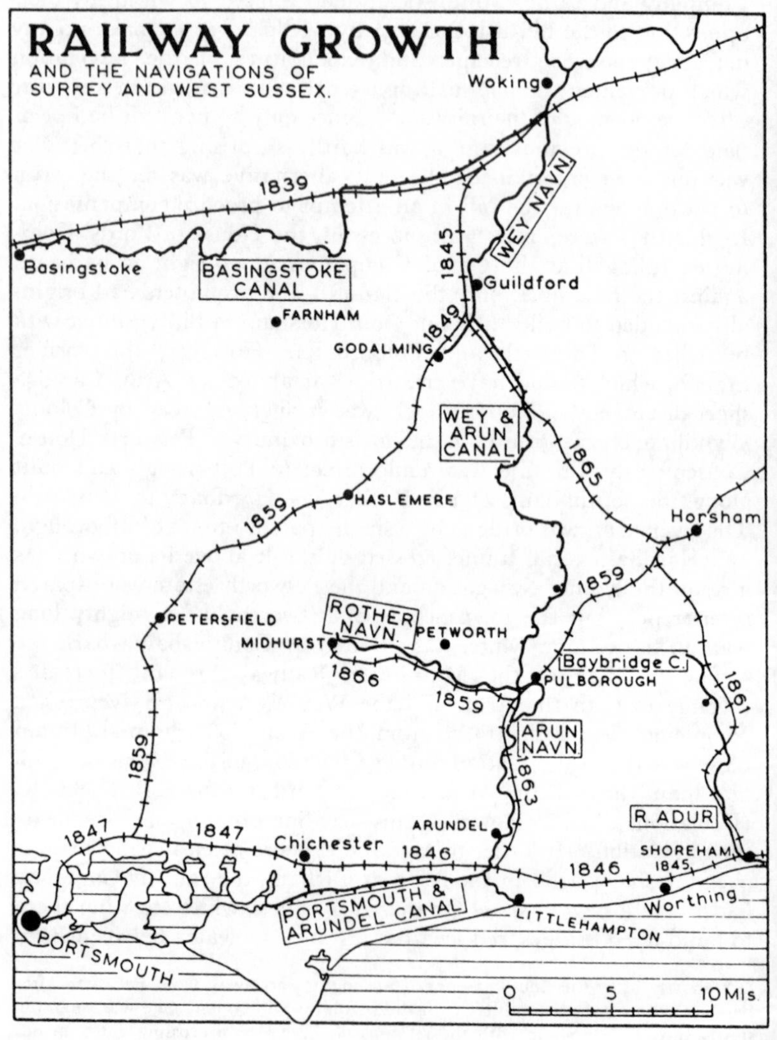

Map 11

RIVER WEY NAVIGATION
FOR SALE.

TO PUBLIC COMPANIES, CARRIERS, CONTRACTORS,
AND PERSONS CONCERNED IN A LARGE TRAFFIC IN GOODS AND MERCHANDISE.

To be Sold by Auction,

IN THE MONTH OF FEBRUARY OR MARCH NEXT,
Under an Order of the High Court of Chancery, in a Cause of "LANGTON v. LANGTON," unless previously disposed of by Private Contract, of which Notice will be given.

ONE MOIETY OF THE NAVIGATION
Known as the River Wey, running from the Thames at or near Weybridge, to the Basingstoke Canal at Guildford, in the County of Surrey.

ONE MOIETY OF THE TOLL
Of 2½d. in every 4s. received on the Gross Tonnage.

ONE-FOURTH OF THE GROATS OR TOLL
Of 4d., and 11/22nd parts of the Toll of 4d.

The above may be purchased as One Lot, and comprises the entire of One Moiety of the Navigation and the Tolls and Profits thereon, and produces on the average

A NET INCOME OF ABOUT £700 A YEAR.

Fig. 40.—Wey Navigation Auction Particulars, c. 1862

WEY AND ARUN JUNCTION CANAL.

ABSTRACT OF ACCOUNTS FOR THE YEAR ENDED MAY 1ST, 1864.

		£	s.	d.			£	s.	d.
1863. May 1	To balance in the hands of the Treasurer ..	181	8	5	1864. Apr. 30	By Payments, viz.—			
1864.	Received for Tolls on the Canal during the					Clerk's Salary	50	0	0
	Year	917	19	2		Thomas Pullen, Superintendent	54	19	[illegible]
	" for Rents of Wharfs	40	12	6		Chas. Baverstock, Collector, Lock-keeper,			
	" from the Horsham and Guildford					&c.	41	17	4
	Direct Railway Company, for Compen-					William Stanton, ditto	10	0	0
	sation	600	0	0		Repairs and Incidental Charges	184	11	8
	" for Sale of Sedge Grass	5	0	0		Taxes, Tithes, &c.	83	17	5
						Rents of Reservoir, Wharfs, &c.	173	14	11
						Law Expenses	14	8	4
						Printing, Advertising, Stationery, &c	3	5	2
						Dividends paid on			
						5 Shares for 1857 ...... 1 5 0			
						5 " " 1858 ...... 1 17 6			
						5 " " 1859 ...... 1 17 6			
						5 " " 1860 ...... 1 5 0			
						5 " " 1861 ...... 1 5 0			
						826 " " 1863 ...... 206 10 0			
							214	0	0
						Balance in Treasurer's hands	914	6	3
		1745	0	1			[illegible]	[illegible]	1

Fig. 41.—Wey & Arun Junction Canal Abstract of Accounts, 1864

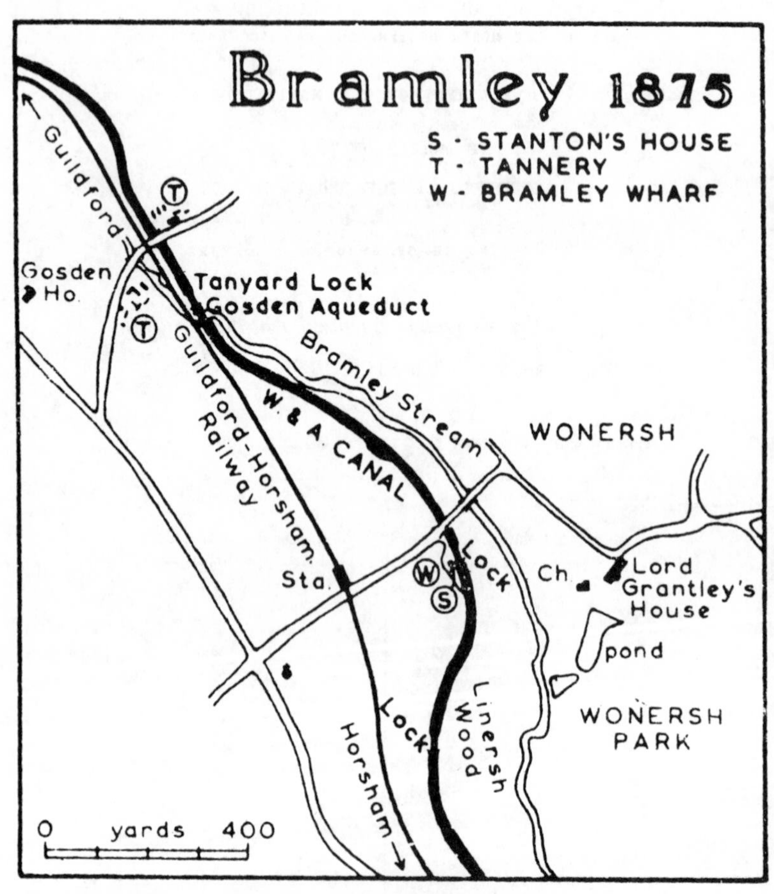
Bramley 1875
S - STANTON'S HOUSE
T - TANNERY
W - BRAMLEY WHARF
Guildford
Gosden Ho.
Tanyard Lock
Gosden Aqueduct
Bramley Stream
Guildford-Horsham Railway
W. & A. CANAL
WONERSH
Sta.
Lock
Ch.
Lord Grantley's House
pond
WONERSH PARK
Lock
Linersh Wood
Horsham
0 yards 400

Map 12

CHAPTER XIII

Pleasure Boating

Pre-1850—boating on the Thames—first passenger steamer 1844—*The Oarsman's Guide* (1857)—pleasure boats on the Wey & Arun—Dashwood's account of a voyage from the Thames to the Solent in 1867—its uniqueness—impressions and adventures *en route* from Weybridge to Littlehampton.

THE presence of pleasure craft upon the waters of Wey and Arun was rare until the latter half of the nineteenth century. In the accounts of the opening of the Portsmouth & Arundel Canal, both the Duke of Norfolk and the Earl of Egremont are reported as having sailed in their own pleasure barges but, without evidence to the contrary, it can be presumed that these were ordinary barges specially decked out for the occasion, which reverted to normal commercial use after the celebrations were over. The earliest references to pleasure boats on the Wey date back to before 1800 and tolls appear to have been collected fairly regularly. For instance, eight pleasure, five fishing, and two sailing boats passed through Thames lock in 1830 and tolls were also taken for four pleasure boats at Guildford.[172] Sometimes barges themselves carried these boats as cargo. In 1828 the *London* carried a half-ton pleasure boat to Send, in 1830 the *Sovereign* brought one from Arundel to London, and in 1833 the *Southampton*, coming from Portsmouth, unloaded one at Stoke. On one occasion in August 1829, with a view to drawing public attention to the practicability of operating passage boats between Portsmouth and London, the *Portmore* went on an all-day excursion cruise from Guildford with forty of the local gentry on board. Two horses towed the barge, four musicians played, and, according to Hodgson, 'everybody seemed determined to be happy and expressed their thanks to the proprietors of the navigation for thus enabling them to do that which they had never before had the opportunity of doing'.[138] In May 1838 the Wey & Arun Collectors' accounts mention that James Carter paid 1s. for taking a pleasure boat from Loves bridge to the Arun Canal. It is also recorded that Lord Henry Cholmondeley ('Chumney' in the Wey ledgers) brought his yacht up from Littlehampton through the Wey & Arun to the Thames. Whether his craft was in need of repairs, or whether Lord Henry was in search of some mild *divertissement* is pure surmise upon which it is interesting to speculate, since he was the only owner of a pleasure vessel to be specifically mentioned in the Wey registers.

On the Thames, tolls had first been introduced for pleasure craft above Staines in 1771 (1s. for four-oared row-boats and 6d. for skiffs and punts), but it was not until May 1829 that the Thames Commissioners instructed lock-keepers to bring these receipts into their accounts. However, this practice was discontinued the following year, presumably not only because of the negligible amount, but because of the dissatisfaction of the lock-keepers, who regarded them as 'perks'.[101] In 1844 the 60-ton *Locomotive* became the first passenger steamer to use the Thames above Teddington. This vessel created quite a furore, on the one hand because her wash was damaging the towpath and undermining riverside lawns, on the other because the City Corporation claimed she was liable for tolls, whereas her owners classed her as a pleasure boat.[102]

Boats could sometimes be hired on the Wey and at some villages bordering the lower reaches of the Arun, but the only 'boating stations' established along the canal consisted of Stanton's skiffs at Bramley and a few punts at Cranleigh. Even on the Thames most forms of boating were associated with athletic activity rather than pleasurable pastime and the only regular sporting venture on the Wey & Arun was that indulged in by young urchins who swam there naked on summer afternoons. So regular a practice had this become that, when in 1819 the second Portsmouth & Arundel Canal Act was passed, a clause was inserted to prohibit such frivolity under penalty of fine or imprisonment. Indeed, so serious a view was taken of the matter that any witness could lawfully 'apprehend and deliver the person into the custody of a peace officer', who could then issue a warrant for the victim's arrest.

Canalside residents were entitled under the Act to build their own boat-houses and moorings and could use their skiffs toll-free providing no locks were drawn, but little advantage was taken of this concession. Some farmers possessed a 'boat of husbandry', others had punts but, except in the grounds of Whipley Manor, no boat-house was ever erected. The toll of 1s. a lock did, of course, make a through journey very expensive and it was not until 1856 that the Management Committee, while deciding that the 1s. lock fee should continue, conceded a maximum charge of 10s. instead of 18s. On the Wey 1s. a lock was also demanded, but the through passage could be made for 5s. On the Arun Navigation pleasure boats paid 1s. whether they passed through one or all the locks and this toll remained unchanged until 1868, when an investigation was carried out, which resulted in the Committee deciding that small boats and canoes should be charged 2s. and steamers 5s.

It was not in fact until the late 1850s, when a new edition of *The Oarsman's Guide*[103] informed the aquatic public that a trip from the Isis to the Arun was a feasible proposition, that the pleasure boat began to make its short incursion into the canal's history. The *Guide* was dedicated to the Oxford University Boat Club as a small tribute to their skill in the art of rowing and the success of the first edition had prompted the author subsequently to include descriptions of the Thames' tributaries. The editor stated in the preface that he was 'sincerely desirous to promote the practice of rowing, believing that long trips like those recommended in these pages, are good for body and soul, and promote sound and practical philosophy, in improving the health and bodily vigour, and in sweetening the blood and the tempers of men to no mean extent; and he will be much obliged if at any time the errors of this work should be pointed out, and additions and alterations suggested, that the benefit of a useful hint should not be lost hereafter.' This tiny guide-book (less than 3 in. square) devoted several pages to describing the Wey to Arun route, tendering advice on such matters as accommodation, tackle, lock-keepers, and the opening of locks. At Send Heath, for instance, the voyager was informed that there were two or three beds to be found at the 'New Inn public house', and that 'Uncle Tom's Cabin' was recommended for beer. The chance of finding a bed in the 'Sea Horse' at Shalford must have sounded attractive, but the pleasure boatman was warned that the 'Onslow Arms' at Loxwood—'three beds or so'—was the only stopping-place between Bramley and Pulborough, that water was very scarce, and that passing through the locks in Sidney Wood was the 'great grind of the trip'. As their pounds had to be left empty, progress became extremely slow when descending and it was suggested that the quickest method of passing them was to take two winches and send your more energetic companion running on ahead to prepare the next lock for the boat's entry. The lock-keeper at Bramley had to be forewarned of each intended journey, since there was no one resident at Stonebridge to provide a winch for opening the different system of locks on the canal. Lastly, the adventurer was ominously reminded 'not to forget a tow-line and spar to track with, as weeds are abundant and the water sometimes low'.

This not altogether encouraging counsel was followed by a detailed itinerary, together with the tolls and estimated times for the journey, which were given as:

Stage	*Distance* (*miles*)	*Locks*	*Toll* (*s.*)	*Estimated Rowing Time* (*hours*)
Weybridge–Guildford	15½	10	5	6
Guildford–Loxwood	14½	20	3	7
Loxwood–Pulborough	13	8	1	5
Pulborough–Midhurst	12½	8	1	5
Pulborough–Littlehampton	20	Tidal	None	4*
Pulborough–Littlehampton (via Hardham tunnel)	18	3	1	4*

* with tide

While some Victorian families were content to spend sunny summer afternoons peacefully in a punt, the more youthful and daring embarked on adventures of their own. Exploits of yesteryear are even now recounted. In rural riverside inns, aged locals may still recall simple stories like that of the Dark Blue who sculled his way from Oxford to Midhurst, or of Grandmama who, when sweet sixteen, was reprimanded for allowing her young man to take her through Hardham tunnel unchaperoned and without a torch. There are tales, too, of those who, in the canal's last days, had to carry their boats round the locks and spend time and energy dragging them through the reeds. It is doubtful if much of pleasure boating is, or indeed was, *per se* a pleasure. In any case, it is evident that those more desirous of sailing preferred the breezes and hazards of the open sea to the placidity of the canal, whose shallow draught, locks, and low bridges offered little enough attraction, even as a short cut home.

The latter part of the 1860s and the 1870s saw a noticeable growth in the popularity of boating. Pleasure boat tolls on the Wey, which had amounted to only £5 in 1830 and £8 in 1860, rose to £17 in 1867 and £30 in 1870 and reached £60 in 1874. In 1864 the Thames Commissioners considered the possibility of reintroducing tolls on pleasure craft and instituted an enquiry as to what the annual return might be under this head, for which purpose the keepers were instructed to keep daily accounts.[104] In 1867 a tax on pleasure boats was discussed and lock tickets for pleasure craft introduced. In the same year the Commissioners of the

Godalming Navigation introduced annual licences for 6s. and day tickets for 1s. Several incidents arose through lock-keepers having trouble with those who tried to portage their canoes and small boats at the locks to avoid payment of tolls, a state of affairs not remedied until an Act of 1878.

Tourists were never greatly encouraged by the Wey & Arun authorities to use the canal, nor for that matter were they by other canal managements, since the amateur oarsman was apt, through carelessness or ignorance, to interfere with barge traffic.* He was known to cause obstructions and to waste water as a result of inexperienced lock working. On the other hand, toll rates for pleasure craft were comparatively high and the Wey & Arun could not fail to appreciate that, at a time when commercial traffic was rapidly on the wane, any boat owner was a source of revenue whom they could ill afford to discourage. Through rates were accordingly reduced to 5s. for sailing boats and 2s. for skiffs. However, the Company began to receive more reports of water being wasted. There was no doubt which class of user was thought responsible, but it may have been an idle lock-keeper who closed the canal for six weeks in the summer of 1866 by leaving one of the lock paddles drawn at the summit.† Nevertheless, to prevent further loss, notice was given in July 1866 'that no pleasure boat, steam boat or other vessel be allowed to pass this canal without an experienced man who is acquainted with the navigation'. The pilot's fee was generally 10s. and, in consequence, the tourist virtually disappeared from the canal. So little known did the route remain, that in 1868 an account of an exploration of the dying waterway was published for half-a-crown.

The Thames to the Solent by Canal and Sea, or the Log of the Una Boat 'Caprice' was written by J. B. Dashwood with the intention of making known a novel way of spending a holiday afloat. The narrative is of particular interest because it forms one of the earliest published accounts of a canal expedition, and heralded a new dimension to pleasure boat literature by being the first account of a family outing.[105]

There was nothing particularly heroic or exciting about journeying by canal in the nineteenth century and possibly there is no method of travel upon which so little has been written in the way

* The Thames Preservation Act of 1885 accepted the fact that the river had come to be largely used as a place of public recreation and resort, and in 1897 it was ruled that passenger steamers at Richmond and Teddington had to be given precedence over barge traffic.

† *See* page 180.

of personal reminiscence. Books about inland voyages are relatively scarce and it is only lately* that this form of literature has gained a wider readership. More comprehensive guide-books to waterways began to appear during the last quarter of the nineteenth century. Henry Taunt's *Illustrated Map of the Thames* (1872) contained a detailed itinerary, photographs, and large-scale maps for the tourist, boatman, and the angler. The third edition, published in 1878, was extended to include a dozen adjoining waterways and four pages described the Wey Navigation. The fact that an illustrated sixth edition was published by 1897, at a cost of 15s., besides the issue of many pocket and cheap editions, reflects the popularity which boating had gained by the turn of the century.

Except for an article in the *West Sussex Gazette*,† Dashwood's is the only extant account of the Wey & Arun during its working days. The book has become something of a rarity—of which the publishers lost all record during the London blitz—and it is doubtful if more than a dozen copies are to be found in private hands.[173] On some front covers is embossed a gilt una boat under sail. Illustrating the narrative are seven wood engravings of a somewhat imaginative and crude character which nevertheless have a certain charm. The inaccurate map shows a railway passing through the midst of Arundel castle, the descriptions of the localities owe much to Aubrey or Murray's handbook, yet local colour is not altogether absent and the whole gives a good impression of the semi-derelict state of the canal. Little reference is made in its ninety pages to the navigation's commercial activities nor, perhaps more surprisingly, is there mention of the barge folk, which is in contrast to present-day nostalgia for things past and people picturesque. The author reveals himself to be a keen yachtsman and the advice and hints given on sailing were no doubt useful, although the account of his experiences must have served more as a deterrent than an encouragement to the would-be excursionist. Frustrating delays certainly arose in the shape of numerous gates across the towpath, and the opening of locks was a most laborious process. There were also occasions for alarm when *Caprice* was threatened by charging oxen outside Guildford, nearly sunk in Hardham lock, and almost swamped in the Solent. The story of their adventure can be briefly recounted as follows.

* In recent years the better-known works have been Temple Thurston's *Flower of Gloster* (1911), Bonthron's *My Holidays on Inland Waterways* (1916), and Rolt's *Narrow Boat* (1944).

† *See* 179.

On 8 July 1867 Dashwood set off from Weybridge in sunny weather, accompanied by his wife and dog, to watch the naval review being held at Spithead in honour of the Sultan of Turkey's visit. An odd assortment of stores had been loaded on board, which included rugs, umbrellas, cooking apparatus, a large hamper, a ship's compass, a keg of beer, and an india-rubber bath. The low clearance of many of the bridges had necessitated the substitution of a 7-ft towing mast for the 20-ft mast (which was lashed to the boom) while a pony and groom had been hired to tow the boat.

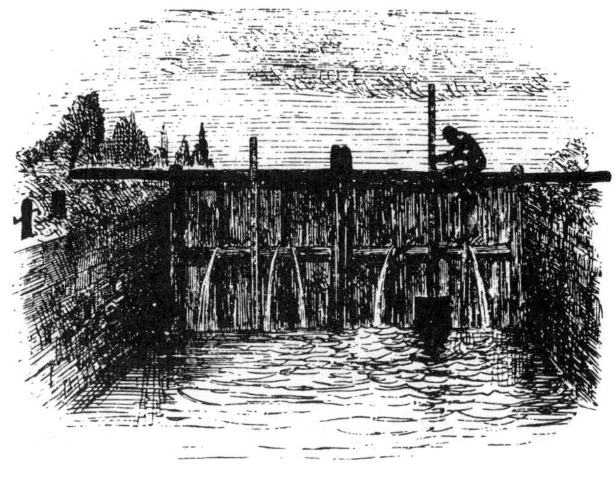

WORKING THE LOCKS.

Fig. 42.—*Working the locks on the Wey Navigation, 1867*

At Thames lock the toll of 5s. was paid to Guildford and a 'most civil and obliging' lock-keeper* provided them with a 3-ft-long crowbar for opening the locks. On the Wey the lock paddles were placed in the centre of the gates so that it was necessary to insert the point of the crowbar in the teeth of the paddle-bar while sitting astride the gates and, by a series of violent jerks, raise it inch by inch. Most of the hatches were very stiff and difficult to raise or lower, and since success depended on good leverage, the crowbar had to be worked from the extreme end of the handle so that if the point slipped out of the niche while the wrench was being made,

* Probably William Strudwick whom Taunt described as 'careful and intelligent' (1878).

away went the user headlong into the water. No mishaps occurred on this voyage, but the fruits of Dashwood's labours were a not inconsiderable number of cuts and bruises.

Leaving Weybridge, the party traversed a long avenue lined with tall alders and spanned by rustic bridges. 'The day was hot and the cool shade most refreshing; the banks were covered with luxuriant ferns and wild-flowers, and the white and yellow water-lilies, floating on the smooth surface of the water, lent enchantment to the view.' Emerging upon Newhaw lock, they came up with a barge, whose crew offered them their services which they readily

ALARMING POSITION.

Fig. 43.—Dashwood in an alarming position near St Catherine's lock

accepted, and so ascended together into a more open country of meadowland and corn-fields (one of the few references to barges during the voyage). Admiring the woodlands of St George's Hill, they soon sighted West Hall Lodge, where an enthralling game of croquet was in progress. Passing Wisley Common and the ruins of Newark Priory, they procured bread and cheese and drank beer with the weary haymakers at the little inn by Pyrford lock. Proceeding through Walsam and Peppercourt locks, they lunched by the water's edge at Send before reaching Triggs lock and the grounds of Sutton Place, the former home of Sir Richard Weston. By now the day was far advanced and the great heat had given place to a calm and lovely evening. 'We glided along the banks gay with water-iris, both yellow and blue, the pretty little forget-me-nots in quantities, the large yellow ranunculus, with no end of other pretty wild flowers, the air fragrant with the scent of new mown hay and the delicious smelling meadow-sweet.'

Beyond Bowers lock, the voyagers entered Stoke Park and at the flour mill showed their way-bill to the toll-keeper. Then, as night was falling, Guildford was reached. The town was alive with excitement as the Foresters' Fête was in progress with the bands of Volunteers parading the streets in every direction. Mooring *Caprice* under the bridge, they left her in charge of the boatman on the quay and spent the night at the 'White Lion'.

Leaving the town early next morning their enthusiasm was dampened at the sight of a small screw steamer just arrived from Brighton lying thoroughly disabled. It appeared that the weeds on the lower part of the canal had been so thick that they had completely fouled her screw and, to make matters worse, she had burst her boilers. However, Dashwood consoled himself with the thought that he could penetrate where the steamer had cleared a passage and was relieved to find that the new series of locks could be operated with a windlass from terra firma, although the hatches remained terribly stiff.

The first serious check to their journey occurred at St Catherine's lock. Some hundred yards after passing through the upper gates *Caprice* stuck fast in the mud in less than a foot of water. Unable to move or to land, the party were espied in their dilemma by an old lady, who informed them that they had no business to be there as the water had been let off for nine days to effect mill repairs. Dashwood pleaded their plight and she, becoming more amiable, told them where they might find the lock-keeper who alone could help. Sitting under umbrellas in the broiling sun while their groom went off to find him, some alarm was occasioned by a large herd of 'formidable-looking oxen' in the adjoining meadow who, drawing themselves up in line, 'charged down upon us with lowered heads and tails erect, threatening us with instant annihilation'. But, as Dashwood says, the animals, on reaching the bank, were almost as astonished as they were to find the river empty and, after much snorting, turned away.

Eventually, the couple was released from their predicament (half-a-crown did the trick) but already it was too late for them to reach Loxwood that night. At Shalford a toll of 1s. was paid to the Godalming Navigation and at Stonebridge they entered the Wey & Arun, where the water was again very shallow (due no doubt to the silt from the Bramley stream). However, they had just sufficient draught to enter the first lock and, passing the large tanyard at Gosden and two more locks, they reached Bramley wharf, where they met William Stanton, the 'good-natured superintendent of the canal at the Guildford end, and a coal-merchant whose barges travelled regularly between London, Bramley, and Littlehampton'. Stanton told Dashwood all about the Wey & Arun and offered the party 'the run of his kitchen garden, rich in gooseberries and currants'. However, they also learnt to their dismay that the Ford

Fig. 44.—A low bridge on the Wey & Arun Canal

section of the Portsmouth & Arundel Canal no longer existed. In consequence of this discovery and in view of the hazards of taking such a frail craft into the open sea (the bulwarks rose only 6 in. above water), they decided, after much deliberation, to return to Guildford, only to run aground again in the shallows at Shalford. While waiting for more water to be released, a passing bargee's encouragement and the toss of a coin caused them to change their minds and return to Bramley, where they planned to spend the night. 'In process of time we got to Bramley once more, much to the surprise of Mr Stanton and the natives. It was too late to proceed further so we deposited our goods in safe keeping in Mr Stanton's stores and set out in search of dinner and a lodging for the night.' However, fresh difficulties beset them, for no suitable accommodation was to be found and they had to take the train to Guildford. The 'Grantley Arms' at Wonersh clearly displeased them, for it was referred to as a 'pokey little inn', while the 'White Hart' was described as 'the best hotel in Guildford, where we regaled ourselves with a capital dinner and were thankful that we were not in the "Grantley Arms"'.

The fourth chapter described their third day's trip from Bramley to Newbridge. In consequence of the shortage of water in the canal and the Company's new rule regarding pleasure craft, they had to take with them George Cox, a 19-year-old bargee, who worked for Stanton. The toll to Newbridge was 5s. and there was in addition

THE TUNNEL

Fig. 45.—Hardham Canal Tunnel

the pilot's fee of 10s. to be paid. The weather continued fine, and the scenery beyond Bramley and through Lord Grantley's property, where the canal wound its way under the shade of woods reaching down to the water's edge, was greatly praised. Many of the bridges had a bare 7-ft headroom and the small iron drawbridge at Whipley Manor had to be opened. However, their pace was quickened by the forethought of young Cox, who ran ahead, in spite of the heat of a broiling sun, to prepare the locks. Only the double swing-gates hampered their progress; as they were impossible to ride through, the groom had to dismount at almost every field to free the tow-rope. After passing heather-covered common and water-meadows, the party entered the summit cutting, which was dug through great oak plantations and spanned by a series of low stone bridges.

On reaching Sidney Wood, they wended their way 'through a most refreshing and picturesque country of a broken and undulating character, densely clothed with a forest of oak trees, opening out and giving peeps into deep hollows verdant with luxuriant ferns and purple heather. Here and there were breaks in the woodland, and the small round hills, rich in pasturage, appeared—the ancient folds of the Weald. We now commenced to make our descent towards the sea, and lock after lock followed each other in rapid succession.' At half-past one they reached Loxwood and noted the 'neat clean little inn* close by the canalside'. However, the decision to take lunch *al fresco* in the shade of a big oak (eating meat-pies of doubtful content bought at Guildford), gave Dashwood the opportunity of observing an unusual way of catching fish. 'Whilst I was quietly enjoying my pipe after lunch, my curiosity was raised by seeing a man amusing himself throwing a large stone into the canal attached to a long line, which he hauled in and flung back over and over again. On approaching him, I soon discovered his little dodge, for I beheld a number of small branches floating about in all directions, to which fine-gut lines and hooks were attached, wherewith to ensnare the wily fish, somewhat on the principle of the trimmer. These boughs he got to land by means of his stone, which he flung over them, drawing them slowly ashore. I did not see him catch anything, although I watched him for some time; but he assured me he had been very successful by this plan, and had at times secured pike and other fish of a large size.'

Pressing forward to Newbridge, the countryside was felt to be 'decidedly ugly, with flat water-meadows on either side', an opinion that could hardly be substantiated by its present-day appearance. The canal became exceedingly weedy as they neared Rowner lock and it was necessary to stand forward to clear the bows. Cox, who had been of the greatest assistance, disembarked at the lock and went off back to Bramley.

Newbridge was reached at half-past five, where they anchored and set off on foot to Billingshurst, 1½ miles away, to spend the night at the 'King's Arms'. Its hospitality appeared to leave nothing to be desired. Dashwood was full of praise for this neat, clean inn where 'everything was fresh and good of its kind; eggs, butter, bread, fruit, cream, all excellent; and our mutton-chops done to a turn, with excellent beer and very fair sherry'.

* The 'Onslow Arms'.

Next morning Dashwood was awake at half-past four and roused the house in order to make an early start, for the first ripples of the ebb tide would be felt at Coldwaltham lock by noon. 'After a bit the little inn was in a bustle—hot and cold water for shaving, and baths, to any amount, and boots polished like mirrors.' A capital breakfast, followed by a brisk walk to Newbridge, and they were off again by seven. The fine weather continued. At Orfold lock no mention was made of the aqueduct, but the lock-keeper's wife and her two pretty daughters were observed making butter. The *Oarsman's Guide* stated that slight refreshment might be obtained here, 'scanty accommodation also, but to a very limited extent'. Indeed, as the lock-house had only two tiny bedrooms in which a family of four or more was housed, the traveller would have been lucky to have obtained a chair in the parlour.

Dashwood now found the flat meadows and the scenery more to his liking, although substantially the same as that described as 'decidedly ugly'. The early morning sunshine, the meadows dotted with cattle, the larks in full song, and the canal banks clothed with flowers of every hue and colour accounted perhaps for the difference in outlook. At length the 'great Pallingham lock' was reached, the largest he ever saw—'about 40 feet long and 30 feet deep and wide enough for two good-sized barges to lie alongside each other'. Inaccurate, of course, but Dashwood was no judge of distance and, as he had had to fill the basin single-handed, the exaggeration was perhaps understandable. A shilling toll was paid at the lock house—referred to as the receiving-house of the Arun Canal Company, which they learnt was still paying its way in spite of the railway, and formerly produced a very comfortable dividend. Into the Arun proper and after a couple of miles Stopham bridge was passed. To avoid the detour around Pulborough, they took the short cut to Coldwaltham. However, at Hardham lock the boat nearly sank with Mrs Dashwood on board when it became wedged under the iron footbridge as the lock was being filled. 'The groom's timely warning saved the day.' Dashwood punted *Caprice* through Hardham tunnel by pushing the boat-hook against the roof. 'In the middle it became quite dark, and we could only just guide ourselves by means of the bright outlet at the end. The roof was covered with stalactites, and in places the water fell upon us from crevices above in heavy drops, so that we had to try to steer clear of them where we heard their splashes on the water below.' After passing through this subterranean passage in about ten minutes, they had to wait for their groom who, having had to lead the pony over the top as there was no towpath through the tunnel, had mistaken his way. However, by half-past twelve they had come upon the last lock at Coldwaltham, where they found the tide had begun to ebb.

Thereafter great difficulty was experienced in persuading their pony to pass several obnoxious swing-gates, three-barred and weighted, and the delay meant that it was nearly 2 o'clock before they reached Amberley, but even so they made a brief halt to visit the castle. The towing-path ceased at Houghton and, while the groom and pony went on to Arundel by road, they were forced to row the remaining 8 miles to the town, partly against the tide.

OBNOXIOUS GATES.

Fig. 46.—Arun Navigation tow-path

'The tide was running strong when we passed under the old bridge at Amberley, eating our luncheon as we drifted on. We went by Bury Hill at a great pace, and soon came to the overhanging wooded cliffs of Arundel Park. The river is here strikingly pretty, and we met a great number of pleasure boats rowing and fishing. . . . We soon left the shelter of the woods, the river winding out into the plain, with high mud banks on each side of us, covered with extensive beds of tall-growing sedges. The tide soon began to work up the centre of the river, and we had to hug the banks to try and cheat it. It was now becoming hard work.' A mile from Arundel they met some barges coming up with the tide and were rejoined by their groom—'we flung him a towing-rope and made him pull us up to the bridge'. Then, after several unsuccessful attempts against the force of the tide, *Caprice* was hauled under Arundel bridge by means of a boat-hook and tied up at the quay.

The last stage of their journey to the sea now commenced, with the pony towing them towards Littlehampton. 'The appearance of the river now showed us that we were evidently approaching the sea. Its great width, the shipping in the distance, and the number of small craft of every description dotted about—some busy fishing and some anchored, some under sail—presented a very animated appearance.' Cautioned against the chains of the

'THE CAPRICE' UNDER WAY.

Fig. 47.—The Una boat 'Caprice'

floating bridge, they reached Littlehampton at about half-past eight and spent the night at a small riverside inn.* The total sailing time taken to cover the 62 miles from Weybridge to Littlehampton during the four days was about 28–30 hours, in the course of which they passed through 43 locks and were charged 22s. in tolls and pilots' fees.

Dashwood interviewed a prospective skipper to pilot the boat through the Channel and the Solent. 'He appeared somewhat unsteady on his pins, hummed and hawed a great deal and said he did not much like the job, that he had been out all day fishing off Selsea Bill, that there had been a nasty bumpy sea which would be almost too much for our boat and that he could not think of undertaking the "voyage" with a lady aboard.' However, the skipper changed his mind the next morning and, with a steady breeze, *Caprice* made eight knots towards Portsmouth.

The sixth chapter described their hazardous journey by sea to the Solent and the imposing sight of the fleet off Spithead, while the last was devoted to describing the capabilities and rigging of una boats. In conclusion, Dashwood thanked his readers for their perseverance in perusing his 'little tale' and hoped that it might encourage those who possessed a small sailing-boat to spend a holiday in this way without much expenditure of either time or money.[174] But in the same year as Dashwood's book was published the Act of abandonment was passed and, within four years of his voyage, the Wey & Arun Canal was closed.

Details of the life and profession of J. Bacon Dashwood are sketchy. His home was at Christchurch, but as his work 'called him to spend his existence within daily reach of London', he also lived on the banks of the Thames. Yachting was his hobby. He owned a fore-and-aft boat for bad weather and a una boat for fine weather sailing. He also enjoyed fishing for mackerel and whiting off Hengistbury Head.

Besides the account of his voyage to the Solent he also produced *The Scholar's Assistant and Standard Table Book*, published by Dashwood Bros. and Charles H. Law of London in 1856. This sixpenny, 47-page booklet contained arithmetical tables, measurements, conversions, foreign currencies and useful information, like the dates of the kings and queens of England.

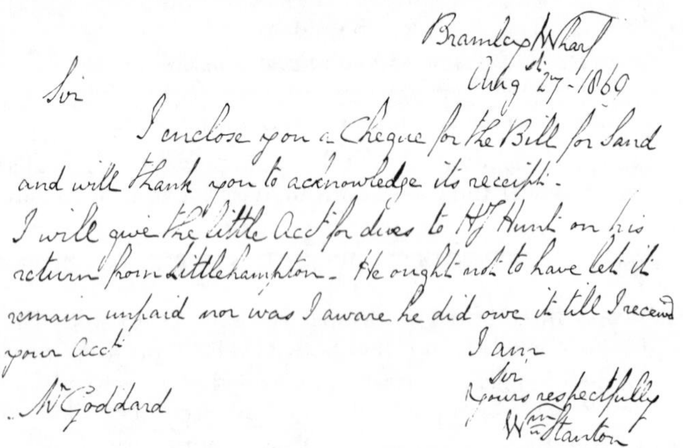

Bramley Wharf
Augst 27-1869

Sir

I enclose you a Cheque for the Bill for Sand and will thank you to acknowledge its receipt.
I will give the little Acct for dues to Mr Hunt on his return from Littlehampton. He ought not to have let it remain unpaid nor was I aware he did owe it till I received your Acct

I am
Sir
Yours respectfully
Wm Stanton

Mr Goddard

Fig. 48.—Facsimile of letter from William Stanton, 1869

CHAPTER XIV

The End of the Wey & Arun Canal (1865–1871)

Future in doubt—Stanton makes an offer—eye-witness account of trade in 1866—the Arun Navigation offers to help—in Chancery—application to Parliament for bill to close the canal—opposition to the bill—evidence in the House of Lords—abandonment Act passed, 1868—opportunity for reprieve—canal for auction, 1870—an assault by bargees—Wey & Arun closed in July 1871—death of William Stanton—last barge to Bramley wharf, 1872—canal sold back to riparian owners.

THE promoters of the Horsham & Guildford railway envisaged, as had formerly those of the canal, both a substantial local and through-traffic, and with this in view had inaugurated a direct service between Guildford and Brighton via Shoreham. The line, too, had been constructed in singularly optimistic vein. Although there was only single-track working except through stations, embankments and some bridges had been constructed to allow for double-track working. One station, set far apart from the nearest village, simply served the historic Tudor mansion at Baynards Park; at Slinfold a railway hotel was built (now a private house), but traffic never developed to justify such facilities.* Indeed, it soon proved to be a more picturesque than profitable section of the London, Brighton & South Coast Railway. Within eighteen months of its opening, fares and freight charges had had to be raised, while as early as August 1867 the spur at Stammerham Junction was closed and through traffic to Brighton ended.

However, even though the railway was not flourishing, it attracted sufficient business away from the canal to halve its revenue and reduce the amount of traffic to uneconomical proportions. The loss of the Cranleigh coal trade and export of Run Common charcoal could not be redressed from any other source, and the canal's prospects looked bleak. It was not therefore surprising that at the

* The station at Christ's Hospital, designed in a comparatively lavish manner in anticipation of housing development that is still awaited, was not opened until 1902.

Company's annual meeting in May 1866, it was proposed, in consequence of traffic having been so much reduced that it was impossible to provide the necessary funds for keeping the canal open, that steps should be taken to dispose of the property.

On the eve of the meeting the chairman, John Napper, wrote to Smallpeice explaining that he would be unable to attend, and stating that since 'I feel so mixed up as a landowner and a shareholder, that if the Committee should do me the honour of proposing me again as chairman, I shall beg to decline it.' He also added that he had received a letter from Stanton which seemed to insinuate that water had been wasted from the reservoir, but also contained an offer to buy any number of shares at 56s. 6d. 'I should recommend all those gentlemen who wish to sell theirs to accept his offer, as I think it is more than they will get by selling it to the landowners.'

Stanton's bid was no idle offer. When in the late fifties William Stanton had taken over his father's coal and timber business, his barges had already begun to displace those of the Arundel Lighter Company, the most powerful of the rival carrying concerns. Whereas in 1837 the Arundel men had loaded over 4,000 tons on the London to the coast route, by 1860 this figure had fallen to less than 1,000. The Company's managers continued to find it extremely difficult to provide regular cargoes for their fleet and the trips made by the remaining two barges on this run became increasingly rare. In May 1861 the *Norfolk* made her final voyage back to Arundel and in June 1863 *Britannia* passed Bramley wharf for the last time laden with London beer. Two months later the opening of the railway through the Arun valley enabled Arundel to be reached from the capital in two hours instead of three days by water. However, the linking of Guildford and Bramley by rail—and the station was only a stone's throw from the wharf—also constituted a grave threat to Stanton's barge trade. As a shareholder he had regretted the Committee's decision not to oppose the railway bill and it seemed clear that the directors were apathetic to the Company's future. He therefore decided to try to obtain a controlling interest in the Company and by injecting a little more life into it wage war against the railway and perhaps come to some arrangement with the adjoining navigations. Already he held thirteen shares, and as they were now changing hands at around £3 each, his offer stood some slight chance of success. However, neither Lord Leconfield nor the majority of shareholders wished to sell at this price and Stanton's bid failed. As the Company's assets included over 200 acres of land together with some property at Guildford and several cottages and buildings along the canal, the shareholders doubtless hoped that they would realize more than £2,550 if the canal was auctioned and the Company went into liquidation.

After the annual meeting in 1866, counsel's opinion was taken and in August the Management Committee resolved to recommend to the shareholders that the Company should be wound up. However, the barge-masters of Arundel and Littlehampton, foreseeing the loss of direct communication with London, decided to take immediate action, and eight of them did that same month purchase for £3 apiece the 61 shares belonging to Samuel Sharpe the gunpowder manufacturer. It came as no great surprise therefore when at the special meeting held in October no less than ten of the seventeen shareholders present opposed the resolution. Lord Leconfield, holding 230 shares, had let it be known that he would fall in with the majority view, so with a total of 81 votes being cast both for and against, William Newland, acting as chairman in Napper's absence, cast his vote against the resolution. Consequently, a Committee of Investigation was appointed under the chairmanship of Richard Holmes, who was both on the Arun Committee and clerk to the Commissioners of the Port of Arundel (who were also shareholders) to ascertain whether, if the canal were kept open, it could reduce its expenses. Except for the rather unfortunate incident when somebody let out the water and closed the navigation for six weeks, the canal continued to function much as usual. On 14 June 1866 an unsigned article had appeared in the *West Sussex Gazette* entitled 'Past, Present and Future', which was a colourful and prolix eye-witness account of the dying waterway. The author appeared to be in little doubt as to its future and had no confidence in Holmes' efforts.

> 'That the canal will become a thing of the past is certain to our minds; but there are gentlemen of great commercial experience who think differently. These zealous calculators can figure out a statement of expenditure and receipts on the back of an old envelope, to show in a twinkling that, with proper management and a curtailment of expenses, it may yet be made to pay; and further than this, they urge a canal is essential to the trade of the Port of Arundel, and for preserving a competition with the railway. Heaven help us! Competition with the railway!
>
> 'It was our pleasure to navigate very pleasantly these eighteen miles of canal a few days ago. Without exception the scenery throughout is the most charming and delightful ever witnessed. A trip up the Shannon is not half so picturesque. The glory of the scenery is its rural simplicity and its richness. At every bend of the canal you see a picture ready for the artist. The landscape is not distorted by cockneyfied villas, or

"villers" as they are called, in derision—indeed you see but a few old farm houses on the journey, and they are very old and picturesque indeed. What the population may be surrounding the 18 miles of canal we know not, but we should hardly suppose it to exceed 2,000 or 3,000, taking some distance from its banks. It lies in a purely agricultural district, and a large quantity of woodland flanks the canal on both sides, and here grows some fine oak. As far as local traffic is concerned the trading would consist of timber and bark. In a passage through this delightful district one almost fancies himself in an unexplored country, away from the haunts of man. About half-way along, by the side of the canal but in the midst of a wood [Sidney Wood] extending over 300 acres, we find the hut of THE man who has to see to the Wey & Arun repairs. He has his neat cottage here, like a Robinson Crusoe, and his occupation appears to be constructing lock-gates, after the rude style of the past half-century. Still his cottage has an air of comfort with its flower garden in front, and his life must be the essence of simplicity.

'A word as to the commercial position of the Wey & Arun canal. Considering that there is a lock on an average every mile, the travelling is somewhat slow on this canal; to pass a lock occupies about a quarter of an hour. In our progress up this canal we were anxious to learn its prospects and witness the business doing there. We believe that we saw but one bona fide commercial operation in progress. This was at Ifold, where stands the very pretty mansion of J. Napper, Esq., who is the chairman of the canal company. Here were signs of something doing, for a man was wheeling out of a barge some gravel, or something of the sort. He was evidently a man familiar to the canal and its ways, as one of our companions addressed him thus—"Hallo, Jerry, you're a pretty long time about that!" Jerry who has not the most amiable countenance in the world was evidently annoyed at this rebuke, but his reply was characteristic of the Wey & Arun. Jerry thus spake—"I unloaded her once at the wrong place and had to load her again." This was almost the only evidence of traffic we witnessed on the canal. Bye the bye, there was yet another barge, in which an individual known as Moses was working. Moses is evidently an institution on the Wey & Arun, and we put him down as belonging to the Company. He, like most of his race, was not the cleanest shaven. He asked for some beer to drink our healths and ran along the banks after us like a wild man of the woods. The remaining barge on the Wey & Arun was a wreck. It was called, we think, the "Providence", and was half-filled with water. The only other exciting incident we heard of, connected with the commerce of the company, was that during the past year Jim Somebody carelessly let the water out of one part of the canal.* The consequence of Jim's carelessness was the suspension of traffic for about six weeks.

* It was alleged that the superintendent had left the gate of a pound open near Sidney Wood. This he denied. The loss of water, he said, was due to the dry weather. Minutes of Evidence, H. of L., 24 March 1868.

'Withal, the calculating gentlemen, to whose superior experience we ought to bow, think "something" can be done with the Wey & Arun. This hope scarcely has been entertained by the Company itself; for on inquiry we learned that the directors have not paid a visit of inspection for twenty years. It is rumoured that an application is to be made to Parliament for permission to sell the canal to the adjoining landowners at £25 an acre. We should imagine that few who own property would object to this. For the Ifold estate it is a charming feature and would certainly be retained as a piece of ornamental water by its owner. We are not aware whether the property is entirely in the market or not—we should rather incline to think not, as Lord Leconfield is the principal shareholder—but if it is we invite some gentleman of an adventurous turn to take it up. It cannot be a worse speculation than the London, Chatham & Dover Railway. Brighton has just started a four-horse coach called "Old Times Revived". The proprietors boast of doing the journey to London in five hours. Where are the men to take up the Wey & Arun with the same spirit of reviving the good old times? The eighteen miles can be done in ten hours—say about the time taken on a journey from London to Paris—providing Jim doesn't let the water out by accident, or a sharp frost doesn't set in and freeze up the whole affair for a few weeks.

'Reader! We have a word or two to add by way of a moral. As we near Guildford we see "the enemy" scampering along by our side. The railway runs for some miles parallel with the canal. Our boat-men are sweating under the hot sun pumping out the lock. The horse that draws our boat is quietly feeding from the herbage growing on the banks of the canal. As we remain here, languidly waiting to be liberated from the lock, along comes "Puffin' Billy" flying over the iron rails like a mad thing.

' "Phew", whistles the locomotive. "Puff, puff, puff, puff", retorts the engine; and as we look round the whole train of carriages whisks out of sight leaving the smoke from the funnel to slowly settle itself and evaporate in the air. The contrast is funny. While we have been "fudging about the lock" the engine has possibly flown ten miles with its freight. This is the enemy the Wey & Arun has to compete with. Well, well, railways are now in their prime. As we write, a parliamentary battle is going forward to decide if another line shall or shall not be made to Brighton. The law proceedings alone will cost £100,000!

'The Wey & Arun has passed through all the glories of its age. Is there anyone among us who can read the future and tell us whether the great iron highways which now spread over all the land will not some day be grown over with grass, having succumbed to a superior power of locomotion? It is a singular subject to reflect upon, but it certainly calls forcibly to mind the transitory state in which all things are and impresses upon us a feeling of humiliation and lowliness at the pride, pomp and vanity of that intellectual animal, Man.'

In spite of some inaccuracies and the writer's tendency to exaggerate, the article gave a fair picture of the state of the navigation. Indeed, it is surprising that in view of the stoppage and the uncertainty regarding the canal's future over 10,000 tons of merchandise should have been carried during the year, or, on average, two barges a day. The Company's coffers had almost run dry and in October the Hon. Mrs Norton was informed that it was regretted that the rent for the reservoir could not be paid.

Holmes' investigation had only lasted four weeks, when early in November he wrote to Smallpeice on behalf of the sub-Committee to say that they had held several meetings and made enquiries of the merchants and others as to the future trade likely to be carried; 'and the Committee regret that they are not able to make a favourable report, and therefore leave the matter in the hands of the Committee of Management to deal with the whole question as they may feel disposed.'

It might be assumed that such a report would have decided the canal's future without more ado. But the shrewd and energetic Holmes did not intend to let the matter rest there. The Arun, of course, had good reason to want the Wey & Arun kept open. If the canal was closed some 4,000 tons of traffic would be lost to the Arun Navigation, which was the equivalent in tolls to a dividend of 2 per cent. In other words, as the Arun's dividend for the previous year had been only 2 per cent, further payments to its shareholders were unlikely if through-traffic ceased, and the navigation would inevitably soon become insolvent. The date of the next meeting of the Wey & Arun was fixed for 30 November. Meantime, the Arun Committee had met and agreed a plan of action. Holmes was well aware that several members of the Wey & Arun Committee wanted the canal's assets liquidated as soon as possible in the hope that some final payment might be made to the shareholders; on the other hand, he knew that both Napper and Lord Leconfield, who also held a substantial block of Arun shares, would not readily consent to this measure if there was a practicable alternative. As Holmes had foreseen, after his report had been formally received at the November meeting, both Napper in the chair and Bryden, Lord Leconfield's agent, expressed the view that it was most desirable that the canal should be kept open if any scheme could be devised. Whereupon Holmes seized his cue and proposed that the Arun Navigation should vote a subsidy of, say, £100 a year towards the canal's expenses subject to a new Committee being appointed and his proposals to effect economies being approved.

A reduction in expenses could be obtained, he suggested, firstly by halving the clerk's salary: 'We thought that would stand very well indeed. I explained to Mr. Smallpeice being a professional man, that we must make a beginning'; secondly, by sacking the superintendent; 'Entirely useless I thought his services were and he kept a shop or something of that kind', who was to be replaced by the manager of the Arun Navigation, 'Mr. Sprinks, a very acute and intelligent kind of man, who had a great number of offices combined in one and was to manage both Navigations'; and thirdly, by dismissing some of the labourers; 'We refused to go in as a Committee of Management unless the old servants had notice, so that we might deal with them as we thought proper.'[106]

The meeting doubted whether this offer was sufficient but, according to Holmes, conceded that an increased subsidy of £120 would be practicable. Holmes was later to state in the House of Lords that although no vote was taken and the meeting adjourned, he understood that his proposals were agreed and that all that remained outstanding was for the Arun Navigation to approve the additional £20 p.a. And to some extent his suggestions were acted upon, for immediately after the meeting notice of dismissal was given to Pullen and to Field and Meecham. A new Management Committee of nine (Holmes, Lear, French, Henly, Tribe, Isemonger, Shaft, Sparkes, and Stanton) was provisionally formed to go into operation on 1 May 1867, and so confident was Holmes as to the outcome of the adjourned meeting of the Wey & Arun on 11 January 1867 that he went to Guildford without a seconder of his proposal—'Some few friends and Commissioners of the port asked if they should go and I said that there was no occasion as the matter was settled, that it was only to take up the resolution from the Arun proprietors, and I did not think that they need go to the trouble and expense of coming.'[107] But only seven proprietors attended and evidently there was a change of heart on the part of the shareholders, for the minutes of the meeting read that 'it having been stated by Mr. Holmes that the Arun Navigation Company have resolved to contribute £120 a year towards the expenses provided the Wey & Arun Canal be kept open, he moved that this offer be accepted; the proposition was not seconded. It was then moved by Mr. F. S. Irving, a shareholder, and seconded by Mr. D. Hayden, that the company be wound up under the provisions of the 99th section of the Companies' Act, 1862; and that the clerk take the necessary steps for that purpose; carried.'

Now the accounts for the previous year had shown a deficit of over £400 (allowing for payment of a dividend costing £270) while annual running costs had averaged £700 over the previous five years, about half of which was taken up by salaries and wages and the remainder was for repairs and rents. Holmes' proposed economies were estimated to reduce expenditure by £200 and it was these figures, submitted to the meeting in January, 'which appeared to take them very much by surprise for they doubted whether it [the canal] could be carried on at those figures'. As tolls and incidental receipts were in the region of £500, Holmes considered that the Arun's offer of £120 a year would suffice to make the canal pay its way. The meeting, however, bearing in mind that the balance of the Company's reserves had been withdrawn in November, did not.

Neither Napper nor Lord Leconfield attended the January meeting, the former excusing himself on the grounds that he was unwell and the latter writing that if the majority of the proprietors wanted to wind up the Company, he would fall in with their wishes. The meeting, with Newland in the chair, discussed the Arun's offer and rejected it as being totally insufficient for the purpose since '£200 was the least possible sum needed to keep the canal open'. No approach was made, however, to the River Wey Commissioners for the balance, presumably because the Arun wanted sole control of the Wey & Arun, and the Wey & Arun regarded liquidation as a preferable solution. It was only in the House of Lords fourteen months later that Holmes referred to the fact that he had had 'interviews with merchants at Godalming and Guildford lately, and they were all ready to fall into any scheme devised for keeping it open'.

A letter written to Smallpeice shortly before the January meeting ran as follows:

'Dear Sir,

Having attended one or two meetings of the Wey & Arun Canal Company at Guildford with no beneficial results, I hope the shareholders will soon determine without many more meetings, upon some final decision, before the little they have left is swallowed up in expenses.

I am, dear Sir, the unfortunate holder of 20 shares,

Yours truly,

John Braddick.'

It was clear that many Wey & Arun shareholders wanted to rid themselves of an incumbrance and equally certain that with the opening of the railway there was faint chance of water-borne trade increasing. But the closing of a canal is a difficult matter. Statutory powers are not easily repealed and whereas upon petition to the High Court of Chancery it was ordered in March 1867 that the Company should be wound up, doubts arose as to whether the powers conferred by the Companies Act were sufficient for the court to authorize the closure and sale of the canal. The summer was to pass before any decision could be reached. In the meantime the navigation had to be kept open for traffic under the direction of the official liquidator, Smallpeice. The old canal servants, Edward Field and Meecham the carpenter, gave up possession of their cottages early in the new year and in May, Pullen left after nearly ten years as superintendent and Stanton was requested to take charge of the works. He and Baverstock alone remained to collect the tolls, while the three labourers (Field, Heather, and Rogers) were left to carry out a minimum of maintenance. At the annual meeting a further reduction of £50 was reported in the toll receipts, but economies had lessened the annual deficit to a mere £60. However, the balance in the hands of the treasurer had fallen to £365. On 17 June uncertainty regarding the future of the waterway was only increased by the posting of a notice on the quayside to the effect that the canal would be kept open for traffic until 13 August. In fine July weather Dashwood made his voyage from Thames to Solent and remarked, 'How long this connecting link will be available seems most doubtful, for the whole of this canal is, I understand, to be put up immediately for auction. In fact considering the great expense in procuring water, the competition of the railway and the small amount of traffic, it is impossible it can pay its way.' In September the Company gave up possession of Loxwood wharf and incurred some expense in putting Lock XVI in condition, since it was leaking badly. Then in November the Vice-Chancellor, Sir Richard Malins, pronounced sentence. As the court had insufficient powers to shut the canal, he would direct that the official liquidator should be at liberty to present a bill to Parliament for its abandonment. The shareholders received the news with weary forbearance and scarcely gave a thought to the fresh demands on the services of Smallpeice.

Although the Canal Company had gone into voluntary liquidation, it made little difference to the working of the canal. On Pullen's departure, no superintendent had been appointed and Charles

Baverstock, the lock-keeper and toll-collector at Rowner, was responsible for supervising the carrying out of repairs south of Sidney Wood, while, according to Dashwood, Stanton was designated superintendent of the canal at the Guildford end. The latter's barges, now showing signs of age, still continued to ply between London, Guildford, and Bramley with occasional visits to Cranleigh, Pulborough, and Arundel. *Providence*, however, was already a wreck lying below the summit level half-filled with water, and in January 1868 he nearly lost the *Lark* through the negligence of a bargee, who endeavoured, without sufficient aid, to take the vessel out of the placid waters of the canal into the turgid torrents of the flooded Wey. Its tow-ropes broken, it floated at six miles an hour downstream, narrowly missing Broadford bridge. 'Had the barge run against the bridge', a local newspaper commented, 'that unsightly and rickety structure must have fallen, which few persons would have regretted.'

The Wey & Arun Junction Canal (Abandonment) bill, introduced into the House of Lords in February, was given first and second readings and then referred to a Select Committee under the chairmanship of Lord Methuen. Seven petitions were entered against the bill. The L.B. & S.C.R. sought the insertion of a clause to transform the viaduct at Whipley Manor into an embankment. Both the Commissioners of the Port of Arundel and the Wey (Godalming) Commissioners and the proprietors of the Arun Navigation opposed the bill on the grounds that traffic from the Thames and the Wey would be lost to their navigations. The landowners adjoining the canal were concerned at the prospect of their fields being flooded should the embankments collapse and by the loss of usage of the towpath which served as a passage for cattle between enclosures. There was a petition by a Mr Rowcliffe, and another by Lord Grantley who was perturbed at the cost of filling in his section of the canal at Wonersh Park.

The hearing opened with the cross-examination of the former superintendent by John Clerk, Q.C. (acting for the promoters of the bill) as to the present state of the canal:

'With regard to the state of the locks, what state are the paddles of the locks in?—I found in the IVth and Vth locks two paddle-bars gone.

'In what state are the walls?—The walls are all out of condition from the IVth up to the XVth.

'At the Xth lock, are the gates in a bad state?—Of the lower gates one is broken quite asunder.

'Are they very leaky?—Yes; the head lock-gate is very good but the lower lock gates are very unsound.

'In what state is the wall?—The head wall is out of condition.'[108]

Pullen had himself inspected the canal ('for 12 or 13 miles') only four days before the hearing and except for Lock XVI, which had been recently repaired, he reported that all the locks above Bramley were out of condition, and that the banks in Sidney Wood were cracked at the water's edge and had sunk quite a foot within the last nine months so that the water had been running over very much. However, further cross-examination showed that the state of the canal had hardly changed in the past ten years and was not as bad as the petitioners for the bill wished to make out. Pullen himself ventured the opinion that 'the locks might be put in order without any very great outlay' and that the canal could be restored without much expense if taken in hand at once. The bill's opponents also alleged that water had been deliberately wasted in order to stop traffic and by so reducing receipts give cause for the canal to be closed. This allegation, however, was not proven. Further witnesses were called whose evidence established the genuineness of the Arun Navigation's offer to contribute towards the Wey & Arun's upkeep, the wish of the Godalming Navigation to do the same, and that both the Arun and the Godalming Navigations would suffer a reduction of revenue if the canal was closed. The Arun estimated its annual loss at about 4,000 tons and the Godalming at over 6,000. One witness stated that he had an outstanding contract to deliver 1,000 tons of timber from Arundel to Godalming and that the railway refused to carry timber in some shapes and sizes, and could not offer adequate storage accommodation. On behalf of several landowners with property adjoining the canal, it was stated that they had agreed to subscribe, for a period not exceeding five years, an annual sum in proportion to the length of their canal frontage, up to a sum not exceeding £5 per mile per bank, which meant that if all the riparian owners subscribed the maximum, some £180 p.a. could be raised.

After the tenth witness had been called, the chairman intimated that their Lordships were of the opinion that sufficient evidence had been adduced and on the third day of the hearing the bill's opponents secured the insertion of seven additional clauses whose effect was to allow a reprieve for the Wey & Arun if certain conditions were fulfilled. The petitioners for the bill agreed as a compromise that the canal should not be closed or sold in lots before 30 September 1869 if, within six months from the granting of the

Act, sufficient money was guaranteed for running expenses; furthermore, that if the canal were disposed of in its entirety, it should not be sold back to the riparian owners until it had been closed for traffic for six consecutive months.

The bill, as amended, was reported to the House of Lords on 26 March, read a third time on 3 April, referred back to the Court of Chancery and sent to the Commons (where only Lord Grantley opposed it). It was returned with amendments on 17 July, which amendments were approved by the Commons on 24 July. On 31 July 1868 the bill received the Royal Assent.

The landowners and both the Arun and the Godalming Navigations guaranteed a sufficient sum to keep the canal in working order until the end of September 1869. Although the abandonment Act had been passed, it was not inevitable that the canal should be closed if a purchaser could be found. Meanwhile a small and fairly regular traffic continued to use the waterway. Tolls actually slightly increased during the year ending April 1868, when the navigation's abandonment was being so actively discussed. This may have been due to the Guildford to Horsham railway raising its charges for the carriage of goods soon after its opening, and for a while it seemed that the canal might retain sufficient traffic to warrant its continued upkeep. However, no resuscitation occurred and tolls dwindled to £393 and £359 in 1869 and 1870.

Finally, on 30 August 1870, the canal, together with some property at Guildford, was put up for auction as a going concern. The sale was advertised as 'affording a rare opportunity for barge owners, capitalists and speculators to secure an important and extensive canal property, long established and which has produced an average annual gross sum per annum of £620 in tolls'. The vendors optimistically claimed that 'if a judicious outlay was made in extending the wharves and in improvements of the property generally, it is believed the traffic upon the canal would be increased and a larger income obtained.' These statements deceived no one. The figure quoted was the average of tolls for the past ten years. Five of these, however, were pre-railway years when the average was £820 p.a. compared with £440 p.a. for post-railway years. The auction took place at the Mart, Tokenhouse Yard, London. There were four lots. The house occupied by John Moon, the timber merchant, which stood in the High Street by Guildford bridge, together with the timber-yard, was sold to Moon for £550. A bid of £200 for the stone-mason's yard failed to reach the reserve price fixed by the Chancery Judge. For lot IV, 'The canal, banks,

Plate 37. Entrance to Pallingham Lock, c. 1918

Plate 38. 'Reliance of Fittleworth' moored above Stopham Bridge, 1905

Plate 39. Hardham Mill and Lock, 1843

Plate 40. Hardham Mill, c.1910. The mill was destroyed by enemy bombs in 1941

Plate 54. Arundel Docks, c.1820

Plate 55. Arundel Docks, c.1870

Plate 56. Topsail schooners at Arundel after a painting by L. A. Wilcox, c.*1870*

Plate 57. Sailing barge approaching Arundel, c.*1900*

Plate 58. Entrance to the Portsmouth & Arundel Canal at Ford, c.

Plate 59. Ford Lock from an oil painting by W. H. Mason, c.*1855*

Plate 60. Chichester Canal, c.*1870*

Plate 61. Southgate Canal Basin, c.*1910*

Plate 62. Circus elephants bathing in Southgate Basin, 1903

Plate 63. Casher Lock, Birdham, 1954

Plate 64. 0–6–0 Sidlesham crossing the Chichester Canal at Hunston, c. 1920

Plate 65. The Hundred of Manhood & Selsey Tramway's lifting bridge at Hunston, c. 1900

Plate 66. Sea Lock I, Milton, 1964

Plate 67. Sea Lock II, Milton, c.*1900*

Plate 68. W. Grove, Master Carpenter on the Wey Navigation (1885–1930)

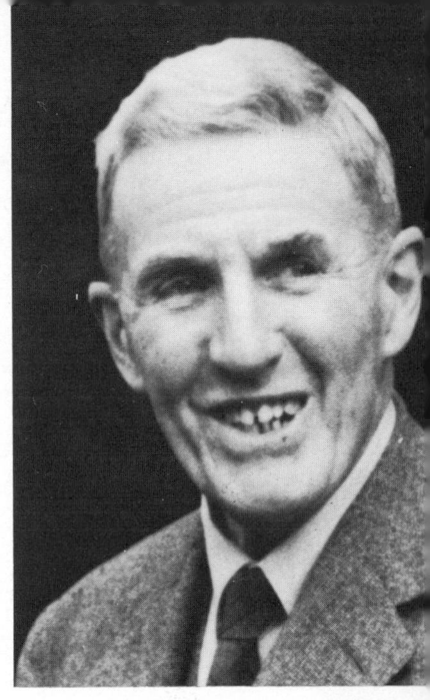

Plate 69. Harry Stevens, Manager of the Wey Navigation (1930–1965)

Plate 70. Benjamin Stone with Annie, his wife, Pallingham Lock, 1934

Plate 71. George Henly, barge-master on the Arun Navigation until 1898

Particulars and Conditions of Sale

OF THE

WEY & ARUN JUNCTION

CANAL PROPERTY,

AS A GOING CONCERN,

COMPRISING THE

LINE OF CANAL EXTENDING FROM STONE-BRIDGE,

ONLY A SHORT DISTANCE FROM THE IMPORTANT

Market Town of Guildford to New Bridge at Pulborough,

Forming the connecting link between the Navigable Rivers the Wey and the Arun, thereby affording direct Water Communication between the Port of Littlehampton, and the Town of Arundel, in the County of Sussex, and the River Thames, passing through sundry Parishes in the Counties of Surrey and Sussex, a distance of about 18 miles, which, with the Banks, Reservoirs, Wharves, Buildings, and the Appurtenances attached, occupy an Area of

ABOUT 200 ACRES,

ALSO

IN THE TOWN OF GUILDFORD,

VALUABLE FREEHOLD PREMISES,

CONSISTING OF

A RESIDENCE AND BUILDINGS,

With Timber and Slate Merchants' and Stone Masons' Yards;

Which will be Offered by Auction, by

HENRY CRAWTER,

(The Person appointed by the Vice-Chancellor, Sir Richard Malins)

AT THE MART, TOKENHOUSE YARD, LONDON,

On TUESDAY, the 30th AUGUST, 1870,

At TWELVE o'clock precisely, in FOUR LOTS.

Particulars may be had of Messrs. W. H., M. & F. F. SMALLPEICE, Solicitors, Guildford; of Messrs. PYKE, IRVING, & PYKE, Solicitors, No. 43, Lincoln's Inn Fields, W.C.; at the "White Hart" Inn, Guildford; Principal Inns at Cranley, Pulborough, and other Inns in the Neighbourhood of the Canal; at the Mart; and of the AUCTIONEER, No. 5, Bedford Row, W.C.

N.B.—Particulars can also be had of Mr. WILLIAM STANTON, at the Wharf, Bramley, Manager of the Canal, and Wharfinger, and who will shew the Property.

Fig. 49.—Wey & Arun Junction Canal Auction Particulars, 1870

buildings and appurtenances totalling 200 acres' of which 61 acres consisted of reservoir and feeding streams, there was no bid.

It was evident that closure was imminent unless immediate action was taken, and again it was the indefatigable Holmes who proposed at the Arun meeting on 5 December 1870 that the Arun Navigation should consider taking a repairing lease of the Wey & Arun at a nominal rent provided that the canal was purchased by a company of landowners. The resolution was seconded by Mr French but, being opposed by both Lord Leconfield and Mr Cooper, was inevitably defeated.

In spite of the railway, barges still occasionally plied between Guildford and Arundel and a case is reported in the *Sussex Express* on 21 June 1870 of two bargees being summoned at Guildford for assault. Thomas Smith, a bargemaster of Arundel, and James Hetherington of Cranleigh were engaged in unloading chalk from a barge at Davis' wharf in Quarry Street when the plaintiff, Daniel Longhurst, came to the wharf to draw water. The evidence revealed that Longhurst, who was a bricklayer, had called the bargees 'grubbers' and 'bastards', the result of which provoked Hetherington into throwing Longhurst into the river. The magistrates dismissed the case against Smith but found Hetherington guilty and imposed a fine, drawing the conclusion that Longhurst, who had sustained injuries to his ribs, had suffered more than he deserved. In August the last of the Wey & Arun barges, Stanton's *Active*, put into Pallingham dockyard for repair.

The end of the canal now hoved in sight.[175] Bridges and locks were sadly in need of repair, but the wherewithal was lacking. Tolls for the twelve months to April 1871 totalled only £277 which represented the carriage of barely 5,000 tons of cargo. The official liquidator had therefore no option but to apply again to the Court of Chancery for authority to close the Wey & Arun. On 26 May 1871 Vice-Chancellor Malins ordered that notice of this proposal, which was intended to take effect from 1 July, should be inserted in the London and local papers and posted along the banks of the canal. Stay of execution, however, was allowed when Sprinks lodged an affidavit on behalf of the Arun Navigation with the Court of Chancery so that steps could be taken to protect the navigation from loss of water at Newbridge, to make it clear that the Wey & Arun were responsible for the repair of the canal bridge there, and that the land south of the bridge belonged to the Arun proprietors. This matter settled, the order to close the canal was made on 5 July and took effect from 22 July 1871.

So, with the navigation abandoned, the chain was broken and London lost her only inland water link with the English Channel. The event passed unrecorded in the national press, but there are

Wey and Arun Junction Canal.

In Chancery.

In the matter of the Companies Act, 1862,

and

In the matter of the Company of the Proprietors of the Wey and Arun Junction Canal.

BY AN ORDER made by his Honor the Vice Chancellor, SIR RICHARD MALINS, in Chambers in the above matter, dated the 26th day of May, 1871, on the application of the Official Liquidator of the above named Company, it was ordered as follows: "It is ordered that Notice be inserted in the *London Gazette*, the *Times Newspaper*, the *West Sussex Gazette*, the *Surrey Standard* Newspaper, and the *Surrey Advertiser* Newspaper; and by Bills posted in the Towns of *Arundel* and *Guildford*, and along the Route of the said Canal, that an application has been made to the Court for the closing for traffic of the said Canal (extending from Stonebridge in the Parish of Shalford, in the County of Surrey, to Newbridge in the Parish of Wisborough Green, in the County of Sussex, the property of the above named Company), and the extinguishment of all rights of way, or user, and other rights in reference thereto, or in connection therewith, on or after the 1st day of July next: And that such application will be further heard and considered on the 24th day of June next, at the Chambers of the said Judge, No. 3, Stone Buildings, Lincolns Inn, in the County of Middlesex, at 12 of the Clock at noon: And it is ordered that the said application be adjourned for further consideration to the said 24th day of June next, at the place and time aforesaid, with a view to the Court then making an Order in accordance with the application or such other Order as the Judge may think to be proper under the circumstances."

J. A. BUCKLEY,
Chief Clerk.

W. STENT, PRINTER, 33, HIGH STREET, GUILDFORD.

Fig. 50.—Wey & Arun Canal—Notice of Closure, 1871

still today works of reference stating that Cranleigh and Loxwood are situated on the banks of the Wey & Arun Junction Canal, as if implying commercial importance rather than rural enchantment

Although the waterway had been officially closed, William Stanton's barges continued none the less to come up from the Thames laden with coal for discharging at Bramley wharf. No one appears to have objected to this state of affairs and presumably the northern end of the canal would have continued in use until the locks had become unworkable if the old merchant had not suddenly died on 13 January 1872 at the age of 61. Stanton's death came as a sad loss to Bramley, where he had become a well-known and much loved figure, respected by the villagers and water-folk alike. The obituary in the local paper referred to 'his

PALLINGHAM LOCK.

18

No.

Fig. 51.—Pallingham Lock Voucher

many admirable traits of character and acts of benevolence which gained the affection and esteem of all with whom he came in contact'. For the past decade he had been the only bargemaster of consequence on the canal. Every day his venerable figure would be seen outside his house on the red brick wharf where he was wont to stand, clad in high hat and long smock, worn black or white as occasion demanded, chatting genially to the boatmen; most were local men, but others came from towns as far away as Basingstoke, Brighton, Oxford, or Midhurst, and there was always some new story to be told or gossip exchanged. If the navigation had lost money for its shareholders, it had brought a fair degree of wealth to Stanton. His coal and timber business had prospered to such an extent that his bid to gain control of the canal had not been an idle one. Noted for his generosity during his lifetime, he bequeathed in his will a legacy of £1,000 to the villagers of Bramley, the interest on which still provides for the distribution of coal to the poor at Christmas time.* His executors continued to run the barges for a few more months but on 27 June 1872 the *Active* carried her last load of coal to Stanton's yards.

H. E. Malden in his *History of Surrey* stated that in 1873 the canal was barely passable for a small boat. It is recounted that the year before the Surrey historian and a friend attempted to work a boat through, but that near Alfold they were halted, as not only were the locks unworkable, but the dense growth of water plants and overhanging bushes barred further progress. A cart had to be procured to return their boat to Godalming while they continued on foot to Pulborough, where another boat was hired to complete the 'intended' voyage to Littlehampton.[109] The Arun Navigation ledgers at Newbridge suggest that there may still have been some activity at the southern end of the canal, for timber and planking were delivered to the Wey & Arun in May 1872. A more likely conclusion is that this was used in making the dam to seal off the water between the two navigations.

After 1872 only one labourer, who lived in a small cottage on Run Common, remained on the pay-roll of the bankrupt canal Company. Rogers' task was primarily to keep the towpath clear by cutting hay and trimming hedges, the fruits of his labour being sold to increase the canal's meagre revenue by a few shillings. Parish rates and tithes had still to be paid and the only hope the shareholders had of obtaining any return for their holdings was that the money received from the sale of the land and property would enable a small final payment to be made. Indeed it is doubtful whether any payment was made to the shareholders from the official liquidator's account. The outlay involved in obtaining the Act of abandonment, the legal costs, the expense of putting in 'good substantial repair any public bridges, roads or culverts' and the compensation paid to landowners in return for the Company's relief from liability to maintain bridges and fences, had all to be borne out of assets. However, at the end of 1875 there was a balance of £400 and little of the Company's land had been sold, but there is no evidence that claims for compensation had then been received or settled.

* On an average, some sixty residents benefit annually from this gift. *Surrey Times*, June 1949.

The official liquidator had the task of offering the land back to the riparian owners, but few of them wanted to increase the size of their property by becoming the possessor of a stagnant ditch, even if it was sold to them at a nominal price. The cost of filling up a canal is almost as expensive as digging it, and, with few exceptions, the lots of the canal which were purchased at varying intervals for small amounts were usually left untouched and remain today in almost their original state. However, Taunt, writing in 1878, stated that the Wey & Arun was entirely filled up in places and in some instances steps to level it had been taken by the purchasers.[110] The stretch through Whipley Manor was sold back for £50 in 1878; the Grantley family, who had received £2,000 compensation for inconvenience and loss of land when the waterway was built, were able to repurchase their 770-yd section for £75 in 1882. Its value today must be very considerably greater, since the bed forms part of the gardens of a housing estate. A lot of over 24 acres, including Southland, Brewhurst, Malham, and Rowner locks, with the latter's cottage and garden, was sold for £200 in 1893 by John Napper, who had presumably purchased it some years earlier. The canal company was not formally dissolved until 1910.

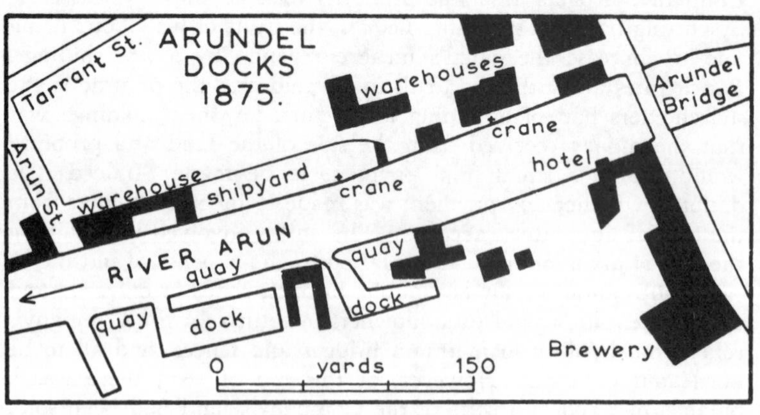

Map 13

CHAPTER XV

Liquidation and Abandonment of the Arun and the Portsmouth & Arundel (1871–1896)

The Arun Navigation appoints a new clerk—introduces economies—pays its last dividend (1874)—appeals for funds—reduces toll on coal—completes its centenary and is closed (1888)—opposition from landowners to winding-up order—Board of Trade enquiry (1893)—Arnold's trials and tribulations—warrant of abandonment (1896)—application to wind up the Portsmouth & Arundel Canal (1888)—objections—Chichester Canal Transfer Act (1892)—the rife at Barnham—warrant obtained (1896).

In 1870 Edward Arnold, solicitor and town clerk of Chichester, was appointed clerk to the proprietors of the Arun Navigation. James Powell, who had held the position since 1842, had been slowly going mad and because of his lunacy Arnold had in fact been acting for him since the beginning of the previous year. The appointment of the new clerk came at a time when the Arun's future had reached a critical stage. The threatened closure of the Wey & Arun, involving the inevitable loss of through-traffic between Arundel and the Thames, jeopardized the whole future of the navigation. Already substantial economies had had to be introduced in the summer of 1867, when the Committee had decided that William Muggeridge, who lived in one of the cottages at Newbridge, should be dismissed and that the salary of the general manager should be reduced by a third to £50 p.a. Sprinks resented this proposal and promptly resigned at the end of June 1868. The Committee thereupon recalled Muggeridge, increased his salary to 18s. per week and told him to manage the wharf. The wharfinger's house, with four acres of land, was let to a Mr Dunkerton and Sprinks, who had moved to Arundel, was requested to superintend the accounts for £6 p.a. and the navigation for £17 p.a. In 1870 the Committee rather apologetically reappointed him as superintendent and collector at £15 p.a. 'if he can accept the appointment'.

The salaries of the three lock-keepers had also been reduced from £6 to £2 p.a. Not unexpectedly Henry Webb at Coldwaltham,

Samuel Fiest at Hardham, and James Stone at Pallingham all objected and they were therefore ordered to leave their houses by the end of October. Stone refused to move and in the following June Mr Sharp was requested to see him and 'desire that he should leave as speedily as possible'. In December the clerk was instructed to obtain possession of Stone's house without delay and if necessary to take court proceedings. The cottage was advertised to let but there were no takers and in June 1869 Stone's arrears in rent (£10) were forgiven providing that he would find a guarantor for punctual payment in the future. The Company were certainly generous, for Stone had been forgiven a similar amount of rent ten years before.

In 1869 the first Lord Leconfield had died, leaving his 34 shares to his eldest son, Henry Wyndham. In 1871 the crane at Newbridge—sadly in need of repair—was sold to Holmes for £10 and Benjamin Stone was appointed lock-keeper at Pallingham following the death of his father. In 1874 the Company ceased to act as wharfingers at Newbridge and declared a final dividend of 1 per cent. More economies had to be made and wages further reduced. Muggeridge was again given notice, also Henry Wood, a labourer, and unsuccessful attempts were made to let the warehouse at Newbridge. In 1881 it was decided that George Dunkerton, who rented the wharf house from the Company and was paid 12s. a week to keep an eye on the wharf and provide refreshments for the Committee on their annual visits, was not to receive more than 6s. a week in view of the depressed state of business. A lengthy correspondence ensued. Dunkerton rejected the offer and suggested 10s. a week 'as it takes a man all day to look after the wharf all the year round', and pointed out that when he first took the job Muggeridge got paid more. However, Dunkerton was told that no increase in the offer could, 'regretfully', be made and was consoled with the advantages of storage and garden and the knowledge that the attention he had given to the wharf was really 'very slight'. In 1885 he was offered 4s. a week; this he refused and so, because there was work to be done, the arrangement was continued. However, the following year he was offered 3s. a week plus use of a store. Dunkerton didn't bother to reply.

Every source of possible revenue was explored. Counsel's opinion was sought on the Company's power to levy tolls on the river above Greatham bridge. The Board of Trade was informed that no funds were available for applying the Explosives Act to the Arun Canal. Corn for Brewhurst Mill was stored at the warehouse. A Mr Ellis

ARUN NAVIGATION.

NEWBRIDGE WHARF.

IS HEREBY GIVEN, THAT

ON AND AFTER THE 1ST OF APRIL, 1874,

THE

ARUN NAVIGATION PROPRIETORS

Will cease to be Wharfingers or receive or deliver Goods at NEWBRIDGE WHARF, in the Parish of Wisbro' Green, or be answerable for any Goods deposited there; the Wharf may, however, still be used at the risk of the Persons using the same.

Dated this 1st day of December, 1873,

(BY ORDER)

EDWARD ARNOLD,

CLERK TO THE PROPRIETORS.

PULLINGER, PRINTER, NORTH STREET, CHICHESTER.

Fig. 52.—Arun Navigation—Vacation of Newbridge Wharf, 1874

Chichester,

May 24th, 1883.

Sir,

ARUN NAVIGATION.

The Expenditure of this Navigation being now in excess of the Receipts, it has been found necessary to devise some means of augmenting the income, with a view to the Canal being kept open by the Proprietors as a going concern. In the absence of sufficient support being obtained the Proprietors will be compelled to close the Canal.

Subscriptions ranging from £10 a year to £2 per year for the next two years, amounting together to about £25 a year have been promised by persons interested in keeping the Canal open; and I am instructed to ask you whether you will kindly add your name to the subscription list, and if so to what amount.

It is estimated that a sum of about £25 a year for the next two years, in addition to the subscriptions already promised, will be required, in order that the Navigation may be kept open for two years longer.

I am, Sir,

Your obedient Servant,

EDWARD ARNOLD,

Clerk.

Fig. 53.—Arun Navigation—Appeal for Funds, 1883

of Bermondsey considered an offer to store hatched bark for 3d. a ton a month 'too heavy'. Sixteen ash and twenty-nine oak trees standing at Newbridge wharf and at Middle lock were sold for £52 in 1882. A further application by Stone for a reduction in rent was refused, since 40s. a year was already considered low and he was able to carry on business as a baker and wheelwright.

Every winter after the annual meeting the proprietors had dinner together at the 'Norfolk Arms'. Sprinks made the arrangements for the meeting and the dinner, and was always told by Arnold 'to get the people at the Norfolk to have a good fire ready'. It was a jolly evening and Arnold, writing in 1878 following the death of the chairman, William Shaft, laments that with the loss of Mr Shaft and Mr French, and with Mr Holmes not being well, 'the whole party seems to be almost broken up'. The dinners continued until 1890, although in 1884 Arnold wrote to Lear, then chairman, that while he would be exceedingly sorry to see their 'games' go the way of the survey, he feared that the time had come. In reply to a shareholder's allegation of extravagance in 1891, Arnold teasingly informed him that the dinners had only been able to be given because the clerk, whose salary was in arrears, did not press for payment.

In 1870 tolls had totalled nearly £500; within five years they had dropped to less than £200 and between 1876 and 1885 averaged only £138. On 10 June 1882 the proprietors viewed the whole navigation by barge for the purpose of determining its future. It was observed that parts of the canal appeared to be rapidly closing up with weeds and that the works were falling into decay. Farmers complained that several bridges were not 'fit for a horse and cart' and were particularly critical of the condition of Greatham bridge. Expenditure now exceeded income and traffic was dying out. Although Lord Leconfield, the second largest shareholder, did not take an active part in the management, his agent wrote in September in regard to the future of the navigation, saying 'we all of us think that his Lordship is really much more interested in the question than anyone else'. Accordingly, preparations were made for a visit to Petworth House by Lear, Holmes, and Arnold, at which the Company's predicament was fully discussed.

In January 1883 Arnold wrote, 'It is I think practically hopeless to look for any material revival of the business of the navigation. On the other hand it is urged that keeping open the canal tends in itself to keep down the railway rates and that in the interests of the public, it is desirable that the waterway should not be closed.' A meeting was therefore held at Pulborough in February, with Lord Leconfield in the chair, at which the proprietors and landowners were invited to subscribe £50 or so a year for two years towards the cost of running the navigation, in the hope that during that period trade would revive. However, except for £10 from Lord Leconfield and £5 from both Holmes and Sir Walter Barttelot, only nominal sums from four or five others were received. Arnold sent out a further appeal in May, stating that 'the expenditure of the navigation being greater than the receipts it has been found necessary to devise some means of augmenting the income with a view to the canal being kept open by the proprietors as a going concern. Subscriptions amounting to some £25 a year having been already promised, a request is made that your name be added to this list as it is estimated that about £50 will be required for keeping the navigation open for a further two years.' Only £65 was, however, donated for the years 1883–5.

In May 1884 Arnold suggested to the chairman that the time had come to wind up the Company, but no one appeared willing to press the matter, for in November he wrote to Charles Cooper asking 'how are we to do anything unless the larger proprietors are with us?' In November Arnold doubted that the canal could be auctioned as a going concern—'that was the difficulty the Wey & Arun got into'—but suggested all the shares might be auctioned. Nevertheless in December a final effort was made to revive trade and by agreement with Lord Leconfield the toll on coal on both the Arun and Rother Navigations was reduced to 3d. a ton for 1885. The experiment lasted two years but the coal merchants appeared to take little advantage of the concession.

In 1887, the Arun Navigation's uncelebrated centenary year, little more than 2,000 tons were carried; tolls dropped to less than £50 a year leaving only Henry Doick's two barges working the canal and a debit balance of £12. A final appeal by the chairman to shareholders asking for contributions of 10s. a share met with a very poor response, 'only 3 shareholders with 3 shares had so far consented to pay' and the letter to the largest shareholder had been returned through the dead letter office. In December Arnold stated that he had received no contribution from Lord Leconfield and only 10s. altogether, this from Mr Smart 'which it would not perhaps be fair to appropriate'. Since receipts only totalled £102 against outgoings of £137 steps had inevitably to be taken to close the navigation and notices were erected along the towpath to take effect from 1 January 1888. The lock-keepers were offered tenancies of their cottages at 1s. a week, the osier beds and dock ceased to be let, and the clerk was instructed not to defend any action brought against the Company but to let judgement go by default.

In March 1888 the Coopers sold their shareholding of 44 shares for a nominal sum to a speculator named Williams who hoped that the assets might prove of value; a false hope in the light of Arnold's remarks the previous October, for he considered the shares

ARUN NAVIGATION.

NOTICE.

The Navigation will be

CLOSED

on and from the 1st day of January, 1888, the Traffic being insufficient to meet the working expenses.

BY ORDER,

Chichester,
13th December, 1887.

EDWARD ARNOLD,
CLERK.

ADCOCK, PRINTER, NORTH STREET, CHICHESTER.

Fig. 54.—Arun Navigation—Notice of Closure, 1888

worthless and thought it doubtful if there would be any surplus for division amongst the shareholders. In spite of the notices the navigation did in fact remain open to any traffic which presented itself. However, on 20 June 1888 Doick left Houghton carrying his last load of chalk; 10 tons for Lee Farm and 20 bound for Newbridge. As usual he returned light. That same month Arnold is writing that 'it is unfortunate that the public discontinue to use the canal but as they have ceased to maintain it, there appears to be no alternative but that it should be closed as soon as possible.'

Danger notices were stuck on Hardham and Lee Farm bridges. In the autumn, John Stephney and a boy took an empty barge up to Newbridge where it was broken up, while former bargees drank ale and sang what was the nearest thing they knew to a dirge. It was a sad occasion. Some months later, in January 1889, the last barge loaded with chalk passed through Hardham tunnel.

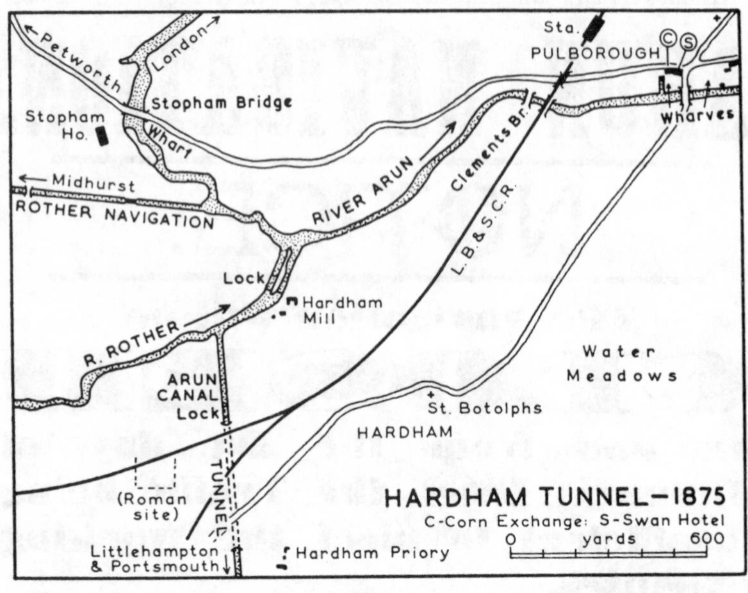

Map 14

Meanwhile the proprietors were unanimously of the opinion that the Company should be liquidated as soon as possible. On the other hand, there were several landowners who raised strong objections to being saddled without compensation with the obligations of maintaining the canal on their property. The petition presented to wind up the Arun Navigation Company in June 1888 was heard by Mr Justice North in August. It was suggested that counsel for the objecting landowners had no *locus standi* to be heard, but they were allowed to address the court as *amici curiae*. Mr Justice North decided that as an Act was likely to be passed shortly which would contain provisions for dealing with useless canals, he proposed to stand over the petition until the next sitting. It was for the promoters to state then whether they wished their petition restored.[111]

at Orfold (value £40) were ceded to him. This demand inspired Sir Walter to say that he would only agree if he obtained Pallingham lock house (value £100) which prompted more claims from Napper and Arnold to comment: 'I do not think that Mr. Napper ought to have claimed Orfold cottage, he is very grasping. He is not content with the Orfold cottage, and the whole of Tithinglee but he insists on having the whole of the bed of the canal on his own land.' Before the end of July Sir Walter had seen Napper again, but he refused to come to terms so that matters had come once again to a jarring halt.

However, in February 1895 Napper withdrew his claims for both sides of the canal, tried to obtain fresh conditions and failed. It was not therefore until April, after a second meeting with Hopwood at Arundel, that the outstanding objectors could be induced to come to terms and 'the B.o.T. is requested to issue the warrant with as little delay as practicable'. On 27 April the warrant was anticipated daily and Arnold received his salary for 1892. Then came another unexpected delay. Arnold was summoned some weeks later to London to learn that the Duke of Norfolk had suddenly decided to oppose the application. Meetings in August and September revealed that the Duke was anxious that the towpath should not be continued as a highway and another meeting was held at the B.o.T. in October at which the atmosphere got 'rather breezy'. By November his objection had been boiled down to the repair of a small bridge carrying the towpath over a ditch at Bury, and Sir Walter was requested to use his influence with the Petworth R.D.C. to persuade them to accept this responsibility. In December a draft agreement was awaiting the Duke of Norfolk's signature but two hurry-ups sent to the Duke's solicitors only raised more queries. Not until the first flowers of spring had arrived was a settlement reached and the agreement signed.

Meanwhile John Sprinks had died in the summer of 1895 while still receiving a salary of £10 p.a. as superintendent. Benjamin Stone's rent had also remained unpaid for two years, and seven months later Arnold was asking Dunkerton if he had seen anything of Stone. 'He has not paid any rent for a very long time.'[176] Yet another return had to be made to the Registrar of Joint Stock Companies at Somerset House.

The warrant of abandonment was applied for again on 5 March 1896. Further delays occurred and on 9 June Arnold wrote, 'they are rather slow at the B.o.T. Somewhat old fashioned, we have to humour them, it will be alright in the end. Considering the vehement opposition of Sir Walter Barttelott followed by the underhand action of the Duke of Norfolk we may be satisfied that with persistence and patience we have pulled it off. There are rocks ahead in the fact that we have no chairman and the company is practically moribund.' Arnold also thoughtfully asked their London firm of solicitors to remember to ensure that the winding-up order provided for him to be remunerated for all he had done. 'The shareholders expect nothing.' His feelings, however, can be imagined when he heard from the B.o.T. in July that Thakeham R.D.C. objected to the warrant on the grounds that no repairs had been done to the canal bridge at Greatham. Again it was pointed out that there were no funds available and that this was an additional reason for the warrant so that it could be taken over by the county or district council. Silence, more follow-up letters and then, on 23 September 1896, Arnold's day of triumph came when the piece of paper arrived announcing that the navigation was officially abandoned with the Board of Trade's authority.

The time and trouble involved in closing the Arun Navigation shows why many waterways have either never been legally closed or only many years after they have fallen into disuse. They followed a familiar pattern. After receipts had dwindled to nothing, meetings would cease to be held, offices would be closed, and employees dismissed. The locks became unworkable, their pounds unnavigable. Creditors might be left with no more assets than marshy land and stagnant water. The Rother Navigation simply faded away and was forgotten for nearly fifty years.

The disposal of the Portsmouth & Arundel Canal, whose phantom-like existence had so sorely troubled the promoters of railway lines and the highway authorities, was a more complicated matter since in spite of the railway along the South Coast and the closing of the barge canal at Ford, the ship canal from Birdham to Chichester continued in operation. However, no meeting of any sort had been held by the Company since 1855 and the Chichester Canal had been managed by the wharfinger, Richard Purchase, who took the receipts and carried out repairs. A tonnage of 5,000 in 1858 had increased to over 7,000 tons in 1868. Tolls, however, slightly declined—£104 in 1847, £86 in 1866, £46 in 1874, and averaged £53 between 1882 and 1888. For a number of years traffic remained fairly constant and only began gradually to decline towards the turn of the century. In 1888 some 4,500 tons of sand, bricks, and coal for the gasworks were still being unloaded at Southgate basin. In that year James Ozzard, a retired naval paymaster,

general wish to reduce railway rates brought a resurgence of interest in waterways. Shortly after the turn of the century experiments were made with electrically driven barges on the Wey Navigation which might have led to the opening of another link from the Thames to the English Channel. The current was generated by an engine-driven dynamo at Dapdune wharf and, since accumulators would take up too much space in a barge, overhead leads were employed similar to those developed many years later for the trolley-bus system. Between Guildford and Woodbridge a system of wires was stretched across the river and supported 15 ft above the water by what a newspaper report called 'a series of irregular drunken-looking posts, evidently once respectable scaffold poles'.

This experiment, which the local press said would ruin the river for pleasure boating, produced nevertheless very favourable results, particularly in cheapness of motive power. More experiments were carried out and a scheme was produced in 1902 for a canal, 64 miles long, from the Itchen and Hamble rivers at Southampton through Botley, Droxford, Alton, Godalming, and Guildford to the Thames at Ditton. The waterway was to be 80 ft wide, 11 ft deep, with 12 locks capable of passing barges carrying 250 tons. Three generating stations were to be built to provide current to an overhead trolley system which would enable the canal to be lit throughout and for barges to be hauled from the towpath by electric traction at a cost estimated not to exceed 1/50th of a penny per mile. In this manner it was hoped to tow cargoes of 1,500 tons, the equal of six fully loaded boats. The undertaking, described as second only to the Manchester Ship Canal, was designed to attract to its banks industry which was alleged to be suffering through the heavy cost of land carriage.[115] The estimated cost of the Southampton Canal project was £2,500,000, but it failed to attract support.

The Basingstoke Canal too was slowly failing. After the original company had gone into liquidation in 1866, the waterway fell into the hands of a succession of speculators, few more successful than the last. A rather hesitant barge traffic continued to Basingstoke until 1901 but the closing of the brick-works at Nately Scures in 1908 took away most of the traffic above Aldershot. The upper reaches fell derelict, a burst embankment below Aldershot caused no loss of life, but damage of £1,000, and when in 1913 Alec Harmsworth attempted to force a passage to Basingstoke with 10 tons of sand, the voyage had eventually to be abandoned at Basing Wharf for lack of water.

After the Great War few craft ventured beyond Ash Vale and in

1932 a section of the 1,200-yd Greywell tunnel collapsed. However the tonnage carried to Woking averaged some 30,000 tons between 1933 and 1936 when the coal trade ceased. A desultory trade in timber was carried on until 1949, in which year the navigation was sold to the New Basingstoke Canal Company for £8,000. (The history of the Basingstoke Canal is told in '*London's Lost Route to Basingstoke*, 1968, David & Charles.)

The Chilworth Gunpowder Company, Limited.

CHILWORTH.

FREIGHT per Barge "Kate" to Royal Arsenal, Woolwich 23 - 12 - 1914.

POWDER.	HOW PACKED.	SHIPPING MARK.	TOTAL. lbs.
MD Cordite.			
Lots B549 & 555 Size 8	144 Cases		10080
" B550 & 556 " 4¼	134 "		10050
MD I Cordite			
Lot B. 557 Size 20	144 " [illegible]		10,080
	[illegible]		30210

Fig. 57.—Chilworth Gunpowder Company Invoice, 1914

The Godalming Navigation had a small amount of trade (2,806 tons in 1888, 2,919 tons in 1898) until soon after the end of the Great War. In 1913 one of Stevens' barges brought the 18-ton steel centre girder from London for the replacement railway bridge over the river at Shalford. Then the Chilworth powder traffic ceased in 1921 and only two barges regularly worked the river above Guildford between the wars. During the Second World War supplies of canned goods were carried to the emergency food storage depot by Unstead lock and coal was landed at Stonebridge wharf for the Vulcanized Fibre Works up to 1946. Godalming wharf, however, has not been used commercially since 1925 and no cargo has been unloaded at Stonebridge wharf since 1950.

Although the Arun and Rother Navigations were closed by the late eighteen eighties, the tidal reaches of the Arun remained a waterway for all who chose to use it. As no tolls were payable, however, the only records of traffic are the barge books kept by the owners.

Henry Doick (1847–1902) who owned a third share of no. 64* worked from Pulborough. In the space of seven years (1895–1901) he made 521 voyages up and down the Arun carrying 17,096 tons of cargo between Littlehampton and Pulborough.† Gross earnings averaged £163 p.a. The average load weighed 33 tons, the maximum 38. The principal consignments were chalk, coal, culm, gravel and sand, but from time to time Doick carried ballast for Littlehampton

HOUGHTON BRIDGE.

Fig. 58.—Houghton Wharf and Bridge, c. 1905

brigs, steam coal for Arundel, bolts of reeds and osiers for Pepper & Son at Houghton, gas coal to Greatham and flints for the Duke of Norfolk at Timberley and for the Rector of Pulborough. Additional earnings arose from pile driving and usually once or twice a year no. 64 was hired out to Mr Slaughter of York House School, Brighton for barge parties to the 'Black Rabbit' and picnics in South Woods. Doick delivered a barge load of coal to Greatham Wharf on 19 April 1902. It was to be his last. Six months later he was dead. He was 55. For thirty years he had been one of the bell-ringers at Pulborough

* Numbering was a relic of the Arun Navigation's system of licensing.

† Cargoes were collected or unloaded at 8 intermediate wharves. Ford, Arundel, Offham, Houghton, Bury, Timberley (for Amberley), Thorndale (for Watersfield) and Greatham. The same barge book gives details of Thomas Doick's voyages between London Docks and Shalford 1883–5.

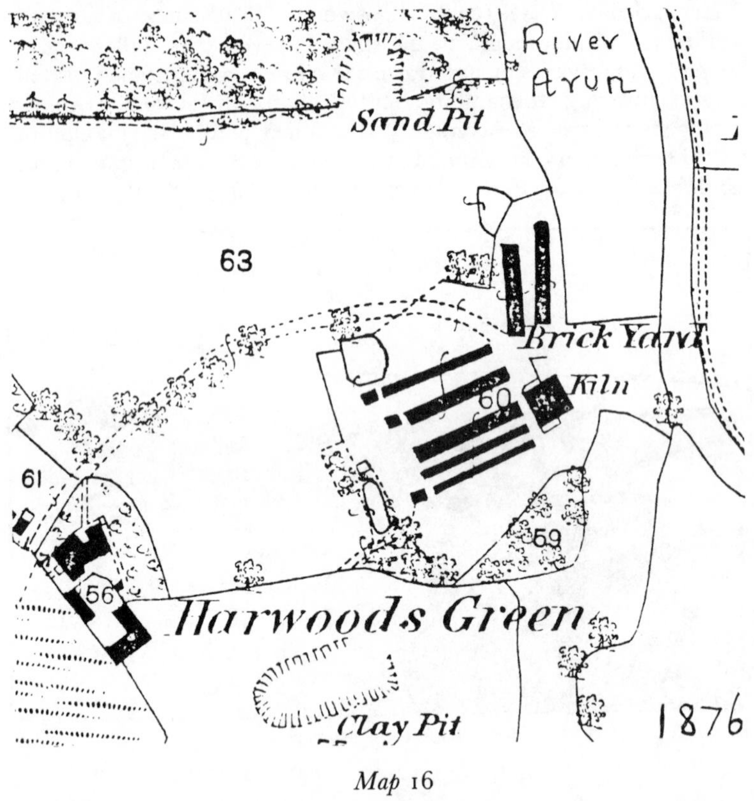

Map 16

Church. The Rector, Churchwardens and bell-ringers erected and inscribed his tombstone 'as a mark of their respect and esteem'.

Another barge-master, John Strudwick of Fittleworth died six weeks later in 1903 aged 82. In his will dated 3 December 1888 he bequeathed his furniture and one cow to his wife and the remainder of his livestock, his house and his ageing barge *Eleanor* to his son, Sam (1864–1933), who had her replaced by the *Reliance* (*see* Plate 38) in 1905. It was about this time that traffic above Stopham Bridge ceased with the closing of the brickworks at Harwoods Green. For eighteen years the *Reliance* operated between Pulborough and Arundel. In 1923 however Strudwick sold her to the Arun Brick Company. This company had speculated in a clay pit at Rackham with the idea of building a light railway to Greatham Wharf. Strudwick's work with the company lasted little more than a year before it failed and in July 1925 the Harbour Master at Littlehampton reported that the brick company had agreed that the abandoned *Reliance* should be given to the commissioners in return for its removal from the tideway.[117]

George Henly, whose family had been bringing coal, sand and timber to Bury Wharf for the best part of a century, continued carrying until the late nineteen twenties when the advent of the motor lorry resulted in the demise of water traffic. *Mayflower, Neptune* and *Old 69* were sold and barges ceased to be floated on to the east bank by the church at high water spring tides for repairs to be undertaken at low water. (see Plate 49.)

The quays above Arundel soon became deserted and overgrown. Two barges were abandoned in the cutting by the south wharf at Houghton soon after the outbreak of the Great War in 1914 when the crane was moved to Littlehampton. For nearly forty years their crumbling hulks retained a certain majesty and grace as the water rose up about their prows on every tide; but on the ebb they appeared a melancholy sight. Now after seventy years only the ribbed skeletons of rotting timbers remain in the forlorn and neglected channel.

In 1898 the L.B. & S.C.R., foreseeing the possibility of subsidence, decided to block up Hardham tunnel at the points where it was crossed by the lines to Arundel and Petworth. This was not a simple operation. First a shaft several feet in circumference had to be bored a few feet from the main line and carried down 10 ft to the crown of the tunnel, which was pierced; thereupon tons of chalk and gravel were conveyed to the spot in trucks, tipped down the hole, and thrown up on either side to touch the roof of the tunnel immediately beneath both lines.[118] So were brought to a close the boating parties and river expeditions which had found the tunnel an intriguing site of exploration during the eighteen nineties.

The tidal portions of the Sussex rivers continued to be used to a greater or lesser extent for commerce until the 1930s. Bonthron described the lower reaches of the Arun as giving 'a good impression of a fine commercial river, the banks of which are well protected, being made up of chalk blocks. Considerable tonnage is carried up to Arundel, Amberley and Greatham'. There was a constant demand for chalk and lime from the Houghton Bridge Agricultural Lime Works which was dispatched both by water and by rail; large and small chalk for road making and as a dressing for pasture land, large blocks for building purposes. However, the outbreak of the Great War necessitated the removal of the crane to Littlehampton and the Government's requisition of the port for the dispatch of munitions and stores to France brought river traffic to a halt; over 2,000 transports had been loaded with $\frac{3}{4}$ million tons before the Armistice was signed; after the war it was decided to use only land transports at Houghton as this enabled trucks or lorries to be loaded at the cliff-face.

Trade on the Chichester Canal had also begun to dwindle before the turn of the century and in 1898 only 704 tons of goods were carried. By 1914 the canal had ceased to be used for commercial traffic, the last recorded trading activity being the collection of shingle in 1906 from Chichester harbour in a sailing barge by the brothers Combe of Bosham, who unloaded it at the basin.[119] In 1907 the *Victoria County History of Sussex* merely referred to the canal as the resort of the heaviest fish, carp up to 14 lb; bream up to $4\frac{1}{2}$ lb; fine perch and roach; a few tench and eels, a pike of $18\frac{1}{2}$ lb taken not long back. However, in spite of attempts by local councils to have the swing bridges replaced at Donnington and Birdham, the Chichester Corporation endeavoured to keep the canal open, but when it became evident that there was unlikely to be any revival of trade, the canal was blocked in 1924 at the two road crossings on the understanding that the swing bridges could be reinstated at six months' notice. On 6 June 1928 the Corporation formally closed and abandoned the canal undertaking, which in 1957 was sold to the West Sussex County Council for £7,500.[120]

Whereas both the Wey & Arun Navigations had been officially abandoned, the Rother Navigation, which had fallen into disuse in the late 1880s, was still legally an open navigation. Technically anyone could come along with a boat, offer the proper toll dues, and wait for the owners to rebuild the locks and put the Navigation in order. An Oxford undergraduate drew attention to this position in 1934 and prompted the Cowdray and Petworth estates to regularize the matter at a cost of over £500 in legal fees, a less expensive alternative to restoring the waterway[121]; if the Midhurst brickworks, with its considerable output, had suddenly decided to use water transport an interesting situation might have arisen. A notice in the *West Sussex Gazette* on 19 September 1935 stated that joint application had been made by the Rt. Hon. Baron Leconfield and the Trustees of the Cowdray Estate, the present owners of the Rother Navigation, to the Minister of Transport for a warrant to abandon the Navigation on the grounds that it was unnecessary for the purposes of public navigation.

It appears almost inevitable that as soon as a public announcement is made of an intention to legalize a situation which everyone has hitherto accepted without protest, objections are sure to be received. In this instance they came from the River Arun Catchment Board on the grounds that the efficiency of the river as a drainage channel might be affected, and from a local Canoe Club. However, on 15 April 1936 the warrant was granted. As with the Portsmouth & Arundel Canal, some fifty years after the last boat had passed through, the obituary would be published in a local newspaper.[122]

The post Second World War years saw a gradual decline in freight traffic on nearly every waterway in the Kingdom and due to the formation of the Inland Waterways Association in 1946 several of the more moribund navigations remained open. Most people's image of canals in those days visualized dilapidated locks and desolate stretches of reed choked channels filled, in urban areas, with the flotsam and jetsam of household waste.

The Wey Navigation remained free from the reins of nationalization and tolerably busy with some dozen craft working the river and along the Thames. However in spite of Harry Stevens' firm control every year from 1944 (29,883 tons) to 1956 (16,105 tons) revealed a drop in freight as the users faded away. The Basingstoke Canal traffic finished in 1949. The collapse of the waste-paper business ended the downstream traffic from Guildford in 1955 and without back carriage the upstream ceased in 1958 with the closure of Moon's timber wharf. In 1957 the flour mill at Stoke closed and in 1963 the linseed oil mill above Thames Lock was burnt down. By now the only regular commercial traffic was the carrying of grain, 80 tons at a time, from freighters in the Pool to Coxes Mill at Weybridge. But even this traffic was threatened by the changing pattern of trade. The London Docks were in decline and bigger cargoes were being discharged at Tilbury where barges collected proportionately less as road transport took the lion's share. In 1963 as a result of the fewer but larger consignments of wheat arriving on the lower reaches of the Thames, the navigation carried less than 10,000 tons for the first time in over two hundred years. The substantial fall in revenue—30 per cent in 1963—prompted Harry Stevens to make a wise and sensible decision and in the following year he generously transferred the ownership of the Navigation to the National Trust (who also took over the Godalming Navigation in 1969).

This rural waterway had changed very little with the passing of the years. Not until 1960 did horses cease to be the barges motive power. Their departure did little to speed things up as tug and barge had to proceed singly through the locks. A visitor to the Company's offices at Guildford was immediately struck by their Dickensian atmosphere. Particularly was this so on winter afternoons when the flickering light from the coal fire cast wavering shadows on the Victorian panelling and low ceiling of Harry Stevens' study. The walls were stacked with musty ledgers and glancing back through the old canal registers, a pageant of barges passed by: names that recalled the strength and majesty of those sturdy, gaily-painted craft, as well as the virtues of their crews and the names of their families. Heading the list were the Arundel Company's aristocratic *Norfolk*, *Egremont*, and *Sovereign*; then came *Perseverance* and *Endeavour*; further down were found *Nancy* and *Harriet*, *Eliza*, and *Anne*. There was a ring of permanence about the *Sussex Oak*, a suggestion of speed on the *Rocket*, and of fragrant aromas from the *Rose in June*. Bargees on the *Guildford Miller* waved cheerfully to the *Prince Regent*; the *Fly* and *Bee* were larger than might be supposed while doubtless the *Algebra* had problems of her own.

The Stevens family had controlled the river for over a century and their continuous association dated back to 1812 when the great-grandfather of Harry Stevens started work as a lock-keeper at Triggs. The old-fashioned locks, with their pounds of sloping turf banks and timber framing, were only being gradually reconstructed; the boat repair yards at Dapdune, run by the Edwards family for three generations, were kept busy although no barges had been built since *Diligent* was completed in 1940. At Guildford wharf stood a massive oak treadmill 18 ft in diameter, worked by man-power, which operated a crane on the water-front. It had not, however, been used since 1908 when concrete piles were brought up the river for the foundations of the Technical Institute.

Although the toll on wheat was reduced in both 1964 and 1966, traffic dwindled as the mill owners found road transport more reliable and not much more expensive.

On 4 July 1969 the West Country type barges *Perseverance* and *Speedwell*, skippered by Steve and John White delivered their last cargoes of grain to Coxes Mill at Weybridge.

Thus ended three centuries of water carriage. Within months the Navigation Office in Friary Street and the old stables and storerooms by the wharf had been demolished to make way for a supermarket. Only the crane was spared. On 13 January 1970 at the age of 82 Harry Stevens died. An obituary notice recalled that he was 'an exceptionally kind man for whom nothing seemed to be too much trouble. He was a man of the greatest integrity and with strong principles'.[123]

CHAPTER XVII

The Lost Route Explored (1900–1950)

Arousal of interest in derelict waterways—views expressed about the Wey & Arun Canal by H. E. Malden (1900), Walter Jerrold (1901), Hope Moncrieff (1906), P. Bonthron, Hilaire Belloc (1906) and Martin Cobbett—article in *The Times* (1915)—the holiday adventure of Mr P. J. Davenant—exploration of Sidney Wood by artist Donald Maxwell (1923)—the Wey & Arun Canal researchers—F. S. Blomfield (1934), Roger Sellman (1935) and Richard Goodchild (1937)—R. Thurston Hopkins visits Pallingham Quay (1935)—John Pitt's verse—Tom Rolt and Charles Hadfield.

Interest in the revival of abandoned waterways began almost as soon as they had been closed. Initially the development of the railway system in Britain so amazed everyone that people were content to think waterways obsolete and to overlook the dangers of monopoly.[124] A letter written to the Secretary of the Royal Society of Arts at the time of a two day conference held in 1888 to consider the possibilities of revival stated 'sixteen years ago anyone advocating water transport was promptly accused of galvanising a corpse'. But advocates of commercial revival ignored the rural waterways of the south and when the Royal Commission of 1906 presented its report in 1909, the commercial prospects of the South of England waterways were regarded as minimal.

The closure of the Wey & Arun Canal had passed unlamented and it was not until the turn of the century that the first signs of interest in its loss began to be mentioned by several writers. Most however referred to it as the picturesque remnant of a past age. The first of these was probably the Surrey historian H. E. Malden who wrote in 1900 that the 'canal is now a thing of the past, as completely as are stretches of the Roman road which runs near it. In 1873 it was barely possible for a small boat. Now it is in many places filled up and abandoned. In others it remains a neglected ditch overgrown with reeds and water-lilies, haunted by the kingfisher and the moorhen.'[125]

Walter Jerrold (1865–1929) the biographer and journalist noted in Dent's series of County Guides in 1901 that the Alfold area was 'unspoiled as yet by disfiguring boards inviting the builder' and how the old Surrey & Sussex Canal enhanced the charm of the countryside. 'What commerce has lost by its disuse has been gained by the picturesque, for Nature has done her best to make man's neglected waterway her own, and there are stretches of the old canal grown with reeds and water-lilies and haunted by water-fowl which must delight the eye of every artist who comes upon them.'[126]

Five years later A. R. Hope Moncrieff made similar reference to the 'junction of the now abandoned Wey and Arun Canal, its grass-grown trench making a peculiar and not unpleasing feature in the valley to the south-east beneath the picturesque crests and clumps that hid Wonersh'.[127] P. Bonthron, who cruised over 2,000 miles on the canals and rivers of Great Britain, chartered a skiff from Sam Strudwick, ('whose father had done service on both the Rother Navigation and Portsmouth & Arundel Canal') at Pulborough and proceeded with friends to Pallingham Quay, where they left their boat and continued along the towpath of the derelict Arun Canal to Newbridge. He recalled that 'Our walk along the bank was such that to us it seemed to open up a new source of pleasure by traversing the disused canals in England with their unfrequented routes and scenes; and another thing, too, one is practically always walking on the level'.[128]

Hilaire Belloc was the first writer to urge the reopening of the Wey & Arun. As the author of A & C Black's finely illustrated coloured book on Sussex (1906) he regretted that the canal system by which the Arun was linked with the rest of England had been deliberately allowed to go to pieces. 'It is typical of our modern politics that a national advantage of this sort should have been thrown away by Parliament in its subservience to the railway interest, and it is to be hoped that that advantage will soon be regained. The trench is still there and the emplacement of the old locks and the sum required to put the canal into use again would certainly be recovered in a few years of pleasure traffic alone.'[129] Unfortunately he declined to allow his name to appear as the author of the book so his call was less than shrill.

Martin Cobbett (1846–1906), the sporting journalist and descendant of William Cobbett, writing at the turn of the century, foresaw the likelihood that some day we would want to restore 'many of the canals now fallen into disuse'. His great regret was that he had been unable to fulfil one of his life's ambitions—to voyage from Putney to Littlehampton via the Wey & Arun. He had missed his chance once and the next time 'cattle were feeding on parts of the canal bed'. He also remarked that correspondents had been kind enough to write giving descriptions of canoe voyages through the canal which involved 'toilsome struggling through weed and reed beds', much carrying and some trespassing, 'always likely to lead to differences with unsympathetic owners'.[130]

The towpath of the old waterway attracted many walkers and countryside explorers. As one writer pointed out 'Each bend is a mystery and rounding it a discovery'. After forty years of disuse nature had come into her own and thrown a mantle over man's ingenuity. The fun was to discover what remained. There were disappointments however. A Mr R. Halliday wrote in his copy of Dashwood's book that he had been to Bramley on 8 June 1914 to inspect the site of the canal and sadly recorded that there 'was no trace of the lock'.[131]

The exploration of the Wey & Arun was however given impetus by an eulogistic article which appeared in *The Times* on 4 December 1915 entitled 'Walks by an Old Canal'. Its author highly praised the charms of the abandoned navigation,* warned intending explorers that the path near Alfold was terribly muddy after long rain though hard as brick in fine weather and that near the Three Compasses Inn 'the canal plunges into a dense thicket where only the most resolute will follow it'. Mention was made of the 'half-rotted lock-gates' and the locks themselves riven by the intrusive roots of thorns and ashes. 'These dry locks have the appeal of all works of man reclaimed by nature; their leafy basins form one of the chief attractions of the old canal. Other allurements of this secret route are the unclipped thickets heavy with red berries which flank the towpath or mask the drier part of the canal's bed. Fieldfares and blackbirds and missel thrushes clamour in them through the frosty autumn afternoons; huge flocks of plovers dapple the level meadows, slim herons heave suddenly into the air like opening parachutes; and magpies and woodpeckers chatter in the stillness of the woods.'

It is interesting to find that in 1916 George Newnes published a book by the fourth son of the Duke of Abercorn who chose as the plot for one of his juvenile thriller stories the idea of two German spies blowing up the Royal Train as it passed over Hardham Canal tunnel only to be foiled by the schoolboy hero at the eleventh hour. The author, Lord Frederic Hamilton (1856–1928) former Etonian,

*Seventy years earlier James Thorne had advised the rambler to avoid following the canal since it presented few attractions. Although it passed through a pleasant country, there was nothing calling for particular notice. (*Rambles by Rivers*, 1844, pp. 112–6).

diplomat and MP entitled his work 'Nine Holiday Adventures of Mr P. J. Davenant in the year 1915'.

In 1908 Eric Parker in the Highways and Byways County series had made only one allusion to the canal. 'Sidney Wood lies between Alfold and Dunsfold, and grows hazel and oak for various industries, besides acres of the purest and palest primroses. Through it runs a curious trackway, marked "disused" on the Ordnance maps. It is a section of the Wey and Arun Junction Canal, now a dry bed studded with hazel stubs and clumps of flowers.'[132]

This same trackway attracted the attention of author and painter Donald Maxwell who described in 1923 how, when in his mid-forties, he embarked on 'the most exciting, most uncomfortable and most interesting' of his studies of the ghost roads of Surrey. The account of this exploration sixty years ago is worth narrating and is of particular interest since all traces of the locks he found and drew had disappeared twenty years later.*

It was winter. The weather was bad. It could only, wrote Maxwell, have been sheer excitement that prompted the party of four to set out at night from Cranleigh to seek the whereabouts of the old locks.

Clad in mackintoshes and woollies, equipped with food, lamps and torches, they reached Alfold and then 'We took a road that gradually became a lane, and then a rough track and then a mud path. The general discomfort of the procession was accentuated by the fact that rain had set in, a steady downpour that did not look like abating.' By ten o'clock they had reached the edge of Sidney Wood. 'There were great numbers of small tracks and footpaths, and at every intersection of our main track we held conferences to debate the best route. Unfortunately, with all the preparations Brown had made, he had neglected to provide himself with a compass. In such weather there was no help from the sky, and we simply did not know our bearings. . . . At last, by the merest guesswork, we found a path leading slightly uphill. It did not seem likely that a canal would ever have existed on rising ground, but sure enough we crossed a dark and overgrown trench which looked suspiciously like the lost canal.

*The author began his research into the history of the canal after reading Maxwell's account and discovering the dry bed in Sidney Wood in 1943. Maxwell must have been fairly familiar with the abandoned waterway since when cruising through Ludwig's canal in 1905 he wrote that 'if the reader can imagine that the Wey & Arun Canal had lost itself upon a spur of the Alps, he would get some idea of the canal's character'. (A Cruise Across Europe 1907 p. 109.)

Fig. 59.—Derelict lock in Sidney Wood, Alfold, 1923

After a few alarums and excursions, different reports shouted from the more adventurous explorers ahead told us that we were on the right track. It was difficult, however, to believe that this could ever have been a waterway for the passage of barges. The fact that there was no water, and the fact that trees of considerable size were growing in it, were not the only difficulties in recognition of its nature. There did not seem to be enough depth to make a good waterway, though it must be supposed that forty or fifty years of undergrowth had added several feet to the floor of the old canal, and it is likely, too, that a certain amount of wear and tear may have lowered its banks in places.

There were rushes and a few pools of water at certain places, and then the wood became so dense and black that we were often afraid of straying away from the old towpath.

We halted for a short rest, and it looked as if these ghostly gates had perished or been taken away. A ration of tea and biscuits brought us back to greater optimism and we decided to push on.

"SCYLLA AND CHARYBDIS HAD DISCOVERED THE GHOST GATES."

Fig. 60.—Derelict lock-gates in Sidney Wood, Alfold, 1923

'While we were still partaking of our midnight refreshment we heard shouts from the direction of the acetylene lamps. Scylla and Charybdis had found the ghost gates. They were close at hand, and we had not seen them on account of the density of bushes and trees on the bank. The children, however, had climbed through and walked along the bed of the canal, suddenly seeing them looming out above them, presenting a very weird sight as they stood half open ready to receive a ghostly barge. The lock within was black, and out of the crumbling brickwork of the lock's sides grew one tree—a birch—quite a foot thick. The whole area was shrouded in woodland growth, thorn and bracken and silver birch, and looked in our lamplight and torchlight sight of it as weird a subject as anything conjured up by a dream.[133]

Maxwell was indeed fortunate to find any lock sites along the southward descent from the summit level since several were demolished to provide employment and a useful supply of bricks during the post Great War depression.

The only contemporary reference to a possible revival of water transport was contained in the regional development plan for the West Sussex Coast and Downs presented by Arthur Schofield (1929).[134] This report recommended that the shipping facilities at Arundel should be used 'to attract a larger trade in corn, fertilizer, road metal, building materials, gravel' etc. and to develop a passenger boat service from Littlehampton to Arundel and beyond. It also felt that canals might recover a share in the transportation of heavy non-perishable goods although the comment that Rennie's Grand Southern Canal was 'scarcely likely to be brought back into use' suggests that the Committee believed it to have been built! It was also suggested that the bed of the Arundel and Chichester canal might be utilized for a motorway.

By the nineteen thirties writers ceased to consider the possibility of revival but continued to praise the beauty of the Wey & Arun's course through the countryside. Even on a national basis few people regarded canals as still commercially viable. The Ward Lock guide books referred to the canal links 'which existed no longer save as rural walks for stray pedestrians'. The chapter on Inland Waterways by Ladbroke Black in Hammerton's *Wonderful Britain* (1928–9) singled out the Wey & Arun as a derelict canal at its best. 'Though some ordnance maps mark the original line of the canal in blue there is nothing to be seen but weeds and trees and grasses. The lock gates are rotten and gaping, memorials of a glorious past. If the traveller stops at Lakers Green he can visit what remains of the canal—now a

Fig. 61.—Portsmouth & Arundel Canal—Ford Bridge, 1932

series of pools, blocked by banks and as beautiful as a virgin forest. The beauty of the country, the strange remoteness of the scenery, is the reward of much patience required in contending with obstacles.'

In 1932 a book of drawings entitled *West of Arun* by students of the City of Chichester School of Art was published which concentrated on subjects which while representing characteristic features of the district had not been drawn by others and included sections on the Portsmouth & Arundel Canal, the valley of the Western Rother and the Arun. *The Times* published another nostalgic article on the Wey & Arun in 1936 (4 September) and a half page photograph on the back page showing the lily-covered channel looking south from Compasses bridge.

Not until more than sixty years had passed since the closing of the Wey & Arun did the first signs of interest into the canal's history appear in print. In 1934 F. S. Blomfield's well researched article entitled 'A Bygone Bargeway' lamented that although the beginning of the canal was decently furnished with water, pursuing it southwards 'the rambler will find it but a melancholy relic of the past, choked with weeds and overhung with low growing branches or so naked of water that even a stickleback would strand. Only here and there, where the road strides rudely over it, does the canal

Fig. 62.—Portsmouth & Arundel Canal—Yapton, 1932

disappear entirely. Elsewhere its lifeless shadow runs through the countryside straight as a Roman road or yielding in a long slow bend to the curve of the contours. Beside it a broad clay rampart, with grassy banks topped by a towing path churned into mud by cattle, sets one thinking of the patient labour that raised these endless massive walls, built to endure for centuries but doomed to uselessness within a generation or two'.

Blomfield considered that the prospect of the Wey & Arun being restored to life in more than imagination was remote. However the recent reopening of Salterns lock on the Chichester Canal (in 1932) suggested 'a possible revivifying tonic. There is a growing craze among motorists for yachting caps, but they find the surface of the sea disgracefully inferior to that even of a third-class road. Now their family cruisers can creep thankfully out of the storm-tossed waters of Chichester Harbour through the restored lock and into a cleaned-out stretch of the canal'.*[135]

More detailed research on Sussex Waterways by Oxford under-

* The events leading up to the reopening of Salterns Lock are described by Douglas Burrage in a booklet issued by the Chichester Yacht Company in 1936.

Fig. 63.—Portsmouth & Arundel Canal—Salterns Lock, Birdham, 1932

graduate Roger Sellman[136] and by Richard Goodchild on the Port of Guildford and Bramley Wharf[137] aroused a certain amount of local interest. So also did R. Thurston Hopkin's account of his visit to Pallingham Quay and his engaging conversation with Benjamin Stone shortly before the octogenarian lock-keeper died in 1935. Stone had been lock-keeper from 1871 until the canal closed but he had also been a shepherd on the hills and after the closing of the canal had done a fair amount of carpentry including making shepherds' stools. Thurston Hopkins described how he 'found an old man sitting on a very curious stool at the wooden bridge. It was a home-made contrivance rather in the nature of an up-to-date cane and nickel-plated shooting stick'.

'Good-morning,' I said. 'Morning, zur,' he replied, removing his pipe and spitting neatly into the red-bricked well of Pallingham Lock. Stone then related how groceries and manufactured goods came down to the farms from London. Wheat and timber went up to the towns, or down to Arundel Port. He also spoke of the considerable traffic in 'plum pie stone' or Petworth marble. 'You will see two whopping slabs of it on the floor of the porch at Billingshurst Church.' The old man got up and limped to the middle of the wooden bridge. He pointed his stool-walking-stick over the side.

'See this lock. It was made in 1789. I found an old piece of sandstone with that date on it.'[138]

In 1939 John Pitt published a lengthy illustrated account in descriptive verse of the Thames which included the stanzas:

'When rivers were canalized in England, long ago,
For economic transporting of commerce to and fro,
The Wey stream's navigation was to Godalming begun,
And first became a water-way in 1651;
Connecting with the Basingstoke canal, now in decay,
And with the Wey and Arun one, long derelict to-day.

The Wey is canalized throughout the main part of its course,
And, in the neighbourhood of Alton, Hampshire, has its course.
A little way past Godalming, constructed to unite
The rivers Wey and Arun, a canal diverged, on right;
Long derelict, in former years it joined the Arun near
The Sussex town of Pulborough; a transport pioneer.'[139]

The formation of the Inland Waterways Association in 1946 brought together a group of enthusiasts dedicated to saving the canal system from obliteration. Among the founder members were Tom Rolt and Charles Hadfield. Rolt is best remembered for his classic accounts of boat travel but he was also an accomplished engineer and writer. In *The Inland Waterways of England* (1950) he regretted the lack of informative works on canal history and urged a study of early records combined with field work. On the question of reviving the Wey & Arun he wrote: 'Keen though I am on canals, I hardly think it would be a practicable proposition for apart from its state of complete dereliction, it always suffered from the lack of adequate water supply to its summit level.'[140]

It was left to Hadfield to become the father of canal history. His twenty-five and more volumes covering a span of nearly forty years have done much to develop the public interest in our waterways heritage and to inspire dozens of young people to join the restoration movement. It was however during the Second World War that Hadfield found the odd moment from his duties with the river service of the London Fire Brigade and the fire staff of the Home

Office to begin his detailed research into the history of British canals. It was he who located in Guildford in the cellars below the offices of solicitors, Smallpeice & Merriman, the chests of old documents relating to the firm's interest in the Wey & Arun Junction Canal. It was due to Hadfield's efforts that this most interesting hoard of papers was saved from destruction and transferred to the Surrey Record Office. It was only after this discovery that the story of the Wey & Arun could be told.

CHAPTER XVIII

Restoration in Progress (1970–1996)

The waterways restoration movement–formation of the Wey & Arun Canal Society (1970)–aims and objects–becomes a trust (1973)–its achievements–success of working parties–reopening of Rowner Lock (1982)–publication of discussion document (1984)–the Halcrow report (1993) and cost feasibility study (1995)–attitude of landowners–boat trips at Loxwood (1995)–future still indefinite.

Undoubtedly the strong urge to restore the water route between the Thames and the English Channel that began twenty-five years ago had its roots in the views expressed by the writers mentioned in the preceding chapter. This revival of interest has developed as a result of two main factors. Firstly the increase in leisure time; secondly, greater communication.

The former has led to positive action being taken and Roger Squires has ably presented in his story of the waterways restoration movement the processes involved.[141] Writers like Tom Rolt have made people more aware of their environment and the need to retain interesting and useful relics of the industrial era. This awareness has led to the formation of societies to support these endeavours. Public support gained, the ultimate aim has been to commit those in authority to provide additional help. West Sussex has been particularly fortunate in the establishment of the Weald & Downlands Open Air Museum at Singleton and the Chalk Pits Museum at Amberley. There is still a long way to go however. Commercially minded men, property developers, road haulage users and town planners have often more lobbying power than conservationists. It seems that only rarely are the latter found amongst the former. How else can the wanton demolition of buildings like the Euston Arch or the Coal Exchange be explained and their destruction has been emulated in most towns and villages. There have been too few defenders of disused Victorian barracks, canal basins, corn exchanges, picture houses and railway stations which so often are laid waste before alternative uses can be proposed.

A turning point in the campaign to save canals from being erased was the passing of the Countryside Act in 1970 which allowed county councils to spend money on recreational facilities. Another was the

Manpower Services Commission recommendation in 1983 that the Community Enterprise Programme for those out of work should include projects for cleaning canals and derelict areas. And so in spite of the continued demands for land to meet changes in living standards, derelict waterways are now at least enjoying recognition by local authorities and Government agencies as being worthy of restoration.

The formation of the Lower Avon Navigation Trust in 1950 culminated in the re-opening of the waterway by Her Majesty The Queen Mother fourteen years later. This successful enterprise led to restoration societies being started to re-open some fifty former navigations. The Surrey and Hampshire Canal Society created in 1966, after many years of valiant effort on the part of its volunteer labour force and with the help of the county councils concerned, succeeded in 1991 in reopening 31 miles of the Basingstoke Canal as far as Greywell. Now there are plans to reopen Greywell Tunnel and complete the restoration of the waterway into Basingstoke town centre.*

The background to the formation of the Wey & Arun Canal Society can be traced back to Hillaire Belloc's plea in 1906. Both a letter to the *Daily Telegraph* in June 1952 and a synopsis of the Wey & Arun's history published by *Country Life* in 1953 provoked correspondence. Robert Aickman, the then chairman of the Inland Waterways Association, feared a weakening in concentrated effort and expressed the view that there were more important waterways to save from closure before attempting to re-open those officially abandoned.

In August 1965, the *Littlehampton Gazette* devoted a four column spread to readers' letters which urged the Littlehampton Urban District Council to take the lead in re-opening the canal and developing a pleasure steamer service up to London. However, even in 1970 the I.W.A. felt unable to support the proposal. At the Guildford rally to promote the restoration of the Basingstoke Canal the I.W.A. reiterated that canal restoration schemes should be concentrated on those having the best chance of success in the short to medium term. The Wey & Arun was still felt to be too much of a lost cause, that voluntary labour could be more profitably used on restoration schemes elsewhere. Nevertheless the Wey & Arun Canal Society was formed in 1970 under the chairmanship of Mr. John East and with Lord Egremont as president.

The object of the Society (since 1973 a Trust) is to reopen a navigable link between the rivers Wey and Arun. In the past twenty-six years it has achieved some notable successes. The first working party met at Rowner

* See Basingstoke & North Hampshire Gazette, 17 September 1993 *et seq* and London's Lost Route to Basingstoke 1994 ch XVI.

Lock on 28 March 1971 and in October 1982 the lock was reopened after extensive renovation and new lock gates. Work on six other locks has now been completed with the reopening of Brewhurst Lock at Loxwood this year (1996). With the consent of landowners restoration work has been carried out at a number of sites. Nineteen bridges have been rebuilt including Gosden Bridge which was restored by members of the Shalford Conservation Society in 1977. Similarly the Pulborough Society assisted with the rebuilding of Pallingham Quay Canal Bridge, reopened in 1976.

The Trust has achieved a membership of over 1400 and has successfully raised money through sponsored walks, jumble sales and donations. In 1995 300 walkers raised £9,000. On most weekends in summer and winter voluntary working parties can be found trying in all weathers to halt the ravages of nature and to remove the silt and debris of the past century. Keeping the bed tidy is not unlike painting the Forth Bridge since without water in the canal bed the growth of vegetation is rapid. So far over ten miles have been cleared and dredged and significant lengths are in water.

A discussion document compiled by the Trust in November 1984 set out the problems of complete restoration; however it was not until 1992 that Sir William Halcrow and Partners were commissioned to study the feasibility and cost of restoration from Shalford to Pallingham. Their engineering assessment confirmed that there were no insurmountable obstacles and that the project could be completed at a cost of around £13 million excluding the cost of land purchase.

The report takes into account the main constraints; namely land ownership, the need for new road and river crossings, accommodation bridges, water supply, ecology, landscape and water quality. The necessary engineering works are quite substantial particularly as a new line will have to be found in the Shalford/Bramley area where urban development has obliterated the original route. Land ownership is a major difficulty because since the canal was legally abandoned, its bed and tow-path have been returned to the riparian landowners. It is therefore a *sine qua non* that all, or nearly all, the present owners should agree to their land being transferred to a new canal authority before complete restoration can occur.

In spite therefore of the work carried out to-date, there has also to be a realistic assessment of the purpose of reopening the canal, its future management and its economic viability. In 1995 Halcrow set out in a cost-benefit study the likely revenue and non quantifiable benefits for the community which restoration would bring about. The study concluded that once the canal was reopened, there would be an annual potential of 42,000 canal cruises and the need to open four visitor centres to cater for the 850,000 visitors a year who might be attracted to its banks. Clearly this would involve a change in land use and the need for both additional accommodation bridges and fencing along the canal banks. This possibility is not one to encourage farmers and residents who have been custodians of the former channel for the past 125 years to support the proposal whole heartedly. Indeed one cannot refrain from thinking that it is one thing to maintain and improve the extant remains of the rural canal and quite another to build a new waterway whose banks have of necessity to be kept clear of undergrowth and oaks. Nevertheless some of the landowners who formed the 'Old Canal Association' to protect their interests, have wavered in their views towards restoration and may well support a modified programme which would allow boats and ramblers to use sections of the canal; what some fear is an unbroken public right-of-way being opened through their property which may effect their privacy and ownership.[142] The current chairman of the canal trust, Peter Beresford, has therefore wisely emphasized that the reopening of the canal can only be achieved with the goodwill and cooperation of the 50 or so riparian residents.

It is also sensible to have formed a local authority liaison group representing the councils and river authorities concerned to advise on planning approvals, future management, maintenance and funding which may help to put in perspective the longer term aims of the trust.

In 1965 I entitled the last chapter 'Future Indefinite'. Now that restoration is in progress the future looks much less indefinite. The rebuilt bridges and renovated locks give evidence of the Trust's serious intentions. Various stretches of the canal have been dredged and rewatered to provide angling facilities and the banks cleared of undergrowth to allow tow-path walks along stretches where the private landowners do not object to ramblers.

The most interesting development has been the beginning of boat trips on a recently reopened section of the canal. As a result of the help of a local landowner, Peter Foulger, the generous donation of a narrow boat by Mr. Thorne of Ash and its conversion to passenger carrying under the guidance of Roy Broadhead, it is now possible to cruise for two miles from the Onslow Arms at Loxwood to Drungewick Lane. Already over 1000 passengers have passed through the recently restored locks and this number should rise considerably now that an adequate water supply has been procured.

Clearing the canal bed has unearthed more of the canal's history. Winston Harwood and his colleagues have over the past few years spent considerable time and energy in investigating the site of the former water-wheel by Orfold aqueduct and the nearby flood gates at Orfold (shown as they were in 1952 in plates 69 & 70 of West Sussex Waterways). In the process they have discovered that here was once a turf sided lock. This lock was completed in 1823 as part of the improvements required to be made to the Arun Navigation by the proprietors prior to the opening of the Portsmouth & Arundel Navigation in order to raise the water level below Orfold lock (see pages 74–5). The lock can be seen marked on the Pulborough Tithe Map, 1841.

In February 1996 the Trust applied to the Millennium Fund for a grant to complete the restoration and this is still under consideration. Meantime efforts are being concentrated on rebuilding the aqueduct (plate 27) over the Western Arun river at Drungewick and the adjoining road bridge. The cost is estimated at £250,000. Thereafter it should be feasible to reopen the canal to Newbridge since the locks at Drungewick, Malham and Rowner have already been reconstructed. This proposal has been welcomed locally. With the continued support of voluntary labour parties and the financial encouragement of such fine concerns as Horsham brewer King & Barnes, Canon U K, Connolly Associates, Harwoods of Pulborough, Sun Alliance and Seeboard (among many others), it is to be hoped that this can be achieved by the year 2000. The 180th anniversary of the opening of the Wey & Arun Junction Canal occurs on Sunday 29 September 1996, but it may take another 20 years before the reopening can be celebrated.

Notes

1. Daniel Defoe, *A Tour Through the Whole Island of Great Britain*, 1724, Letter II, pp. 59–60.
2. Stanford, *Civil War in Sussex*, p. 210.
3. F. S. Thacker, *The Thames Highway*, 1914, pp. 12–36.
4. Preamble, 3 James I, c. 20.
5. W. T. Jackman, *Development of Transportation in Modern England*, pp. 178–9.
6. W. Stevenson, *General View of the Agriculture in the County of Surrey*, 1809, p. 560.
7. Loseley MSS. Letter from Viscount Mountague to the Commissioners upon the Waters of Wey, 6 April 1566.
8. R. Scotcher, *The Origin of the River Wey Navigation*, 1895, p. 20.
9. *Ibid.*, p. 20.
10. *Ibid.*, pp. 25–26.
11. Daniel Defoe, *A Tour Through the Whole Island of Great Britain*, 1724, Letter II, p. 87.
12. Thacker, *The Thames Highway*, p. 112.
13. MSS., 16 December 1758.
14. *J.H.C.*, 5 February 1759.
15. *V.C.H. Surrey*, Vol. II, p. 247.
16. Rev. W. Gilpin, *Observations on the Western Parts of England*, 1789.
17. Hadrian Allcroft, *Waters of Arun*, 1930, p. 130.
18. *Ibid.*, pp. 66–80.
19. *The High Stream of Arundel*, edited by J. Fowler, 1929, pp. 20–21.
20. *V.C.H. Sussex*, Vol. II, p. 233.
21. *The High Stream of Arundel*, Fowler, p. 55. *See also* W. Camden, *Britannia*, 1607, and p. 286 of 1806 edition.
22. *Ibid.*, p. 49.
23. Defoe, *A Tour*, Letter II, p. 65.
24. *V.C.H. Sussex*, Vol. II, p. 235.
25. H.L. petition, 28 February 1792, relating to Arun and Rother Navigations.
26. Rev. Arthur Young, *General View of the Agriculture of the County of Sussex*, 1808, p. 419.
27. *Ibid.*, p. 424.
28. *Ibid.*, p. 422.
29. MSS. 'Abstract of expenses of building the Rother Navigation'.
30. Plan at Petworth House.
31. W. Marshall, *Rural Economy of the Southern Counties*, 1798, Vol. II, p. 98.
32. Holland House MSS.
33. Quoted in H. A. Wyndham *The Wyndham Family*, 1950, Vol. II, p. 333.
34. Plan by Thomas Gream in Petworth House.
35. Plan by Thomas Gream in Horsham Museum.
36. Young, *General View of Sussex*, pp. 421–422.
37. *Ibid.*, p. 426.
38. Arun Navigation Minutes.
39. *Ibid.*, June 1796.
40. 5 March 1804.

41. C. E. Lee, *Early Railways in Surrey*, p. 12.
42. C. Hadfield, *Canals of Southern England*, 1955, pp. 97–98.
43. Arun Navigation Minutes.
44. *Ibid.*, June 1806.
45. *Ibid.*, December 1809.
46. Hadfield, *Canals of Southern England*, p. 113.
47. Arun Navigation Minutes, April 1811.
48. Letter to John Smallpeice, 26 January 1816.
49. Arun Navigation Minutes, December 1839.
50. J. Rennie, *Report and Estimate of the Grand Southern Canal*, 1810.
51. MSS. dated 11 October 1822 entitled 'Remonstrance to the Proprietors of the Wey Navigation'.
52. W. G. Gates, *Illustrated History of Portsmouth*, 1900, p. 574.
53. The Poor Employment Act, 1817, set up Exchequer Bill Loan Commissioners with power to lend money to concerns that would employ the poor, especially unskilled labourers, and so help relieve the distress following the Napoleonic Wars.
54. *V.C.H. Sussex*, Vol. III (1935), pp. 15 and 16.
55. *West Sussex Gazette*, 10 September 1936.
56. J. Williams to C. Sandys, 31 March 1823.
57. MSS., *Ibid.*, 31 March 1823.
58. *The Hampshire Telegraph*, 28 June 1823, reported that a voyage up had been accomplished in 2 days 20 hours and back in 2 days 16 hours.
59. Gates, *History of Portsmouth*, p. 575.
60. *The Times*, 19 September 1826.
61. Wey & Arun Canal Co. Abstract of Accounts, 1827.
62. Gates, *History of Portsmouth*, p. 575.
63. Report of the Committee of Management, 7 June 1831.
64. Figures calculated from the Wey Navigation ledgers at Guildford.
65. F. D. Heneghan, *The Chichester Canal*, 1958, p. 24.
66. N. W. Cundy, *Reports on the Grand Ship Canal*, 1827, p. iv.
67. *Autobiography of Sir John Rennie*, 1875, Chapter VI.
68. *The Times*, 30 October 1827 and 1 November 1827.
69. *Ibid.*, 3 November 1827.
70. *Ibid.*, 9 November 1827.
71. *Ibid.*, 13 November 1827.
72. Reprinted in *The Times*, 17 November 1827.
73. *Autobiography of Rennie*, Chapter VI.
74. Wyndham, *The Wyndham Family*, Vol. II, p. 252.
75. MSS., C. O. Hodgson to J. S. Langton, 8 December 1829.
76. *Ibid.*, 12 March and 11 August 1831. The proprietors hinted at misappropriation. Hodgson replied 'whatever errors I may have committed for want of instructions . . . expenses can be vouched for with a correctness and regularity which I believe to have been previously unknown to the proprietors of the Wey.'
77. P. Marshall, *An Examination into the Respective Merits of the Proposed Canal and Iron Railway from London to Portsmouth*, 1803.
78. Quoted by R. R. Sellman in *Sussex County Magazine*, 1935, p. 214.
79. H.L. Minutes of Evidence, 10 July 1866.
80. *Hampshire Telegraph*, 6 September 1823.
81. Heneghan, *Chichester Canal*, pp. 15 and 24.

82. F. Carr, *Sailing Barges*, 1951, p. 173.
83. As depicted in W. F. Witherington's 'Fete in Petworth Park', 1835.
84. Young, *General View of Sussex*, pp. 426–427.
85. Hadfield, *Canals of Southern England*, p. 19.
86. Basingstoke Canal Company Annual Report, 1836.
87. MSS., C. O. Hodgson to J. S. Langton, 10 March 1830.
88. Minutes, Godalming Navigation, 10 November 1852.
89. q.v. Arun Navigation Letter Book (1843–1857).
90. H.L. Minutes of Evidence, 13 June 1844.
91. C. F. Dendy Marshall, *History of the Southern Railway*, 1936, pp. 291 and 298.
92. *Railway Magazine*, 1938, p. 108, and 1955, pp. 517–520 and 570.
93. H.L. Minutes of Evidence, 25 June 1845.
94. *Ibid.*, 13 June 1844.
95. *Ibid.*, 23 March 1846.
96. *Ibid.*, 28 July 1845 (printed *J.H.L.*, Vol. 77, p. 1022).
97. J. B. Dashwood, *The Thames to the Solent by Canal and Sea*, 1868, p. 27.
98. Godalming Navigation Minutes.
99. H.L. Minutes of Evidence, 10 July 1860.
100. The original estimate had been £150,000 and the authorized capital £160,000.
101. Thacker, *The Thames Highway*, p. 179.
102. *Ibid.*, p. 226.
103. *The Oarsman's Guide to the Thames and Other Rivers*, 2nd edition, 1857, by a member of the Leander Club, published by Searle & Sons, boat builders to Her Majesty, H.R.H. The Prince of Wales, and the Emperor of the French. Price 2s.
104. Thacker, *The Thames Highway*, p. 192.
105. P. A. L. Vine, *Pleasure Boating in the Victorian Era*, 1983, p. 52 and bibliography.
106. H.L. Minutes of Evidence, 25 March 1868.
107. *Ibid.*
108. *Ibid.*, 24 March 1868.
109. Rev F. W. Cobb, *Alfold, the Story of a Surrey Village*, 1935.
110. *Illustrated Map of the Thames*, 3rd edition, p. 78.
111. *The Times*, 8 August 1888.
112. q.v. Arun Navigation Letter Book (1876–96).
113. *The Times*, 6 August 1888.
114. Hadfield. *The Canals of South and South East England*, 1969, p. 146.
115. *The Times*, 10 December 1902.
116. I am indebted to John Strudwick (b. 1909) for this information. (August 1984).
117. Minutes of the Commissioners of the Port of Arundel, 21 July 1925.
118. Letter from former Chief Clerk, Civil Engineers' Dept. (S.R.) Brighton published *Sussex County Magazine*, May 1953.
119. *Chichester Observer* and *West Sussex Advertiser*, 14 March 1906.
120. Heneghan, *Chichester Canal*, pp. 19 and 24.
121. MS Gerald Randall to Roger Sellman, 16 May 1936.
122. *West Sussex Gazette*, 16 May 1936.
123. Bulletin of the Inland Waterways Association no. 92, March 1970, pp. 18–19.
124. Hadfield, *British Canals*, 1950, p. 204.
125. H. E. Malden, *History of Surrey*, 1900, p. 284 and Rev F. W. Cobb, Alfold, 1935, p. 6.

126. Walter Jerrold, *Surrey*, 1901, p. 51.
127. A. R. Hope Moncrieff, *Surrey*, 1906, p. 70.
128. P. Bonthron, *My Holidays on Inland Waterways*, 1916, p. 65.
129. [Hilaire Belloc] *Sussex* (A & C Black) 1906, p. 188.
130. Martin Cobbett, *Wayfaring Notions*, 1906, pp. 22–6.
131. Information courtesy of Mr Peter Fenemore, B. H. Blackwell Ltd., Oxford.
132. Eric Parker, *Highways & Byways in Surrey*, 1908, p. 167.
133. Donald Maxwell, *Unknown Surrey*, 1924, pp. 197–206.
134. Arthur Schofield, *The West Sussex Coast and Downs*, 1929, p. 134 and pp. 146–7.
135. *Sussex County Magazine*, April 1934, pp. 233–6.
136. *Ibid., The Waterways of Sussex*, January–May 1935.
137. Guildford City *Outlook*, The Port of Guildford, June–September 1937 and Bramley Wharf, June 1939.
138. *Sussex Rendezvous*, 1938, pp. 80–4.
139. *The River Thames from Source to Mouth* [1939], pp. 34–5.
140. MS LTC Rolt to Paul Vine, 20 May 1951.
141. Canals Revived, 1979 and The New Navvies, 1983.
142. Wey South bulletin no. 32, August 1980, p. 15.
143. The water-bailiff was probably William Barttelot (1592–1667) who lived at the Manor House, Stopham. (q.v. p. 21)
144. In a petition to Queen Elizabeth in 1567 Jean Carre, the glass-maker, mentions that he had set up two glass houses at Fernfold Wood, Wisborough Green. Winbolt identified the site as being east of Loxwood. In the enquiry held on the petition Carre stated that he proposed to obtain wood for the furnaces from Arundel which would also suggest that the river was now navigable to Pallingham. (S. E. Winbolt, Wealdon Glass, 1933, p. 13. Jean Carre's Glass Furnaces, Transactions of the Society of Glass Technology, 1936, vol. 20). (q.v. p. 22)
145. The accounts of the Overseers of Wisborough Green include payments of 14s to Thomas Pavey for the carriage of 5 chaldrons of coal from Newbridge on 8 October 1788 and 6d for bringing weights from Newbridge to the Poor House on 5 January 1796. (q.v. p. 29)
146. The history of the Rother Navigation entitled *London's Lost Route to Midhurst* by P. A. L. Vine is due to be published in 1987 or thereabouts. (q.v. p. 33)
147. About 1800 the Earl of Egremont purchased land at Amberley for the purpose of opening chalk pits to supply the region with manure. He also made in 1802–3 a 350 yd cut southwards from the Arun at Houghton Bridge at a cost of £400 to enable barges to come closer to the pits. (MS Palme & France requesting counsel's opinion respecting duties being levied on chalk at Littlehampton, 6 July 1820.) Francis Jarrett, the tenant at the chalk pits had erected lime kilns at Amberley and the case had arisen because the Arundel Port Commissioners were charging pier dues on the export of chalk. (q.v. p. 34)
148. On 23 August 1790 William Jessop reported to Lord Egremont on the practicability of linking the Rother and Wey rivers. 'I am afraid it will at all events exceed the ordinary expense of similar undertakings, but I am much inclined to believe that if executed, there would be trade upon it to pay interest for the expense'. (q.v. p. 35)
149. A schedule of papers relating to the Wey Navigation in July 1793 refers to Lord Egremont's proposals to unite Petworth with the Godalming Navigation in opposition to the one proposed by Dorking and to the Earl of Portmore's opposition to any new navigation that might hurt the river Wey. (q.v. p. 35)

150. At a meeting held in Horsham on 12 January 1793 (the Duke of Norfolk in the chair) it was resolved to pay the Arun Navigation 75% of the maximum tunnel toll and either to purchase the Pallingham–Newbridge canal at cost price or that tolls should be reduced when Arun Navigation profits exceeded 10%. It was also agreed to have a survey made to determine the best line from Newbridge or Shoreham to Dorking, a survey from Dorking to Thames Ditton having already been made. (q.v. p. 39)

151. In 1820 the *Brighton Herald* recorded that the Commissioners of Shoreham Harbour contemplated forming 'a junction of the rivers Adur and Arun by which a navigation would be opened between Shoreham and the Metropolis. (quoted by Henry Cheal, *The Story of Shoreham*, 1921, p. 160). (q.v. p. 46)

152. Josias Jessop (1781–1826) was the second son of William Jessop (1745–1814) the distinguished engineer from whom he received much of his training. In October 1802 at the age of twenty-one Josias was appointed joint engineer with his father of the Croydon, Merstham & Godstone Iron Railway Company. Besides giving evidence to the Parliamentary Committee he set out the line before going to Bristol in February 1804 where he had been appointed resident engineer of the Bristol Floating Harbour Project, under the direction of his father, at the substantial salary of £500 p.a. The works were completed in 1809 but Josias stayed on until the end of 1810 and in February 1817 the directors of the Bristol Dock Company wrote 'Mr Josias Jessop with whose accuracy and attention to the Interests of the Company, they have every reason to be satisfied; and to whom it is no more than justice to state, that he acquitted himself in the important trust reposed in him with the most unsullied reputation and honour, (C. Hadfield & A. W. Skempton, *William Jessop, Engineer* 1979 pp. 241–2). (q.v. p. 49)

153. Traffic on the river Arun exceeded 30,000 tons in 1814 (*Hampshire Telegraph*, 25 September 1815). (q.v. p. 80)

154. The Portsmouth & Arundel Canal prospectus dated August 1817 attempted to prove that an ample return on the investment might be expected and that even if only half the anticipated tonnage materialised, the shareholders could expect an annual return of nearly 10 per cent. However correspondence between '*Zeno*' and '*Atticus*' in the *Hampshire & Sussex Chronicle* during the autumn of 1816 criticised the scheme on the following grounds:
   (i) The estimate of trade between London and Portsmouth was over optimistic;
   (ii) Merchants preferred to send their goods by land or by sea;
   (iii) Labour needed for the canal would put 8 coasting smacks out of service and prevent 60 or 70 horses being yoked to the London and Portsmouth wagons;
   (iv) The enormous capital required.

   The only positive advantage given in reply was that foreign goods transhipped at Portsmouth would avoid customs clearance at London if they were moved by canal instead of by sea. (q.v. p. 80)

155. Work began on the Chichester section at Merston on 1 September 1818 and on 17 November the *County Chronicle* reported that the works were proceeding 'with celerity at seven different places and that the first bridge had been completed'. (q.v. p. 80)

156. The engine was intended to be worked for half a day once a week to replace water lost through lockage (*Hampshire Chronicle*). (q.v. p. 81)

157. The opening day arrangements were left perhaps rather too much to chance. Apparently although Williams, the Manager, had planned an early start in

order to take advantage of the tide, shortly before sailing at 9 a.m. a Mr Burdett appeared on the deck of the tug *Egremont* and offered his services to Williams claiming knowledge of the tricky route through Langstone Harbour. Williams, anxious to spend more time with his guests, was glad to hand over the task of steering the procession to a man he thought to be an experienced pilot. Burdett's first action was to delay the start because of his doubts about the depth of water by Hayling Island, so not until 11 a.m. did the vessel enter Langstone Harbour. Here more doubts were expressed about the depth and further stoppages occurred. However both Williams and a passenger, Mr Hicks, were dubious about this further delay since they considered there was 6 ft of water and the *Egremont* only drew 4′6″. With all these delays it was not until 5 p.m. that the ship left the Emsworth Channel to enter Chichester harbour. Then disaster struck. The tug was just turning the last angle of the lake. The canal entrance was in sight not $\frac{1}{4}$ mile away, when the pilot steering the vessel himself ran aground on a mud bank even though he was negotiating a deep channel 180 yds wide. The procession held fast waiting until the tide turned or some larger vessel came to the rescue, and so those aboard were 'precluded from participating in the principal object of their excursion'. Williams tried to excuse himself by stating that the procession had had to struggle against a north east gale and the ebb of a spring tide. (*Hampshire Telegraph*, 12 April 1822). (q.v. p. 82)

158. In 1826 only £18 was taken in tolls between Salterns and Ford compared with £428 between Salterns and Chichester and £564 between Ford or Chichester and Salterns. There was no revenue from the Portsea Canal and when John Rennie saw it in July 1827 he reported 'there was no water in it, nor has it, we understand, been used to any considerable extent on account of the very defective manner in which it has been executed, as it is incapable of holding water'. (The Rennies' MS Reports, Institution of Civil Engineers Library.) It seems unlikely that the Portsea Canal was used after 1825. (q.v. p. 87)

159. A 1,200 yd causeway with a 320 yd bridge was opened in September 1824 to link Havant and Langstone with Hayling Island. The toll bridge 'handsomely and substantially built on piles of African oak and other choice timber' was described as one of the finest structures in the kingdom. A forty foot section in the centre could be swung to allow barge traffic to pass. A contemporary guide mentions that 'great quantities of manure may be obtained from Portsmouth and chalk from the pits on the northern shores of the harbour at an easy rate of water carriage'. The island also exported barley, wheat, oats, peas and butter, but this traffic did little to help the company's finances as it paid no tolls when using the dredged channels of the navigation which were tidal waters. (I. Skelton, *A Topographical and Historical Account of Hayling Island*, 1826, pp. 9–11 and 26). (q.v. p. 88)

160. A confidential letter from George Palmer to James Mangles dated half past two 30 April 1833 referred to Admiral Halkett's wish to be rid of a long standing debt (presumably relating to the canal) and 'as to the men of business at Portsmouth, I am sorry to say to you privately and confidentially that I think one of them (Mr Casher) at least who might assist us a good deal, is a very wavering man and to use a vulgar expression I think he earwigs the Admiral. He is a man I can never make out'. He also mentions that Mason the wharfinger has reported that their barge trade is 'going on favourably'. (q.v. p. 95)

161. In September 1829 the Collector of Dues for the Port of Arundel had to seize a barrel of gold for non-payment of harbour tolls amounting to over £700. The Collector was to guard it for two days before the Arundel Commissioners agreed at an emergency meeting that the bullion should be removed to 'the Banking

House of Messrs. Hopkins & Co.' in Arundel. (q.v. p. 96)

162. Colonel E. L. Botting of Westbury (his family were millers at Brewhurst, Loxwood from 1815 until 1920) relates that his Great Uncle Tom was drowned between Brewhurst Lock and the Onslow Arms on 25 January 1827 when he was 12 years old. (Wey–South, November 1973). (q.v. p. 118)

163. Mr Puttock of Billingshurst used his own barges to send his hoops to London. (q.v. p. 121)

164. W. C. Smith writing about Guildford in 1828 refers to the import of slates from Wales by means of the Wey & Arun at a cheap rate. In 1840 it was found that coal could be brought more cheaply to Guildford from Littlehampton than from London on account of the several extra expenses in and out of the Port of London. 4s 9½d compared with 5s 5d a ton. (q.v. p. 121)

165. From the evidence of an elderly inhabitant quoted in the *West Sussex Gazette*, 10 September 1936, it appears unlikely that these collier brigs frequented the canal, although some time after the canal had been opened two brigs were built at the wharves.'One was called Richmond and the other Chichester. There was a great "to do" when they were launched. Hundreds of people came from all parts of the country. The ships were towed down the river, but they never returned as they were too large to do so with a cargo'. And so it is more probable that coal was transferred from brig to barge in the channel of Chichester Harbour and consequently this time-wasting process coupled with the limited size of the canal remained a permanent disadvantage and discouragement to larger vessels. (q.v. p. 123)

166. I am indebted to Mr R. F. Buckley for drawing my attention to Hampshire's book published by Lake & Co. of Falmouth. (q.v. p. 136)

167. James Thorne walking from Littlehampton to Arundel in 1843 noted at Ford 'the pleasing example of a rustic church standing close by the Arundel and Portsmouth Canal.' (*Rambles by Rivers*, 1844, p. 99). (q.v. p. 144)

168. The last entry in the Wey Ledgers is dated 29 December 1847 and refers to the passage of two pleasure boats at Thames Lock bound for Portsmouth. (q.v. p. 144)

169. The bridge carrying the tow-path over the entrance to the Portsmouth & Arundel Canal at Ford continued to be mentioned in the minutes of the Commissioners of the Port of Arundel, who were forced to rebuild it in 1856 for horse-tracking at a cost of £20 5s 3d. In 1893 the commissioners suggested to the new landowners (the Governors of Christ's Hospital) that it be taken down but apparently the bridge was repaired and it was not until after February 1917 that the tow-path was levelled across the old canal. (q.v. p. 146)

170. The Wey & Arun Committee had also been trying to reach an accommodation with the L.B. & SCR. The railway company's minutes reveal that early in 1859 a plan was conceived to convert 16 miles of the canal into a railway. On 4 August a deputation led by John Napper met the directors of the L.B. & SCR. to seek their views on the proposal to build a railway along the line of the existing canal which would link Guildford with Pulborough. However after it was discovered that no survey had yet been carried out, the L.B. & SCR. informed the promoters that they would not form a definite opinion unless a 'matured scheme' was submitted that appeared practicable and had the support of owners of agricultural land who would grant 'every facility to sell the land at agricultural prices'. There is no further mention of the canal conversion scheme and the L.B. & SCR. contented itself with petitioning against clauses of the Horsham & Guildford Railway bill. The Wey & Arun Canal Company's draft minute book makes no reference to this proposal although on 14 February 1960

the seven members of the Committee of Management with Napper in the chair resolved that no opposition be offered to the bill for the Horsham–Guildford railway. (q.v. p. 155)

171. In the eighteen forties there was a considerable increase in barge traffic from the newly developed Amberley Chalk Pits where in 1847 five pits were being worked. Balcombe Pit adjacent to the wharf south of Houghton Bridge had three kilns in operation. The busiest wharf however was north of the bridge where a steam crane operated. Until 1863 when the railway reached Amberley all the lime produced had to be taken away by barge or cart (Lime Burning and the Amberley Chalk Pits, 1979, pp. 7–10). (q.v. p. 155)

172. The keeper at Thames Lock kept a record of notable happenings. On 15 June 1831 he noted that 'Lord and Lady Portmore and three others came through Thames Lock in H. Purduc's punt'. Six weeks later he also reported the arrival of Mr Birnie's yacht at Weybridge Lock. (q.v. p. 161 and *London's Lost Route to Basingstoke*)

173. Many publishing houses in London were damaged or reduced to rubble by enemy action. Six million books were lost in a single night and by the end of 1941 over 21 million books had been destroyed. (National Book League The Fifty Books, London 1945). (q.v. p. 166). *The Thames to the Solent* was reprinted by Shepperton Swan in 1980. In 1984 Blackwell's of Oxford advertized a first edition for sale at £150.

174. Within a fortnight of Dashwood's departure from Littlehampton to the Solent, John MacGregor, the canoeist of Rob Roy fame, arrived there from Le Havre in his 3 ton yawl having sailed across the English Channel singlehanded. However whereas the Dashwoods spent the night at a little inn by the ferry, MacGregor stayed at the Beach Hotel and wrote at once to *The Times* about his feat. In June 1868 MacGregor sailed from Erith up the Thames to the Wey and on the 16th wrote in his diary the brief cryptic note 'By Wey River. Adventures in Locks'. Two days later he entered the Arun and on the 19th reached Littlehampton. That autumn MacGregor left for Egypt and Palestine to begin the cruise which was narrated in 'Rob Roy on the Jordan' and which included the famous incident when he was captured by Arabs and carried forcibly ashore while still seated in his canoe. (P. A. L. Vine, *Pleasure Boating in the Victoria Era* 1983, p. 40). (q.v. p. 176)

175. The difficulties of trading on the Wey & Arun were worsened by the severe winter. The *West Sussex Gazette* reported on 25 January 1871 that in spite of the thaw the canal was so frozen as to render navigation impossible. At Birtley the ice was nearly 5 inches thick and in Sidney Wood it was thicker. 'On Friday afternoon Thomas Doick, captain of one of Mr Stanton's barges and his employee attempted to break in the ice at Birtley with heavy hammers but could not make the slightest impression'. (q.v. p. 190)

176. Auction particulars of the sale of part of the Stopham Estate (13–14 July 1911) include reference to the lock cottage at Pallingham. This consisted at that time of a living room with cupboard, kitchen, scullery with down fireplace, bakery and grocer's shop, 3 bedrooms, one with fireplace. Outside brick and stone built and tile heeled shed; also privy and good garden. Let to Benjamin Stone at £7.4.0 p.a. The Lock and Carpenter's shop covered 1r 36p; the carpenter's shop was a timber built and thatched workshop which stood on the south side of the docks. (q.v. p. 203)

Notes 114 to 176 are new to this edition

APPENDIX A

Bibliography

(I) ACTS OF PARLIAMENT

1651 An Act for making the River Wey navigable from the Town of Guildford in the county of Surrey to the town of Weybridge in the said county. (Wey Navigation Act.)

1671 An Act for Settling and Preserving the Navigation of the River Wey in the county of Surrey. (Wey Navigation Act.)

1732 An Act for erecting Piers in, and for repairing and keeping in repair, the Harbour of Littlehampton, called Arundel Port, in the County of Sussex and for empowering the Commissioners, acting under the said Act, to improve the Navigation of the River Arun from the said Harbour to the town of Arundel in the said county. (Littlehampton Harbour Act.)

1760 An Act for extending and continuing the Navigation of the River Wey, otherwise Wye, in the county of Surrey, to the town of Godalming in the said county. (Godalming Navigation Act.)

1785 An Act for amending and improving the navigation of the River Arun from Houghton Bridge in the parish of Houghton in the county of Sussex to Pallenham Wharf in the parish of Wisborough Green, in the said county, and for continuing and extending the navigation of the said River Arun from the said wharf called Pallenham Wharf, to a certain bridge called Newbridge, in the parishes of Pulborough and Wisborough Green, in the said county of Sussex. (Arun Navigation Act.)

1791 An Act to enable the Earl of Egremont to make and maintain the River Rother navigable, from the town of Midhurst, to a certain Meadow called the Railed Pieces, or Stopham Meadow, in the parish of Stopham, and a navigable Cut from the said River to the River Arun, at or near Stopham Bridge, in the county of Sussex; and for other Purposes. (Rother Navigation Act.)

1793 An Act to explain and amend an Act made in the sixth year of the Reign of his late Majesty King George the Second entitled (as for 1732). (Littlehampton Harbour Act.)

1813 An Act for Making and Maintaining a navigable canal to unite the rivers Wey and Arun in the Counties of Surrey and Sussex. (Wey & Arun Junction Canal Act.)

1817 An Act for making and maintaining a navigable Canal from the River Arun to Chichester Harbour, and from thence to Langstone and Portsmouth Harbours, with a Cut or Branch from Hunston Common to or near the city of Chichester and for improving the Navigation of the Harbour of Langstone, and Channels of Langstone and Thorney. (Portsmouth & Arundel Navigation Act.)

1819 An Act for giving further Powers to the Company of Proprietors of the Portsmouth and Arundel Navigation, and to the Company of Proprietors of the Wey and Arun Junction Canal, and to confirm an Agreement entered into between the said Companies. (Portsmouth & Arundel Navigation Act.)

1821 An Act for giving further Powers to the Company of Proprietors of the River Arun Navigation, and for confirming certain Agreements entered into between the said Company and the Company of Proprietors of the Portsmouth and Arundel Navigation. (Arun Navigation Act.)

1825 An Act for the more effectual security of the Harbour of Littlehampton called Arundel Port. (Littlehampton Harbour Act.)

1828 An Act for granting further Powers to the Company of Proprietors of the Portsmouth and Arundel Navigation. (Portsmouth & Arundel Navigation Act.)

1868 An Act to provide for the closing of the Wey and Arun Junction Canal, and the sale of the site thereof; and for other purposes. (The Wey & Arun Canal (Abandonment) Act.)

1892 An Act to provide for the transfer of the Chichester Section of the Portsmouth and Arundel Canal Navigation to the Corporation of the City of Chichester and for other purposes. (Chichester Canal Transfer Act.)

1894 An Act to confirm a Provisional order made by the Board of Trade under 'The Railway and Canal Traffic Act 1888' continuing the Classification of Merchandise Traffic and the Schedule of Maximum Tolls and Charges applicable thereto, for the Aberdare Canal Navigation and certain other canals. (Canal Tolls and Charges Provisional Order (No. 3) (Aberdare & Co Canals) order Confirmation Act 1894.)

1927 An Act to dissolve the Commissioners of the Port of Arundel and Harbour of Littlehampton; to change the name of the harbour; to constitute a new Harbour Board and to transfer the harbour undertaking to them; to empower the West Sussex County Council to raise sums of money and to pay such sums to the Harbour Board; to provide for contributions by local and other contributing authorities; to amend the West Sussex County Council Bridge Act 1918; and for other purposes. (Littlehampton Harbour & Arun Drainage Outfall Act.)

1938 An Act to authorize the mayor, aldermen and burgesses of the borough of Guildford to execute street works and to acquire lands for those and other purposes to empower the Corporation to purchase by agreement the Godalming Navigation and to confer further powers upon them in regard to their water, electricity and markets undertakings and the health local government and improvement of the borough and for other purposes. (Guildford Corporation Act 29 July 1938.)

1967 An Act to confer further powers upon the mayor, aldermen and burgesses of the borough of Guildford; to make further provision with respect to the health, local government and improvement of the borough; to provide for the transfer of the Godalming Navigation of the National Trust for Places of Historic Interest or Natural Beauty; and for other purposes. (Guildford Corporation Act 21 July 1967.)

(II) BOOKS OF REFERENCE

The following publications contain references of particular interest:

1675 John Ogilby *Britannia Depicta.*

1724 Daniel Defoe *A Tour through the whole Island of Great Britain.*

1798 William Marshall *The Rural Economy of the Southern Counties.*

1804–14 Rev. O. Manning and W. Bray *The History and Antiquities of the County of Surrey.*

1808 Rev. Arthur Young *A General View of the Agriculture of the County of Sussex.*

1815–32 J. Dallaway *The History of the Western Division of Sussex.*

1817 L. Allen *The History of Portsmouth.*

1826 William Cobbett *Rural Rides.*

1827 N. W. Cundy *Reports on the Grand Ship Canal from London to Arundel Bay and Portsmouth.*

1828 N. W. Cundy *Mr. Cundy's Reply to anonymous and other Authors of Malignant Abuse and Misrepresentation on his projected line, etc.*

1828 Richard Dally *The Bognor, Arundel and Littlehampton Guide.*

1828 W. C. Smith *Rambles round Guildford.*

1831 J. Priestley *Historical Account of the Navigable Rivers, Canals and Railways throughout Great Britain.*

1833 *Lengths and Levels to Bradshaw's Maps of the Canals, Navigable Rivers and Railways.*

1844 James Thorne *Rambles by Rivers, The Adur, Arun and Wey.*

1856 George Jackson *History of Bramley.*

1857 *The Oarsman's Guide to the Thames and Other Rivers* (2nd edition).

1868 J. B. Dashwood *The Thames to the Solent by Canal and Sea.**

1879 H. W. Taunt *Illustrated Map of the Thames* (3rd edition).*

1895 R. Scotcher *The Origin of the River Wey Navigation*—written in 1657.

1896 F. E. Prothero and W. A. Clark *A New Oarsman's Guide to the Rivers and Canals of Great Britain and Ireland.*

1897 H. R. De Salis *Chronology of Inland Navigation.*

1900 W. G. Gates *An Illustrated History of Portsmouth.**

1900 H. E. Malden *History of Surrey.*

1901 Walter Jerrold *Surrey.**

1912 A. S. Cooke *Off the Beaten Track in Sussex.**

1916 P. Bonthron *My Holidays on Inland Waterways.**

1916 W. T. Jackman *The Development of Transportation in Modern England.*

1924 Donald Maxwell *Unknown Surrey.**
1929 Anon. *The High Stream of Arundel.* Written *c.* 1637. Edited J. Fowler.
1930 Hadrian A. Allcroft *Waters of Arun.**
1932 *West of the Arun**—a book of drawings by Chichester School of Art
1933 E. Robinson and J. S. Howard *Reminiscences of Littlehampton.*
1935 Rev F. W. Cobb *Alfold, the Story of a Surrey Village.*
1935 Lady Maxse *Story of Fittleworth.*
1936 Douglas Burrage *An Old Waterway Revived.*
1936 T. S. Willan *River Navigation in England 1600–1750* (reprinted 1964).
1938 L. Collison-Morley *Companion into Surrey* (reprinted 1949).
1938 A. Thurston Hopkins *Sussex Rendezvous.*
1948 Lilian Brown *All About Bury.**
1950 Charles Hadfield *British Canals:* (7th edition, 1984).
1950 L. T. C. Rolt *Inland Waterways of England.**
1950 H. A. Wyndham *The Wyndhams,* vol. II.
1951 J. Hillier *Old Surrey Water-Mills.**
1958 F. D. Heneghan *The Chichester Canal.**
1962 R. H. Goodsall *The Arun and Western Rother.**
1968 Rev E. N. Staines *Dear Amberley.*
1968 P. A. L. Vine *London's Lost Route to Basingstoke.**
1969 Charles Hadfield *The Canals of South and South East England.**
1969 Hugh McKnight *The Shell Book of Inland Waterways.**
1969 L. T. C. Rolt *Navigable Waterways.**
1979 F. Aldsworth *Lime Burning and the Amberley Chalk Pits.**
1981 D. W. Horsfall *Adelina.**
1982 Donald Smith *The Horse on the Cut.**
1985 P. A. L. Vine *West Sussex Waterways.**

* illustrated

(III) PERIODICALS

The following articles have also been published:

'The River Wey and its Navigation', H. W. Stevens (*The Keep,* April 1914).
'Stories of Loxwood', J. C. Buckwell (*Sussex Archaeological Collections,* vol. LVI, 1914).
'A Bygone Bargeway', F. S. Blomfield (*Sussex County Magazine,* April 1934).
'The Waterways of Sussex', Roger Sellman (*Sussex County Magazine,* January–May 1935).
'Branches and Bridges of the Arun', S. E. Winbolt (*Sussex County Magazine,* May–October 1937).
'The Port of Guildford', 'Iscanus' (Guildford City *Outlook,* June–September 1937).
'Bramley Wharf', Richard Goodchild (Guildford City *Outlook,* June 1939).
'Seeing Sussex by Water', John North-More (*Sussex County Magazine,* July 1939).

'The Lost Canal', L. W. Bromley (Guildford City *Outlook*, February 1942).
'The River Arun', P. A. L. Vine (*Motor Boat & Yachting*, December 1951).
'Canoeing Under Sussex', A. G. Marshall and W. Norris (*Sussex County Magazine*, March 1953).
'London's Lost Route to the Sea', P. A. L. Vine (*Country Life*, 27 March 1953).
'The Desolate Quay', K. Ashworth (*Country Life*, 10 February 1955).
'The Wey and Arun Canal', P. A. L. Vine (*Motor Boat & Yachting*, March 1955).
'From the Wey to the Arun', J. Spencer Gilks (*Sussex County Magazine*, March 1956).
'By Boat through Surrey and Sussex', P. A. L. Vine (*Sussex County Magazine*, July 1956).
'A Remote Surrey Waterway', H. McKnight (*Country Life*, 12 December 1963).
'The Haslingbourne Navigation', G. D. Johnston (*Sussex Notes and Queries*, November 1964).
'Lost Highway to the Sea', P. A. L. Vine (*Weekend Telegraph*, 21 May 1965).
'The Wey Navigation Claims of 1671' ed. Hector Carter (*Surrey Archaeological Collections*, vol. LXII, 1965).
'In Search of Dashwood', J. de Manio (Drive Autumn 1967).
'Early Seventeenth Century Schemes to make the Wey navigable', Michael Nash (*Surrey Archaeological Collections*, vol. LXVI, 1969).
'Barge traffic on the Wey Navigation in the second half of the Seventeenth Century', Michael Nash, (*Journal of Transport History*, 1970).

Reference should also be made to the Collections of the Surrey and the Sussex Archaeological Societies, Sussex Notes & Queries, bulletins of the Inland Waterways Association, *Windlass*, the journal of the south east region of the I.W.A., (first issue October 1956), Wey-South, the bulletin of the Wey & Arun Canal Trust (first issue May 1971, fiftieth April 1985) and the issues of the Sussex Canal Trust (July 1973–75).

(IV) FICTION

The only reference to the Arun Canal in the realm of fiction is to be found in Lord Frederic Hamilton's *Nine Holiday Adventures of Mr. P. J. Davenant in the year 1915*, published in 1916.

One of the nine adventures takes place in Sussex when Mr. Davenant, playing the rôle of schoolboy detective, thwarts an attempt by two German spies to blow up the royal train as it crosses over the canal tunnel at Hardham on its way to Portsmouth. All very naïve, and there is more than a little literary licence in the way the tunnel is used for the plot.

APPENDIX B

Table of Locks and Distances from London Bridge to Littlehampton, Godalming, Midhurst, and Portsmouth, 1840

Navigation	*Lock*	*Place*	*Distance* (*miles*	*flgs*)	*Distance from London Bridge* (*miles*	*flgs*)	*Height above datum at Liverpool at head of locks* (*feet*)
Thames		From London Bridge to:					
(30 miles)	1	Teddington	18	5½	18	5½	24
		Kingston Bridge	1	6	20	3½	
		Hampton Court Bridge	2	7	23	2½	
	2	Molseley	0	1½	23	4	30½
	3	Sunbury	2	7½	26	3½	36
		Entrance to Wey Navigation	3	7½	30	1	
Wey	4	Thames	0	1	30	2	46
(13½ miles)	5	Weybridge	0	6	31	0	52
	6	Coxes	0	5	31	5	59
	7	Newhaw	0	7	32	4	66
		Junction Basingstoke Canal	0	5	33	1	
	8	Pyrford	2	0	35	1	72
	9	Walsham (flood gates)	1	0	36	1	73
	10	Newark	0	4½	36	5½	78
	11	Paper Court	0	6½	37	4	85
		Send Bridge	1	3	38	7	
	12	Worsfold (flood gates)	0	2	39	1	86
	13	Triggs	0	5	39	6	92
	14	Bowers	2	0	41	6	99
	15	Stoke	1	2	43	0	106
		Dapdune Wharf	1	6	44	6	
		Guildford Wharf	0	5	45	3	
		Guildford Bridge	0	1	45	4	
Godalming	16	Mill Mead	0	1	45	5	111
(2 miles)	17	St Catherine's	1	1	46	6	115
		Stonebridge Wharf and Junction Wey & Arun	0	6	47	4	

Navigation	*Lock*	*Place*	*Distance* (*miles*)	*Distance* (*flgs*)	*Distance from London Bridge* (*miles*)	*Distance from London Bridge* (*flgs*)	*Height above datum at Liverpool at head of locks* (*feet*)
Wey & Arun Canal (18½ miles)		Stonebridge	0	1½	47	5½	
	18	Stonebridge	0	1	47	6½	122
	19	Tanyard Lock and Gosden Aqueduct	0	4½	48	3	129
	20	Bramley	0	3	48	6	135½
	21	Wesby	0	2	49	0	142
	22	Park	0	3	49	3	149
	23	Lock XVIII	1	2	50	5	156
		Run Common Wharf	0	7	51	4	
	24	Lock XVII	1	1	52	5	162¾
		Elm Bridge Wharf (for Cranleigh)	0	6	53	3	
		Compasses Bridge Wharf (for Horsham)	2	1	55	4	
		Tickners Heath and Cobdens wharves	0	6	56	2	
	25	Sidney Wood XVI	1	3½	57	5½	162¾
	26	Sidney Wood XV	0	2	57	7½	156
		Lock House	0	0¼	57	7¾	
	27	Sidney Wood XIV	0	0¾	58	0½	148
	28	Sidney Wood XIII	0	1	58	1½	140
	29	Westland Copse XII	0	1	58	2½	132
	30	Westland Copse XI	0	1½	58	4	124
	31	Bonfire Hangar X	0	1	58	5	116
	32	Gennets Wood IX	0	1	58	6	108
		Surrey and Sussex border	0	0½	58	6½	
	33	Gennets Bridge VIII	0	1	58	7½	100
	34	Southland	0	3	59	2½	92
	35	Devils Hole	0	3	59	5½	84
		Onslow Arms, Loxwood	0	3½	60	1	
	36	Brewhurst	0	2	60	3	75½
	37	Baldwins Knob (Stubbs)	0	6	61	1	68
		Drungewick Aqueduct	0	6½	61	7½	
	38	Drungewick	0	4½	62	4	60
	39	Malham	1	5	64	1	52
	40	Rowner	1	1	65	2	44
		Newbridge	0	6	66	0	

Navigation	*Lock*	*Place*	*Distance* (*miles*	*flgs*)	*Distance from London Bridge* (*miles*	*flgs*)	*Height above datum at Liverpool at head of locks* (*feet*)
Arun	41	Orfold Aqueduct	1	2	67	2	36½
(4½ miles)		Orfold (flood gates)	0	1	67	3	
	42	Lee Farm—Middle	1	5	69	0	31
		Pallingham Quay and Docks	1	3	70	3	
	43	Pallingham (double lock)	0	1	70	4	24
River Arun		Stopham Bridge	2	4	73	0	14½
(3 miles)		Junction Rother Navigation	0	1½	73	1½	14½
	44	Hardham	0	2½	73	4	19
Arun	45	Tunnel	0	2½	73	6½	17½
(2 miles)	46	Coldwaltham	1	2½	75	1	17½
River Arun		Junction River Arun	0	2	75	3	
(17 miles)		Bury Wharf	2	3	77	6	
		Houghton Bridge	1	2	79	0	
		Arundel Bridge	6	5	85	5	
		Ford Railway Bridge	3	5	89	2	
		Junction Portsmouth & Arundel Canal	0	2	89	4	Tidal
		Littlehampton Swing Bridge	2	1	91	5	
		Littlehampton Harbour Mouth	0	7	92	4	
Basingstoke Canal (37 miles) (29 locks)		From Junction Wey Navigation to:			33	1	66
		Basingstoke	36	7	70	0	260½
Godalming (2¼ miles)		From Junction Wey & Arun Canal to:			47	4½	115
	1	Unstead	0	3½	47	7½	122
	2	Catteshall	1	2½	49	2	128½
		Godalming Wharf	0	3½	49	5½	

Navigation	*Lock*	*Place*	*Distance* (*miles flgs*)		*Distance from London Bridge* (*miles flgs*)		*Height above datum at Liverpool at head of locks* (*feet*)
Rother (11½ miles)		From Junction River Arun to:			73	1½	14½
	1	Stopham	0	1	73	2½	21
	2	Fittleworth	1	3	74	5½	28
		Shopham Bridge	1	5	76	2½	
	3	Shopham	0	3½	76	6	35
		Junction Petworth Canal	0	3	77	1	
	4	Coultershaw	0	7	78	0	41
	5	Ladymead	3	0	81	0	48
	6	Lodgebridge	1	2	82	2	55
	7	Moorland	0	4	82	6	62
	8	Todham	1	0	83	6	68½
		Midhurst Wharf	1	0	84	6	
River Arun (5¼ miles)		From Junction Rother Navigation to:			73	1½	Tidal
		Pulborough Bridge and Wharf	1	0½	74	2	
		Greatham Bridge	3	4	77	6	
		Junction Arun Canal	0	6	78	4	
Portsmouth & Arundel Canal (27 miles)		From Junction River Arun to:			89	4	
	1	Ford I	0	0½	89	4½	13
	2	Ford II	0	1½	89	6	21
		Hunston Bridge and Junction	9	6	99	4	
	3	Casher	0	7	100	3	21
	4	Salterns	0	4	100	7	13
Closed in 1830	5	Milton I	13	1	114	0	11
	6	Milton II	0	1	114	1	21
		Portsea Basin	2	2	116	3	
Chichester Canal (1¼ miles)		From Hunston Bridge to:			99	4	
		Southgate Basin, Chichester	1	2	100	6	21

Note: Heights are measured from a point 6 ft 10 in. below the sill of the Old Dock gates at Liverpool.

SUMMARY

From London Bridge to:	*Shortest Distance (miles)*	*No. locks*	*Navigation*	*Maximum size of vessel admitted by locks* ft in. ft in.
Weybridge	31	5	Thames	140 0 × 22 0
Guildford	45½	15	Wey	73 6 × 13 10½
Godalming	49½	19	Godalming	73 6 × 13 10½
Basingstoke	70	36	Basingstoke	72 6 × 13 6
Pulborough	74	43	Wey & Arun	68 6 × 12 2
Arundel	85½	46	Arun Canal	68 3 × 11 9
Midhurst	84½	51	Rother	73 0 × 12 0
Littlehampton	92½	46	P. & A.	75 0 × 12 6
Chichester	101	48	Chichester	86 0 × 18 8
Portsmouth	116	52	Portsea	101 0 × 24 1

Note: The P. & A. lock details are from Bradshaw (1833) and have not been verified. The minimum draught throughout was 3 ft 1 in.; the minimum headroom 7 ft. The length of Hardham tunnel was 375 yards. The making of the cut in the Arun at Offham in 1862 reduced the distance between London Bridge and places south of Arundel by ¾ mile.

APPENDIX C

Officers and Servants

THE ARUN NAVIGATION COMPANY

Chairman:		*Clerk:*	
1785–1794	Sir Harry Goring	1785–1800	W. Carleton†
1794–1837	Earl of Egremont	1801–1808	P. Hart
1837–1855	Not appointed*	1808–1835	R. Wardroper I
1855–1877	W. Shaft	1835–1842	R. Wardroper II
1877–1890	G. Lear	1842–1870	J. Powell
1891–1894	R. Holmes	1870–1896	E. Arnold

* *Management Committee:*

1837–1842 W. Cutfield, J. P. Henly, G. Sharp
1842–1855 J. P. Henly, W. Shaft, G. Sharp

Treasurer:		*Superintendent:*	
1785–1793	H. Digance	1790–1793	H. Digance†
1793–1796	J. Cutfield	1790–1807	T. Seward†
1796–1813	E. Carleton	1807–1827	J. Seward
1813–1842	W. Cutfield	1828–1856	R. Seward
1842–1846	J. Stoveld	1857–1895	J. Sprinks
1846–1850	R. Luard		
1851–?	J. W. Orsborn		

Lock-keepers:

Coldwaltham		*Pallingham*	
1792	Medwin	1792–1808	T. Stone I
1808	T. Overington	1808–1814	W. Stone
1852–1888?	H. Webb	1828–1832	T. Stone II
		1832–1871	J. Stone
		1871–1888	B. Stone

Orfold

1792–1808	J. Sandham
1809–1828	R. Seward
? –1868	T. White
1868–1871?	Baverstock

† Honorary

THE WEY & ARUN JUNCTION CANAL COMPANY

Chairman:

1813–1837	Earl of Egremont
1837–1838	J. Mangles
1838–1844	J. King
1845–1850	W. Newland
1850–1855?	Hon. Rev. A. Perceval
1855–1867	J. Napper
1867–1869	Lord Leconfield

Deputy Chairman:

1813–1821	Rev. John Austin
1821–1837	J. Mangles

Joint Treasurers:

1813–1871	R. Sparkes & Co.
	J. Haydon & Co.

Clerk:

1813–1837	J. Smallpeice
1837–1844	J. Smallpeice W. H. Smallpeice
1844–1871	W. H. Smallpeice

Superintendent:

1813–1818	M. Upton
1819–1857	J. Stanton
1857–1867	T. Pullen
1867–1871	W. Stanton

Lock-keepers:

Bramley:

1819–1849	J. Stanton
1849–1871	W. Stanton

Rowner:

1816–1823	Not known
1824–1871	C. Baverstock

THE WEY NAVIGATION

Attorney:

1776–1808 G. Stubbs

Agent:

1764–1766?	J. Smith
1770–1775	T. Ward
1775–1796	J. Granger
1798–1807	Smith
1808–1817	C. Brooks
1818–1821	H. Sandys
1821–1822	C. T. Cracklow
1822–1823	Nicholson
1823–1826	C. Sandys
1827–1831	C. O. Hodgson

Manager:

1844–1868	F. de Visme
1890–1930	W. Stevens III
1930–1965	H. W. Stevens
1965–1974	E. E. Avery
1974–	B. O. Ratcliffe

Wharfinger (Guildford):

1707–1718	H. Dean
1778–1797	T. Bateman
1797–1823	T. Matthews
1823–1856	W. Stevens I
1856–1890	W. Stevens II

Master Carpenter (Worsfold Gates):

1764–1778	J. Dean
1778–1780	R. Jones
1780–1793	J. Aldridge
1793–1851	S. Chandler
1851–1865	C. Chandler
1865–1885	Jesse Stone
1885–1930	W. Grove
1930–1966	N. Grove

Lock-keepers:

Thames

1775–1779	J. Armytage
1779–1810	W. Alladay
1810–1820	J. Jenkins
1820–1823	W. Stevens I
1823–1857	J. Mathews
1857–1864	W. Mathews
1864–1894	W. Strudwick
1895–1939	E. Grove
1939–1955	A. Edwards
1955–1972	V. Edwards

Newhaw

1795–1825	W. Glaysher
1825–1862	B. Glaysher
1863–1884	W. Glaysher
1884–1937	E. Grove
1937–1939	W. Grove
1939–1940	P. Grove
1940–1949	W. Denyer
1949–1955	V. Edwards
1955–1959	W. Turner
1959–1983	J. Harris

Walsham

1812–1832	J. Percy
1832–1842	P. Percy
1842–1851	T. Stone
1851–1862	J. Ottoway
1862–1865	W. Eastland
1865–1878	T. Jackman
1878–1887	J. Smither
1887–1903	R. Corpes
1903–1914	W. Manderville
1914–1929	T. Bicknell
1929–1937	A. Trussler
1937–1947	W. Jacobs
1947–1950	E. Jacobs
1950–1956	A. Kirby
1956–	J. Payne

Paper Court

1830–1832	J. Hart
1832–1839	W. Hunt
1840–1856	James Wickens
1857–1866	John Wickens
1866–1889	John Stone
1889–1901	H. Wye
1901–1941	A. Wye
1941–1945	C. Hardy
1945–1954	J. Grant
1954–1961	J. Miller
1961–1965	E. Casey
1965–1968	W. Harrington

Triggs

1812–1820	W. Stevens I
1820–1833	J. Bonsey
1833–1840	James Wickens
1840–1854	W. Styles
1854–1856	W. Walden
1856–1915	W. Grove
1915–1933	J. Wye
1933–1945	W. Moseley
1945–1949	W. Burton
1949	F. Waterman
1949–1950	P. Crofts
1950–1972	R. Kirby

Stoke

1800–1813?	J. Payne
1830–1854	W. Day
1854–1888	W. Styles
1888–1890	Joseph Stone
1890–1908	W. Edwards
1908–1925	W. Martin
1926–1934	J. Durrant
1934–1943	A. Batchelor
1943–1946	G. Dicker
1946–1949	A. Smith
1949–1963	G. Britton
1963–1969	W. Elliott

THE GODALMING NAVIGATION

Clerk:

1760–1800	E. Yaldon
1800–1803	T. Blunt
1803–1840	H. Woods
1841–1861	C. Woods
1861–1864	H. Stedman
1864–1868	R. Whitbourn

Manager:

1869–1890	W. Stevens II
1890–1930	W. Stevens III
1930–1969	H. W. Stevens

Wharfinger (Godalming):

1763–1774	R. Stedman
1774–1789	T. Davis
1789–1790	W. Davis
1790–1799	T. Payne
1800–1812	J. Aldridge
1812–1825	J. Fry
1825–1854	S. Richardson
1854–1864	C. Billinghurst
1864–1886	J. Goddard
1886–1906	E. Boxall

THE ROTHER NAVIGATION

Proprietor:

1791–1837	Earl of Egremont
1837–1869	Col. George Wyndham (created Lord Leconfield 1859)
1869–1901	2nd Lord Leconfield
1901–1936	3rd Lord Leconfield

Clerk:

1791	J. Upton
1820	Stoveld
1831	W. Tyler
1838–1850?	H. Upton
1866–1871	H. Brydon

THE PORTSMOUTH & ARUNDEL NAVIGATION COMPANY

Chairman:

1817–1827	Admiral Sir Peter Halkett
1827–1830?	Lord Selsey
1831	W. C. Newland

Manager:

1817–1826	J. Williams
1827–1833?	G. Palmer

Clerk:

1817–1818	G. L. Greetham
1819–1824	J. G. Williams
1824–1832	J. Fowler
1832–1851	T. Edgcombe I
1851–1888	T. Edgcombe II

Committee of Management:

1817 Rear Admiral Peter Halkett (Chairman), Earl of Egremont, Viscount Keith, Sir Lucius Curtis, James Brown, William Cutfield, Thomas Edgcombe, Moses Greetham, Trevor Letham, Robert Park, John Snook, William Turner, John Williams, William T. Williams.

APPENDIX D

Arun Navigation Traffic Returns, Dividends, and Share Prices, 1787–1890

Year ending 31 *July*	*Tolls* (£)	*Estimated Tonnage*	*Dividend* (%)	*Average Share Price*
1788	310	4,500	2	£100
1789	293	4,500	—	£100
1790	376	6,500	—	—
1791	856	14,000	—	—
1792	782	13,000	4	—
1793	864	14,000	2	£100
1794	872	14,000	2	£100
1795	914	15,000	3	£101
1796	1,034	17,000	2½	£100
1797–1806	?	?	—	£50/100
1807	1,372	?	—	—
1808	?	?	—	—
1809	?	15,760	—	—
1810	?	17,600	—	—
1811	?	15,160	—	—
1812	?	14,200	—	—
1813	?	23,440	—	—
1814	?	18,300	—	—
1815	?	15,700	—	—
1816	?	15,500	—	—
1817	?	?	—	—
1818	?	?	—	—
1819	?	?	—	—
1820	?	?	—	—
1821	?	?	3	—
1822	1,360	20,000	—	—
1823	1,322	20,000	—	£121
1824	1,760	26,500	—	—
1825	1,750	26,000	—	—
1826	1,450	22,000	—	—
1827	1,400	21,500	—	—
1828	1,300	20,000	—	—
1829	1,385	20,000	—	—
1830	1,300	20,000	—	£200
1831	1,471	23,000	7	—
1832	1,729	26,000	12½	—
1833	1,604	24,000	12	—
1834	1,534	23,000	11	—
1835	1,529	23,000	11	—
1836	1,628	25,000	11	£150
1837	1,738	26,000	12	£181
1838	2,020	30,000	12	£183
1839	2,426	36,000	12	£200
1840	2,407	36,000	12	—
1841	1,539	23,500	8	£200

Year ending 31 October	*Tolls (£)*	*Estimated Tonnage*	*Dividend (%)*	*Average Share Price*
1842	1,588	24,000	4	—
1843	1,727	26,000	7	£185
1844	1,483	23,000	8	£160
1845	1,878	30,000	10	—
1846	1,920	30,000	11	—
1847	1,890	30,000	10	£150
1848	1,700	27,000	9	—
1849	1,460	29,000	8	—
1850	1,460	29,000	8	—
1851	1,230	25,000	7	£120
1852	990	20,000	4½	—
1853	1,060	21,000	6	—
1854	1,220	24,000	6	—
1855	1,170	23,000	6	—
1856	1,150	23,000	5½	—
1857	1,420	28,000	7½	£70
1858	1,380	27,000	7½	—
1859	1,150	23,000	7	—
1860	1,020	20,000	5	—
1861	1,070	21,000	6	£75
1862	1,090	22,000	6	£70
1863	1,100	22,000	6	—
1864	1,066	21,000	6	—
1865	791	16,000	4	£55
1866	664	13,500	2	—
1867	610	12,500	2½	£50
1868	567	11,500	1	—
1869	477	10,000	1½	£50
1870	497	10,000	2	—
1871	481	10,000	2½	—
1872	444	9,000	1½	£7
1873	255	7,500	—	—
1874	292	8,750	1	—
1875	222	6,500	—	£20
1876	195	6,000	—	—
1877	207	6,250	—	—
1878	165	6,500	—	—
1879	164	6,500	—	—
1880	152	6,000	—	—
1881	143	5,500	—	—
1882	93	4,500	—	—
1883	110	5,500	—	—
1884	91	4,500	—	—
1885	63	5,000	—	—
1886	82	4,000	—	—
1887	46	2,000	—	—
1888	34	1,145	—	—
(29 Jan.) 1889	2	135	—	—
1890	—	—	—	90s.

Note.—The accounts from 1821 onwards were for the twelve months ending 31 October. All except nominal share transfers have been recorded. The Arun's tonnage includes a variable proportion of traffic passing to and from the Rother Navigation which was in commercial use between 1794 and 1888; between 1809–15 the average annual tonnage was 8,600.

APPENDIX E

Wey & Arun Canal Traffic Returns, Dividends, and Share Prices, 1815–1871

Year (*to* 1 *May*)	*Tolls* £	s.	d.	*Tonnage* (*approx.*)	*Dividend* £100	*Average Share Prices*
1815–16	2	14	9	165	—	—
1816–17	977	6	7	7,000	—	£94
1817–18	1,167	6	0	8,000	—	ND
1818–19	1,481	12	11	10,500	—	£60
1819–20	1,286	9	3	9,000	—	ND
1820–21	1,342	13	8	9,000	£1	ND
1821–22	1,426	16	10	10,000	—	£60
1822–23	1,252	17	10	10,000	—	ND
1823–24	1,989	2	0	16,000	—	£50
1824–25	2,165	3	11	17,500	—	£50
1825–26	2,355	8	4	19,000	—	£40
1826–27	1,952	4	5	15,600	—	£35
1827–28	1,981	6	6	15,750	£1	£25
1828–29	2,028	15	5	16,250	£1	£36
1829–30	1,813	11	8	14,500	£1	£35
1830–31	2,180	12	11	17,500	£1	£33
1831–32	2,169	0	2	17,250	£1	£30
1832–33	2,009	18	8	16,000	£1	£27
1833–34	2,157	18	4	17,250	£1	£30
1834–35	2,024	10	7	16,200	£1	£25
1835–36	1,938	7	10	15,500	£1	£24
1836–37	2,084	15	9	19,250	£1	£25
1837–38	2,226	16	5	20,500	£1	£25
1838–39	2,479	4	8	22,750	£1	£25
1839–40	2,524	1	1	23,250	£1	£25
1840–41	2,188	10	6	20,500	£1	£23
1841–42	1,713	2	8	15,750	—	£25
1842–43	1,569	11	0	14,250	£1	£19
1843–44	1,637	13	6	17,000	£1	£20
1844–45	1,628	18	10	19,000	£1	£20
1845–46	1,515	10	10	17,750	15s.	£20
1846–47	1,374	6	3	16,000	15s.	£16
1847–48	1,308	13	11	15,550	10s.	ND
1848–49	1,218	13	9	14,250	10s.	£10
1849–50	1,236	6	10	14,500*	10s.	£9
1850–51	1,036	6	6	15,121*	7s. 6d.	£10
1851–52	873	7	1	15,832*	5s.	£8

Year (*to* 1 *May*)	*Tolls* £	s.	d.	*Tonnage* (*approx.*)	*Dividend* £100	*Average Share Prices*
1852–53	819	1	11	14,614*	—	ND
1853–54	879	7	11	16,000	5s.	ND
1854–55	753	16	1	13,000	—	£4
1855–56	1,025	19	3	20,500	5s.	£4
1856–57	1,120	19	8	22,350	5s.	65s.
1857–58	1,118	5	10	22,300	7s. 6d.	70s.
1858–59	966	10	1	19,000	7s. 6d.	70s.
1859–60	914	15	1	18,000	5s.	70s.
1860–61	787	2	7	15,750	5s.	65s.
1861–62	773	9	1	15,500	—	65s.
1862–63	811	6	9	16,000	5s.	70s.
1863–64	917	19	2	18,250	7s. 6d.	ND
1864–65	807	2	7	16,000	6s.	60s.
1865–66	512	12	11	10,000	—	60s.
1866–67	463	1	3	8,750	—	60s.
1867–68	469	6	10	9,500	—	—
1868–69	393	16	10	7,750	—	—
1869–70	358	19	5	7,000	—	—
1870–71	277	17	3	5,500	—	—
1871 (30 June)	53	9	10	1,000	—	—

* Exact. ND—No Dealings.

APPENDIX F

Wey Navigation Traffic Returns, 1724–1969

Year	*Tolls (£)*	*Tonnage*	*Year*	*Tolls (£)*	*Tonnage*
1724–25	2,754	20,000*	1739–40	2,119	15,500*
1725–26	2,306	17,000*	1740–41	2,025	14,500*
1726–27	2,227	16,250*	1741–42	2,248	16,000*
1727–28	2,144	15,500*	1742–43	2,416	17,500*
1728–29	2,014	14,500*	1743–44	2,682	19,500*
1729–30	2,394	17,500*	1744–45	2,730	20,000*
1730–31	2,629	19,000*	1745–46	2,385	17,250*
1731–32	2,145	15,500*	1746–47	2,550	18,500*
1732–33	2,307	16,500*	1747–48	2,447	17,500*
1733–34	2,373	17,000*	1748–49	2,800	20,500*
1734–35	1,773	13,000*	1749–50	2,840	20,500*
1735–36	2,050	15,000*	1750–51	2,707	19,500*
1736–37	2,280	16,500*	1751–52	2,440	17,500*
1737–38	2,334	17,000*	1752–53	2,022	14,750*
1738–39	2,169	15,500*	1753–54	2,460	17,750*

Year	Tolls (£)	Tonnage
1754–55	2,636	19,000*
1755–56	2,618	19,000*
1756–57	2,753	20,000*
1757–58	3,045	22,000*
1758–63	NK	NK
1764	3,175	21,515
1765	3,089	22,500*
1766	2,900*	21,000*
1767	3,350*	24,500*
1768	2,748	20,000*
1769	2,893	21,000*
1770	2,880	21,000*
1771	2,834	20,750*
1772	2,973	21,750*
1773	2,486	18,000*
1774	2,535	18,500*
1775	3,012	23,500*
1776	3,188	23,000*
1777	3,044	22,380
1778	3,165	22,818
1779	3,081	21,740
1780	3,349	24,006
1781	3,702	29,280
1782	4,131	35,668
1783	4,458	30,412
1784	4,287	30,646
1785	4,459	32,470
1786	4,207	31,295
1787	4,356	31,220
1788	3,872	28,643
1789	4,103	31,335
1790	4,236	32,981
1791	4,599	36,799
1792	4,561	35,581
1793	5,118	36,250*
1794	4,827	36,000*
1795	4,750	35,500*
1796	NK	45,500*
1797	NK	48,000*
1798	NK	47,000*
1799	NK	52,000*
1800	5,860	57,500
1801	NK†	63,000*
1802	NK†	60,000*
1803	NK†	50,000*
1804	NK†	60,000*
1805	NK†	62,000*
1811	NK†	65,000*
1812	6,009	65,279
1813	5,964	57,638
1814	6,208	60,000
1815	5,753	58,800
1816	5,478	55,612
1817	5,392	53,913
1818	6,313	58,465
1819	6,995	63,193
1820	5,678	56,400
1821	4,792	46,196
1822	4,350*	43,000*
1823	4,469	45,000*
1824	4,300*	43,000*
1825	5,120	51,182
1826–28	NK	NK
1829	6,144	57,200
1830	5,571	55,035
1831	5,956	58,289
1832	5,842	59,922
1833	5,739	61,700
1834	6,217	64,164
1835	6,376	67,673
1836	7,148	75,908
1837	7,292	75,787
1838	7,763	86,003
1839	7,642	78,878
1840	6,881	75,990
1841	5,200	64,504
1842	4,968	61,540
1843	5,180	62,710
1844	5,619	63,240
1845	5,571	72,701

† Distributed profit averaged £3,533 p.a. for these years and reached £4,708 in 1819.

Year	*Tolls (£)*	*Tonnage*	*Year*	*Tolls (£)*	*Tonnage*
1846	4,374	59,580	1889	1,226	26,146
1847	4,616	63,045	1890	1,136	24,581
1848	3,985	58,820	1891	1,086	26,322
1849	3,579	50,940	1892	1,039	25,372
1850	3,173	47,250	1893	1,184	28,675
1851	2,763	42,540	1894	1,248	30,936
1852	2,344	39,340	1895	1,241	26,455
1853	2,812	46,710	1896	1,359	33,487
1854	2,813	46,655	1897	1,205	30,902
1855	2,839	52,172	1989	1,179	33,517
1856	3,027	63,705	1899	1,028	30,925
1857	2,808	55,636	1900	896	28,297
1858	2,835	50,793	1901	931	28,561
1859	2,929	53,561	1902	1,002	30,625
1860	3,001	60,707	1903	1,045	31,973
1861	2,913	63,502	1904	1,083	31,540
1862	2,845	62,745	1905	1,090	32,430
1863	2,598	58,521	1906	1,067	32,245
1864	2,412	54,564	1907	1,041	31,635
1865	2,337	45,740	1908	1,076	30,800
1866	1,928	41,350	1909	1,199	36,990
1867	1,906	40,296	1910	1,269	41,125
1868	2,013	43,832	1911	1,226	39,655
1869	2,007	41,125	1912	1,344	41,026
1870	2,083	41,585	1913	1,489	46,611
1871	1,942	37,435	1914	1,525	47,507
1872	1,879	35,020	1915	1,501	46,706
1873	1,814	37,087	1916	1,325	46,659
1874	1,696	37,658	1917	1,567	46,714
1875	1,583	33,246	1918	1,745	51,115
1876	1,601	33,360	1919	1,572	43,916
1877	1,601	31,737	1920	1,934	47,052
1878	1,705	32,819	1921	1,555	36,980
1879	1,580	31,202	1922	1,957	42,875
1880	1,549	29,414	1923	1,782	45,517
1881	1,405	31,839	1924	1,803	48,196
1882	1,369	25,792	1925	1,810	48,632
1883	1,324	25,984	1926	1,784	47,954
1884	1,221	25,644	1927	1,981	55,622
1885	1,211	27,881	1928	1,695	50,334
1886	1,128	25,324	1929	1,651	48,600
1887	1,221	26,232	1930	1,763	52,220
1888	1,203	26,130	1931	1,634	52,474

continued on page 279

APPENDIX G

Analysis of Barge Traffic on the Wey Navigation in 1830

Name of Owners	*From*	*No. of Barges*	*Names of Barges*	*Tonnage Carried*			*Principal Cargoes*
				Northward	*Southward*	*Total*	
Arundel Barge Co.	Arundel	7	*Arun* *Commerce* *Egremont* *Norfolk* *Sovereign* *Swallow* *Union*	1,778	2,873	4,651	Bark, coals, corn, cyder, flour, furniture, hoops, pottery, soldiers' baggage, timber
Barnard, Thomas	Petworth	1	*Sussex Oak*	100	—	100	Timber
Birnie, John	Basingstoke	12	*Andover* *Alton Fly* *Commerce* *Friendly* *Harriet* *Pilot* *Rachel* *Salisbury* *Alresford* *Union* *Wellington* *Winchester*	4,435	5,025	9,460	Beer, cheese, coals, flour, furniture, hoops, malt, sugar, wool

Brickwood, James	Guildford	2	*Rocket* *Union*	1,695	1,868	3,563	Coals, timber
Casher, Edward	Portsmouth	1	*Fly*	77	1	78	Bullion
Crowley, A. & H.	Alton	1	*Independent*	479	1,022	1,501	Ale
Davis, John	Guildford	1	*Endeavour*	570	—	570	Chalk
Downs, John	Richmond	1	*Edwin*	—	—	—	Bricks
Eager, Richard	Newark Mill	1	*Lighter*	—	—	—	Corn
Edwards, George	Guildford	2	*Economist* *Guildford Miller*	—	—	—	Chalk, lime
Gay, George	Aldershot	2	*Endeavour* *Hope*	352	1,680	2,032	Coals, flour, potatoes
Gurr, Samuel	Hardham	1	*Mary*	—	—	—	Corn
Hatch, William	Shepperton Lock	1	*Lighter*	21	—	21	Sand
Hillyard, Benjamin	Chertsey Bridge	1	*Elizabeth*	2	108	110	Coals
Isemonger, Richard	Littlehampton	4	*Chichester* *Hampton* *Perseverance* *Union*	410	575	985	Bark, coals, carrots, corn, groceries, hops, oil-cake, tallow, wine
Keeme, John	Weybridge	1	*Mayflower*	68	227	295	Iron
Lacoste, J. & G.	Chertsey	2	*Harriet* *Rosa Ann*	10	41	51	Coals, faggots
Marshall, George	Godalming	5	*Hope* *London* *Royal Oak* *Triumph* *Wey*	2,844	2,934	5,778	Corn, firewood, groceries, oil-cake, timber
Mason, William	Guildford	1	*Chance*	—	—	—	Clay

Name of Owners	From	No. of Barges	Names of Barges	Tonnage Carried			Principal Cargoes
				Northward	Southward	Total	
Mills, William	Guildford	3	*Ann* *Vanguard* *Victory*	2,498	3,092	5,590	Bullock horns, alder poles, carrots, coal, hoops, malt
Nye, Benjamin	Pulborough	1	*Maria*	—	—	—	Hay
Oakly, Isaac	Chertsey	1	*Raft*	—	7	7	Faggots
Pimm, William	Bowers Mill	2	*Briton* *Hero*	1,497	2,069	3,566	Cement, pollard
Russell, C. & R.	Godalming	4	*Industry* *Providence* *Safety* *Unity*	2,605	2,285	4,890	Barley, corn, glass, peas; timber, wheat
Russell, Hugh	Guildford	2	*Chance* *Hope*	130	163	293	Gunpowder
Seward, John	Loxwood	2	*Bee* *Hope*	370	193	563	Hoops, oak, timber
Smart, Charles	Offham	1	*Eagle*	252	115	367	Corn, manure
Smart, George	Fittleworth	1	*Algebra*	100	—	100	Hoops
Smart, Joseph	Fittleworth	2	*Dart* *Lark*	28	29	57	Deal
Smith, John	Frimley	1	*Nancy*	5	495	500	Manure
Spong, John	Ripley	2	*Rose in June* *Trial*	625	1,430	2,055	Coals, corn, hoops
Stanton, James	Bramley	1	*Eliza*	448	50	498	Hoops, potatoes

Stone, Thomas	Pallingham	1	*Bee*	218	103	321	Hoops
Strudwick, William	Fittleworth	1	*Albion*	137	9	146	Hoops
Webb, Thomas	Newhaw	3	*Prince Regent* *Victory* *Wellington*	359	1,207	1,566	Coals, ash poles, gypsum, hurdles
Wilkins, J. & J.	Guildford	3	*Lighter* *Regulator* *Reliance*	1,125	1,477	2,602	Coal, cyder, groceries, stone
Wilkins, J. M.	Guildford	3	*Charlotte* *Friendly* *Maria*	1,110	1,609	2,719	Bark, bog earth, carrots, coals, osier reeds
	Total			24,348	30,687	55,035	

Note.—Approximately 80 per cent of the Wey Navigation's northward traffic and 85 per cent of its southward traffic in 1830 was recorded in loads or chaldrons and these have been converted on the basis that each load or chaldron weighed 25 cwt.

APPENDIX H

Tonnage carried between the Thames and the Portsmouth & Arundel Canal (1823–1840)

Year	*To the Thames*	*From the Thames*	*Total*
1823	425	1,475	1,900
1824	1,158	2,492	3,650
1825	1,001	1,581	2,582
1826	421	958	1,379
1827	193	78	271
1828	285	95	380
1829	125	77	202
1830	101	92	193
1831	115	296	411
1832	670	1,335	2,005
1833	1,102	1,458	2,560
1834	820	1,130	1,950
1835	409	721	1,130
1836	547	636	1,183
1837	303	602	905
1838	259	494	753
1839	285	502	787
1840	192	282	474
Total	8,511	14,204	22,715

Portsmouth & Arundel Canal

Year	*Tolls (£)*	*Tonnage*
1822	142	3,000*
1823	669	10,000*
1824	827	11,500*
1825	944	12,500*
1826	1,010	13,351
1827	1,000*	13,000*
1828		
1829		
1830	1,028	

Chichester Canal

Year	*Tolls (£)*	*Tonnage*
1847	104	3,000*
1858	191	5,111
1866	86	3,250*
1868	185	7,070
1874	46	1,750*
1888	133	6,001
1898	18	704

APPENDIX I

An Act for the Making a River Navigable for Boats and Barges to Pass from the Haven of Arundell through the Counties of Sussex and Surrey into the River of Thames 1641

WHEREAS it is most apparent that some of our neighbouring Counties are more enriched by making of rivers navigable from town to town, whereby the one supplying the other with such commodities as they want, at more easier rates than they possibly can do by land carriage in respect of the great charges charged, because that every Barge that will carry but Twenty Tons doth save the charge of keeping six score horses (which is very great) accompting six horses to every waggon or cart, whereby there will be more ground for tillage and more pasture for pasturing of cattle and sheep besides Nine hundred pounds that will be saved in the six score horses accompting them at 8d. a horse one with another, besides other casual losses by death or laming the said horses which doth ordinarily happen to those that are land carriers.

AND whereas a river that runneth from Cranley in the County of Surrey into the River of Wey and runneth through the town of Guildford and from thence into the River of Thames near a town called Weybridge in the said County of Surrey, and whereas another river that runneth from a place called Dunsfold in the said County of Surrey and from thence to a place called Newbridge in the County of Sussex and from thence to Arundell and so through the Haven of Arundell into the sea near Little Hampton in the said County of Sussex where the said river falls into the marine sea, the said river that runneth from Cranley and the said river running from Dunsfold are about two miles in distance and the one may be cut into the other without any great difficulty and by locks, weirs, sluices or turnpikes as is usually accustomed in cases of like nature may be made navigable and passable for boats and barges of convenient burthen to pass from London to Guildford and so unto Arundell and Hampton and unto divers other parts of the Counties of Surrey and Sussex as occasion shall require to the great commodity, ease and benefit of the said Counties of Surrey and Sussex and of the Towns of Guildford and Arundell and of the Cities of London and Westminster, by transporting of the commodities to and fro from London to the sea through the main lands of the Counties of Surrey and Sussex at all times of the year without danger and hazard, and by carriage of Chalk to be burnt into Lime whereby the said Counties have been already more enriched and will be more enriched in respect the said Chalk will be had at an easier price by reason of the water carriage. AND it will be also a very great help for the conveying of Corn, Timber, Wood, Iron, and the manufacturing thereof, together with each and such other commodities as these Counties do offer unto the Cities of London and Westminster which otherwise cannot be conveniently conveyed thither in the winter season by reason of the foulness of the highways in the most distant parts of the said Counties, it being almost impossible for carts and carriages to pass through the said ways being now extraordinary foul and dangerous for His Majesty's people to travel in will be much bettered by reason there will be less occasion for the use of them. AND such materials as Gravel and Stone will be the more easily conveyed for mending of them.

BE IT THEREFORE ENACTED by the King's Majesty, the Lords Spiritual and Temporal and Commons in this great Parliament assembled, and by the authority of the same, that the Lord Chancellor or Lord Keeper of the Great Seal of England for the time being or Commissioners for the Great Seal of England for the time being from time to time after the end of this present Session of Parliament, shall and may appoint and authorize by commission under the Great Seal of England, Twelve Commissioners whereof Six to be of the County of Surrey to be nominated and certified to the Lord Chancellor or Lord Keeper of the Great Seal of England or to the Commissioners of the Great Seal of England for the time being by the more part of the Justices of the Peace of the said County assembled at the first, second or third general Quarter Sessions to be holden for the said County next following this present Session of Parliament, and Six of the County of Sussex to be nominated and certified to the Lord Chancellor or Lord Keeper of the Great Seal of England or to the Commissioners of the Great Seal of England for the time being by the more part of the Justices of the Peace of the said County of Sussex assembled at the first, second or third general Quarter Sessions holden for the said County next following this present Session of Parliament, which said Commissioners, or the more part of them, shall have full power and lawful authority to compound and agree with every such person or persons as shall or may sustain hurt, loss, detriment or damage by any act or thing necessary to be done for the compounding, effecting or perfecting of the said free passage of the river or new cut or cuts to be made from London unto Guildford and so from Guildford unto Arundell and unto other parts of the said Counties of Surrey and Sussex as shall be thought fit and convenient by the more part of the said Commissioners so as it may be passable and navigable for barges and boats to the parts and places aforesaid.

AND in case any person or persons through whose land the said River or Rivers or any other waters or rivers within the said Counties of Sussex and Surrey shall be renderable to the navigation aforesaid must be cut and surveyed shall be obstinate and refuse reasonable compensation, then the said Commissioners, or the more part of them, shall determine, appoint and set down what and how much recompense and satisfaction every such person shall have that shall be damnified either in their lands or wills or by any other warrants or orders for effecting the said work, and when the same shall be paid, And after such recompense so agreed upon and set down by the said Commissioners, or the more part of them, then it shall be lawful for them or any other person or persons by them appointed, to dig or cut away so much of the land, ground, soil and inheritance of any person or persons as shall be thought meet and necessary for the cutting of the said river and waters beforementioned, both into one, for doing what shall be thought necessary for the effecting or perfecting the said work for the more free passage of the said river, and the making of the same meet to carry vessels, boats or barges to the towns or places above mentioned or any other places within the said Counties of Surrey and Sussex.

AND for that it is right and equal that those who partake in the benefits of any work should in a fit manner contribute to the costs and charges thereof. BE it therefore enacted by authority of this present Parliament, that the said Commissioners, or the more part of them, shall and may have full power and lawful authority to tax and assess such of the inhabitants of the said general Counties as shall in their opinion be likely to receive ease or benefit by the said passage and river so to be cut as aforesaid, at such reasonable sums of money and payments as they in their discretion shall think fit, and convenient, and the said sum or sums and every one of them to be disposed and imployed, for, and towards the satisfaction as well as the persons damnified or to be damnified as aforesaid, and also of, and for other necessary charges touching the effecting of the said profitable work and the maintaining, supporting and continuance of the same, and that the said Commissioners, or the more part of them, shall at all and every time and times hereafter, have power and authority by this present Act to nominate, appoint and agree such person or persons as they shall think fit for the doing of the said work, and likewise to nominate and appoint whom they shall think fit to collect and gather the aforesaid general sums for to be assessed and taxed as aforesaid, and that such person and persons as the said Commissioners, or the more part of them, shall appoint for the gathering and levying thereof shall have hereby full power and authority by way of discretions upon denial, refusal or non-payment within twelve days after demand thereof made to levy the sum and to make sale of such discretions and upon the sale thereof to receive and detain all the moneys so taxed upon such persons as aforesaid, and if the value of the discretions be better, then to deliver to the owner the residue thereof and the same money for to be levied to be delivered over and paid unto the said Commissioners who shall make the said appointment, or such other person or persons as the said Commissioners shall appoint, who shal limploy the same with as much speed as may be to the purpose aforesaid. AND if any person or persons within the said Counties who shall be taxed or rated to pay any sum or sums or money informed aforesaid, do refuse the payment thereof or otherwise withstand their distresses, or if any other which shall be charged to gather or levy any such moneys aforesaid shall wilfully refuse, neglect, deny or impugn to accomplish the order or command of the said Commissioners, or such more part of them, then every such person or persons shall be imprisoned without bail or mainprize by the discretion of the said Commissioners, or the more part of them, until such time as each or every one of them so offending shall be conformable to perform and abide by such order of the said Commissioners, or the more part of them.

AND moreover be it enacted by the authority aforesaid, that if any person or persons appointed to collect the said money having received any such part or parts of the money aforesaid towards the good and profitable works aforesaid, do detain such part or any part thereof in his or their hands and do not pay the part in all convenient speed unto the Commissioners, or such person as they shall appoint to receive the sums, but shall put it to his or their own private profit, commodity or behalf, to the detriment of the said good works, That every such person so offending for every such default shall lose the treble value of every such part so detained or not imployed. One moiety whereof shall be imployed toward the performance of the said good works and the other moiety to him or them which shall sue for same in any of His Majesty's Courts of Record by action of debt Bill, plaint or information wherein no essoigne or protection or wager or law shall be admitted or allowed. AND if any shall find themselves grieved, wronged or unjustly charged or damnified by reason of any act, order or determination of the said Commissioners, or in default of satisfaction to him or them given or appointed, that then upon the complaint of every such person within six months after his supposed wrong done to the Justices of the Peace of the said Counties in which such wrong shall be done or such want of satisfaction sustained at the general Quarter Sessions of the year, the said Justices, or the more part of them, at the said Sessions shall and may order and appoint such redress or relief and information therein as they in their discretion shall think fit and that in default thereof every such person shall and may upon suit accepted in the King's Majesty's High Court of Chancery have such relief as Justice, right and equity shall prove meet. AND be it further enacted by the authority aforesaid, that it shall be in the power of any Four of the said Commissioners, whereof Two to be of the County of Surrey and the other two of the County of Sussex, from time to time to order all things about and touching wharfage in or at the said town of Guildford and in or at the said town of Arundell or in or at any other place or places within the said Counties and touching all payments for the same to be made, AND touching the towing of boats and doing of all other things necessary for the settling of the free passage of boats and barges aforesaid. Provided always that no inhabitant of any of the said general Counties shall be taxed or imprisoned as aforesaid without the consent of Two of the Commissioners, or more of them being Commissioners thereof for that County wherein the person taxed or imprisoned is or shall be an inhabitant at the time of his taxing. Provided always and in case of any of the Commissioners to be nominated, certified and appointed as aforesaid shall depart this life or refuse to be a Commissioner and signify the same unto the Justices of the Peace at the Quarter Sessions to be holden for that County wherein he was nominated as a Commissioner, that then, and in such case, the said Justices of the Peace, or the more part of them, shall, at the next or second Quarter Sessions after such death or refusal upon notice respectively given unto the said Justices, nominate and certify unto the Lord Chancellor or Lord Keeper of the Great Seal of England or the Commissioners for the Great Seal, some other person or persons to supply the vacant place or places. And for that in the compassing, effecting and perfecting this great and beneficial work divers particular cases, questions and difficulties may arise which cannot at this present be foreseen and so expressly provided for by express and particular words, therefore to the end that the said great work may receive no delays nor hindrance but be advanced with all convenient and possible speed, BE it enacted by the authority of this present Parliament that it shall and may be lawful for the said Commissioners, or the more part of them, bindingly to determine, decide and direct all particular cases and questions that may arise of and concerning the said work, Provided always, and it is the true intent and meaning of this present Act of Parliament, that in case the Justices of the Peace for the Counties of Surrey and Sussex, or the more part of them, shall at the first or second general Quarter Sessions holden for the said Counties at Arundell and Guildford next ensuing this present session of Parliament, generally and respectively refuse in the behalf of the said general Counties to undertake the said work for and in the behalf of the said Counties, that then and in such case it shall be lawful for any undertaker or undertakers at their own cost and charge to begin and finish the said work in the manner as aforesaid. And the said Commissioners, or the more part of them, shall be aiding and assisting the undertaker or undertakers in all things for the compassing and perfecting of the said works. And shall have full power and authority by this present Act to do any act or thing in such manner and by such ways as is before expressed to help the undertaker or undertakers to perfect the said work or works as if the said Counties had done the same, saving that the said Commissioners or such number of them as is before expressed in case of such refusal shall not have power or authority to tax and assess any of the inhabitants of the general Counties to be contributory unto the charges and costs of the said work. Provided always that the undertaker or undertakers shall have the sole benefit and profit that shall accrue by transporting of commodities to and fro. That the said undertaker or undertakers, keeping the rates and prices to be set by the said Commissioners or the more part of them, the said rates and prices to be assessed under their hands and seals before the said work be undertaken and the said rates and prices so assessed not to be altered without the consent of the undertaker or undertakers.

19 February 1641.
Read 1ª, L.J., IV. 167.
Read 2ª and Committee 168.
No further proceedings.

Index

Plate numbers of illustrations shown in bold type.

Note: Names appearing solely in the appendices have been excluded.

Wey Navigation (Appendix F) continued from page 261

Year	Tolls (£)	Tonnage	Year	Tolls (£)	Tonnage
1932	1,586	49,794	1951	1,129	20,000
1933	1,501	49,522	1952	1,114	17,826
1934	1,543	51,430	1953	1,123	17,748
1935	1,507	51,520	1954	941	16,212
1936	1,413	50,064	1955	874	16,119
1937	1,278	40,895	1956	850	16,105
1938	1,010	33,212	1957	837	17,280
1939	910	31,319	1958	813	16,305
1940	978	26,932	1959	773	15,596
1941	1,299	34,126	1960	761	14,701
1942	1,087	29,669	1961	762	15,754
1943	1,160	27,169	1962	756	15,615
1944	1,309	29,883	1963	536	9,880
1945	1,055	28,918	1964	400	8,006
1946	1,337	26,876	1965	360	7,200
1947	1,239	25,910	1966	168	6,320
1948	1,398	25,334	1967	128	5,134
1949	1,374	23,034	1968	183	7,301
1950	1,274	20,502	1969 (5 JULY)	66	2,658

Note.–The Wey Navigation recorded its traffic in loads or chaldrons and these have been converted on the basis that each load or chaldron weights 25 cwt. Between 1816 and 1871 a certain amount of cargo passing to and from the Wey & Arun was recorded in tons and allowance has been made for this fact.

The Wey's tonnage includes a variable proportion of traffic passing to and from the Basingstoke Canal which was in commercial use between 1794 and 1949. Trade was, however, desultory after 1865 and no regular traffic plied above Woking after 1923. Even so over 30,000 tons was carried in 1934 and 1935 and the sudden drop in 1937 and subsequent years was mainly due to the loss of the coal freight to Woking.

T & D Murrell revived commercial traffic from Tilbury to Coxes Mill Weybridge 1978–1983.

Reference to the carriage of soldiers' baggage between London and Portsmouth will be found in 'The Military on English Waterways 1798–1844', Hugh Compton and Carr-Gomm, 1991 pp. 47–9; details of many such consignments between 1823 and 1838 are listed in the Wey Navigation Ledgers deposited at Guildford Museum.

Note 146.–London's Lost Route to Midhurst, an Historical Account of the Earl of Egremont;'s Navigation and the Building of the Petworth Canal was published in 1995. This updates the information given on page 255. The dates of commercial use of the Petworth Canal shown on Map 1 should now read 1795–1826.

Epilogue – Chapter XIV page 194

The Wey & Arun Junction Canal Company went into voluntary liquidation in 1867, failed to find a purchaser when put up for auction in 1870 and was closed for traffic in July 1871. The official liquidator reported in 1888 that 29 acres of the original 200 remained unsold including the lock house at Rowner. However, by 1901, only seven lots totalling eight acres had still to find new proprietors. The liquidator stated that the lord of the manor of Braboeuf had declined to purchase half the bed of the canal at Shalford although Williams Stevens, the Manager of the Wey Navigation had offered ten shillings (50p) for the six perches.

Finally, in April 1910, Gilbert John Smallpeice who had taken over as liquidator on the death of William Hayden Smallpeice in 1872, and had been receiving an annual fee of 100 guineas for his services, requested the High Court of Chancery to dissolve the company and destroy the books and papers. The balance was shown as £1,742. 4s. 11d. The file in the Public Record office remains silent as to how this request was received and as to how the balance of the money was distributed.